The Rule
of
Saint Augustine

An Essay in Understanding

by

Sister Agatha Mary, S.P.B.

Augustinian Press

1992

Nihil Obstat: Andrew J. Golias
Censor Librorum

Imprimatur: Anthony J. Bevilacqua
Archbishop of Philadelphia
3 October 1991

Cover illustration: A folio of the concluding words of the *Rule* of Saint Augustine: *Non sicut serui sub lege, sed sicut liberi sub gratia constituti.* By permission of the British Library, Royal MS 8 D IX, fol. 78.

Cover design: Jaroslaw Dziewicki

Library of Congress Cataloging-in-Publication Data:

Agatha Mary, Sister, 1916-
        The Rule of Saint Augustine : an essay in understanding / by
    Sister Agatha Mary.
                p.   cm.
        Includes bibliographical references.
        ISBN 0-941491-48-X. —ISBN 0-941491-47-1 (pbk.)
        1. Augustine, Saint, Bishop of Hippo. Regula. 2. Augustinians-
    -Rules. 3. Monasticism and religious orders—Rules. I. Title.
    BX2904.Z5A43   1992   91-36154
    255′ .406—dc20   CIP

Augustinian Press
P.O. Box 476
Villanova, PA 19085

Printed in the United States of America

In memory

of

Luc Verheijen, O.S.A.

Contents

Foreword

During the celebration of the 1600th anniversary of the Conversion of Saint Augustine of Hippo (1986-1987) I was preparing for publication Adolar Zumkeller's commentary on the *Rule* and also had read two other books in preparation for publication: van Bavel's commentary on the *Rule*, and Zumkeller's book *Augustine's Ideal of the Religious Life*. Zumkeller and van Bavel's commentaries are excellent; each in their own way they are different and yet complement one another. At the same time I received a manuscript on the *Rule* of Saint Augustine from Sister Agatha Mary of the Society of the Precious Blood. It seemed to me that the *Rule* had been explored quite thoroughly and there was not much left to be said. However, as I was reading the manuscript of Sister Agatha I realized how unique her approach was and not at all a duplicate of either of the above books. Several people read Sister Agatha's commentary, and they too were impressed with it and urged Augustinian Press to publish it. Unfortunately publication had to be delayed several years because of previous commitments to other books. So it is with delight on my part that this commentary now sees the light.

Sister Agatha is a true disciple of Father Verheijen and has been greatly influenced by him and his works. She represents his thought accurately as well as advancing her own insights. The uniqueness of this book is that she sets down the background from her own insights or from other scholars and then seeks to connect one particular thought to another. Scientific insights, prayerful reflection, and modern day approaches to religious life are all blended together so that the *Rule* of Augustine is not examined in various parts or chapters but as a composite whole.

This is precisely what impressed me when I first read her manuscript — everything is connected. It is like a piece of crocheted work. When you see it at the beginning, it looks different; when you see it half way completed, again it looks different; when you finally see the completed piece, everything that you looked at before fits together very nicely in a pattern.

Sister Agatha brings this unity to her commentary on the *Rule* of Saint Augustine. She shows the relevance of each chapter of the *Rule* to the other chapters so that in the end the reader feels the overall spiritual and sociological forces behind Augustine's guidelines to this followers.

I think that the delay was fortunate. Readers have absorbed the insights of Zumkeller and van Bavel in their commentaries. Now, with that background, they will be ready for the next step of insights which Sister Agatha gives in her commentary — an essay in understanding, as her subtitle indicates.

Sister Agatha finished her formal education in 1939. She spent the war years first with Reuters press news agency, and then with an organization engaged in getting books on all subjects and in all languages out to Africa for use in Catholic, Anglican, and Protestant mission schools and colleges. She gained experience of community living as a student at London University, as a missionary living and working in South Africa black townships for eleven years, and as an enclosed Anglican religious in the Society of the Precious Blood in England since 1957. She began to explore the *Rule* of Saint Augustine seriously while novice mistress between 1967 and 1973.

Augustine taught his followers to follow the life of contemplation and action and that part of their activity is to share their contemplation with others. In a true Augustinian fashion Sister Agatha shared her contemplation of many years with the novices of her congregation; she now shares it with us in *The Rule of Augustine — An Essay in Understanding*.

20 October 1991   John E. Rotelle, O.S.A.

Preface

The subtitle of this book explains what it is and also what it is not.
It is an exploration, rather than an exposition, of the *Rule* of Saint
Augustine. An exposition would presuppose far more knowledge
than I possess, and what I have written is in the nature of an
attempt to understand the things which he gave as "precepts to
be observed" by a particular group of people in a particular
monastery at the end of the fourth century.

Evidently this short document, which the author could easily
have thought out and written down or dictated in two or three
hours, made an impression in monastic circles, for it has had a
long and complicated manuscript history which has now been
unravelled by the great Augustinian scholar, Luc Verheijen,
O.S.A., whose two-volume study, *La Règle de Saint Augustin*, was
published in 1967.

It is Verheijen's critical edition of the text that I have used.
Readers who are familiar with older versions will notice that his
division of chapters and paragraphs differs from that of his predecessors. Augustine's thought in the *Rule* has a close adhesion
which make analytical division difficult, but this new edition
gives shape and consistency to the text in a very convincing way.

The provision of an English translation has been my first aim in
the process of exploring the *Rule*. For that reason, and following
the practice of others who have produced modern translations in
other languages in recent years, I have set it out in sense lines and
not in continuous prose form. This is to facilitate slow reading.
With a short and compressed text such as this it is all to easy to
miss the fullness of meaning that lies in the words and phrases
that are used.

My second aim has been twofold: to set the precepts against
their biblical and their social backgrounds. The first of these has
been easy to follow through because the *Rule* is crowded with
scriptural quotations and allusions. I myself have seen two biblical
analyses of the text, one produced in France and one in England;
each refers to over one hundred passages, but a comparison of the
two lists has shown only about twenty-five percent of overlapping. And in my reading and re-reading of the *Rule* I have found
other echoes which have helped me to understand a little more of
what Augustine was saying and what made him say it.

Discovering the social background has been more difficult and I am aware of how little I have uncovered. Perhaps foolishly I have rushed into this area where it would be of great value to know more accurately what the *Rule*'s first readers would have understood by this or that detail, or the use of one word rather than another. It would be good if my foolhardiness urged some angels to tread with greater delicacy in this field and so unearth many rich things that I have overlooked.

My third aim has been to set the *Rule* within the context of community life today. It has been one of the formative documents of the religious life down the centuries, and for a considerable number of today's religious it is their *locus classicus*. I have followed Augustine in moving gradually from one level of experience to another. He takes a concrete external situation, discusses it, and then interiorizes it as he searches for meaning; then having found, as it were, one platform of meaning he turns to another concrete aspect of community life and repeats the process — until at the end he is able, in his last chapter, to show the monks for whom he wrote, whose difficulties he has so sensitively laid bare, that they can live their lives as "free persons established in grace."

Mention of the word "monk" in the previous sentence leads me to explain at this point how I have attempted to differentiate levels of interpretation in what I have written. It has been my practice to use the words monks/men and their appropriate pronouns when I am trying to explicate Augustine's own ideas, and to use inclusive words and phrases when I am expressing my own thoughts about what is set down in his *Rule*. Sometimes as I have been working through a passage of the text I have found myself moving from the language of one level to that of the other; but this shifting reflects an aspect of Augustine's own writing throughout his life and so I make no apology. As for the word "monastery," I have with few exceptions used it throughout to describe any dwelling place where a committed common life under vows is lived.

I have accepted Verheijen's conclusion that the *Rule* was written soon after Augustine became bishop of Hippo and so had to leave the monastery that he had established near the church when he was ordained priest; and that the purpose of setting down the precepts was to give his former companions advice which he could no longer give by his presence among them. Nevertheless in the course of my exploration I have come to realize that what Augustine gave to a small body of monks living in a specific monastery does have great relevance for members of other kinds of community. The central position that he gives to the common life itself can, I believe, make the *Rule* a valuable guide for many groups. My own understanding of the precepts comes from living in lay communities as well as in religious ones. It comes also, intangibly, from spending most of my religious life in an abbey which housed other Augustinians from 1266 until its dissolution as a religious house in 1539 and which was restored to its original use in 1916.

As readers will note, I have relied on and found aids to my understanding in many places — in the works of scholars, spiritual guides, and other writers. My debt to them is enormous and if I have misunderstood and therefore misrepresented any one of them, I am sorry and ask to be forgiven. At the very least, they have helped me to understand Augustine.

Verheijen's division of the *Rule* into eight chapters has greatly facilitated the work of interpretation and it has helped me to see both the continuity of thought throughout the document as well as the gradual emergence of its developing themes. For that reason I have given a title to each of my chapters and have provided subtitles which may be regarded as analogous to the lines of latitude and longitude on a map: you do not experience them when you are traveling, but they help you to know where you are.

Many attempts have been made to describe the structure of the *Rule* and my own differs from those that I have met. As I see it, there are two distinct parts to what Augustine has to say, and the division comes almost half-way through, at chapter IV, 10. The first part is concerned with the place of individuals in the community — their aspirations, their weaknesses, and their sins; the second part is concerned with the life of the group as a whole. The turning point comes with the first mention of the word "love" (*dilectio*). According to my understanding Augustine writes about: (1) Unity; (2) Prayer; (3) Asceticism through poverty and the common life; (4) Asceticism through chastity and mutual concern; (5) Love in action; (6) Forgiveness; (7) Obedience, and (8) Mature Freedom. There is a great deal of recapitulation, of the sort that one would expect to find in a document written continuously or almost continuously, when ideas and words would be at the forefront of the mind. In some cases I have indicated in my text how one thought of Augustine's is related to something he has written earlier or that will emerge further on in the *Rule*. But to do this with every such overlapping would have been boring and confusing for a reader because it checks the impetus of Augustine's river-like thought which I have tried to interpret.

My chapter headings show how the main principles and practice of fourth-century monasticism are reflected in the *Rule*. In regard to principles (though that is probably too strong a word for this early period of monastic history), it is instructive to find that the notions of poverty, of chastity, and of obedience are not dealt with *en bloc*. Dispossession of personal goods and the demands of celibacy are discussed in the first part of the *Rule*, under the general aspect of asceticism which follows naturally after a chapter on prayer. Obedience is explored in the penultimate chapter, and not until after there has been a long discussion of forgiveness and its importance in the common life. As for the pattern of the common life that the precepts describe and take for granted, there is little allusion to obedience before the second half while chapters 1-4 mainly discuss the ideal of unity in God and how individuals react to the experience of living with other people, regardless of the form that their life takes.

I have paid particular attention to Augustine's language. As an experience *rhetor* and a prolific writer, he was a master of words and did not use them lightly. When we use words carefully, we chose them on the basis of their resonances for ourselves and also for those that we expect our language to have in our hearers and readers. The passage of time tends to flatten words, even to change their meaning; and that is why I have looked at dictionary meanings more than is customary nowadays. It is impossible to judge the impact of an idea upon a hearer unless one knows the chords that it will strike. We know that as a fact of common experience, together with the misunderstandings that can arise. In trying to understand the *Rule* of Saint Augustine the same fact holds good. The word *pater* (father) is a case in point: when we hear the word we immediately place it in the context of male parenthood or of a nuclear family, but in the fourth century it implied a whole network of relationships and responsibilities within a household. And so one could go on, for "family" is another word that has become narrowed in its meaning.

One further point needs to be mentioned. Attention to Augustine's use of language applies both to his own words and to the words of scripture which he quoted. For that reason I have, where necessary, explored the Latin words of the Bible rather than the

Greek because it was Latin words that Augustine handled and shared with others.

I have been helped by many people in the preparation of this book, and I am grateful to every one of them for what they have given me from their own creative living. My first debt is to all with whom I have shared my life and that includes my family. My community has given me the time and space for writing. More than that: it is through my sisters in the Society of the Precious Blood that I have learned how Augustine's *Rule* can be lived creatively in circumstances so different from his own. In understanding what the *Rule* meant in Hippo at the turn of the fourth-fifth centuries I have been helped by three scholars who have read and criticized by chapters as they were written: Denys Lloyd, Andrew Louth, and Luc Verheijen, O.S.A. Without their encouragement I should have given up the attempt to explore the *Rule*. Without two other people I should not have been able to make my journey: June Jansen and Vera Stevens, of Burnham Public Library, who never failed to obtain the books for which I asked them. And then since my typescript has been completed it has been John Rotelle, O.S.A. and his co-workers in the Augustinian Press, Villanova, who have used their editorial and other skills in the process of publishing this book. To all of these people, as well as to the authors whose writings have helped me, I am very grateful.

Burnham Abbey   Agatha Mary, S.P.B.
28 August 1991

1

Unity

Rule, Chapter I, 1
These are the things which we give as precepts
to be observed
by you who live in the monastery.

AN OVERTURE

In music, the tone of an opera is expressed in its overture. The composers are then doing three things: stating their own points of view in relation to the themes and the action that are to follow, evoking what they expect the singers and the orchestra to make explicit in the course of a performance, and inviting the cooperation of the audience in freeing their ideas and the musicians' skill into the consciousness of all the participants present in the opera house.

The first sentence of this *Rule* is just such an overture. We need to heed it carefully. Yet it is baffling, because it says so little. But that in itself is a characteristic of the *Rule* as a whole; it is so short. It does not spell out the answers to every conceivable contingency and facet of life in the monastery; it offers precepts, guidelines, with some discussion of a number of typical problems that have to be solved in the course of the community's developing experience. In terms of the musical analogy, the author sets down his ideas which each monk will make explicit according to his capacity and which the community as a whole, by its very togetherness, will absorb and spread through its witness far beyond the limits of the monastery itself.

Precepts? The limits of language trip us up at the very beginning of our exploration — and perhaps this itself is a salutary reminder of how often within any group, within any attempt at communication, language itself fails to express all that our heart and our head cry out to make plain. Indeed much of the *Rule* is an attempt to get behind words as well as behind actions into the depths of each person in the group, to plumb those depths for the truth that makes each person and makes possible the incredibly difficult thing that community life is — the corporate expression of each one's singularity and value in the sight of God.

Precepts? Less than that, really, for in the Latin text the precept-form is contained in the verb and the subject of the sentence lies in two pronouns. *Praecipio* means to give rules or precepts, to advise, admonish, warn, inform, instruct, direct.[1] It is a pity that translators are not musicians: if they were, they could with their notes on their staves express each of these words in one chord or phrase. But they cannot and are forced to choose and, in this case, are forced to express a verb with a noun and leave all possible other nouns unwritten. Nevertheless, in the course of the *Rule* as a whole, first one and then another of the alternatives have more force: advice, admonishment, warning, information, instruction, direction.

In that list, one possible word supplied by the dictionary is missing: rules. And that points to a telling fact: nowhere, either in its title or in the text, does the word rule (*regula*) appear. This is important because the absence of that word acts as a warning lest we approach the precepts-advice-instruction too literally. What follows in the text is offered for consideration and interpretation in countless different ways and by equally countless different people. The subjects discussed are to be observed, not — as one might expect — obeyed. Again here, in the choice of word, the author has taken the position of a composer. He shares his ideas with the performers and the audience, and it is for them to sift, to interpret, to express, and each expression will either diminish or enlarge the original idea. The full richness of the ideas lies deep; it is for each one to find that depth and make room for it within his own depth. Of course, not every discovery is durable; unless it carries within it a dynamism, the dynamism that is of the Spirit, it cannot endure but only wither. The testing-place of every spark of understanding that a monk may attain to is the life of the community as a whole. What is true on a world-scale is equally true of a monastery: the deadening futility of attempting to codify ideals and to build a free society on and within the strict limits of any one set of propositions. There must always be movement, flexibility and adjustment based on fresh appreciation and related to fresh circumstances. That is why the word observe is so telling.

Obseruo carries a wide spectrum of meanings: to watch, note, mark, heed, observe, take notice of and pay attention to, keep, comply with, respect, regard, esteem, and honor. That implies that the meaning of the thing observed can only be found within that thing itself, it cannot be assessed in terms of any preconceived theory or regulation. Neither negative nor positive commands or commandments can carry the weight of a fully-lived, deeply-felt, and patiently understood monastic life. Only an all-embracing acceptance of all that is involved will suffice. And what is involved is all, the all of each, the all of each community, the all of the Church, the all of humankind. In consenting to observe these things given as precepts, a monk is committed to a total way of living.

We must look very carefully at this word observe, for it was not lightly chosen. This is shown by the fact that it occurs three times in the text, and always in a key position: here in chapter I, 1, again in chapter IV, 10 and finally in chapter VIII, 1. In due course each passage must be carefully studied. Here it suffices to point out that in chapter I, 1 it indicates the manner and spirit in which the following guidelines are to be approached; in chapter IV, 10 it occurs near the end of a very long discussion of the way of dealing with serious moral problems that may harm the community: "What I have said . . . should be applied (*obseruetur*) carefully and faithfully . . . with love of the persons and hatred of the offenses"; and in chapter VIII, 1, at the beginning of the final chapter of the *Rule*, it is used to describe how all the foregoing considerations are to be made real, turned from precepts into a living thing which is the life of the community: "May the Lord grant that you may observe (*obseruetis*) all these things with love, as lovers of spiritual beauty, radiating by your good life the sweet odor of Christ, not as slaves under the law but as free persons established in grace." These two passages show what observance means in the *Rule*'s language.

The Rule? There is no tenable alternative to using this word as a handle to hold it by. Although, as we have said, it occurs nowhere in the text it is the only word that describes what the things given as precepts really constitute: the basic, formative document that has guided and continues to guide one monastic tradition through the centuries. In using the word monastic of this tradition, one is firmly within the tradition itself, and equally firmly within the word and the spirit of the text. Although the adjectival form is not to be found there, nor the word monk (*monachus*), the word monastery (*monasterium*) is found in nine places. The fact of its weighty repetition in chapter I, 1, 4, 5, 6, 7; chapter III, 4 (twice); chapter V, 3 and chapter VI, 2 underlines the monastic quality of the community's life. The very flexibility of the *Rule* has made possible a remarkable variety of patterns of this monastic ideal; and although this has had its dangers internally and externally from time to time, the fact is now again recognized that this *Rule* portrays an authentic monastic spirituality.

The word translated living together (*constituti*) need not detain us long. It occurs five times in the text — in chapters I, 1, II, 1, 2, V, 3 and VIII, 1 — and always in a relatively weak sense, sometimes meaning little more than "happen to be." Its occurrence here, along with the moderate word *praecipimus*, underlines once again the gentle, unobtrusive spirit of the *Rule*. Yet, paradoxically, living together in a monastery is anything but an unobtrusive aspect of the life of the Church. As we shall see later, the life and witness of each monk or nun has a function that surpasses his or her importance as an individual person; we stand for something more than we are. And here we come to the heart of the matter.

LIVING IN THE MONASTERY

Why do some men and women live in monasteries? What, or who, began the train of events that leads them to a monastery and how is this impetus continually animated? Millions of people, down the centuries, have given themselves to this way of life, and none of them would produce an identical answer. Yet some things have remained constant, and it is these that both sustain the individuals and also draw them toward others who are similarly drawn. There is the human being's constant thirst for God, the unfulfilled longing to know and be known in God, to find and be found in God, to live within the contradictions of experience in the assurance of understanding. And there is the desire to serve and to be used.

The yearning for God, for truth, for goodness and beauty is by its very nature insatiable; and taking it seriously involves living with a paradox. God in his transcendence is always beyond the horizon, like the secret pale light of the sun before dawn or the brilliant, unpredictable colors of the sky after sunset. God is beyond a person's most satisfying thought of him, whether that be expressed in a line of a poem, in a long book or in the silence of wonder. God is beyond what can be thought, let alone expressed. Yet it is God who comes close enough to beckon and to whisper as people search for him; and it is God's insistent invitation that impels some men and women to set aside other occupations and ways of life in order to seek him within a monastery.

Seek, and you shall find (Mt 7:7): but you cannot possess what you find, it remains God's and there is always more to seek. So we continue the search, through the years spent within the monastery, with an ever-growing awareness of the value of what is given, with increasing courage when the search is dark and unfulfilled for long years, with growing gratitude for the glimpses of God's loveliness that we are occasionally allowed to see and to hold and always to remember. Without this contemplation, life in a monastery would be insupportable.

If there is anguish in seeking the hiddenness of God, his very nearness often brings agony as well as joy to those who love and long for him. As with human relationships that suddenly burst into a dimension of living that opens the heart to another's understanding, and in the humility of love makes fear of being known to fall away, so in their encounter with God in the very life which they live people may be liberated into a rich and rewarding awareness of his beauty and of their potential likeness to him. But what they must also see and accept are the many dark and ugly aspects of themselves which spoil their relationship with God and with each other. God's care and providence in the little life of each one, in the staggering fact of creation which in our generation is being more wonderfully revealed to us, in the ingenuity and the beauty of which the human mind is capable — the miracle of humanness at its best — in the lovableness of people, in books, pictures, music, and in all that is a meeting-place with others: all of these gifts of God are the foci of his immediacy to which the contemplative responds with love and with humility. As we shall see throughout the *Rule*, the integral place of love and humility within the life of the community arises out of the spirit of contemplation which is the primary motive that each monk has for committing himself to life in the monastery.

The way of contemplation embraces every aspect of monastic life, and every part of that life has to be tested again and again in the light of this primary vocation. If the single-minded search — the repeated threefold rhythm of seeking and finding and adoring — is lost sight of, a religious and even a whole community may be close to living a sterile existence. This means that there must always be movement within the community. Growth and change are the fruit of contemplation, for they express the humble recognition of the not-yet-achieved end of the search itself. For contemplation draws people into the dynamism of God and enables them to share his power which he expresses in millions of different ways all the time. We have to become very supple, if God is to use us as a channel of his immanence; we must have eyes to see his slightest movement and ears to hear his whispered word; we may hold nothing back if he is to use us for the continued making of his world and the building of his Church in each generation. All of this helps to explain why the *Rule* lays down no hard-and-fast obligations but instead presents precepts to be observed.

The impulse to contemplation lies very close to the second source of monastic vocation, the desire to place oneself entirely at God's disposal and to be of service to him in whatever way he wants. In biblical terms, too, to seek God sometimes actually means *to serve him faithfully* (see Dt 4:29, Pss 40:16, 69:6, 105:3, Am 5:4). The first monks were often known as servants of God, and it is significant that when Athanasius wrote his life of the man who came to be called the father of monasticism he said that Antony gained renown not for his writings, nor for worldly wisdom, nor for any art but solely for his service to God.[2] The desire to be of use, to be recognized as valuable, lies deep in the human condition and is itself a good thing. It has its roots in awareness of oneself and also in awareness of other people, of the fact that they have needs as I have, that they are worth helping. In other words, it is closely related to people's capacity to love and also to their need to have their love recognized. It implies, too, the willingness to be at the disposal of another.

No one can be willing to serve God without knowing him, worshiping him, loving him: to try to serve him without this disposition could achieve nothing, for there could be no point of meeting. Experience of God, recognition of his activity, response to him as one person to another: all these things draw people out of themselves, out beyond an awareness of other people, into a threefold relationship in which God, someone else, and I-myself are bound together. It involves more than knowing another; it means seeing, worshiping, loving God's activity in the other and seeing the other through God. A work of interpretation and intercession is constantly going on within the life of a servant of God. Heart and head are given over to this labor of serving the Lord; flesh and blood, bone and muscle too. There is nothing that he does not need to use in us, and nothing that we may hold back from the service of others because of him. Yet we do hold back, very often — pride, anger, laziness, or sheer weak-will can make us unprofitable servants. It takes heroism of a high order to be willing to give oneself away all the time, and the Church of the fourth century was quick to make the discovery that this utter giving way of life demanded the same courage and bravery as that which had made the martyrdoms of the years of persecution the supreme witness of fidelity to Christ. Indeed, monasticism was still in its early days when its way of life was seen to be itself a way of martyrdom.[3]

Martyrdom was not simply a laying-down of one's life; it was regarded as an expression of sanctity; and because sanctity is always an attribute that is given and never earned, it is supremely a witness to the grace of God at work within human beings. The testimony of the Christian martyr, monk, nun or servant of God proclaims one thing: that God was in Christ, reconciling the world to himself.[4]

The present time is teaching us much more of what it means to be a reconciler in personal relationships, between groups and between nations. The cost is great and it is endless. The capacity to see both sides of an argument is not something that comes easily to most of us, nor does the ability to suspend judgment. To stand in the firing-line between opposing forces as a mediator demands great self-awareness and selflessness. It demands a willingness to lose all, to be challenged as to our objectives and our resources, to give ourselves away to the point of seeming emptiness; and it can only be undertaken to the extent that we are dedicated to this work.

PRIMARY RESPONSIBILITY FOR OBSERVANCE

Augustine's understanding seems to be somewhat as follows. In a monastery there are X number of persons each responding within his own self to the double call of God, to seek and to serve. No one man can be more than himself, nor can he be other than himself. Each is subject to enormous fluctuations — physical, temperamental, emotional, intellectual — and, indeed, the only constant is God alone. Within the monastic group, one of the most costly and never-ending tasks is that of making room for all its members. This is the responsibility of the community as a whole, not only that of the superior. This important fact is implicit in the structure of the *Rule*: the precepts to be observed are directed to those who live in the monastery, and whereas the first eight references to the prior are mainly functional it is only the last two that describe his moral standing in the community. Chapter I, 3 states that the prior is responsible for the distribution of food and clothing; chapter IV, 9 advises that serious misdemeanors should be reported to the prior, if an offender has failed to respond to a brother's warning, and correction is to be given according to the prior's judgment and that of the priest; chapter IV, 11 states that illicit receiving of letters and presents should be dealt with by the prior or priest; chapter V, 3 says that gifts received are to be handed over to the prior so that he can distribute them according to need; chapter V, 4 makes him responsible for laundry arrangements, while in chapter V, 5 it is his duty to decide whether or not the public baths are to be used; and in chapter V, 7 it is he who must choose a monk's companions for any expedition from the monastery. It is not until the penultimate chapter, at chapter VII, 1, that the relationship between the prior and the rest of the brethren is described (and that in surprisingly unconventional terms which will be discussed in due course); and in chapter VII, 2 his obligation to see to the fulfillment of the precepts is explicitly stated.

The primary responsibility for observance thus lies with each member of the community, according to his individual capacity; and this in itself is an important factor in freeing the group (which is bound by certain rules, customs, conventions) from the risk of stultifying rigidity. Each one can, in fact, express his ever-growing understanding and appreciation of the precepts and the life of the community within his own person; what he does, though, impinges on every other member, influences them, and to a certain degree changes them. The willingness to be changed by one's brethren lies close to the heart of one's growth; and the willingness to make room for the growth of one's brothers lies even closer to that heart, for it demands a total self-surrender. But such a surrender is only valid, and can only result in new life in a monk, if he is convinced that the call to such a yielding comes from the Lord whom he is seeking and serving. It is God at work in others, in circumstances, to whom the response is made. Yet not every impulse comes directly from God; what God is saying may be blurred or blocked by stupidity or sin and, as Saint John warned his beloved congregation,[5] the spirits must be tested to discover whether they are of God (and the rest of this important chapter of the letter is devoted to a description of the nature of love for God and for one another).

SEPARATION FOR SERVICE

It is because of love that the monastery is important, the monastery with its self-limiting way of life that at the same time has to be wide open for every encounter with God and with people. The monastic life, historically speaking, began with individual separation (and it still requires that dimension in the case of every single religious). But although solitude and distancing continued to hold a certain pre-eminence the necessity for togetherness gradually emerged as a factor that is hardly less prominent. Witness and service are the twin conditions that bind together and give validity to the need for solitude and for companionship.

Since these factors have been particularly important in the monasticism that has been formed by Augustine's *Rule*, it will be useful to explore the development of separation for service within the early Church. The separation of celibates in New Testament times was closely linked with both witness and service. In the earliest text,[6] written about the year 57, Paul discusses the freedom of an undivided loyalty that is possible for the man or woman who is not committed in marriage. Luke, writing sometime between the year 64 and 70, mentions the four virgin daughters of Philip the evangelist of Caesarea who had prophetic gifts — a costly and often isolating vocation.[7] In Matthew's gospel, which dates from about the year 80, there is recorded Jesus' discussion with the Pharisees on the question of marriage and divorce, which was followed by a further conversation with the disciples who had been present. In the course of this, someone said to him that maybe it is better not to marry and it was this that precipitated his challenging remark that some do go to the length of making themselves eunuchs for the sake of the kingdom of heaven.[8] And in the Johannine tradition the book of Revelation, which may have been written as early as 70 or as late as 95, gives a special place in the choir of heaven to celibates.[9]

All these passages indicate that very early in the Christian era there was a particular and readily identifiable role for those who committed themselves to celibacy for the sake of Christ. Thus for some but not for all, as Matthew 19:11 makes clear, there was a kind of withdrawal from the ordinary pattern of life by men and women who in other ways lived ordinary lives. In Revelation 14 the honor given to celibates is said to be because they were willing to follow the Lamb wherever he goes (verse 4); and this is followed immediately, in verse 6, by the appearance of the angel charged with preaching the everlasting gospel to all who dwell on the earth, to every nation and kindred and tongue and people. The juxtaposition of these two views of a specially dedicated life suggests that celibacy and service were at a very early period seen to be related.

The important place of service in the early Christian communities is borne out by 1 Timothy 5:3-10, which may date from about the year 65. Here, the particular function of widows is described; they are free to consecrate all their days and nights to petitions and prayer, and their selection for service in the Church must depend on their being known for their good works, their hospitality to strangers, their care for their fellow-Christians (washing the feet of the saints), their help for people in trouble, and their activity in all kinds of good works. Even if it could be argued that this passage was no more than a counsel of perfection, what Luke has to say in Acts 9:39-41 allows of no doubt that widows were in some way special people within the community. He is describing Peter's raising of Dorcas:

> All the widows stood beside him weeping, and showing tunics and other garments which Dorcas made while she was with them. But Peter put them all outside and knelt down and prayed; then turning to the body he said, "Tabitha, rise." And she opened her eyes, and when she saw Peter she sat up. And he gave her his hand and lifted her up. Then calling the saints and widows he presented her alive.

Clearly, those who were willing and free from other obligations could be set apart in order to render special service on behalf of the Church. This seems to have been characteristic over a wide area. 1 Corinthians was sent to that city from Ephesus; Acts 21:8-9 describes a situation in Caesarea; Matthew's gospel relates to the Christians in Palestine; Revelation has its home in the western part of Roman Asia; 1 Timothy was sent to Ephesus from Macedonia; and Acts 9:39-41 describes events that took place in Jaffa.

This impulse toward apartness for the sake of attention to the things of God seems to be the root of the Christian monastic tradition, and by the second century the function of those maintaining the single state emerges more clearly.[10] Eusebius, in his *Ecclesiastical History* written at the end of the third century, provides continuity with the apostles in stating that two of Philip's four daughters remained virgins till death and were buried, as their father was, at Hierapolis while a third "rests at Ephesus."[11]

It would seem that they remained associated with their father's work and witness until the year 117 at the latest.

In about the year 96 Clement of Rome provided evidence of a gradually deepening understanding of the meaning of celibacy. He reminded the "one who is physically chaste" of the paramount importance of humility; such a one "must not brag about it but know that the ability to control his desire has been given him" by another, that is, God.[12]

Ignatius of Antioch (c. 35-107) is also a witness to a further development. When he was on the way to Rome and martyrdom, he wrote from Troas to the Christians of Smyrna and concluded with "greetings to the families of my brethren who have wives and children, and to those virgins whom you call widows."[13] The title widow could here refer either to status or to function or to both. Réne Metz considers that it was from this time, the beginning of the second century, that the observance of virginity constituted a sort of profession, a state to which certain members of the Christian community vowed themselves.[14]

Ignatius' contemporary Polycarp (d. 155 or 156) gives explicit expression to what is expected of women who thus serve the Church. They are

> to observe discretion as they practice our Lord's faith: they should make constant intercession for everyone and be careful to avoid any tale-bearing, spiteful tittle-tattle, over-eagerness for money, or misconduct of any description. They are to recognize that they are an altar of God, who scrutinizes every offering laid on it, and from whom none of their thoughts or intentions — no single one of their heart's secrets — can be hidden.[15]

Here for the first time there is a reference to sacrifice and offering.

Justin the Martyr, writing toward the end of Polycarp's lifetime, claims that he "can produce abundance of both sexes who have from their childhood been disciplined unto Christ, and lived in a constant course of spotless virginity to sixty or seventy years of age." He goes on to say that he "cannot but give glory in being able to produce so many instances of Christian purity out of every nation."[16]

Some twenty years later Athenagoras, who is described in the earliest manuscripts as the Christian philosopher of Athens, refers to "many men and women who have grown old without marrying in the hope of being of service to God."[17] Thus by the last quarter of the second century the link between celibacy and service is firmly established.

It is pertinent to notice again the places with which these later writers are connected. Justin the Martyr's "out of every nation" may be hearsay or rhetoric, but he could have encountered living examples during the course of his Christian life in Ephesus and Rome. Apart from this conjecture, there is reasonable certainty in Hierapolis and Ephesus (Eusebius), Troas and Smyrna (Ignatius), Philippi (Polycarp), Rome (Justin Martyr) and somewhere within news-distance of Athens (Athenagoras). It would seem, then, that the impulse to commit oneself to such a life of separation had its origin in ordinary Christian living in any place. Later on, imitation and emulation certainly played their part and contributed to the evolution of a common pattern of life; but in the early stages there was no easily identifiable way of expressing one's given-ness. Separation itself was the outward and visible sign of an inward and spiritual dedication to the service of God.

This correlation between separation and dedication lies deep in biblical spirituality extending over a long period. The same word that occurs in Acts 13:2 (*set apart for me Barnabas and Saul for the work to which I have called them*) is used in the Septuagint in a number of contexts. Exodus 13:12 concerns the consecration of the firstborn to the Lord. Numbers 8:11 and Exodus 29:24-27 enjoin the setting apart of the Levites and of Aaron and his sons as a wave offering to the Lord. In Numbers 15:20, a cake from the first baking of fresh dough is to be set aside and presented to God. In Deutero-Isaiah, those who bear the vessels of the Lord are to be separate and to purify themselves because of the office which they have to perform (52:11). David himself, in being separated from his people in order to do the work of the Lord, is compared to the fat that is separated for God from the peace offering (Sir 47:2). And in the New Testament, Paul regarded himself as specially set apart for the gospel of God (Rom 1:1), that he might preach Christ among the Gentiles (Gal 1:15).

This separation and this service are seen as a two-sided coin. First, the person or the thing is to be reserved for God's use and not to be expended in any other way or for any other purpose. Second, the calling to such separation and service is an act of God's initiative and it makes its imprint, sets its seal, on the person or thing that God chooses. Seen in terms of the developing Church of the first three centuries, this means that the man and woman who committed themselves to a life of celibacy for the sake of Christ were laying themselves open to a threefold way of living: they were to be separated from ordinary life, yet at the same time they were to be available to serve God and their fellow human beings as they should be needed, and in obedience to him they were to become the expression of his love and mercy to all whom they encountered. There is nothing essentially spectacular in any of this; it was meant to be humble, hidden, and unobtrusive. Justin the Martyr may have rejoiced because he knew many such men and women, but the life that they lived was itself unassuming. As one historian has put it, "The Apologists, Justin the Martyr about the year 150 (sic, but the date is not now generally agreed), Athenagoras about 180, and Minucius Felix about 200, all refer to the chastity and sobriety which characterized the (Christian) sect, the celibacy practiced by some of its members."[18]

In the early centuries, the fame of the celibates was not of their own seeking. In a sense, their self-offering to God was exploited for the sake of the development of the Church which they themselves were called to serve and to reinforce. The long panegyric on chastity which Methodius of Olympus wrote toward the end of the third century[19] set a fashion which was followed by later Christian leaders who, like him, were in positions of responsibility in relation to the ethics and spirituality of their fellow Christians. It is noteworthy that among the outstanding later writers who praised and advocated celibacy were some who were not themselves virgins, Jerome and Augustine, for example.

So, the individual man or woman who withdrew from normal social obligations in order to draw near to God was, by the third century, in an embarrassing position; his very withdrawal attracted the attention of both the needy and admirers. Withdrawal could defeat its own end. The stages by which the monastic life itself evolved from more than two hundred years of experiment in individual seeking and service is until now unknown (perhaps one day research will reveal them). What must be stressed is the answers which life in a monastery gave to the problems posed by individuals whom God called away from ordinary patterns of living into an intimate search for and commerce with himself.

First of all, the monastery restores things to their true proportions. The individual who lives out his life of celibacy alongside others who are doing the same thing does not see himself with the eyes of a Methodius, or a Cyprian, or Tertullian. He knows that the costly and often lonely way by which he goes takes him close to all those who are never called heroic, whose self-giving and self-denial hold them in circumstances that attract little praise: those who give themselves completely to whatever is asked of them in the ordinary things of life. Celibates in a monastery are aware of the heart's cry in themselves, in each other, in all people everywhere. They know the joy of recognition and the sorrow of rejection; they experience increasing depths in relationships and the agonies of isolation. They are challenged to an integrity that is consistent with the way of life to which they are committed, in exactly the same way as every other conscientious person is challenged. In other words, they are not special people. They are ordinary people with an extraordinary job.

Secondly, the monastery provides an external protection from the extravagant evaluation which would say that religious are extraordinary people, giants in the land. In the monastery a religious learns just how ordinary, even perhaps substandard, he or she is in capabilities and attitudes, as well as physical, psychological, and spiritual equipment. Because they have given themselves into the hands of God to be purified and molded and made ever more fit for service, they grow in self-knowledge and in an ever-deepening dependence on the power of God to hold them in life. This dependence on God lies at the heart of monastic poverty. The poor of the earth are, in biblical terms, those who wait upon the Lord in adoring trust, knowing that to strive for their own well-being is to erect barriers to the free-flowing generosity of God. The ability to wait, to set aside self-seeking, is only possible as religious abandon their false self-concern and grow in awareness of their true needs. And as their self-knowledge increases, so does their understanding of one another. As they constantly renew their own self-giving, they grow in admiration at the self-giving of others. In other words, they grow in understanding and love.

So, thirdly, the monastery is a place of love and compassion, as a happy family home is. The single, unique call to which each one is responding is a unifying factor among the members. God's call to one is echoed in each of the others, as a theme played on different instruments. It is the recognition of the vocation of each one that actualizes a depth of love and fellowship which witnesses to the power of God and attracts people to the monastery. Each monastery, even within one order or congregation, is different because what it depends on is the people within it; yet each monastery reflects or makes explicit some facet of the love of God and of his activity within people's lives. And a tradition can and does outlive one generation of religious, because the love that the tradition makes explicit is itself external. To enter into such a tradition, when one follows God's call, is to place oneself trustingly in his hands, to be willing to be used by him.

Fourthly, then, the monastery is the place where the religious learn how to live in true freedom. For if they enter into a way of life that already has its own tradition, they must also be able, through growth in love and compassion, to learn how to give themselves without grudging or constraint to all that the ongoing life of the community asks of them. To recognize the Spirit at work in changing situations, to evaluate motives and experiences, to grow in discernment and to grow away from an attitude of criticism, to be willing to take risks when necessary, to give others the benefit of the doubt, to be willing to be wrong: all of this is a true liberation from the false supports that we cling to. And it is more than this: it is an opening out into a dimension of living in which God is found, God for whom the search itself is undertaken. When we live in this way, freedom and obedience are found to be close partners. True obedience does not show itself in a life strictly regulated by an explicit code of behavior; it is recognized by the loving generosity with which we can assess the needs of the moment and give ourselves to them according to our capacity. True obedience does not take its stand on an unbreakable tradition: it knows that the letter kills and that the Spirit gives life — and life implies change. True obedience is, above all, unself-conscious because it is animated by the spirit of love. The dynamics of love which Paul describes in 1 Corinthians 13:4-8 could equally well be used of the spirit of monastic freedom. In fact, love and obedience are what make possible the true freedom that a religious may come to within his or her monastery.

Life in a monastery takes a person more deeply into himself or herself and more deeply into the community. The references to *monasterium* in the *Rule* begin with the monk as an individual, as he inserts himself (or is inserted) into the life of the group; and they gradually go deeper, as the *Rule* proceeds, to describe the place of the individual within the community as a whole. There are altogether nine references to the monastery in the text. As we have seen, chapter I, 1 addresses the subsequent precepts to those who live in the monastery. Chapter I, 4 states what a man is to do with his property when he enters the monastery. Chapter I, 5 discusses the attitude of mind of those who have no property before they enter. Chapter I, 6 takes a step forward from the attitude of this or that individual monk to an illuminating discussion of the effect of life in monasteries on both rich and poor alike. And chapter I, 7 takes a further step in discussing the sharing of all possessions in the common life of a community. The next discussion of a monastery occurs at chapter III, 4 where the word is used twice. Here a deeper level of acceptance of one another is at stake. Different backgrounds and ways of life have produced different weaknesses and strengths, and the problem that has to be resolved for the well-being of the group as a whole is the degree of consideration that has to be given to each individual in relation to the person that he is; for only in this way can the community itself be harmonious and effective. In chapter V, 3 the discussion concerns the sharing of gifts and making them available to all who are in the monastery. And in chapter VI, 2 there is further deepening in the exploration of the need for humility and a growing willingness to ask pardon of one's brothers.

What happens with the treatment of the word *monasterium* is characteristic of the *Rule* as a whole. It begins with the man where he is at the first stage of his monastic life, desiring all but knowing little, having everything to learn. And gradually, by probing and discussing first one and then another of the problems that face brethren in community life, the *Rule* takes them all deeper and deeper into an understanding of themselves and of what monastic life really means. We shall see, as we proceed, that with a few exceptions this is also true of each separate section: it begins by discussing the superficial aspects of a matter and bit by bit takes its readers to profounder levels of consideration. (The exceptions are chapter II, 1; III, 1; IV, 2.4.11; V, 10.11 and we shall need, later on, to look at each of these in order to uncover the reason for the deviations from the common pattern.)

The purpose of the precepts is to remove obstacles to love and unity, the obstacles that are built into each one of us when we enter the monastery, as well as into the very structure of community life. That is why the key words are "precepts" and "observance" and not "commands" and "obedience." The latter imply a person who gives commands and to whom one is obedient, while words precepts and observance suggest a way of life where certain ideals are protected by the observance of certain precepts. The way must always be open for flexibility, revision, change. Only so can dynamic love grow among the members; only so can deep unity and not superficial uniformity become a characteristic of the group. There has to be room and opportunity for growth, both for each individual and for the community as a whole. What the corporate observance of the precepts is designed to ensure is the building up of a stable community in which each person has an opportunity to seek and to serve God; and when this is a common possibility for every member, then a true community has been created.

Rule, Chapter I, 2

In the first place —
and this is the very reason for your being gathered together in one —
you should live in the house in unity of spirit
and you should have one soul and one heart
entirely centered upon God.

This very next sentence sets the scene and provides the score for the — no, opera is not the right analogy now — symphony that is to be composed by the brothers in monastery: the monks are to be one in spirit (*unanimes*) and to have one soul and one heart (*anima una et cor unum*).

On the face of it, it would seem that for the man whose whole life is set on the search and the service of God, a life lived in the constant company of others might be more of a hindrance than a help. And, indeed, a life of separation from others was the seed from which all monastic history has grown. Separation and solitude are necessities for those who are called to this life of self-effacing sacrifice, but normally the human spirit can tolerate this discipline only for short periods and in some cases never at all. For most people, being with others is a necessary safeguard in the search for God, for in this is the surest way of remaining fully human and consequently fully alive to receive the God who comes to meet them in their search.

NEED FOR EACH OTHER

We need one another, in the first place, because we are not self-sufficient. We support each other, we console, correct, and encourage each other. Through the closeness of others, with their

individual characteristics, we grow in compassion and understanding, in tolerance and in the ability to forgive. Through awareness of others, our horizons are widened and our perspectives
become truer, and above all, our capacity to love and to accept is
developed. These are the terms of our giving, in the common life.
And what we receive is something infinitely greater, for while we
can only give from within our own single self we receive from
each member of the group according to his capacity to give and
so to enrich.

We receive the love and the acceptance of the group. For most
newcomers the experience of welcome and loving care of the first
days and weeks is the thing that strikes them most, when they
have come to the monastery from the wear and tear of work and
play in ordinary life. And so we go on, discovering meanwhile the
things in the self that divide one from another; we learn to discern
the deep, tolerating, and accepting love that binds us together as
a group — as a unity in Christ. It is from this experience of loving
acceptance that compassion for others grows: we only dare suffer
with others when we know ourselves to be cared for, to have
meaning in the lives of others. (There is an essential difference in
quality between this sort of sharing of love and the doing-good-
to-others which is unconsciously motivated by the need for self-
compensation. This inferior form of service is, of course, always
ready to go into action; but its recipients recognize its quality
before the do-gooder himself does so.) It is only when we have
ourselves experienced being understood that we can commit
ourselves to the self-loss that is an inevitable part of a deep
understanding of others. I use the word self-loss here because
every profound encounter with another must involve a giving
away of a part of oneself, must involve a change in our own
position and a shifting of our equilibrium; and such self-giving
and self-loss is one of the chief contributing factors in the growth
and development of the group — it is a way forward as well as a
way down into deeper unity. It is only as we risk all in a situation
that we can learn to tolerate the weakness and ineptitude of others
and to forgive the sin which harms our self, the group or humankind. It is only when we have taken the risk and then discovered
the enveloping love and upholding of God that we can extend
such love and upholding to others. And, finally, it is only when
we have plumbed the depths of our own weakness and incompetence which life in the group shows up that we can receive in

humility the abrasive correction, the strengthening consolation, and the enduring encouragement of our fellows. This is the common experience of each one, made known to us in our own unique person but recognized by us in every member of the group; this is how the unity of the group becomes a living and growing reality.

UNITY OF SPIRIT

As our life becomes more real, as we recognize ourselves for what we are, and as we recognize the action of God in our own life and in the life of our companions, so we grow into true unity which is perfected in Christ. As Bishop John Taylor has written:

> One Faith, one Lord can only mean that there is one absolute Way and Truth and Life, but for those who follow him the different degrees of their attainment are far less noticeable than the similarity of their insufficiency, and their unity comes from the divine grace which makes up the short measure of each to a common completeness in Christ.[20]

These twentieth-century words describe the experience that is explored in the fourth-century *Rule* of Augustine. Unity is set forth at the beginning as the primary reason for life in the monastery; the insufficiencies of us all for this life and the ways of meeting them are probed and discussed in a number of characteristic situations of community life; and finally we discover that it is the grace of God which brings us to a common completeness in Christ which is both the term of the search and the witness of service for each individual in the monastery.

The first mark of the community's life is to be its unity of spirit, but this is not brought about by a uniform conformity. As we have seen, there has to be room in the community for a wide range of temperaments, gifts, needs, and modes of expression. There has to be room for every form of prayer, for many forms of service; there has to be scope for honest inquiry as each one is led forward in his search for God. If that be so, how is unity possible and why is it above all things desirable? We can only reach the answer to our first question by examining the second.

Unity of spirit within the group stems from the very fact of the search in which all are engaged. Each individual has been called by God into one particular community, to fulfill a particular ministry at a particular point in time, and all are engaged in making a response to the truth of God. As he is one and truth is one, so unity is reflected among those who seek him and his truth. As the One is made known to us and is experienced by us in the relations of the Trinity, so the experience of many, centered in the Trinity, may express a unity of spirit that is a reflection of the unity of God.[21]

Unity is never reached by striving; it is always a gift. Yet at the same time, it can only be achieved if there is honest and costly scrutiny of ideas, motives and actions. There is no room for falsehood in unity, and that is why unity and truth are inseparably linked. So in Augustine's *Rule* the monk finds his thoughts, indeed his very self, being constantly challenged and sifted by the mere fact of his being gathered together with others in the monastery. Togetherness is a necessity for all at the beginning of their monastic life, and for most it remains a necessity. For along with the challenge there is also companionship on the journey. "Why, I ask," Augustine asks himself in his *Soliloquies* (I, 20, 20), "do you wish your friends to live and to live together? That with one mind we may together seek knowledge of our souls and God."

Paradoxically, one of the things that makes unity difficult to express in community life is idealism. The person who has got his high ideals sorted out and tabulated finds it hard to adjust to the ideals of others. Similarly, perfectionism has a hard time in coming to terms with the values and priorities of others. As Bishop Taylor put it in the passage quoted above, the thing that really unites is the similarity of insufficiency. To set out to find a way of living in unity of spirit is a very courageous thing to do, and what it entails is something that we have hardly any inkling of when we enter the monastery. For it is all-embracing, and most of us are too little to dare, or even to want, to include all patterns in the design. So the problems involved begin to leap from this page. Perhaps the best thing to do is to make a list of them now, and to find the answers to them as they are developed in the text.

The monks are bidden to live in the house in unity of spirit, but how can such unity develop between them when they are all so different? How are their inevitably differing attitudes to material goods to be brought together and harmonized? How, with unity of spirit as the goal, are the diverse needs of individuals to be met? What sort of pattern of a common life can be achieved among people with all their individual needs and attitudes? How is each member of the group to assimilate the different traditions of the other members, and how is he to adapt himself to them?

These are the problems that are considered in the remainder of this chapter of the *Rule*. The same method of inquiry is followed in each specific case. First the surface is examined and described; then the deeper implications are explored and finally the heart of the matter is reached — the center where God, and God's answer to the problem, are to be found. It takes courage to attack difficult situations in community life, as in every other area of living, and it is this very quality that gives richness and an appropriateness to the probing of problems in the *Rule*: the conclusions are reached out of living situations. Unity of spirit is the goal in all circumstances of the common life, and that implies no rigidity but a constant movement. What Peter Brown has written of Augustine's thought as a whole is certainly true of the *Rule*: "This thought never appears as a 'doctrine' in a state of rest: it is marked by a painful and protracted attempt to embrace and resolve tensions."[22] That is why a quick glance at the *Rule* might give the impression that it deals only with difficult situations. But in fact it is through seeking stability in such situations that the *Rule* endeavors to establish a community on that rock which is Christ.

The community's first witness to God at the heart of its life is to be unity of spirit based on a common vocation to serve him in that house and within that group. The recognition of this common vocation within each other is itself a powerful factor in resolving the tensions that inevitably arise, but that in itself is not sufficient to surmount all the difficulties. So, as a first step in deepening the experience of the group the *Rule* proposes imitation of the common life of the first Christians in Jerusalem who had *one soul and one heart* (Acts 4:32). This was the model of community living which Augustine adopted when he established his first community at Hippo,[23] and he frequently referred to it in a monastic context throughout his life.[24] At the beginning of our religious life, imitation is the commonest way of entry into the traditions of the group: the first stage consists of finding one's bearings in the ways of the house, then comes learning the meaning of these ways, and after that the real process of assimilation begins. It is then that the ideal begins to be translated into the actual, and experience tests, evaluates, and eventually comes to accept the demands of the common life.

The ideal of shared living is a high one, and the collapse of that first apostolic attempt in Jerusalem has never deterred later followers of Christ from trying to achieve it. In fact, it is only by failure that such an ideal can in any sense be achieved, for failure and not success takes people into their innermost self where they can dare to live in truth with others. Accepting failure into the pattern of life requires time, and perhaps religious communities are more fortunate than the first Christians were in having time on their side. In normal circumstances, communities have the opportunity to redeem the time, to learn from their mistakes, to make concessions and — here I refer again, and not for the last time, to one of the fundamental requirements of monastic life — to make room for each and every member in his or her present dynamic situation. A community is always on the move.

IN DEUM

At the beginning of life in the monastery, generosity and love make it comparatively easy, both in theory and practice, to set aside one's own feeling and to be caught up in the outlook and attitudes of the group. Problems begin to arise as soon as a conflict of interests emerges — as was the case in Jerusalem. Then the nature of the challenge begins to appear. This challenge concerns a person's identity, meaning, and aspirations. What I am, what I am meant to be, what I desire to become: this and much else becomes articulate, and it can very easily suffocate us as we go on. But the *Rule* redirects us — nothing that we do in the monastery has any meaning unless it is "entirely centered upon God." God is the center to which we must return again and again. He is the still center of our search; he is the center from which we go outward to serve. He is our safeguard and our security. He is our meaning, and we find our meaning in him.

"Entirely centered upon God" is actually a periphrasis of Augustine's almost untranslatable *in deum*. What I have tried to do is to express something of the all-embracing experience of Christian life lived together. To be with others in a life that is entirely related to God in love and adoration is to live the life of heaven. The unity of those in the monastery is to be *in deum*. It is to be a way of movement toward God, a movement into him, an ascent up to him from our weak human situation. It is to go on, perseveringly and in the face of failure, always striving to find him. This unity is for his sake and to be striven for only for his sake and not for the sake of unity as such; indeed, it is only worth striving for because it brings us all closer to him. For our lives are to be founded on his life which he shares with all, and we are to show that we are always about his business. All that we do is to be related to him, is to be a positive sign of our nearness to him. Our one purpose is to express his purpose for the world and we are to be the means by which he works. More than that, we are to work in the manner in which he works.

All of these phrases are what my dictionary[25] tells me are translations of the Latin word *in*, and I decided to use the words "entirely centered upon" as a way of expressing the purpose and also the richness of the relationship between each monk and God which this phrase implies. God is the companion on the way as well as the end of the journey, and this is the truth that binds the monks together in soul and in heart so that, in the measure that they are faithful, their life reflects his life lived among men.

IMITATORS OF CHRIST

We have already noted that at the beginning life in the monastery tends to be imitative. But the monks are not only bidden to follow the example of the common life of the first Christians; they are also to be imitators of Christ, for it is he who has revealed the unity of God to his followers. *Holy Father, keep those you have given me true to your name, so that they may be one like us* (Jn 17:11). This is to be the quality of our unity. This prayer of Jesus expresses the kind of relationship that he desires should exist among his followers. John 17 is a chorale on the unity within God which Jesus experienced as man. How God, as God, understands and knows this unity is something that we cannot know; but as man Jesus expressed it in human terms. Moreover, he prayed that it might be the experience of his friends. The sixfold repetition of the word *Father* (in verses 1.5.11.21.24 and 25) expresses both dependence and trust. In verse 1 the reciprocity of the relationship between Father and Son is described in terms of *glory*; and the real meaning of this glory is made explicit in verse 24 — it is *the glory you have given me because you loved me before the foundation of the world*. Unity is above all a reciprocity of love, and from this are derived all the other facets which are described in this chapter. There is shared power and mutual trust (verse 2) which is paralleled by identity of will and purpose expressed in obedience (verse 4), and through these the glory of the Father is reflected in the glory of the Son (verse 5). In verses 6-10 the theme is the receiving and giving which, again, is reflected in glory (and all of this with dereliction and death awaiting him!). But even that holy word *glory* does not express the fullness and wonder of the intimacy and trust between Son and Father, and indeed nothing can adequately describe it, so that Jesus in this prayer can say no more than *that they may be one like us*. Yet out of his very humanness he still tries to express, because love is compelled to try to express, some of the consequences of such unity. His joy in the Father must be shared with his friends (verse 13); he longs for them to be aware of and live within the truth such as he himself knows (verses 17-19); he desires that they may know the mutual indwelling which he has with the Father (verse 21), that even they may know it in terms of glory. He prays that his friends, in their experience of union with God, may be *so completely one* (verse 23) that their transparent companionship may be a witness to love itself; and through that companionship they will both know each other and be known to each other. So the friends of Jesus in their relatedness will be mirrors of the relatedness of the Father and the Son and vehicles of the self-giving love of the Son for all humankind.

This, then, is the quality of the unity that the *Rule* describes as being the *raison d'être* for living together in the monastery. A unity that is going to aim so high, as it were, will necessarily have to dig deep foundations. It will test every man to the core of his being, and to the heart of his faith. In human terms it would not even be sensible to expect that such a way of living could be possible; it is only when men are *in deum* that such an attempt can be made.

In one sense, all our effort and striving is a search for that unity; in another sense, the effort and striving can only be sustained because those involved are already united, or are at least committed to unity. The reason why true unity is so painfully come by and why uniformity on the one hand and courteous forbearance on the other are no substitute for it is that in itself unity differentiates. At first it seems surprising that the idea of unity which is so strongly stressed in this passage at the beginning of the *Rule* is only referred to specifically in one other passage: *united in mind and heart* (chapter I, 8). But this makes sense in the light of John 17: Unity is the expression of the glory of love. And that is what the common life of the monastery is meant to be. As William Johnston has put it: "Jesus prays that his disciples may be one, that they may be completely one — *even as thou, Father, art in me, and I in thee.* And yet they are not one, because each retains his own personality."[26]

It is the retention of one's own personality that is both the strength and the bane of the common life, for we are hampered on all sides. Within ourselves we are hampered by lack of self-knowledge, by fear and by guilt, and the like; within the group we are inhibited by lack of perception and knowledge of other people, by our own limited horizons, by all the sins, negligence and offenses that hinder us from seeing other people as they really are: pride, resentment, the desire to dominate, and all the rest. That is why the remainder of the *Rule*, and of this chapter in particular, is concerned with exploring the obstacles to unity that are to be encountered by those living in the monastery. Some of these go to the depths while others seem more trivial; but all of them constitute very real problems which we all have to try to solve.

The method of exploring situations and relating them to theological truth is used frequently in Paul's letters, and what has been written of 1 Corinthians can be applied to the *Rule* which also shows "theology at work, theology being used as it was intended to be used, in the criticism and establishing of persons, institutions, practices and ideas."[27] Moreover, as is pointed out in the discussion of 1 Corinthians 1:10b (translated as *unity of mind and opinion*), "disunity is fundamentally a matter of mind and opinion, that is, of doctrine, and it is here that restoration and reconciliation must take place."[28] What the *Rule* does for the monk is to lead him from the ideas expressed in chapter I, 2 — that is, imitation of the apostles and imitation of Christ — step by step through all the happenings of monastic life, down into the great climax of theological and spiritual understanding of chapter VIII, 1 where all that the monks do and are is seen to stem from the fact that they have become free persons established in grace.

THE MONASTERY SHARING ITS LIFE

Before we begin our exploration of the rest of the *Rule* there is one primary situation that must be looked into. The *Rule* for the most part is concerned with what happens in the monastery, but the place of the monastery within a larger whole is important both from the point of view of the individual members but also for that whole itself. This is not spelled out word-for-word in the text, but it is implicit in the very wording of the paragraph which we are now considering. We have seen that the oneness of the community is expressed as a dwelling together; even the dwelling together *in domo* (in the house/in the household) is mentioned. The evocation of the life of the first Christians in Jerusalem, who were one in mind and heart, and the setting of the whole life of the monastery *in deum*, in God, coupled with the idea of the household which we have just mentioned, all stress the important fact of the close relationship between the monastery and the Church.[29] Indeed, the unity of the monks cannot be a true unity unless it is an expression of the Church's life and witness. More than that, it cannot be true unity unless there is oneness with and in the Church: a Christian monastery is unthinkable outside the context of the life of the Church. It is, of course, possible to build a community without reference to the Church and, indeed, many such do exist. But the special character of a monastic community is that its life is a part of, an expression of, the whole Church. The overriding reason why the life of the monks must be a continual striving for unity is the nature of the unity of the Church itself: its union with Christ and in Christ. "All men are one in Christ, and the unity of the Christians constitutes but one man" (*Expositions of the Psalms* 39, 2). So says Augustine, and in another place he is even more emphatic: "This man is one, and all men are this man: for all are one, since Christ is one" (*Expositions of the Psalms* 127,3). This *totus Christus* is, though, more than the meaning of and the reason for the unity of the brethren: the one Christ is their very life.[30] And it is this fact that makes it possible for each and every monk to set heart and mind to the task of resolving difficulties and breaking down barriers, for the life of Christ is a continuing work of salvation and he is still active in every situation to redeem and to cherish if men do not hinder him.

That much may be said of the Church-situation of the men within the monastery. But we need to go further and look at the place of the monastic community itself in the life of the Church. It has taken a long time for Christians inside and outside monasteries to understand that the religious life is only one way of living a fully committed life. The inflated idea of monastic vocation, which seems to have come first from outside rather than from inside, is belied in the *Rule* by the very ordinariness of the problems which it faces: few of them are unique to monastic situations. The similarity of insufficiency, to use Bishop Taylor's phrase, is — if men are humble — a binding force and also a strength in the life of the Church. But this is only possible if there is real communication between Christians inside and outside monasteries. Perhaps one of the most important areas of witness for religious today is the sharing of their ordinariness within the whole life of the Church. The claiming or according of privilege is a destructive element within the Church, and certainly in the life of a monastery. Perhaps the *Rule*'s insight, although it is related to a different area of need and consideration from the one that we are looking at here, is relevant to this matter also. Chapter III, 4 states that if those in weakness are given special treatment they are not thereby given honor but only a concession to their weakness. The fact of the self-limitation of monastic life is a source of weakness in relation to the ordinary affairs of men, and we should not regard them as a reason for being given deference. If on any occasion which involves people outside the monastery we or our community as a whole are accorded special treatment, this should be regarded as a concession to weakness and not an expression of honor (and that by both giver and receiver). On the other hand, all that a community may properly do with the experience and understanding that has come to it through its particular vocation is to make that available in whatever ways seem possible to the Church and to the world. Religious do not know all the answers, and all must recognize that in many areas those outside the monastery have more to give than those inside. We have tended to forget that as part of the *totus Christus* we are sharers, and the give-and-take that is learned in community life must be extended to the whole body, and through the body to the world. For that, both heart and mind, always centered upon God, must be ever alert to the heart and mind of others, both within and outside the Church.

Rule, Chapter I, 3

And, then, you should not call anything your own,
but rather you should have everything in common.
Food and clothing should be allotted to each of you by your prior,
not equally to all because you are not all equally strong,
but to each one according to his need.
For thus you read in the Acts of the Apostles:
They had everything in common
and distribution was made to each as any had need.

Having set the scene — the monastery (chapter I, 1) — and stated the purpose of its existence — unity, centered upon God (chapter I, 2) — the *Rule* then goes on to consider in general what the day-to-day life of the monks should be like.

ALL THINGS IN COMMON

The very first counsel is a deep challenge: "you should not call anything your own" (*non dicatis aliquid proprium*). This goes to the heart of a man's readiness to give away all that he has. Can he set aside the longing to possess, to grasp for himself, the things that he sees around him? What about the dominion over creation that Genesis 1:28 states has been given by God to man? What about the urge to establish one's own security which the psychologists say is a part of one's humanness? What about the need to possess largesse in order to be able to bestow it? What about the inescapable fact that no one person can regard with understanding every existing thing and its corollary that some are able to act dispassionately toward certain things while others can do the same toward different ones? What about the fluctuations in awareness that health and age cause in everyone?

The value of things in themselves is not to be minimized; it is the monk's helpless attachment to them that has to be reduced. At first, as the *Rule* points out, the will has to be taken for the deed: "you should not call (*dicatis*) anything your own." Words express feeling and intention, and the choice and use of words is what forms habit. For the newcomer to the monastery who has already parted with or is about to dispose of his possessions, the difficulty is relatively small; he is only too aware of having separated himself from his own things and has nothing he can call his own, and almost everything that he sees around him is certainly not his possession. The challenge begins to emerge as and when the man becomes part of the community, when he has responsibility for the things that he uses — and the greater his developing skills the larger the number will be.

Of course, it is unreal and pedantic to avoid all use of possessive pronouns. It is significant that while in the text the word *your* (singular and plural: *tuus, uester*) occurs some seventeen times, *tuus* occurs only once, at chapter IV, 8, while *uester* is found in this present paragraph and also at chapter III, 1; IV, 3 (twice), 4.6.8 and 9; V, 1 (twice), 2 (twice) and 4, VI, 2 (twice) and VII, 3. Now the important thing is that although not every agreeing noun is that of a material thing (sometimes it describes behavior or relationship), without exception the word *your* occurs in sentences that are concerned with acting responsibly: distribution of food and clothing, self-discipline, the religious habit, social behavior in various aspects, responsibility for one another, the care of and the attitude toward the community's clothing, work in common, prayer, and forgiveness. This provides the clue to the meaning of this first precept: you are not behaving responsibly if you consider things as your own personal property. Everything in the monastery is the responsibility of all. The word personal (*proprius*) only occurs again in chapter V, 2, where it is mentioned four times. A monastery does not work like a factory conveyor-belt, where each person is responsible for one small part and rarely knows the complete product. In the monastery everything is to be known and available: "Have everything in common" (*sint uobis omnia communia*), and that not only for the monks' use but also for their delight.

Joint responsibility, if it is to be effective, has to be based on shared knowledge. Even if one member does not have cause to make use of some objects, nevertheless the fact of their existence should be a part of that person. There is no point in placing a guitar in the hands of someone with no musical sense yet he or she may delight in the knowledge that the instrument is available for those who can play it.

As we have just said, even references to personal possessions — real or assumed — are few in the *Rule*, but the theme of having all things in common (*communia*) is stressed throughout this chapter (twice in this paragraph, in chapter I, 4 and 7), and it is repeated in chapter V, 1, 2 (five times) and 3. In the present chapter it appears with emphasis in the context of striving to establish unity, and in chapter V equally emphatically it is seen as an aspect of love in action. The connection between unity and love scarcely needs to be pointed out.

RESPECT FOR INDIVIDUAL NEEDS

In the broadest sense, the primary unifying experience of having all in common is that of common delight. All may enjoy the fact of the object's existence and presence in the monastery; and if it is a gift, all may feel gratitude toward the giver. A smaller number will put it to use and care for it. (It is worthwhile at this point to mention Augustine's important distinction between

using and enjoying (*uti* and *frui*) which we shall need to consider
further in chapter I, 5). To ensure that a thing is used where it is
most needed, one person with sufficient knowledge of all needs
is responsible for its allocation. In this present paragraph this
general principle refers to food and clothing only, and the responsible person is the prior; but the same holds good for all other
possessions of the community, though in many cases it will be the
leader of a smaller group who will bear that responsibility.

It is at this point that the paragraph moves from the superficial
level of material objects to the deeper level of the persons involved, from the mechanics of administration to the work of
caring. The allocation is to be made "according to need" (*sicut
cuique opus fuerit*). It is unity and not uniformity that is at stake,
and this must always be a corporate work. Although it is the prior
alone who is to allocate, and who also is in the best position to
assess relative needs, the fact of needs must be a matter of sensitive
awareness for all the community. Although only one person can
accept one article of clothing, all must accept his need for it.

People vary so much. For some it is easy to recognize one's own
need and to make it known; others are sometimes deluded (as the
Rule points out in another connection, at chapter V, 5); still others
do not easily know what is needful, either for their work or for
their well-being, and even these will vary in their ability to make
their needs known. Every member of the group has to learn to
keep all these factors in mind in his day-to-day living and in his
relationships within the monastery, and this is by no means an
easy lesson. Family groups have foundered for failing to observe
this precept (strange how that phrase came unbidden to mind!);
monastic groups do the same. If there is common property there
must, above all, be common concern. And common concern is a
milestone on the road to unity.

This certainly does not mean that the critical faculties and native
common sense of religious are to fall into disuse as they acquire
the art of allowing each of their companions to have as many
needs as they have themselves; on the contrary, all their perceptive skills are needed. They have to learn to distinguish, personally
and in others, true needs from false ones, half-knowledge from
understanding; they must also learn tact and discretion and infi-
nite patience; they have to grow in love before they dare to
challenge, and to practice endurance before they ask it of others.
They have to see themselves in their companions, people always

in need. And it is the growing ability to relate one's own condition to that of others that turns us from a person concerned with our own affairs (*propria*) into a person who can accept and cherish others as they are so that with them a true unity can be established.

No two people are alike and for that reason no community can grow on a foundation of egalitarianism: things are not to be apportioned "equally to all because you are not all equally strong" (*non aequaliter omnibus, quia non aequaliter ualetis omnes*). There is no principle of growth in a group that regards each member as a replica of the others, though this has been a hard lesson for humankind to assimilate, and again and again egalitarian blueprints have been produced. In the name of a theory, these ignore humanness and seek an easy solution. But there is no easy solution in community living because, for one thing, there are constant fluctuations in health, strength, and attitudes in each individual, and few needs are constant and unchanging. This last fact is an additional call to each member's perceptiveness, for all have to learn to notice changes in others and be ready to change themselves. As we have said already, a community is always on the move.

In this paragraph, variations in need are discussed in relation to food and clothing, that is, the basic needs of every man. Two different words are used in the text for food: *uictus* here and at chapters I, 5 and III, 3, and *alimentum* which occurs at chapter III, 1 and 4. There is a slight difference, but it does not amount to much. *Uictus* implies provisions, *alimentum* indicates nourishment. In the present context *uictus* is clearly appropriate. Similarly, the text has two words for clothing. *Tegumentum*, a covering, occurs only here while *uestis*, a garment, is used in chapter IV, 1, V, 1.3.4 and 9. *Tegumentum* is the less specific of the two, and, like *uictus*, indicates that in this first part of the *Rule* the considerations are all relatively simple and straightforward. This reflects a monk's experience of life in the monastery.

At first, needs are explicit mainly at this basic level, and for most adults entering a monastery this circumstance is at the least puzzling and is occasionally dangerous. Having one's needs provided for is a condition that one begins to grow out of as soon as one emerges from infancy; thereafter, one learns how to become more and more self-supporting so that the adult who enters a monastery has already acquired skill and resourcefulness in keeping himself alive. By dispossessing himself of his own property and entering a way of life in which all things are held in common, one is at the same time dispossessing oneself of the use of skills and resourcefulness for one's own benefit and placing all the experience that they imply at the disposal of the whole community. Often the impact of this is confusing and it seems to be largely a matter of temperament how easily anyone can in fact adjust to this new way of living without reverting to a childish outlook. There is no way to avoid having to face the danger of slipping back, for it is inherent in the situation. An important test of a newcomer's capacity for living a monastic life is the capacity to overcome the danger, to discover the meaning of this seemingly-strange requirement, and to be able to channel all one's knowledge and ability into the common life of the group.

LIVE LIKE THE FIRST CHRISTIANS

The way through this dilemma is indicated by the last sentence of the paragraph. In chapter I, 2 the reference to the life of the first Christians in Jerusalem was implicit; here, there is an explicit evocation of that life.[31] This immediately deepens the experience of complete dependence on others, for the fulfillment of even one's elementary needs, and adds a new dimension to it. It implies, first of all, a solidarity of outlook with that of the early Church; and by inference it sets the life of the monastery within the life of the Church.[32]

"For thus you read in the Acts of the Apostles." Having all things in common is a deliberately chosen sign of the Church. It is a proclamation of the great power with which the apostles first, and then their followers in succeeding generations, gave witness of the resurrection of the Lord Jesus.[33] For them self-dispossession and common property have as their motive power an emulation of the sacrifice of Christ, of his abandonment to the will of the Father, and a confident trust in the resurrection as the supreme event through which God's love and mercy could reach into the ordinary lives of ordinary people for all time. That is why, in spite of failure after failure, the example described in Acts 4 is still taken seriously. For living in this abandoned way is an expression of belief in the resurrection; more than that, it is an experience of resurrection, of the enabling power given by God through which Christians may live fully within a self-denying pattern of life. This is the personal experience of each individual and the corporate experience of the group. Within a religious community, common ownership relates each one's experience to that of every member of the group: all face the same problems and thus all are acquiring a wisdom in searching for answers. And this wisdom and understanding will inform the common attitude to possessions and basic needs; it will above all create the climate of opinion in which distribution according to need can be made. (Acts 6:1 provides an interesting and salutary example of failure to establish such a climate of opinion at a later stage among the Christians in Jerusalem.)

It is at this point, therefore, that the *Rule* (and the life of the community) begins to take on a deeper meaning. The *one soul and one heart* of chapter I, 2 must express itself first of all in meeting the basic needs of each brother. The important word here is *basic* — something to put on as clothing and something to put inside as food (later, the *Rule* will consider human frailty's fads and fancies — in chapter V, 1.4 and 5). The attitude of the group must be such that each can accept the needs of the others, and each can have confidence in making his needs known. This is a mature capacity, and one of the necessities of monastic life seems to be a recapitulation of development from primitive selfish human attitudes to a spiritual awareness that transcends them. This applies to all the fundamental human urges, but only the need for food and clothing is considered in this early part of the *Rule*. Further on, other impulses will be referred to.

NEED AND INTERDEPENDENCE

Twentieth-century man, post-Freudian and media-conditioned, is developing a highly sophisticated attitude to basic needs alongside a widening and uncritical acceptance of what constitutes necessity. The pattern of experienced needs in adult life reflects one's infantile patterns of self-protection, and thus in a monastery as in any other environment there can never be a hard-and-fast rule defining needs and their fulfillment. Need has a positive function in releasing a person into the reality of her or his situation and in enabling each one to act creatively. An illustration of this fact is given by Anthony Storr[34] when he quotes Nicholas Nabokov's description of Stravinsky's study — the meticulous arrangement of two pianos, two desks, two cupboards with books, scores and sheet music alphabetically arranged, a few small tables with cigarette boxes, lighters, holders, fluids, flints and pipe cleaners, five or six comfortable chairs and a couch. This

Hollywood study is poles apart from a monastery in Hippo at the end of the fourth century, and from every other monastery since then, but I have referred to it because it underlines Augustine's important point which is repeated frequently in the *Rule*: need must be accepted and taken seriously. So we must turn to the *Rule* and try to discover what its author is saying.

Augustine uses two words for *need*. In the present passage (twice) and in chapter I, 5; V, 1 and 8, the word is *opus*; it implies the lack of something, the fact that something is wanting in order to make a situation viable. In a far larger number of cases, the words used imply an element of inevitability in the lack: *necessarius* occurs at chapter I, 5; V, 3 (twice) and 11, and VII, 3. *Necesse* is found in chapter III, 5 and V, 7. *Necessitas* appears in chapter III, 5; V, 2.5 and 7, and VI, 3, while chapter V, 3 also uses *necessitudo*. All of these words carry overtones of deprivation.

Opus, then, is clearly related to the situation in which all goods are held in a common stock. When a monk lacks a thing it will be given to him from the general source of supply. We tend to get into tangles over asking for things because in English usage (and therefore in English thought) it is not easy to distinguish between what describes an ordinary lack and what describes a state of deprivation. *Opus*, one might say, concerns administration; with *necessitas* one enters the world of social service. In practice difficulties arise when the emotional overtones of *necessitas* are given play in an *opus*-situation. The challenge is to our willingness to be simple and direct. To say that your socks are past mending can be an agonizing and complicated proceeding for anyone who is trying to learn what poverty and self-denial mean in his new way of life. But such events as the end of the life of a sock, or great hunger after an exceptionally hard morning's digging, are normal events in anyone's life and the community's resources should be made available to supply what is lacking. Perhaps the lesson of Acts 6 is relevant here: it seems that the early common-property experiment failed just because the administration of those combined resources broke down. Later on, we shall have to discuss the question of how a community limits the quantity and the quality of its common property; but, as the *Rule* rightly shows, this can only be considered in a context that is both profounder and more demanding than the one that is being discussed here in chapter I, 3.

The use of the word *opus* is taken straight from Acts 4:35 (and also Acts 2:45). What is at stake is a simplicity of living that frees Christians, be they first-, fourth- or twentieth-century, from over-concern with their own basic needs and makes them available for the work of witness. If responsibility for making supplies available is vested in the prior or his delegates, then there is no cause for anxiety or distress among the community as a whole. Each monk is then free to give his time and energy to the primary bases of his vocation, the search for God, and a life of service. Thus what begins to emerge is the concept of mutuality in the life of the community, and a growing acceptance of interdependence — and with it a growing sense of security which after all is the need that lies behind that of food and clothing.

Distribution according to need does not inevitably lead to a sense of mutuality. It can, in other conditions, lead to an auto-matic, slot-machine attitude: you have/I ask/I get. Mutuality enters because the source of supply is the common property for which all to some degree have a responsibility. To be the distrib-utor is to be at risk, for that can deteriorate into being a slot-ma-chine; it is significant that this particular problem is not faced until well into the second part of the *Rule* (chapter V). Attention is drawn to it here merely because it has some bearing on the developing theme of mutuality which begins to appear here and which is taken further in the next paragraph. The newcomer begins to move from the sphere of administration into that of social service.

Rule, Chapter I, 4

At the moment of entering the monastery
those who had any property in the world
should hand it over willingly
so that it becomes common property.

A NEW DIMENSION OF LIVING

Here, in this short paragraph, the life of the monk is set in a new dimension of experience and understanding that takes him be-yond the superficial level of living inside a monastery and not outside it. The key phrase of the challenge of this section is *in saeculo*, and the key to interpreting it lies in the fact that it is Augustine who has set it in this sentence. For the moment we must put aside the question of how to translate it; that poses other problems. First we must try to discover what it means when Augustine uses it, as he frequently does throughout his life.[35] Luc Verheijen has made a detailed analysis[36] of the use of the word *saeculum* in the *Confessions* which was written almost contemporaneously with the *Rule*; thus the connotation in the former may be presumed to be the same as that in the latter. Modern devotional language has diminished the meaning of the word by making a distinction between life in a monastic or clerical setting (religious) and life outside it (secular). But such a distinction was not in Augustine's mind; for him the distinction is between Christian life and secular life. And he makes a further distinction, chiefly by the use of words and not by argument, between what we might for the moment call secular life (*saeculum*) and mundane life (*mundus*). Having examined all the texts in the *Confessions* — a work undertaken in order to determine why Augustine found the former more appropriate than the latter in the *Rule* (where it does not occur at all) — Verheijen concluded[37] that while *mundus* (which applies to space) is the symbol for people who, forgetting their creator, live without transcendent perspectives (an attitude which leads to idolatry), *saeculum* (which applies to time) is the symbol of people who conduct their lives without eternal perspectives (which is manifested in avarice, ambition, careerism, possessiveness, the desire to dominate, and the like). In renouncing the *saeculum* and entering a monastery a man undertakes a way of life that is quite different from that of other people.

Thus the use of both *saeculum* and *mundus* describes a one-dimensional way of living which roots men in time and space; and even though it allows room for movement of the human spirit it entirely discounts any relationship between human life and divine life. In the context of the *Rule mundus*, leading to idolatry, would have little meaning; for a monk as a committed Christian has already found the object of his worship through Christ. The *saeculum*, however, describes a state that the Christian must constantly continue to recognize and reject, for it is all around him; more than that, it is within him and manifests itself in avarice, ambition and the rest. It is, as R. A. Markus says, "The sphere of human living, history, society and its institutions characterized by the fact that in it the ultimate eschatalogical oppositions though present are not discernible."[38] And that is why the monk, in particular, must always resist its pressure, just as a healthy body always resists the pressure of disease. As Peter Brown has shown, Augustine actually uses the word pressure (*pressura*) to describe the experience of Christians within the *saeculum* which, he says, is "all-embracing and inescapable."[39] Brown goes on to say:

> The most obvious feature of man's life in this *saeculum* is that it is doomed to remain incomplete. No human potentiality can ever reach its fulfillment in it; no human tension can ever be fully resolved. The fulfillment of the human personality lies beyond; it is infinitely postponed to the end of time, to the Last Day and the glorious resurrection. Whoever thinks otherwise, says Augustine: "understands neither what he seeks, nor what he is that seeks it" (*Agreement among the Evangelists* II, 20).

So, for the monk, resisting the claims of the *saeculum* is an integral part of the search to which he has given himself; he is committed to moving, not once for all but constantly, beyond the *saeculum*. But before we consider what this means in the life of a monk, we must try to discover the best translation of the word itself.

In the *Rule*, *saeculum* occurs four times: here in chapters I, 4, (twice) I, 7 and again in III, 5. *Saecularis* is found in chapter III, 4. The significance of the fact that the word occurs only in the first half of the *Rule* will be explored at a later stage. The word clearly represents something, some experience, that a Christian must reject; and since a turning away from this *saeculum* necessitates for him an entry into some other tradition, it is best to turn to the roots of that tradition and look at the use of the word there. That means that we should look at the biblical use of the term and in particular at the use which Augustine makes of this material. In the *Confessions* he several times refers to New Testament passages which in their Latin form employ the word *saeculum* (Jn 16:33, Rom 12:2, and Eph 2:2).[40] I have consulted the main English translations of the Bible (the Authorized Version, Douay Bible, Jerusalem Bible, New English Bible, Revised Standard Version, the Revised Version, and the New American Bible) and have found that there is a wide consensus of opinion in the rendering of the word:

For Jn 16:33 all versions have "world"
For Rom 12:2 AV, DB, JB, RSV and RV have "world"
NEB has "present world"
NAB has "this age"
For Eph 2:2 AV, DB, JB, RSV and RV have "world"
NEB and NAB have "present age"

So it is the "world" that best describes the way of life that is to be left behind by the monk as he enters the monastery; he is to turn away from a way of living that is merely here-and-now, one-dimensional and without a religious ethos, and he is to set his feet on a road where all the signposts are written in eschatological terms. Some modern Christians find it offensive that the word world is employed to describe something that leaves God out of account, saying (with reason) that the world in the sense of created things is the sphere of his activity, whether men recognize it or not. But the force of this argument lies in the notion of space, not in that of time. The difficulty arises out of the poverty of English which has to use the same word to translate both *saeculum* and *mundus*. For instance, most of the instances of the use of the word world in the English translations of the New Testament have *mundus* as their Latin counterpart, because the concept is spatial[41] while world also translates *saeculum* which concerns time. While it must be admitted that the word world is open to misunderstanding, worldly and worldliness retain wholly the unequivocal sense of the one-dimensional which we have been describing.

It has been necessary to discuss some linguistic aspects of the present paragraph of the *Rule*, because without an understanding of what the words mean in the thought of the author it is impossible to see how at this point he is leading the monk to a deeper understanding of his vocation. When Augustine used the word now translated world in the *Confessions*, he frequently stressed the fact that every Christian must resist its impact on his thinking, and therefore on his behavior.[42] So when he uses the same word in relation to life in a monastery he is making the same point which may be expressed in two equally important ways.

In the first place, we may regard monastic life as an aspect of the life to which all Christians are called. Neither in essence nor in ethos does it differ from the life of other Christians. All who have been baptized are Christ-bearers, enabled by the Spirit to live as sons of the Father. Monasticism has gone wrong, to its own hindrance and that of the whole Church, in accepting the role that in any significant way differentiates its life from that of Christians outside the monastery. In our own day, the concept of the wholeness of Christian life, which Augustine was one of the earliest to make explicit in writing, is being recovered: with the result that no part of the Church's life looks the same as it did some twenty years ago. We now think in terms of, and are trying to make effective, what Paul saw clearly in the first century: that as the Spirit's gifts are diverse so are the ministries which they enable.[43] It is the very diversity of the gifts that constitutes the oneness of the body; and this calls for great reverence among all the members toward their own individual gifts as well as toward those of all the others. In theory it is fairly easy to see that there is no superiority of gifts, but in practice the downward pull of the "world" makes this very difficult to absorb and act upon. The opening words of Wordsworth's Sonnet XXXIII echo Augustine's insight:

> The world is too much with us; late and soon
> Getting and spending we lay waste our powers.

Secondly, while there is continuity and a unity in Christian life wherever it is lived, there is similarly a continued repetition of the act of turning away from the world. That is to say that fundamentally conversion is a process, not an event. Throughout life, there must be fresh movements away from what pulls us toward a shallow way of thinking and behaving; and this, not only because we encounter the same temptations again and again but also because our developing self-knowledge makes us aware of new aspects of our worldly outlook. Before Augustine's time, the life of a monk was regarded as an expression of his penitential turning to God, and after his time conversion became a classical word and concept in monastic tradition.[44] The notion is integral to all forms of monasticism; and the call to reform, to new beginnings, to penitent acceptance of one's weakness and failure is insistent. In the *Rule*, the thought occurs explicitly here in the first chapter and again in the last (chapter VIII, 2); most of the intervening chapters are concerned with first one and then another aspect of the matter.

RELINQUISH POSSESSIONS

So what is being postulated in the present paragraph's requirement that possessions are to be handed over and put into the common stock (*qui aliquid habebant . . . illud uelint esse commune*) is something much deeper than anything found in the preceding paragraph. Indeed, it will be well to look back to the development that began even earlier. Paragraph 2 described in general terms the unity that must characterize the common life of the monks, citing the early Jerusalem pattern for their imitation; paragraph 3 took the monk a stage further by providing for the fair distribution of goods from the common stock; paragraph 4 sees the handing over of possessions into that stock as a symbol of the monk's will-to-conversion, of his placing himself within the ongoing life of the Church. The handing over of possessions requires in a man the setting aside of their meaning for him; the meaning that the community gives to them may be equally valid but may be quite contrary to his own, as Augustine points out in Sermon 142, 8-9. Handing over the things a man brings with him to the monastery has something of the character of a sacramental act; it is an outward and visible sign of an inward and spiritual grace. It is not a mere matter of convenience or expediency; it is not just a gesture of compliance with the mores of the community; nor is it simply a sign of voluntary self-denial. It is an affirmation, the strongest that at this stage can be made next to that of entering the monastery itself, of a man's willingness to give himself completely to following the call of God, turning his back on worldly values as they have presented themselves to him in the past and as they will present themselves to him in the future. It is abandonment to a life of faith, a launching out into the deep, a walking on the water. And repeatedly throughout his life the monk will reaffirm this abandonment. He always has himself to give away.

All through life and at every turn the religious are challenged to think in a worldly way or in a Christian way. By the nature of our vocation, we must be constantly aware of the levels at which we are being challenged to think and act by the force of exterior circumstances. Our attitude to things has always to imply that their value exceeds utility and economics, for everything has meaning, simply because it is a created thing, and creation expresses the mind of God. So we see that a growing reverence for things marks an advance in the search for God. It is this that is at stake in the new monk's willingness to hand over his possessions when his road brings him to the monastery. English is inadequate to express the close relationship of thought that existed for the fourth-century monk between his handing over of his possessions and his voluntary commitment to the life of the monastery. Until well into the fifth century the common word for monastic commitment was not *votum* but *propositum* which in ordinary use meant a plan, intention, design or purpose and also a way of life. The significance of this in a monastic setting is that the noun derives from the verb *proponere*, whose primary meaning is to put forth or to place before. By placing his possessions before the community, the newcomer is committing himself to the life of the community. (Vows, as such, were at the time of the *Rule*'s writing a thing of the future and we must not try to read into the text something that is not there.)

SURRENDER AND FREEDOM

Newcomers to the monastery are to surrender their property willingly. The *Rule* states that they are to want to do it (*libenter . . . velint*; the Latin is strongly expressed). This handing over is a free act in which constraint lies only in the fact of love. Life in a monastery is meaningless without freedom, yet there is this paradox that the first free act that is required of the monk after his arrival is the surrender of all that he possesses, including himself. This free act may be described as the bridge between the world and the monastery, signalizing the repeated conversion to which the monk is called. Every choice is sterile unless it is freely made; assent to the requirements of the common life is without value unless it is freely given. In the *Rule*, the use of the words meaning freedom is infrequent, but the three passages (and their relative positions in the whole text) have a lot to say. The word *libenter* (willingly) occurs here in chapter I, 4; *libens* (translated gladly) is found in chapter VII, 3 where the prior is bidden to be *libens* in his keeping of the *Rule*'s precepts; *liberi*, in chapter VIII, 1 describes the state of monks who have found by God's help their whole meaning within the common life of the monastery — they are "free persons established in grace." A monk's life is a continual growing in the exercise of freedom — and how different this is from the world's understanding of the monastic way! Such freedom takes us deeper into our surroundings, deeper into ourselves, deeper into the lives of others, deeper into the life of God. The *Rule* traces a course which takes a monk beyond himself into fullness of life, but the course is not across a plain but across mountainous ranges where he finds frustration, sin, and pain.

The *Rule*'s use of the other word in the phrase which we are now considering (*uolo*) is a pointer to the crises through which each one will have to work his way if true freedom is to be found. At a first glance, the occurrences of the word seem disparate. Chapter II, 2 speaks of wishing to pray in the oratory (and possibly being thwarted); chapter III, 4 discusses jealousy; chapter IV, 4 refers to a wanton attitude to women while chapter IV, 5 (in two almost identical phrases) attempts to help the monk who is faced with this temptation; chapter IV, 8 is concerned with helping a brother to amend and the necessity of sifting good and bad motives; in chapter V, 5 the same verb is used in a discussion of sheer willfulness and chapter V, 7 takes this a step further by facing the temptation to collusion, while chapter VI, 2 goes to a deeper level and is concerned with those who are never willing to ask pardon. The word *uolo* is not found after chapter VI, and it should be noted that it is not until chapter VII — that is to say, not until false freedom has been exposed and overcome — that the question of obedience is probed. After that, there occur the telling repetitions of the true-freedom theme in the *libens/liberi* of the end of chapter VII and the beginning of chapter VIII. The occurrences of the verb meaning to will/to wish do in fact trace the course of conversion in monastic life. It is first used in connection with a desire to pray, it is then used in relation to temptations to sin, and finally it is used when humility and the need for forgiveness are being discussed. By this route, the monks arrive at a freedom that is not of the world's making but is the free gift of God. God honors the free gift of himself that each one makes willingly at the beginning of his life, and also every subsequent gift, to such an extent that each one finds himself to be not a compelled person following a set of instructions but a free person moving within the sphere of grace. But we will not discuss that prospect further here. There is much hard work that a monk has to take part in before he discovers that crowning glory of his religious life. We must go back to the monk at the beginning of his new life, when he willingly hands over all his possessions to the community.

Paragraph 3, which stated the necessity for having all things in common, was a response to the call of paragraph 2 for a common life of unity in which the group was given the ideal of having *one soul and one heart*. The willingly (*libenter*) of paragraph 4 has echoes of Paul's words in 2 Corinthians 12:15 which in the Latin read *Ego autem libentissime impendam, et superimpendar: ipse pro animabus uestris*. It is easy to find English words for the first part of that sentence: *I will most gladly spend* but *superimpendar* has defied most translators. *To be spent* is not enough: it is the prefix *super-* that takes us beyond the language at our disposal, as it also takes us beyond the experience that we already have. In echoing Paul's words, we are to allow ourselves to be overspent, to be used up completely, giving all that we have. And this is *for your soul's sake*; self-abandonment is for the sake of the deep unity of soul that is to characterize the life of the monastery. Within such a God-centered, God-embracing life, nothing less than a total gift will suffice. This is what a true common life is all about. Dispossession frees us for the only true security. Nevertheless, the obstacles to the achievement of a truly common life are as many as members of the community.

So the *Rule* goes on to discuss the elements that disrupt the common life and which provide the occasions for conversion and a growth toward true freedom.

Rule, Chapter I, 5

As regards those who had no possessions,
they should not seek to have in the monastery
things which they could not have had outside.
All the same if, because of illness, they are in need
they should be given whatever is necessary,
even though their poverty before entering was such
that they could not even obtain necessities.
Only they should not congratulate themselves on their good luck
in finding food and clothing
of a sort that they could not have found outside.

POSSESSIONS AND POSSESSIVENESS

If the handing over of personal possessions at the time of entry is an earnest (a deposit, as it were, made in good faith) of a person's will to continuous conversion from the standards of the world, it is fair to ask: What of those who have nothing to surrender? This is one of the problems which all communities have to face, for there is no getting away from the fact that everyone, rich or poor, is marked by his or her attitude to possessions. Not to have had possessions does not free one from being possessive in outlook; the temptation to be grasping and self-seeking is present all the same, perhaps even more so.

The situation which the *Rule* now discusses appears to be this: it is obviously the duty of the community as a whole (in its outlook) and of certain persons in particular (in the matter of administration) to see that the basic needs of all are supplied (see chapter I, 3) and to see also that there is a just distribution of the further resources of the community (aspects of this are discussed below in chapter I, 7). For some members this will involve a higher standard of living, because of the pooling of goods; for most it will ensure the immediate availability of a larger number of resources than are normally available to a single person in a small family unit. What is to be the attitude — not for the sake of convenience, but for the sake of the unity of the group — of each monk as he finds things available to him which he could not have obtained when he was still outside the monastery?

The fact has to be faced that in these matters pain is inevitable, that each monk may spend many years finding partial solutions to the problem and that he does not move into the area in which a true resolution can be found until his experience of life in the community has become deep and coordinated. In the present chapter, the difficulty is faced here in paragraph 5 and again in paragraph 6; the real answer lies far ahead and does not appear until chapter V, by which time the *Rule*'s description of the life of the community has taken on another dimension altogether.

Neither the former possessor nor the former non-possessor is actually in a more fortunate position than the other; their problems are different, as chapter I, 7 shows clearly. And this is important, because it at once establishes a bond of unity. We often get so absorbed with our own problems that we cannot realize that others are equally burdened with different difficulties. The recognition of the struggles of others is a way to the resolution of our own, and a unity of soul and heart within the group will only come when room is made for the struggles of each member.

For the man who has few or no possessions to bring to the community, the area of conflict is twofold. He has to recognize and understand his own attitudes to the things that he finds in the monastery, and to relate his growing insights to the life of the group; and he must also face the even subtler difficulty of relating his monastic situation to the way of life that he has left behind and to the life of the society in which the monastery exists. Unless each individual member is willing to confront these problems, the credibility of the monastery in the eyes of the world will be very low indeed. This is a matter in which we meet challenges at every turn, and we shall fail if we attempt to justify the monastery's life in worldly terms. The warning of this paragraph is that the monks' life must be consistent with their commitment to search for God in a life of love and to serve others in a selfless ministry.

So the newcomer who has brought nothing with him, who never sees around him things that were once his own, has to be aware of his emerging attitudes to the community's possessions. In general, there are two strands to all that is implied in the injunction not to seek for things that were not available to the monk before he entered — an injunction that would seem naive and simplistic if it stood alone. Its depth of meaning is related to the willing self-surrender that has been evoked in the previous paragraph and to the warning against cheap opportunism that occurs at the end of the present one. The immediate requirement of the passage is that if a monk did not have certain things in the years preceding his entry into the community he should not try to get them now. But if they are things that are commonly available to everyone, clearly he must be a sharer in their benefits: to decline to use things because one did not formerly do so is to stand still; it is to be ostrich-like in a refusal to recognize that all situations are fluid. This becomes clear when we realize that the situation that has been left behind is as much on the move as the one within the monastery. Otherwise, for instance, there could be no growing-point in skills and the use of artifacts, or in the ability to use books more intelligently. The challenge is to the nature of a man's response to the things that are made available to him. The two strands that make up the worldly attitude which this sentence warns against are, first, an attitude of envy toward those who formerly did possess such things, coupled with great resentment at having been deprived of them oneself, and, secondly, a possessive attitude to the things that are now available. We must look carefully at each of these difficulties.

ENVY AND RESENTMENT

In one way or another, every single member of the community will find that the common life makes accessible to him some goods (a word which I use deliberately, with all its ambiguities) which he would not come by elsewhere. In the western world, where there is to some extent a leveling of standards of living, this applies less to the basic necessities of life than it does in other matters; in other parts of the world, wide discrepancies in the availability of food and other essentials still make this an agonizing problem for a religious. There is no ideal answer to any of these problems. The solution that a community works out will only be a partial one, and even within the community this may not satisfy each individual member. Indeed, it seems that the inevitable pain of the members is itself a sharing with the pain of the deprived outside. We are all, in one way or another, in the position of a person in need; more than that, we are all stricken to some extent, distraught by the sheer impossibility of moving out of the area of our need. A community must make room for the grief and suffering of all its members; it must recognize that each distress is something that the whole group has to bear. It is in the context of Paul's understanding of the Church as a body (more than that, as the body of Christ) that he reminds the Christians of Corinth, who were by no means an ideal group, that there should be no discord among them: the members should care for one another and if one member suffers all suffer together.[45]

And while in some parts of the world discrepancies in wealth and the availability of material things have diminished and now present less acute problems, disparities in education, in general experience and in former opportunities for travel present very hurting challenges within a monastery. In that area dispossession is impossible, for those are goods that have made the man the person that he is. It is often a cause of bewildering distress to one who has had these benefits to find that they are a cause of mistrust and dissension within the group. On the other hand, it is equally hard for the one who has never possessed these good things to avoid bitter envy against their existence for others and bitter resentment against the fact that they do not exist for him. What this really illuminates in us is a deep mistrust of ourselves. It takes courage to face up to these real agonies, and we may thank God that Augustine did face up to them and see their importance for the unity of the common life of the monastery. We should not explore these problems, and indeed have no right to do so, unless we appreciate the pain that they involve, and there is plenty of evidence to show that Augustine did know what he was talking about when he set down this bold imperative near the beginning of the *Rule*: "those who had no possessions . . . should not seek to have . . . things which they could not have had outside."

These real distresses must call out from within a monk two distinct responses. The first is a deep generosity, for it is this that is freed into the mainstream of his life by his willing self-surrender to God within the monastery and all that it stands for. The impulse to envy is not itself sin; it is a basic human attitude that springs from the primitive recognition of the fact that here is a desirable object that I do not possess. Envy becomes sin when possession of the object becomes an imperative. The one who is not influenced by envy is able to say, "That good thing is not for me because it is not compatible with the way of life to which I am committed." In the face of enviable goods, each one must make a renewed and ever-renewed act of faith in God's love and power at work in our life. If our whole life is a response to God's glory and goodness, then it matters very little where our starting point is. God has found us; we have found God sufficiently to dare to hand over our person and our life to his safekeeping. For each monk whom the *Rule* addresses, neither his wide gifts nor his obvious limitations have prevented the meeting between God and his selfhood which has made his monastic vocation possible. So he can dare to live with the imponderable ambiguities that make him what he is; all of them make him less than he may be, less than he will be. It is the enabling power of God which will release him gradually into a life that is marked by a trust and a confidence that in his confined humanness he does not possess.

The second response, then, lies in the recognition of a growing reverence for the goodness of the things around him. There must be respect for the integrity of the thing itself and the integrity of the person who uses it (whether it is a new broom or a flair for languages). If he belittles the value of the thing, if he hates it (and it is all too easy to hate the wealth or the intellectual gifts of a brother), he is not giving it its true worth as an object of God's creation and as a sign of his desire to share his goodness with humankind. When he recognizes the goodness of God in this or that desirable thing, then he will not feel bitterness at his own lack of it.

He will have to face up to whatever resentment there is in himself because of this lack. It is one thing not to have; it is another and deeper thing to mind not having. If a man is greatly concerned about the good things that he does not have, this is very likely because he is not aware of the good things that are his — and which in fact do make him the man that he is. This whole matter is fully explored in chapter III, where the establishment of a harmonious common life is discussed. Here the problem is looked at from the point of view of the individual monk who is trying to find himself as a person in relation to all the other persons in the community. After all, when he decided to give himself freely to God he knew instinctively that he was giving all that was best in himself. It is a false modesty and an insult to God the giver to deny the existence of any good in oneself. But people tend to regard what goods they know are in themselves as if they were a do-it-yourself kit. No, they are God's tools which he places in our safekeeping. Counting one's blessings is not an adding-up game that is easily played. Indeed, there is a passivity in it that is nearer to the mathematics of chess where the moves of each player are constantly challenging the thought and action of the other. In fact, the healing of resentments can never take place until the factors presented by the other person (whom we often see as an opponent) are made a part of the pattern of our own life.

We can long to be without resentment, we can struggle against making it explicit in our conduct; but we cannot contrive its disappearance. We may find that it has burnt itself out (though we are never conscious of this happening), as and when we have set our sights in another direction and not looked for fuel for its nourishment. The decisive action for us is an act of conversion: a willing turning-away from the area of tormenting inadequacy into that of grateful recognition of resources that have been placed within our hands. Discovering more of what is within is a way forward toward fuller cooperation with the creativity of God, and it is the responsibility of the community to make this possible for all the members. And that, in terms of its resources and its attitude to them, must mean making room for the developing goods of each member and a willingness to provide whatever facilities are necessary. Not that give-and-take is in itself easy to achieve, for there are so many factors which have to be taken into account and which have validity of their own. As the *Rule* puts it, further on and in another context, "everything should be in keeping with your holy state" (IV, 3); no individual has the right to act contrary to the common good of the community, indeed no one should willingly disturb the goodwill of the community in his own interests. Again and again, as we shall see in the course of our exploring, the *Rule* faces the sort of adjustments that must be constantly made if the monastery is to be a place of life and not of death. Unreined resentment is lethal in its effects on the individual and on the group. With very few exceptions resentments are a part of one's humanness and bearing one another's burdens in this matter is an imperative for the group that would live the life of Christ; and this will express itself not in huge and obtrusive gestures but in small and ordinary ways.

HEALTH AND HEALING

For the sake of argument, as it were, the *Rule* therefore goes on to the statement that if a monk is ill he is to be given whatever is necessary for his healing, even if he would not have had access to these things if he were outside the monastery. That is to say, he is to be treated quite simply as a person in need. It is his present condition that is important, not his past — and that has a bearing on his own attitude as well as that of the brethren. Some might, because of an in-built lack of confidence, decline to receive things — clothing, bedding, warmth, extra food — which were beyond their means before they entered the monastery, but this would betray an inadequate understanding of one's own worth. If the community is the channel of God's love to each monk, then each must allow its resources to meet him. Earlier, in chapter I, 3, the *Rule* pointed out that needs are not equal because strengths are not so either. And this is the point: needs relate to present strength not to past background. In one way this may seem trite and not worth mentioning, but in practice it is not always easy to discern the measure of need just because, in this day and age, we are becoming more and more aware of the place of background in a present situation. There is a tendency to lose the wood for the trees and the *Rule*'s injunction to treat the man as you find him is a useful reminder that things do get unnecessarily over-complicated.

Poor health (*infirmitas*) is mentioned several times in the *Rule*[46] and that is not surprising for it is a factor that has to be taken seriously in community life. We shall need to consider it again more than once, as its different aspects are brought forward. Similarly, the backward look to former poverty (*paupertas*) is not something that makes no further appearance among the monks though, as we shall see later, it is found only in the first part of the *Rule*: here at chapters I, 5; in I, 6 (twice) and 7 (four times), and in III, 4 and 5. It is the discussions of the next two paragraphs of the present chapter that are going to need most attention. What needs to be pointed out now is the fact that the *Rule* takes it for granted, here and elsewhere (for example, chapter III, 1), that within the common life there will be continuing variations in what the monks are given as necessities, and it is the constant responsibility of each one to differentiate between what for him is necessity and what is luxury. This he can only do if he is always aware of the purpose of his life: besides God, any other possession has no meaning. Goods only contribute to our up-building and strengthening when they are valued for his sake and not for their own or even for one's own.

OUR SECURITY IS IN GOD

This is why the last sentence of this paragraph is so important: "they should not congratulate themselves on their good luck in finding food and clothing of a sort that they could not have found outside." Up till now, in this paragraph, we have found ourselves in a bridge-position between worldly attitudes that are one-dimensional and the attitudes of a man who knows that his life is set within the perspectives of eternity. It is this final sentence that leads the monk across the bridge on to the firm ground of his life in God. Augustine's phrase, which we have translated as "should not congratulate themselves on their good luck," is *non ideo se putent esse felices*. The word *felix* has a long history which the gentle English words felicity and felicitous do not reflect. My dictionary tells me that it is related to *fecundus* and primarily means fruitful or fertile. Applied to persons it means happy, successful, fortunate or lucky. By Augustine's time the noun had come to be used as an honorific applied to the emperor: *Felicitas tua*.[47] If these words, then, are used to refer to any other person there is a false resonance. Happy because successful an emperor may be, but *felix* applied to an ordinary man indicates a situation that is not based on true merits or true facts. There is a distortion here which is brought out in the English word lucky (in itself a somewhat cheap word). We shall meet the word again in chapter III, 3.4 and 5, and in VII, 3, and we shall always need to bear in mind the sense of falsity that is inherent in its use. Luck therefore appeared to be the best word to use in the translation of this sentence, for it underlines the fact that to exult in having access to things which were out of reach before one entered the monastery is an attitude unworthy of the man whose life is a search for God.

USE AND ENJOYMENT

Envy, resentment, pain: it takes courage to probe this raw nerve-center of disunity in a community. And we may ask how it was that Augustine had the daring to enter into this exploration so early in his precepts, and that with a group of men who, like himself, had not had more than a decade's experience of monastic life with all that that implies. Now during the year preceding the writing of the *Rule*, and at a time when he was still living among those men to whom it was addressed,[48] he had begun to work through the problem of a Christian's attitude to things in the first book of his *Teaching Christianity* (*De doctrina christiana*). Attitude is the operative word here, for it determines whether we enjoy things, whether we use them, and whether we do both — and why. Some things, he wrote:

> are to be enjoyed, others to be used, and there are others which are to be enjoyed and used. Those things which are to be enjoyed make us blessed. Those which are to be used help and, as it were, sustain us as we move toward blessedness (*Teaching Christianity* I, 3).

And again:

> To enjoy something is to cling to it with love for its own sake. To use something, however, is to employ it in obtaining that which you love, provided it is worthy of love (*ibid.*, I, 4).

Then in the same book he went on to uncover what he calls "illicit use." The example he gave was that of a traveler who wanted to get home because he was not happy abroad. The journey would take him by sea and by land, and vessels and vehicles would have to be used to help him on the way. If the traveler liked staying in inns and being in boats and on the road so much that he contrived to make his journey last as long as possible, then he would be enjoying these traveling amenities instead of using them. This is called illicit use. It is this same inferior attitude that Augustine is pointing out in telling the monks not to congratulate themselves when illness gave them access to niceties which they were not used to having. To enjoy and make use of the good things that are brought to the sick room is a proper thing for the patient to do, and his appreciation itself helps toward his healing; but if the man loses sight of their purpose and simply regards them as something to feather his nest with, then his attitude is cheap and unworthy. "If," as Augustine put it, "we . . . wish to enjoy those things which should be used, our course will be impeded and sometimes deflected, so that we are retarded in obtaining those things which are to be enjoyed, or even prevented altogether, shackled by an inferior love" (*Teaching Christianity* I, 3).

If a monk receives benefits in a spirit of one-upmanship, he has lost his way badly, for he has lost sight of God because of whom things may be enjoyed; instead, he has let himself enjoy things for his own sake. The supplying of special things to a brother who is ill is an act of love and an expression of the goodness of God, and he who receives them must — as Augustine would say — look beyond the things to what they signify. To relish things in themselves is what in Book III, 10 of the same treatise he calls cupidity. And the notion of cupidity/greed/avarice goes back to the world (*saeculum*) from which the monk committed himself to turn when he handed over all that he had when he entered the monastery.

So here in the *Rule* Augustine has once more challenged the monks to a deeper understanding of what their commitment involves. All created things are to be regarded as the gift of God, betokening his generosity to men. And the man with eyes to see God's goodness in the things that are given to him for his strengthening is the man in whom conversion is continually taking place; each new seeing is a conversion. More than that, each separate movement of conversion is a strengthening of the unity of the community, for if God is one every movement toward him draws men to the center where all are made one. In this way, the worldliness of envy and resentment can be courageously looked at; and until they are, there can be no healing of the pain that they cause. Augustine is telling the Hippo monks that the very desire for unity with God and with their brothers — more than that, in God and in their brothers — will give courage to face the problems which the disparity of God's gifts obliges them to experience.

Having, as it were, aired this problem on the level of material goods the *Rule* now approaches the more fundamental difficulty of social relationships and social distinctions.

Rule, Chapter I, 6

Nor should they give themselves airs
because they find themselves in the company of people
whom outside they would not have ventured to approach;
but they should lift up their heart on high
and not be seeking vain earthly things.
Otherwise, monasteries will become profitable to the rich
and not to the poor,
if the rich become humble there
and the poor become puffed up.

SOCIAL DISTINCTIONS

It is all too easy at this point, against the background of the self-consciously egalitarian attitudes of the late twentieth century, to expostulate and to say: How dare he? It is not done nowadays, or so we say, to draw attention to social distinctions. But unless these things are looked at honestly the pain that they cause will go on scraping and irritating until a moral abscess is formed in the life of the community.

As with material goods so in this area also there are difficulties in relation to those outside the monastery as well as to those within; both can give rise to justifiable criticism as well as to false guilt. In this paragraph, the ingrained outlook of the underprivileged is discussed; in the following one the common attitudes of the privileged are considered. Here, it is dissimilarities in social standing, wealth, talents, and education that must be looked at as they affect the life of the group as a whole, as well as the characteristic attitudes of those who are involuntarily dispossessed insofar as that may affect the unity of the group. For few people do these matters produce no problem at all in community life.

It is sometimes said that in approaching this matter Augustine was guilty of sheer arrogance, that he — a highly talented and traveled man, and a bishop — was writing down to the members of the "lower orders" in the community. But I do not think that this is so. Augustine was writing out of his own experience. And he was able to approach this very fragile aspect of human relationships with such frankness because he did not lose sight of the far deeper values which all the monks in the monastery had in common: the search for God and their work in his service. Experience shows that the pain of social and economic distinctions can never be healed by social and economic remedies. For Augustine they can only be really resolved where the dimension of contemplation is the chief thing that the members of the group have in common. In grappling as he does with the hurt and distress that disparities of gifts can cause within the monastery, he looked at them with what in another context he called the eye of the heart.[49]

In the *Confessions* (II, 3) he writes frankly about his upbringing and early years; and then he says: "But to whom am I telling this? . . . And to what purpose do I tell it? Simply that I and any other who may read may realize out of what depths we must cry to Thee."

Most of our information comes directly from the *Confessions* but there are further clues in his other writings and also, of course, in the *Life of Augustine* which his old friend and companion Possidius wrote after his death. According to this account, Augustine was the son of a *decurion*;[50] he himself simply said that his father held municipal office at Thagaste.[51] What these two statements show is that he was the son of an hereditary councilor in a small town in Roman North Africa. The family, he wrote elsewhere, was poor and education was not easily available; his cousins remained uneducated.[52] But, finding that there was a brilliant youngster in their midst, the father scraped together sufficient money for a good education (gaining the praise of his acquaintances for his generosity to the boy).[53] All the same, there had to be a year off school when he was sixteen, as funds were not to be found.[54] Fortunately, Augustine was encouraged by a wealthy patron, Romananius, who was as much at home in Rome as he was on his African estates.[55] When, after a few years of teaching, Augustine decided to seek his fortune in Rome (where, his friends promised him, there would be "greater earnings and higher dignity"),[56] he was sadly disillusioned and became very ill.[57] Fortunately, his talent had not gone unnoticed and he was urged to apply for the post of rhetor in Milan,[58] which was as much the center of the world as Rome was since the court spent a good deal of time there. In modern terms, this makes a good magazine story: the local boy makes good. But the long way that the Thagaste boy had traveled, not only into new places but also into widening intellectual and social circles, had made the marks on him that such a progression makes on anyone who experiences it. The *persona* that such a man develops in such a situation is generally marked by inner uncertainty, self-consciousness (Augustine, for instance, was very aware of his provincial accent),[59] brashness and a kind of brittleness that has a false note in it (if such a mixed metaphor may be allowed in describing a mixed-up person). The brilliant young man from North Africa was clearly attracted to Rome by alluring prospects (and was not a little daunted to find that his social betters were more disinclined to pay their children's tuition fees than their wealth warranted).[60] And the heady life on the edge of the court in Milan where, as he wrote, he had many powerful friends and where, on his own admission, he had been "all hot for honors, money, marriage,"[61] led him to think that a governorship and a rich marriage were not beyond the bounds of possibility.[62]

AUGUSTINE'S WORLD

This was the man who ten years later told the monks he knew so well that they should not give themselves airs (*nec erigent ceruicem*) because they found themselves in the company (*sociantur*) of their social superiors. And there is no cause for surprise that this situation should have to be faced within a monastery, for it had presented difficulties within the Church from the very beginning — inevitably, because the Church existed in a definite society with its own recognizable social structures, as the Church always does at all times. Whether it challenges these structures or reinforces them, they are still there and their existence has to be acknowledged. In the Roman world of the fourth century, unlike the world of today, social structures were created not only financially and culturally but also legally so that the evening out of distinctions was more difficult than it is now. Leaving aside slaves who formed one unit within society, among free men there was a division between *honestiores* and *humiliores*. Among the former were senators, *honorati*, barristers, civil servants, soldiers, members of the liberal professions, the Christian clergy, as well as decurions and veterans who formed the lowest class (Augustine's father was one of these). Those who were not slaves and were not *honestiores* were *humiliores*, generally landless but always poor and underprivileged; they were subject to severer legal penalties than were the *honestiores*, were in certain circumstances claimed for compulsory work for the government, and were always at the mercy of the latter's agents who were responsible for the recovery of debts owed to the state.[63] Thus no man could be indifferent to his social position even though personal relationships might be established across the barriers of status. Augustine himself began life just on the privileged side of the middle wall of the partition and his career took him a considerable distance from the dividing line. But a man rarely loses all the marks of his beginnings, so that when the decision to go home to Thagaste was made this meant a re-entry into a way of life that he had thought to escape from; more than that, it meant a reversal of thought.

Thus when it became necessary to provide guidelines for the community in the establishment of a life of authentic unity, this was one of the issues on which he could speak from singeing experience. In the monastery, where the whole of a man's life becomes exposed, in spite of the unifying fact of a common vocation, every nuance of thought will also become apparent; and the man who has been thrilled at receiving delicacies in illness will probably find himself becoming a social climber if he is not careful. Twentieth-century religious may not experience this acutely in relation to the members of their own group, but for most people who enter a community today this does present a problem in relation to those who visit the monastery. In this respect — and more so in proportion to the effectiveness of the community's ministry — most members do encounter people whom they would not have met in any other place. We have already mentioned the problem of monastic privilege in relation to the inflated respect that is often accorded to us; a further aspect of this privilege is the opportunity to meet and to be helped and strengthened by the talents and generosity of many wise men and women who place their resources at our disposal. Even if this does not often create problems within the monastery, it does create envy and therefore a sense of guilt in relation to our links outside the monastery — with our family and friends for instance. We shall have to look at this again when we consider the next paragraph. The matter is only mentioned here in order to fill out the picture of the difficulties of privilege in any form. A modern reader is aware of a biting edge in this paragraph; a reader in the fourth century would experience this bite in many parts of his life.

At this stage it will be well to discover what tradition had to offer to the monks by way of help in this situation. That is to say, we must look at what the early Church made of this puzzling anomaly in its corporate life. The particular aspect of the problem which the *Rule* considers (the temptation to be a social climber) is not discussed in the New Testament, but the correlative temptation to give especial honor to the wealthy and to discriminate against the poor in a congregation receives scathing treatment in James 2:1-9. The Jerusalem Bible, more than any other version, brings out the force of the writer's challenge: *My brother, do not try to combine faith in Jesus Christ, our glorified Lord, with the making of distinctions between classes of people . . . Can't you see that you have used two different standards in your mind?* Paul in Galatians 6:3 makes the pointed remark that *It is the people who are not important who often make the mistake of thinking that they are.* This brings us nearer to the attitude of mind that the *Rule* uncovers in this paragraph implying, as it does, an unacknowledged lower standard of thinking than the one that life in a monastery must elicit, that is, a worldly approach. And such an approach applies not only to other people but also to oneself. So long as a monk finds himself thinking in the terms of his former life, he will inevitably look at all his brothers in terms of their previous experience. It is impossible to make a frontal attack on this problem and think that it can be solved in one mighty confrontation; this is ground that has to be fought over and fallen into again and again, and rightly so. For this is the stuff of conversion, the gradual way from the world to the kingdom.

The fact of our background will repeatedly meet us, not only in our instantaneous reaction to things and events, but also through our friends and relations whom we in some way carry with us into monastic life. In fact, none of us has moved very far from the small boy who is ashamed of his mother's hat on sports' day. There can be real pain here which we can either deny or accept sensitively. Staretz (which means "the elder" in Russian) Silouan's "our brother is our life"[64] is very relevant here, and that in a literal sense: a brother or sister is a part of me that I either deny or welcome. So, down below the fourth-century tensions between *humiliores* and *honestiores*, this paragraph is instrumental in uncovering the false values and false images that we all attach to ourselves as a protection against our own limitations. These values and images mean so much to us; indeed they may mean everything. We may think that they are what we are, and for that reason we strain to reach them in our relationships as well as in our attitude to things. But the person who is set on a search for truth must discover where falsehood lies even though we may be unable to break away from the treadmill of our compulsive self-compensation.

ETERNAL VALUES

The *Rule*, taking its stand on Paul's words in Colossians 3:1-2, makes the strong point that it is not possible to move away from this crippling attitude to ourselves and to others so long as we continue to think in terms of status and of worldly categories: *They should lift up their heart on high and not be seeking for vain earthly things.*

Before we look for the implications of this passage in any detail, we must note the "should not seek" (*non quaerant*) which is a repetition of the phrase used previously in chapter I, 5. To seek for either food or companions of a sort that was not available before the entry into the community is a denial of the very reason for being there, it is a denial of the seriousness of a man's search for God. All the same, merely to tell anyone to stop looking for vain earthly things but instead to lift up his heart on high does rather leave him faced with a vast distance between these two poles. The passage in Colossians spells out what the *Rule* implies: that the move from a worldly attitude to a heavenly one is a resurrection experience: *If then you have been raised with Christ, seek the things that are above, where Christ is, seated at the right hand of God. Set your minds on things that are above, not on things that are on the earth.*

Within the context of the letter, it is clear that the reference is to death and life through baptism; in the context of life in a monastery, the reference is to a renewal of the commitment of baptism in a continual conversion from the things of the earth to the things above. Earthly circumstances and attitudes are all too well known to the newly baptized as well as to the men or women who now find themselves in a monastery. But we have died to them and are now living in the enabling power of Christ's resurrection. The whole of our being is evoked in Paul's *set your affection* (verse 2). The seeking of the things of Christ, the experience of new life lived with him, the knowledge that in our search we shall look into that place *where Christ is, seated at the right hand of God* — these are the things that make our self-conscious concern with food and status seem what they are, very paltry in the light of eternity.

It is in John's gospel that the immediacy of the power of Christ's resurrection is most fully described. In the account of the conversation of Jesus with Martha before the raising of Lazarus (11:24-26) there is what W. D. Davies calls "the conviction that the resurrection has moved from the future into the present for those who believe in Jesus."[65] But the way to this resurrection is, for Jesus as well as for his followers, the way of the cross; the glory of his resurrection is one with the glory of his crucifixion. We noted earlier that the reason for striving for unity is, as chapter 17 of John's gospel shows, that God's glory may be revealed and released into the human situation. Now we see, in the account of the actual events leading up to Christ's death, that glorification and complete self-giving are one (12:20-26). Thus the work of striving for unity is itself the way of releasing eternal values into the life of the monastery.

Eternal values within the monastery? That is too prosaic a way of describing the light and life of the *Rule's* brief half-sentence. The words of J. B. Lightfoot on the Colossians passage express the heart of the matter: "The change . . . must pervade a man's whole nature. It affects not only his practical conduct, but his intellectual conception also. It is nothing less than a removal into a new sphere of being. He is translated from earth to heaven: and with this translation his point of view is altered, his standard of judgement is wholly changed."[66]

Such a description is a far cry from all that is implied in the *Rule*'s pen-sketch at the beginning of this paragraph, of a man succumbing to pretentiousness because of the sort of people among whom he now lives. It is far, too, from the imitation of a fellowship that was postulated in chapter I, 2, even though the *Rule* there described that fellowship in terms of "one soul and one heart entirely centered upon God." Chapter I, 3 led the monks to differentiate between one another and to recognize what each man is in himself; and then chapter I, 4 presented the challenge of the conversion of person and values that must take place if "entirely centered upon God" is to become a reality. Chapter I, 5 probed a man's willingness to turn from one way of life to another; and now chapter I, 6 describes what the new life truly is: a life where the power of Christ's resurrection may be at work in and among the group, a life where each man's life is *hidden with Christ in God* (Col 3:3). Augustine has reached the point where the way of contemplation is opened up for the monk, even though the word itself does not occur at all in the text. When contemplation, the looking for the deep meaning of things, is the thread that holds together every aspect of the monk's life, then he can face up to the disturbing thoughts and events that obscure his vision and make him lose his way. His ordinary reactions to people and happenings will inevitably be conditioned by what has made him the person that he is; and as he grows in age and experience, if his outlook remains worldly (the word in this paragraph of the *Rule* is not related to *saeculum*, nor even to *mundus*, but to the basic uncultivated nature of things — *terrena*) then his idea of himself and of other people will become false and inflated.

So the *Rule* continues by saying, with a light note of irony, that if the former underprivileged men who are now monks do not live this resurrection life of contemplation and instead get puffed-up ideas (*inflantur*) of the value of status, then life in a monastery can do them no good at all; while if those who had privileges before entry do divest themselves of them and become humble and unpretentious then life in a monastery has done a great work in them. There is no suggestion, be it noted, that the one group does always fail in this respect and the other always succeeds.

There is an "if" (*si*) in the text which is made emphatic by the whole structure of the Latin sentence.

At this point it is useful to remind ourselves that it is unity and the obstacles to it that are being explored in the whole of the first chapter; for now, here at the end of chapter I, 6, the crude distinction between rich and poor is made. But we must notice the delicacy with which this is done. Although poverty (*paupertas*) was mentioned in chapter I, 5, the terrible tension between this and wealth (*divitiae*) is not mentioned until after the thought of the brothers has been drawn into the area of contemplation. While each one, either rich or poor, is still thinking within worldly categories this painful issue can never be resolved, the downward drag of human nature being what it is; but it can be looked at and overcome when it begins to be seen as of less importance in the light of the search of God. Here in chapter I, 6 the problem is only just touched on; in chapter I, 7 it is deeply explored as it affects the ability of individual monks to adapt themselves to the life of the community. In chapter III, 4 and 5 the effects of former poverty or wealth are discussed with regard to the establishing of the common life of the group. Having said that, we may now turn to the next paragraph.

Rule, Chapter I, 7

On the other hand,
those who were regarded in the world
as persons of consequence
should not look down on their brothers
who have entered the religious community from humble circumstances.
They should try to glory
in the companionship of their less privileged brothers
rather than in the rank of their wealthy parents.
They should not be conceited
if they have contributed anything to the common life
from their private means;
nor should they take more pride in their riches
because they are sharing them in the monastery
than they would if they were enjoying them in the world.
For every other vice prompts people to do evil deeds;
but pride lies in ambush even for good deeds,
to destroy them.
What advantage is it to scatter abroad and give to the poor
and become poor oneself,

if the mind in its misery becomes prouder in despising riches
than it was in possessing them?

PRIDE

Here the *Rule* challenges the attitude of the *honestiores* among
the brethren, in order to test whether the standards of the world
or those of the gospel are the motivating factors in their lives. In
the very first sentence we may note the use of the phrase "in the
world" (*in saeculo*) and remark that it was not used in the previous
paragraph. In chapter I, 6 it was possible to face the call to
conversion of outlook without recourse to the heavily loaded
word *saeculum*; for it is mere humanness that tends to envy and
artificiality. But here in chapter I, 7 all the disadvantages of being
a privileged person are summed up in the use of that word, and
this first half-sentence orchestrates the theme: "Those who were
regarded . . . as persons of consequence" is a slight enlargement
of the text's "those who were seen to be something" (*illi qui aliquid
esse uidebantur*). Such men were of consequence in the world
because of what status could achieve and what money could buy;
and now they had chosen the life of a monastery. But no one could
deny what position and wealth had given them — authority,
influence, a network of relationships with family and friends
which could affect the affairs of men widely, a sophisticated and
cultured outlook, the ability to draw on resources not available to
the *humiliores*, security and the protection of the law, freedom to
act responsibly. All these attributes of privilege are good in themselves. The evil and destroying aspects of wealth and high social
position need not concern us for, generally speaking, it is not men
thus motivated who would betake themselves to a monastery. No,
the people whom the *Rule* is addressing at this point are privileged
men of good will whose one desire is to seek and to serve yet who,
because of their former way of life, cannot help expecting to wield
authority, control events, have recourse to persons of influence,
delight in intellectual exchange, have access to whatever is
needed, act with impunity, and look to wide horizons in all that
they do. Men such as these experience in the monastery the exact
opposite of the impact that the life makes on those who were
formerly underprivileged. While these last find their horizons
widening, the men who formerly lived in a broad place, as the
psalmist put it, find themselves constricted. If they consorted in
the monastery only with others from a like background, the

limitations of the life would not be acute; but when they find themselves among men whose basic assumptions are so different from their own, their security is undermined and they find themselves in a weak position. And the worldly defense against isolating weakness in this situation is the snobbishness which the *Rule* attacks: they "should not look down on their brothers" (*Non habeant fastidio fratres suos*).

The use of the word brothers (*fratres*) implies a bond that lies at the heart of the Church's experience of life in Christ. It assumes, that is, a common source of life and a dependence on that source. Its use beyond a physical kinship group before the time of Christ is assumed in the use of it in Acts 3:17 where Peter addresses the people as brethren after he had healed the lame man in Solomon's portico. But in the New Testament generally the word acquires a more-than-courteous meaning and comes to denote the members of the fellowship of which Jesus was the leader: *You have one teacher, and you are all brethren* (Mt 23:8). The Lord himself applied it to all men in his picture of the final judgment: *As you did it to the least of these my brethren, you did it to me* (Mt 25:40). But it is in Mark 3:35 and parallels that the word gains its most explicit Christian meaning. Here Jesus says that kinship with himself lies in doing the will of God. With that as a starting point it was easy for the word to become gradually more widely embracing to include those who stood together in a relationship of love and trust in God through Jesus. Its common use in the New Testament describes those who love Christ and in him strive to love one another, that is, the members of the Church. So the use of the word in a monastic context (and the *Rule* was following an already established tradition) places those within the monastery also within the whole life of the Church. The brotherhood which describes the Church in 1 Peter 2:17 can also be used to describe a community of monks.

Brother or brothers occurs seven times in the *Rule*: twice in this paragraph of chapter I, twice in chapter IV, 8, where the principle of mutual responsibility is being worked out, in chapter V, 1 where the subject is again envy of one another, in chapter V, 9 where service of the brethren is examined, and lastly in chapter VI, 1 where hatred is discussed and 1 John 3:15 is quoted. We may say, then, that the concept of brotherhood and the use of the word brother is a constant challenge to the deepening life of the community. It forces each monk to examine the nature of his commitment to life in the monastery, and it is probably the most effective instrument for dislodging the falsehoods that each one carries in his heart and mind. For a group that is striving to become one in heart and mind, it describes both the aim and the way to attain it. You cannot despise or be disgusted by (*non habeant fastidio*) one of the Lord's brethren, who is also one of your own however different from you he may be. For it is in his brother that a monk may see God's will at work with power; and that is the reality which A. M. Allchin calls "the sacrament of our brother."[67] A brother is not one to be despised.

In twentieth-century western society (wherever it is lived) the vast disparities of wealth and status that characterized the fourth century scarcely obtain, and consequently snobbishness based on family connections and family wealth is not the burning issue that it must have been for the monks whom the *Rule* is addressing. In other modern societies, however, the earlier pattern is readily recognizable and the problems it raises are still acute. (I take it that this was a serious problem among the Hippo brothers since the discussion of this issue is fairly lengthy — only chapters V, 1 and VI, 2 are longer, and IV, 8 is of the same length.) Wherever a monastery is set, in some form or other the problem of possessing privilege has to be faced, together with the temptations that it poses. Even if superiority is not felt because of pedigree and income, there are other forms of privilege which are still a source of pain in community life: education, competence, width of experience, knowledge of affairs, professional training, skill in languages, skill with hands or head, what one might call social graces, even a person's home address — these are the assets which today have largely taken the place of those inherent in being *honestiores* and not *humiliores*. Obviously, the items in that list do cross social barriers, but all the same they are the sources of snobbishness, arrogance, and condescension. There is not one of us who is not guilty in this respect, to some extent. We all look down on one another for some reason; we all regard ourselves as superior in some respect; we are all aware of our own consequence in some fields; we all despise another for what we regard as his poverty.

Today we are faced with another aspect of this difficulty, for we have become aware of an inverted snobbery which takes delight in the absence of privilege and glories in the ability to overcome limitations. A typical example of this attitude is expressed by modern parents when they say that in their young days a fellow student would feel guilty and ashamed because his or her father was a miner, whereas their own sons who are present-day students confess to feeling guilty because their father is a barrister and not a miner. This is an outlook which vitiates the common life of a monastery as much as the other kind can do. We need to be able to discern what is good and creative in each person's background and the ability to profit from it.

We therefore need to grasp the fact that this snobbishness is a universal fault and not one peculiar to the wealthy and well-born. To recognize in myself a weakness that I perceive in someone else is a door opening into truth; it is, in fact, the way to true unity. So in uncovering a sore weakness which all monks share the *Rule* has brought them deeper into an understanding of yet another strand of the unity which is among the primary purposes of the monastery. In arrogance and condescension *all have sinned and fall short of the glory of God* (Rom 3:23). In biblical terms, God's glory is his presence revealed and seen to be at work in the world.[68] Arrogance thus results in an occlusion of the glory of God as he shows it to us and as it exists within us; condescension makes us blind to the glory of another.

There is a link here with the step toward truth that the previous paragraph of the *Rule* pointed out. The reference to the Colossians passage on life in the power of the resurrection led us to look at John's understanding of Christ's suffering and death and to see that, in terms of 12:20-26, his self-giving and his glorification are one. We may now turn back to Colossians and look at what follows the passage that we have already considered. Colossians 3:3 led us to see that it is the hidden life of contemplation that is the way of the search for God. The following verse (4) states: *When Christ who is our life appears, then you also will appear with him in glory.* So it is not surprising that the idea of glory should find expression in the present paragraph which is a corollary of the preceding one: *They should try to glory.*

This phrase needs consideration, for it teaches us a lot. "Try to" translates the Latin *studiant*. The primary meaning of this word is to engage the heart as well as the head. The modern word study describes a disciplined activity of the mind, and this is a long way from the warmth of eagerness, the willingness to take trouble over someone or something, the generosity of busying oneself with others' concerns, the persistence of striving after a good outside oneself, which the primary meaning of the word carried. *Studiant,* therefore, is the exact word for this context; the same can hardly be said of "try to." But to select one good word would have necessitated setting aside many others that are equally telling; so the best thing to do seemed to be to choose a toneless one for the bass note and to build up a chord on that. For approaching people whose way of life and way of thinking is different from our own requires a many-sided activity and a variety of attitudes if a real relationship with them is to be established. Words and phrases such as warmth, eagerness, willingness, taking trouble, generosity, persistence, striving, and pursuing describe a heartfelt goodwill. Trying to understand and get alongside a person who is very different from oneself is only possible if it is entirely devoid of self-seeking. One has only to think of the number of efforts to put right a bad relationship which have proved abortive because of the desire of one or other of the parties to be justified. The work of interpretation only enters the field later. The first need is to see the other one for the person he or she is, not just as the person I see. Such people may have table manners that are not like those my mother taught me, but they are those that their mothers taught them. They may know nothing of the Tintorettos in Venice, but I can never acquire their reverent understanding of a living landscape. To them a Beethoven quartet may be sheer cacophony, but their ears will be the first to hear a lark's song at the height of a February day. I shall not discover their gifts until I have looked for them and ceased from looking at my own. What I shall then find in my companions will be really something to boast of, to glory in. And what we experience together as they share what they have with me is companionship (*societas*). This indeed, even more than their individual gifts, is something to glory in for it is something that I share with them and which has its abiding place deep within each of us. This is true unity. Our diversities of gifts are the very stuff of our unity within the monastery. When we are proud of our own talents or feel threatened by another's, then that unity can never become a reality. So once again we are forced to the conclusion that within the common life there must be room for all.

DIVERSITY IN UNITY

Diversity in unity is explored by Paul in 1 Corinthians 12:4-31, and the tensions reflected in the present paragraph of the *Rule* are closely analogous to those of the Church in Corinth: condescension, envy, arrogance, and all the rest. The point that Paul makes in verses 4-11 is that every personal endowment is not only given

. by God but is bestowed as an expression of his will for that person and as a means to be used in his service. Verses 12-17 show how diversity itself is essential for the making of true unity, for the making of one body. *If all the parts were the same, how could it be a body?* (1 Cor 12:19, JB). And more than that, for Paul goes on to show that each part is affected by every other part: *if one part is hurt, all parts are hurt with it* (1 Cor 12:26a). But he does not conclude this part of his argument with the suffering aspect of the matter, which is obvious enough whether in a human body or in a body of people; he goes on to say what, we have to admit, is not always as true in practice as it ought to be in community life — *if one member is honored, all rejoice together* (1 Cor 12:26b). But let us not be too harsh with ourselves over this humanness. It was the Lord who made the pointed remark that a prophet is not without honor except in his own country and in his own house.[69] Within the context of the *Rule*, then, the use of the word *studiant* (try to) is particularly poignant.

In the Latin version of 1 Corinthians 12:26 we find that the verb which in most English versions is translated as "is honored" is in fact the word which the *Rule* echoes — gloriatur — while the "rejoice together" expresses the Latin symbiotic word *congaudent*. (There is real poverty in the English language in that it is often impossible to express the with-ness of a verb or noun in a single word: compassion and companion are exceptions, but there are not many such.) It is the with-ness of appreciation that helps to build up the religious community and the companionship (*sanctam societatem . . . societate*) which this sentence of the *Rule* is striving to describe. The language of the sentence is a bit stilted, and I suspect that it reflects its author's diffidence (in view of his own ambiguous social standing) in attempting to stand in the shoes of a naturally privileged fellow monk. But as he himself has invoked the help of Paul in working through this difficult discussion, we may do the same.

If any of us is asked what the apostle had to say about glorying, we shall probably answer in terms of infirmities, tribulations, and the cross of Christ. It is true that these are the themes of most of the discussions in the letters.[70] But there is one passage (2 Thes 1:3-4) which brings out the depth of appreciation which the *Rule* aims to encourage: *Your faith groweth exceedingly, and the charity of everyone of you all toward each other aboundeth; so we ourselves glory in you in the churches of God for your patience and faith in all your persecutions and tribulations*. I have preferred to quote the Authorized Version here, because all the others paraphrase and lose the force of *we ourselves glory in you*. This glorying is a response to the presence of the power of God in the Christians of Thessalonica; it is a response to his glory. And that is what the appreciation of the gifts of one's sister or brother must be in the monastery: a glorying in the glory of God which is in each one of them. 1 Corinthians 4:7 (AV) takes us a step further: *Who maketh thee to differ from another? and what hast thou that thou didst not receive? Now if thou didst receive it, why dost thou glory as if thou hadst not received it?* When real values and their true source are discovered in the gifts that each member possesses (even though we ourselves may not recognize them — but that is another problem that need not concern us here), then the wealth and standing of one's parents is a matter of indifference and no cause for pride.

COMPANIONSHIP

It is only in this paragraph that the *Rule* mentions pride. The word recurs three times and it will be best to leave our discussion of it until more of its ramifications have been uncovered. At the stage we have now reached, we ought to look at the use of the word companionship (*societas*) and at the related verb-form which occurred in chapter I, 6. The noun is found twice in this present paragraph and once in chapter IV, 9. The Latin word[71] means partnership, being derived from *socius* which means a partner. It implies a common purpose and outlook within the group; it expresses both the objective existence of the group and its subjective experience. Thus in translation the words that most nearly represent the full meaning are fellowship and companionship. The English word society will not do, because it is too restricted: for example, *societas* can be applied to the family but the word society is ill-fitting in that context. So in the *Rule* we must bear in mind that what is being assumed is a fellowship, and a growing one at that. The use of the words *sociantur/societas* in the four passages of the *Rule* proves an interesting, though probably unwitting, description of the kind of development that takes place in relationships when people are placed together (*constituti*). Chapter I, 6 concerns people of one sort who "find themselves in the company" of those of a different sort. Chapter I, 7 describes that mixed company in the monastery as a religious community, and it then goes on to suggest what, within this setting, should be

the attitude of brothers of one sort to brothers of another sort —
they should glory in their companionship. In these last two passages there is a real progress in relationships. From being individually members of a group whose ideals and way of life are
religious, the monks have become a company in which each is
learning to recognize and appreciate the glory that is in the others.
In companionship, in a real society, there is the constant movement of give-and-take and a willingness to learn from and be
pliant toward the thought and feeling of others. Sheer dogged
individualism is the bane of the life of any society, and willful and
deliberate sin not only spoils the good fellowship of a group but
also can destroy its life. So when chapter IV discusses the problem
of an incorrigible wrongdoer within the community, the only
plausible solution is that he should be dismissed "from your
fellowship" (de uestra societate), chapter IV, 9. The group becomes
a body, a body that can be infected and poisoned by the wrong of
one member, so great is its symbiosis.

The gifts of God, in all their diversity, are to be the marks of the
life of the monastery. References to holiness itself are sparingly
made in the *Rule*, but each one of the four instances strikes deep.
Here in chapter I, 7, the very stuff of the common life is described
as the religious community (sanctam societatem): obviously, because the glory of God is inseparable from his holiness and it is
also inseparable from the holiness of men and women.[72] In chapter IV, 3 the monks are reminded that nothing is to be done that
is not in keeping with their holy state (uestram sanctitatem); in other
words, as we have seen in other contexts, the call to conversion is
insistent and always present. Chapter IV, 5, after discussing the
problem of scandalous behavior on the part of a monk and evoking patience and the wisdom of God in dealing with the frailties
of humankind, goes on to say that awareness of God and the fact
that the monk is a man consecrated to holiness (uir sanctus) should
constrain him to fear displeasing him and so help him to overcome
his weakness. Finally, the inner holiness that clothes a monk's
heart (in illo interiore sancto habitu cordis) is alluded to in chapter
V, 1. So the progression is the same here as elsewhere, from an
exterior manifestation to an inner intimacy that is so close within
a man that holiness can be called the clothing of his heart, wrap-
ping it round, protecting it, fitting his thoughts and desires as a
garment fits a body.

SELF-GIVING

If that is to be the quality of each monk's life, then there is no room for pride in the ability to contribute to the community's funds because one happened to have a lot of wealth at one's disposal at the time of entry. Nor should there be pride — and this is harder to achieve — when one sees one's former property being put to good use in the monastery. The downward drag here stems from the fact that being bountiful may be a way of self-compensation. Except in a phase of possibly false euphoria, abandoning one's goods and one's right of disposal over them is a costly thing to do — as, obviously, it is meant to be. For some, what is done with the head's consent leaves the heart where it was before, attached to one's possessions; for others, what the heart can freely give the mind cannot consent to and there remains an ambivalence of attitude. In both cases, the unresolved conflict may be covered up by a rather subtle self-congratulation on the grounds that others are obviously the beneficiaries of one's bounty. But, comes the challenge of the *Rule*, there is a falsity here because such an attitude makes the erstwhile wealthy man more worldly than he was before. The distinction here is not between a worldly man (the former rich one) and a religious man (he who was formerly poor), for rich and poor alike have come to the monastery for the one thing needful. If his wealth was of comparatively little importance to the rich man so that he could turn aside from it and enter a monastery, and if after entry he in any way consoles himself with the effect of his generosity to the monastery, then clearly he is setting more value on what he once possessed than he ever did when it was his to dispose of. And in this sense, all of us were once rich for we have all contributed some form of wealth to the common life; and there is a real temptation that we all face, that of valuing — and over-valuing — our gifts as a means of compensation for the pain of having given our all to God and left ourselves defenseless and in need.

So it is no accident that this sentence, about not glorying in whatever a man has brought to the monastery, comes after the one which draws him to see and appreciate the gifts that God has placed in the keeping of his brothers. For it is only when a monk desires to go out of himself toward his brother that he gains the courage not to rely on his own gifts as a source of security and well-being.

But there is a further insidious trap here, for generosity is a good thing, and so is the right use of possessions, and to pretend or even to believe otherwise is to be trapped in unreality. The problem is, then, how to value goodness and yet not take pride in it. For, as the *Rule* puts it in the next sentence, while "every other vice prompts people to do evil deeds" the vice (*iniquitas*) of "pride lies in ambush (*insidiatur*) even for good deeds, to destroy them."

PRIDE AND MISERY

In view of the warnings against pride that have played a large part in Christian spirituality down the ages, it is interesting to discover that in the *Rule* this particular vice is only mentioned in this one paragraph, chapter I, 7. But this is not surprising when we find that there is very little reference to it in the New Testament: in fact it only occurs there three times (Mk 7:21-22, 1 Tm 3:6, and 1 Jn 2:16). Are we to say, then, that tradition has got it all wrong and has been seeing a non-existent bogey all the time? No, for the *Rule* is right in saying that pride is very difficult to identify. Conceit, arrogance, boasting, condescension, haughtiness, disdain and all the rest are easy enough to recognize; but the sheer subtlety of pride makes it less easy to detect, especially in oneself. Pride stems from a sense of the value of things, and to be able to appreciate the worth of things is a high and good gift. And there is a sense in which this appreciation amounts to a self-appreciation which, again, is a great good. As we are today beginning to learn, it is one of humanity's greatest assets to be aware of one's own worth and dignity; and self-respect and a shrinking from what is base and mean are real strengths both to their possessor and to those with whom one has to do. Moreover, to undervalue one's own gifts, of whatever sort they are, is a result of a stunting of personality at some stage of development. The safeguard against a destructive kind of pride in oneself is an ability to take pride in one's fellows, as the *Rule* has already stated earlier in this paragraph.

The destructive pride that the *Rule* is now bringing into focus is an in-turned overweening self-esteem that feeds on isolating self-satisfaction. So, for instance, when a monk glories in what his bounty can do but at the same time loses sight of the personhood of those who benefit by it, then the worth of the gift itself is destroyed as well as the relationship that should bind giver and receiver together. A further complicating factor is the very gratitude and just appreciation which such bounty may elicit from the brethren. It was Nilus of Ancyra who advocated life in the desert on the grounds that it "delivers from the praise of men, which ruins even the best works."[73] But the monk who is not a solitary is always open to this temptation, and it takes detachment in heroic proportions to overcome it. As the *Rule* points out, even the bestowal and the sight of one's former possessions in the hands of others may make a man prouder of his goods than he ever was when he himself used them unquestioningly. One's own newly-adopted poverty itself becomes a source of pride, and there is nothing more destructive than this simply because its presence and its power are so insidious. The mind is indeed then in the state of misery.

Some interesting lines of communication lead out of the word misery (*miseria*). It can mean wretchedness, misfortune, or distress, in which case it is contrasted with pride in possessing riches; it can mean poverty and squalor, in which case it contrasts with a former state of wealth; it can mean anxiety, trouble, or defenselessness, in which case it contrasts with pride itself in the sense of high self-satisfaction. Perhaps it is best to regard the word as a chord, each of whose notes strikes a different resonance in our understanding. For in some way or other the description applies to us all, and in many respects we all resist becoming poor; we hate the thought of living without our assets, our attitudes, and the approbation of others. And this, maybe, is our greatest misery of all — that we rely on our pride. The road that leads us away from the pride that waits to distort even the best that is in us leads not even to the best that is in other people, but to the persons themselves. So we are led back to the challenge of the key phrase of this paragraph: "they should try to glory in the companionship . . . ," for it is in others that we meet not only that other person but God himself.

It is this fact with which the *Rule's* first chapter is concluded.

Rule, Chapter I, 8

Therefore all should live
united in mind and heart
and should in one another honor God
whose temples you have become.

GROWING INTO UNITY

The exploration of the meaning of unity, and of the obstacles to its achievement within a community, has brought us to the heart of the matter in every sense of that word. From one point of view, every incident in the life of the group may be regarded as a unique event holding its meaning — perhaps it is right to say meanings — within itself. Certainly each situation that has been analyzed in paragraphs 3-7 has been seen to yield some intrinsic aspect of truth; and the phraseology of paragraph 2: "you should have one soul and one heart" may also point to the distinctness of successive experiences — or, to put it another way — may resemble each separate piece of a jigsaw puzzle which when joined to others form a whole picture.

But there is a deeper way of growing into unity, one that is hinted at by the significant Latin adverbs of chapter I, 8: All the monks are to live *unanimiter et concorditer*. They are not only to manifest unity by their behavior; they are to live (*uiuite*) with mind and heart completely open to the unifying power of the Spirit. The adverbs describe the quality of life that is to be built up within the group. There is to be a oneness (*unanimiter*) and a withness (*concorditer*). All the gifts of reason, intelligence, and affection that each one possesses are to be directed to one end, the worship of the God whom each is seeking and who reveals himself among them, within the very unity which they are bidden to discover and express.

The preceding five paragraphs have looked coldly and dispassionately at the causes of the fragmentation of unity within the group; and in each case it is a facet of God's truth that has been found to provide the way of binding together what has been broken by man's self-regarding. Now, in the chapter's short final paragraph, the warmth of togetherness is found to be both the cause and the effect of discovering where God is.

The English word concord is anemic in comparison with the Latin *concordia* and the adverbial form that occurs in the text; it is too restrained to express the pulsing life that the *Rule* is here picturing with a few strokes. For the Latin does more than suggest unity of purpose, more even than the partnership that the uses of the word *societas* have evoked; *concorditer* calls to mind harmony, friendship, and peace — qualities that a loving heart can bring to birth. But can these be born among a group whose common difficulties have been probed earlier in this chapter? Yes, but not once and for all. Yes, again and again, every time that a monk's mind and heart turn away from self-regarding to see and to worship him who is at the center of the community's life. "Entirely centered upon God" was how chapter I, 2 described the group's unity; now, chapter I, 8 sums up all the hints that have appeared in the succeeding paragraphs so that we find that "in one another" (in the odd, cantankerous, suspicious, and fearful people who make up the community) God is to be honored because these same ill-assorted men are the "temples" of God.

TEMPLES OF GOD

Three Pauline passages are referred to in this paragraph: Romans 15:6, and the image of the temple which occurs in 1 Corinthians 3:16-19 and 2 Corinthians 6:16-17. It will be best to consider the latter before turning to the Romans text which provides the link with chapter II of the *Rule*.

The temple-image has a long history.[74] In the nomadic period of Jewish history the tent (Latin *tabernaculum*) was the dwelling-place of each family's life. It was primarily the family's shelter and protection; destruction of the tent meant the loss of all security (see the imagery of Jeremiah 4:20), the pitched tent was a sign of the togetherness of the family (Jer 10:20). With a growing awareness of the nearness of God to people's lives and his relatedness to them, a special tent where he was to be encountered was a logical development; hence the tent of his presence which was also the tent of meeting (Ex 25:25). But the tent was more than the place where God was; it became a place of revelation, the place where he made his will known (Nm 11:24-25; 12:3-10). The enlargement of a tent implied the increased significance of those whose home it was and also their ability to influence and succor others (Is 54:1-3). And the rich adornment of the tent of the Lord, as described in Exodus 35, was designed to give the highest honor to him whose presence was there as an object of worship, a source of help and a guide to those who turned to him. Thus when Solomon later erected a permanent building to house the ark of God's presence, the temple had the same meaning and function as the tent/tabernacle of earlier times.

As the size of the house of the Lord increased, so did its meaning and function. What had begun as the place where God uniquely was, and where the people's representative, the high priest, made his vicarious acts of worship, now became the place of prayer for all who turned to him (Is 56:7); it became the place of instruction where his way was made known (Mi 4:1-2); it became, as it were, a fountain from which the aridity of daily lives could be watered and made fertile (Zec 14:8 where the equation is Jerusalem = temple). In these last-mentioned passages, the significance of Yahweh has become universal; he is no longer the lord of thousands of nomads but the Lord of the whole earth (Is 54:5; Mi 4:13; Zec 4:14). Within the temple, all men might come to God.

All of these ideas are reflected in the New Testament. The temple is the place of public teaching (Jn 18:20). Jesus himself called it a house of prayer (Lk 19:46, citing Is 56:3) and the house of his Father (Jn 2:16). The temple, then, as God's dwelling-place, is the place of his glory, the place where he has rights of possession, where he is at home and free, the place of sanctuary for the fearful, the place where there is real communication. This is both temple-language and tent-language; it is proper to God and also proper to humankind. And it is in the light of this that two passages in John's gospel have special significance. In the account of the cleansing of the temple it is stated that Jesus referred to his own body as the temple (Jn 2:21), meaning that he himself is the cultic center, the place where God dwells. The words of the prologue are thus seen to bind together all of these ideas, for the editors of the Jerusalem Bible tell us that the literal meaning of John 1:14 is not *lived/dwelt among us* but *The Word was made flesh and pitched his tent among us*.[75] And this happened because *God loved the world so much* (Jn 3:16). Jesus is the point of intersection between God and man, the meeting place of need and love, of seeker and sought; and as Christians ponder on his continuing life and its meaning they discover that in him glory has meaning, belonging gains significance, freedom grows in depth, security may be experienced, and communication can take place. Finally, they find that suffering and sacrifice have meaning and more than meaning — they are found to be integral to our very being as they are also to God's.[76] So when Paul used the temple-image and applied it to that difficult group of people who were the Church in Corinth he was in fact making a very bold statement, and so was Augustine when he borrowed it from Paul and applied it to a group of monks whose faults he and they were very well aware of.

Here once more the *Rule* assumes the close relationship between the monastery and the Church as a whole: what can be said of the one can be said of the other. Each man is a place where God is; each one belongs to him; each can become, because of God's indwelling, a source of freedom to others while at the same time he discovers his own true freedom; through each man security in God is to be found; with each man dialogue with the Holy One becomes possible; and in each man the creative flowering that stems from sacrifice and suffering may come to full fruition. All of this takes full account of the struggles, disappointments, and failures that mark the way of the Christian. Indeed, these are the very things that serve as the machinery (I am tempted to say bulldozers, cranes, and all the rest) which removes bit by bit all the things that separate us not only from one another but from God.

> *Nothing therefore can come between us and the love of Christ, even if we are troubled or worried, or being persecuted, or lacking food or clothes or being threatened or being attacked. . . . Nothing can ever come between us and the love of God made visible in Christ Jesus our Lord* (Rom 8:35-39).

It is small wonder, then, that the monks are bidden to honor God in one another, for it is in the fullness and blessedness of love that he dwells in each one of them. He is there, at the center of every member. He is the cause of their unity. He is the binder of their fellowship. He is the forgiver of their sins and the renewer of their striving. In them he is invisible and he is visible; he is unknown and he is known. The search has always to be made, but the end of the search is always present within that temple which is every Christian's heart. The wording of the first part of this paragraph of the *Rule* is a conflation of Romans 15:6b with the words of Acts 4:32a which we have already examined. The recollection of Paul's *with one mind and one mouth glorify* (*honorificetis*) *God* has been taken up into the total unity which this chapter of the *Rule* has sought to analyze. The thread which is fastened into the fabric in chapter I, 2 seems, then, to be as follows: the whole personality of each disparate monk is to be consecrated to God within the life of the monastery, and despite all the differing identities which a common search for him will bring into focus, his presence will be revealed within the essence of each one; it is his presence which makes of this group of individuals something more than even a fellowship (*societas*); it makes them, severally and corporately, the place where the deepest exchanges between

God and man become a reality. Thus something of the worship which heart and mind instinctively offer to God is to inform the relationships which living together in the monastery makes possible. Later in the *Rule*, we shall find some discussion of what true and false honor are (that is, in chapter III, 4; VII, 1 and 3); and this is right, for the whole of Christian life is a process of purification. Here at the beginning of the *Rule* all that needs to be done is to point out the relationship between what goes on in each one's heart and what is common to the group, and these are seen to be one and the same.

Unity, then, is both the way and the journey's end. "Let the members of Christ understand, and Christ in his members understand, and the members of Christ in Christ understand; because head and members are one Christ" (*Expositions of the Psalms* 35, 3).

NOTES

1. Smith's Latin-English Dictionary.

2. Athanasius, *The Life of Saint Antony* 93 (see Johannes Quasten, *Patrology*, Volume III: *The Golden Age of Greek and Patristic Literature*, Utrecht/Antwerp: Spectrum Publishers, 1960, page 149).

3. This applies principally to monasticism's requirement of celibacy. See the discussion in Gerhart B. Ladner, *The Idea of Reform*, Harvard University Press, 1959, Part Three, Chapter I, and especially page 317 with the relevant notes.

4. See 2 Cor 5:19.

5. See 1 Jn 4:1.

6. See 1 Cor 7:7-8.25-35. The dates for the books of the New Testament have been taken from the annotations of the Jerusalem Bible.

7. See Acts 21:9.

8. See Mt 19:3-12.

9. See Rv 14:2-5.

10. See Réne Metz, *La Consécration des Vièrges dans l'Eglise*, Presses Universitaires de France, 1954.

11. *Ecclesiastical History* III, 31.

12. *First Letter to the Corinthians* 28.

13. *Letter to the Smyrnaeans* 13.

14. Réne Metz, *op. cit.*, page 43.

15. *Letter to the Philippians* 4.

16. *Apologia* I, 18.

17. *Legatio pro Christianis*, quoted in Réne Metz, *op. cit.*, page 44.

18. Henry C. Lea: *History of Sacerdotal Celibacy in the Christian Church*, Williams & Norgate (3rd revised edition), 1907, Volume I, page 19.

19. Methodius, *The Symposium, A Treatise on Chastity*, translated and annotated by Herbert Mursurillo, Newman Press/Longmans, Green, 1958.

20. John V. Taylor: *The Growth of the Church in Buganda*, SCM Press, 1958, page 255.

21. This sentence crystallized while I was reading the last chapter of David E. Jenkins' *The Contradiction of Christianity*, SCM Press, 1976, "The Trinity — Love in the End." I recognize that the thought is not in line with Augustine here.

22. Peter Brown, *Religion and Society in the Age of Saint Augustine*, Faber, 1972, page 260.

23. Possidius, *Life of Augustine* 5.

24. *Expositions of the Psalms* 4, 10; Letter 186, 7; *Answers to Faustus* V, 9; *The Work of Monks* 17, 25.32; *Holy Virginity* 46; *Expositions of the Psalms* 131, 5; 132, 2.12-13; Letter 211, 2; *Expositions of the Psalms* 99, 11; 83, 4; *The City of God* V, 18; Letter 243, 4; Sermon 355, 2; 356, 1; see Luc Verheijen, *Nouvelle Approche de la Règle de Saint Augustin*, Abbaye de Bellefontaine, 1980, page 78 (hereafter *Nouvelle Approche*).

25. Smith's Latin-English Dictionary, and so for all dictionary definitions.

26. *Silent Music*, pages 84-85 (Fontana edition 1976); see also pages 147 and 164.

27. C. K. Barrett, *The First Epistle to the Corinthians* (2nd edition) A. & C. Black, 1971, page 26.

28. *Ibid.*, page 42.

29. Luc Verheijen has explored this idea within the context of Saint Augustine's use of *anima una et cor unum* throughout his writings, in a paper entitled "Spiritualité et Vie Monastique chez Saint Augustin"; see *Nouvelle Approche*, page 75.

30. Perhaps the finest short exposition of Augustine's understanding of the *Totus Christus* is that of Emile Mersche in *The Whole Christ*, Part III, chapter IV, Dennis Dobson, 1949.

31. See Acts 4:32c and 35b.

32. There is a valuable discussion of helplessness and dependence in community life in Ruth Burrows' *To Believe in Jesus*, Sheed & Ward, 1978, page 41.

33. See Acts 4:33.

34. *The Dynamics of Creation*, Secker & Warburg, 1972, page 99.

35. An important study of this subject is that of R. A. Markus, *Saeculum: History and Society in the Theology of Saint Augustine*, Cambridge University Press, 1970.

36. "Mundus et Saeculum dans les Confessions de Saint Augustin," in *Studi e materiali di Storia delle religioni* XXXVIII (1967) 665-682.

37. *Ibid.*, 682 and 678.

38. Markus, *op. cit.*, page 133.

39. See "Political Society," in *Augustine: A Collection of Essays*, edited by R. A. Markus, Anchor Books, Doubleday & Company, 1972, pages 322-332.

40. Jn 16:33: *Confessions* X, 47; Rom 12:2: *Confessions* XIII, 14.30-32; Eph 2:2: *Confessions* VI, 3 and VIII, 3.

41. Mt 5:14; Mk 8:36; Jn 3:16; Rom 3:6; 1 Cor 2:12; 2 Cor 5:19; Gal 6:14; Heb 11:38; Jas 4:4; 1 Jn 2:2. I have used the phrase "Latin counterpart" because of course both the Latin and the English are translations. In New Testament Greek the distinction between αιων (which is usually translated *saeculum*) and κοσμος (which except when it is used as a metaphor in Jas 3:6 is uniformly translated as *mundus*) is far more pronounced: αιων, being concerned with time, is at least open to divine influence but κοσμος, which is spatial, generally carries a "bad" meaning. (It is interesting to note that in what are in one sense the most missionary-minded books of the New Testament, Luke-Acts and Revelation, *mundus* does not occur. Where English has "world," they have *saeculum, civitas, orbis, terra*.)

42. See, among other passages, VI, 19; VIII, 11.18.30; IX, 26; X, 47; XIII, 30.

43. See 1 Cor 12:4-31.

44. For a full discussion see Ladner, *op. cit.*, Part III and especially chapter II.

45. See 1 Cor 12 and particularly verses 25-26.

46. Chapters I, 5; III, 3 and 5; V, 1 and 5; VII, 3.

47. See R. H. Barrow, *Introduction to Saint Augustine, The City of God*, Faber, 1950, page 168.

48. For a full discussion of the dating of the *Rule* and the circumstances of its composition, see Luc Verheijen: *La Règle de Saint Augustin: II. Recherches Historiques*, Études Augustiniennes, 1967, chapter IV, pages 87-116.

49. *Teaching Christianity* IV, 5.

50. *Life of Augustine* 1, Villanova: Augustinian Press, 1988, page 39. Augustine's younger contemporary Saint Patrick was also the son of a *decurion* (see Peter Salway, *Roman Britain*, Clarendon Press, 1981, page 727, and also pages 463 and 575-576).

51. See *Confessions* II, 3.

52. *The Happy Life* I, 6.

53. See *Confessions* II, 3.

54. *Ibid.*

55. *Teaching Christianity* II, 1.

56. See *Confessions* V, 8.

57. *Op. cit.* V, 9.

58. *Op. cit.* V, 13.

59. *Order* II, 17, 45.

60. See *Confessions* V, 12, where he goes on to say (writing some years after the event) that he still hates "such vicious and perverse creatures," though he loves them as subjects for amendment.

61. *Op. cit.* VI, 11.

62. *Op. cit.* VI, 6.

63. For *honestiores* and *humiliores* see M. Rostovtzeff, *The Social and Economic History of the Roman Empire* (2 volumes, 2nd edition revised by P. M. Fraser,

Clarendon Press, 1947), pages 370, 383, 413, 419, 423, 496, and 518; and also A. M. H. Jones, *The Later Roman Empire, 284-602* (3 volumes Blackwell, 1964, reprinted in 2 volumes, 1973), pages 17-18, 519, and 749-750.

64. Archimandrite Sofrony, *The Undistorted Image*, Faith Press, 1958, page 123.

65. W. D. Davies, *Invitation to the New Testament*, Darton, Longman & Todd, 1967, page 412.

66. J. B. Lightfoot, *St. Paul's Epistle to the Colossians and to Philemon*, Macmillan, 1886, page 207.

67. *The World is a Wedding*, Darton, Longman & Todd, 1978, page 90.

68. See Ex 24:16-17.

69. See Mt 13:57.

70. Notably in Rom 5:2-5, 15:17; 1 Cor 1:28-31; 2 Cor 11:12-30; 12:1-9; Gal 6:13-14.

71. See Barrow, *op. cit.*, pages 22-23.

72. Is 6:1-7.

73. See Johannes Quasten, *op. cit.*, page 500.

74. The finest study is that of Yves Congar, *The Mystery of the Temple*, Burns & Oates, 1962. In what follows I am also indebted to the articles in John L. McKenzie, *Dictionary of the Bible*, Geoffrey Chapman, 1966.

75. The Jerusalem Bible, Geoffrey Chapman, 1966.

76. Andrew Elphinstone's *Freedom, Suffering, and Love*, SCM Press, 1977, is a sensitive exposition of the centrality of pain and suffering in all growth and development throughout creation.

2

Prayer

Rule, Chapter II, 1
Persevere faithfully in prayers
at the appointed hours and times.

THE WORK OF PRAYER

The link between chapters I and II is inevitable. "Make for thyself a temple for God within thee. *For the temple of God is holy, which temple are ye.* Wouldest thou pray in a temple? Pray in thyself. But be thou first a temple of God, for he in his temple heareth him who prays" (*Homilies in the Gospel of John* 25, 25). So wrote Augustine some years later. The shift in emphasis is more apparent than real, for what is true of another man is also true of myself: each one is a temple of God and if I am to honor him in others I must also honor him in myself. If I am to love him in others I must love him in myself. The whole of my being must become my prayer. My prayer must embrace the full person that I am becoming. Prayer is love's language and also love's work.

On the face of it, it may seem puzzling that this chapter is so short and says so little. Certainly no treatise on prayer is to be found in the *Rule*. Indeed, Augustine did not ever write one.[1] But almost the whole of his work may be subsumed under prayer, for prayer is the supreme expression of the never ending search: "Your desire is your prayer" (*Expositions of the Psalms* 37, 14), he once wrote. And, as we have already seen throughout chapter I and shall continue to see in the remainder of the text, it is the prayer of contemplation that from the beginning to the end infuses his understanding of monastic life. We do not have to look into this chapter alone to discover what the *Rule* has to say about prayer and its place in the life of a monk. Prayer or praying (*oratio, oro*) occurs in the text at chapters II, 1.2 and 3; IV, 11; VI, 2; and VIII, 2 but these are by no means the only references to the activity of prayer in the *Rule*.

The position of this chapter within the whole text is significant. For every religious in every generation, once we have given ourselves to the life of a particular order, congregation or community, the primary concern is for prayer; this is the activity which we long for above all else. Other activities might be undertaken outside the monastery (and are often done more efficiently there), but it is within a monastic setting that prayer is the primary undertaking of a lifetime. It is the one aspect of life that is not in itself strange to a newcomer. The community's *modus operandi* may stretch the imagination almost to the breaking point, but in prayer we may be completely ourselves.

A further reason why prayer has to be discussed at this point in the *Rule* is that it is the way toward unity. The common life of the group cannot be built up and express a reality deeper than its outward manifestations unless the life of each individual is itself a constant prayer. In *Expositions of the Psalms* 38(37), from which we have already quoted, Augustine gave a new interpretation of Paul's injunction to pray without ceasing (1 Thes 5:17),[2] for he goes on: "If your desire continues without interruption, your prayer continues also. Not without meaning did the apostle say: *Pray without ceasing*. Does he mean that we must kneel, or prostrate ourselves, or lift up our hands without ever ceasing? If this is what we mean when we say that we pray, then I think it is something we cannot do always. But there is another kind of interior prayer, and that is the desire of the heart" (*Expositions of the Psalms* 38[37], 14).

In the sentence of the *Rule* that we are now examining the word for prayer is *oratio*. In his *Expositions of the Psalms* 86(85), 7, Augustine defines *oratio* as "talking to God" (*oratio tua locutio est ad deum*). The same word is used in the passage from the commentary on Psalm 38(37) which we have quoted above. Talking to God and the heart's desire for him are all of one piece; they are the totality of prayer in that the whole of man is a unity within this context — heart, mind, and action are fused. Prayer, as Augustine understands it, is deeply rooted in man's humanness, in his awareness of incompleteness and his longing for wholeness. Prayer is also the situation in which God is to be encountered. In prayer man's inadequacy is met by God's all-sufficiency, his weakness by God's strength, his evil by God's forgiveness, his fear by God's love. That is why Augustine can say that prayer is talking to God; indeed one can express that a bit differently and say that it is conversation with God.

In conversation, attention to the present moment is very important (we all know, for instance, how disastrous it is if we let our attention stray while we are talking with someone, and we find it

even worse when it is the other person's attention that wanders!).
In conversation there has to be a givenness to the situation in
which the exchange is taking place. In one sense there is always
some urgency in an exchange between two or more people; this
is the moment when understanding can be realized, made real.

PERSEVERANCE

It is with this in mind that we should look at the first paragraph
of this chapter: "Persevere faithfully in prayers at the appointed
hours and times." Here, it is not 1 Thessalonians 5:17 that is
evoked (*pray without ceasing*), but a number of other New Testament passages. *Orationibus instate* contains echoes of Romans
12:12 and Colossians 4:2 which both have *instate* in relation to
prayer. The verb is variously translated in the English versions as
continue, keep on, persist in, be constant, be persevering, persevere. Ephesians 6:18 has *Pray at all times in the Spirit, with all prayer
and supplication. To this end keep alert with all perseverance.* Here,
perseverance occurs in all translations of *instantia* and *keep alert*
translates *vigilantes*. The words *keep alert* in this passage echo two
sayings of Jesus which are recorded in Mark 14:38 (*stay awake/be
awake/watch and pray . . . not to be put to the test* — the words spoken
in the garden) and Luke 21:36 (*watch/be alert/stay awake and pray . . .*
for strength to pass through the trials that are described in the
preceding apocalyptic passage). Alongside these verses from various letters and gospels, where the context is hortatory, we find in
Acts a number of references to the experience of the early Church
which itself fulfilled the injunction of Jesus in the Lucan passage:
*Pray at all times for the strength to survive all that is going to happen
and to stand with confidence before the Son of Man* (JB). Acts 1:14, 2:42,
and 6:4 all use some form of the Latin verb *insto* to describe the
constant meeting for prayer of the first Christians.

It has been necessary to pursue these biblical semantics in order
to show how these first words of chapter II summarize the developing theme of chapter I which began with an evocation of the life
of the Church in Jerusalem and ended with the fact that Christians
together are more than a group of people who believe and do
certain things — they are the holy place of God. So we may now
see that prayer is more than the heart's cry and the expression of
a person's need: prayer is a joint activity engaged in by God and
every person as we pray. Talking with God (Augustine's *locutio*)
always involves a person-to-person encounter.

APPOINTED HOURS AND TIMES

It is against this background that we must look at the second half of this precept on prayer: praying is to be done "at the appointed hours and times." There are not enough clues to make it possible for us to discover what exactly Augustine was talking about with his "hours and times," but it seems that he was making room for a recent innovation.[3] From other sources we know that by the fourth century both commemorative services and a regulated use of the book of Psalms had become widespread in the Church as a whole. These practices could have a tremendous impact on those who encountered them.[4] At the same time, corporate vocal worship within monasteries was becoming ordered and controlled, largely as a result of Basil's work in the 370s.[5] (We do not know how much Augustine knew of these reforms. Basil's monastic *Rules* were not translated into Latin for use in monasteries in the West until the year in which Augustine was writing down his precepts-to-be-observed.)[6]

What concerns us at the moment is the connection between the search for God, the striving for unity of heart and mind, and the use of some pattern of ordered worship. As in chapter I, the point of development lies in relationship to the early Church in Jerusalem. There are two passages in Acts which, in continuity with Jewish worship, ascribe special significance to time and associate it with a specific and time-honored act of worship. It was at the ninth hour, on his way into the temple for the usual "service," that Peter met and cured the cripple at the Beautiful Gate (Acts 3:1); and it was at the same time of day that Cornelius had the vision that changed his life. Now this does more than indicate that the time was three hours after noon. It means that it was the time of the evening sacrifice, the *perpetual holocaust from generation to generation* of Exodus 29:42 (JB). This was the time when the offered lamb became the representative of the hopes, aspirations and failures of every devout person; it was the time of turning Godward; it was the time of rededication and renewed self-sacrifice — perpetually renewed, day after day, down the centuries. And it was at this same ninth hour that the Lord died on the Cross (Mt 27:45-50; Mk 15:33-39). Some times for the Christian, as for the Jew, were more than clock-times.

There is more here than what came to be seen as the sanctification of time and of work by a seven- or eight-fold Office. It is the sanctification of the person and of the group that is at the heart of the matter. The will to be sanctified, to be made holy, has been a strand in the fabric of Christian worship since apostolic times. As Robert J. Daly has pointed out,[7] Christians dare to enter the sanctuary (Heb 10:19) and draw near (verse 22) to God (that is to say, to offer themselves to him through their lives seen as a sacrificial act) because Christ himself both sacrificed himself and has incorporated us into his sacrifice. The observed hours and times (whatever the manner of the observation) are a part of the continual conversion which makes a monk's consecration effective, for they are the point of meeting with God and a celebration of the mystery of salvation which makes that conversion possible. But is that statement corroborated by our daily experience of the Divine Office as we now know it? Perhaps we had better set aside that question at present and follow Augustine into the digression of the next paragraph of the *Rule*, for that digression itself has an important bearing on the difficulty that we have raised.

Rule, Chapter II, 2

In the oratory
no one should do anything that conflicts with the purpose of the building,
which is implied by its name,
so that if those who happen to be free
wish to pray there outside the fixed hours
they would not be hindered by anyone
who might think of doing something else there.

THE ORATORY: SOLITUDE AND SILENCE

Continuity with the previous paragraph lies in the words *orationibus* and *oratorio*. It is necessary to express this in Latin because in English the words have to be translated differently. What the words say is of the highest importance in the history of monasticism, as Adolar Zumkeller has pointed out.[8] For in setting aside a special room or building for prayer, Augustine made a monastic provision of which there is no earlier record. In the past, the place for prayer — apart from the church, which was used for corporate worship — was a monk's cell or the place where he worked. This, of course, was compatible with the continuous recitation of the psalms; but the provision of a place of undisturbed quiet was a response to the requirements of a different and more discursive way of praying. An oratory made possible a development of prayer that for most people was and still is unattainable in a busy place. The ability to get away from other people is a sheer necessity to those for whom the search for God is the chief activity of their lives. It is from aloneness-with-God that they can return to the work of service, and also to the work of creating fellowship with others in him. To have a place to go to for a conversation with God when one is free from other duties is one of the supreme privileges of a religious, in the sense that for almost everyone outside a monastery there is no such possibility. This is itself a challenge, for it is easy to abuse a privilege either by over-indulgence or by using it cheaply, and at the same time there is the possibility of divorcing what one does in the oratory from what one does elsewhere (which is a form of infidelity). The whole life of the monk must be related to the life of the Church of which he is a part.

For the person whose whole life is a search for God, there is an important aspect of aloneness that is a contrast with the *Rule's* reminder that we are temples of God (chapter I, 8). While it is true that each man is a place for worship and for learning, God's transcendence always calls him out and beyond what he understands and values. It is when one is alone with God that the dimensions of being are extended. People, things, activities are by their very nature circumscribing in their effect on others — and the human spirit yearns to be beyond limits, to reach out toward the otherness of God. This has a direct bearing on the life of religious who are striving to establish unity of heart and mind among themselves. Because such unity will always have an indefinable dimension that reaches beyond the shared experience of the group, it must make room for the unique contribution of each one. That means that in terms of both time and space each one must have some privacy, must be free to be alone with God — we should perhaps add, in the spirit of the *Rule,* "according to need." The exchanges that take place during our aloneness with God are what provide the quality of our life of togetherness with our companions in worship, work, and play. Togetherness will crystallize and test the experience and insights of aloneness, but without respect for privacy no fellowship can have a deep and lasting value.

Even if physical aloneness is not always practicable — and it is always possible that two or more people might wish to use the oratory at the same time — silence there should always be attainable. It is not so much the presence of another that may hinder private prayer, but noise of any kind can be a real distraction. The problem of noise-elimination is one that we are very much aware of in the twentieth century, and our responses to sound are quite different from those of a fourth-century man (and even of our contemporaries who are able to live far from madding crowds). Although humans seem to be developing a rejection-mechanism which makes them indifferent to certain sorts of sound, the level of tolerance differs widely and is closely related to general health and happiness. It is for each one to ensure the maximum of silence for his companions, if the community's life of prayer is to deepen. And it is only out of the depths of private prayer that corporate vocal prayer can become a living thing. It is in silence that the search for truth and for love is made; it is in public worship that God's gifts are celebrated, and both heart and mind can make their response. So at this point we may go forward to consider the next paragraph of this chapter which relates the prayer of the heart to the prayer of the voice.

Rule, Chapter II, 3

When you pray to God in psalms and hymns,
meditate in the heart
on what is expressed with the voice.

CORPORATE VOCAL PRAYER

The word which we have translated as "meditate" occurs only twice in the text — here, and in chapter VII, 4 — and in each case the English word used is tidier than the Latin. The verb *uersor* means to turn oneself about in, to dwell in a place, to be occupied with something: there is movement here as well as an at-home-ness, a change of attitude as well as a settled abode. *Uersor* implies movement within secure and strengthening limits. It is for this reason that "to meditate" seemed to be the best translation in the present context. Psalms and hymns occupy voice and mind, but the heart must also be engaged in this prayer to God if the whole person is to be involved. The mind which controls the voice must also control the heart, if there is to be unity within the undertaking. If the mind concentrates all its energies in the voice of each person, the choral effect may be well-nigh perfect while the thoughts of their hearts are stifled. If the mind and the heart are exclusively united, sound and even words may go astray. Corporate vocal worship is the most exacting form of prayer, and one is tempted to wonder why the Church (or any other religion, for that matter) has poured so much time, thought, and energy into this activity. The reason lies in the nature of humankind, in the fact that coordination is one of our most highly developed instincts, in the fact also that we are compelled by our very being to find expression for the worship that is in us, and because there is a strong inner impulse to bring together not only our fellows but every part of our own humanness in acts of praise, adoration, and supplication. So once more we are drawn toward the theme of unity. (In passing, we may note that a few years before writing the *Rule* Augustine had done a treatise, *De musica*, which explored these phenomena philosophically, aesthetically and from the point of view of a Christian moralist.)[9]

Now if and when all the members of a group were able to bring to an act of corporate worship a full coordination of voice, mind, and heart then, obviously, the totality of this act would be very rich: it would hold in one all the love, desire, and sorrow of each individual, stretching far out to the limits of their individual experience. But we all know that this can rarely happen. There will always be fluctuations in both quality and quantity of what each one brings to the united act. In fact, this nevertheless gives an added dimension to the undertaking for it calls into play a further human attribute — man's humility in his own inadequacy before God. Each one has also to hold, in this act of worship, both his own failure and that of his brothers and sisters. However rich might be the totality of full consent of heart, mind, and voice, the purity of a corporate act of worship is far greater if in love each is accepting what all others have to bring. What each one brings is the expression of his selfhood as it is at that time.

The word translated "expressed" (*proferetur*) is to be found three times in the *Rule* and in each case it needs a different English word to bring out its wide meaning. Primarily it means "to bring forth, produce, reveal" — always it implies an addition to a situation, the emergence of something that is not merely superficial and immediately apparent. Here in chapter II, 3 the psalms and hymns which the voice utters must be infused with the thoughts of the heart if real prayer is to be made. In chapter V, 1 the word supplied has been used concerning the clothing that is to be issued according to the season, but it should be noted that the text does not use one of the ordinary Latin words, *supplere* or *suppeditare* which simply mean "to provide"; the thought and consideration underlying the provision of clothing according to need seemed to indicate the use of the word supply, with its overtones of making up that which is lacking. And in chapter VI, 2 the Latin word *proferre* is found to have an equally sensitive meaning: when harsh words have been spoken, their perpetrator should "not be ashamed to let that mouth which caused the wound provide the cure." The deep well from which this word draws its meaning is sensitivity.

But how — and every worshiper is forced to ask this question from time to time — how is it possible to maintain that sensitivity that can hold together heart, mind, and voice through the course of a "service"? If this was a difficult undertaking for a fourth-century man, it is much more so for anyone alive today. In the days before sound could be processed, the making of music was in the nature of things always an event — and as such it automatically proclaimed part of its own significance. At the very least, "we sing with the voice to arouse ourselves" (*Expositions of the Psalms* 147, 5), as Augustine put it in a sermon. Singing always marked an occasion, even if it were only the singer's moment of personal happiness or sorrow. But today, when we can have music merely at the turn of a knob, when music can be so degraded that it becomes undifferentiated sound to the hearer, it is much more difficult to "make music make sense." There is so much music to be heard that its meaning is harder than ever to express. Apart from the sheer multiplicity of music that is available to us (a good thing) but which can confuse us (a bad thing), all who have lived since the end of the seventeenth century are at a further disadvantage. For until then music was usually related to words or to dancing. The development of instruments and instrumental music has relegated language to a minor and sometimes an absent factor in music-making — although the music now being written as an accompaniment for the dance has been greatly developed. And we of the twentieth century, who have always had the sound of music available to us without having to understand and make it for ourselves, are very hard put to it to relate and hold together all that music-making implies when it is used as an expression of praise to God. In spite of our sophistication, we today are the poorer for all that we have; and the process of learning to integrate heart, mind, and voice is a challenging one for our spirituality.

Yet we may look to the fourth century for help in our problem. Augustine himself was aware of it and referred to it several times over the years. The passage from the sermon which we have quoted above reads in full: "We sing with the voice to arouse ourselves; we sing with the heart to please Him." In another sermon[10] he tried to spell out one aspect of his answer to the problem: it is a man's whole life and work that is the background to his psalmody. His work must be in harmony with his voice, his work must be his real praise for God; then what the voice expresses will be true praise and not blasphemy. And again, in another sermon,[11] he suggested the opposite approach: the praise that a man utters in church is continued when he goes out if his works reflect that same attitude of Godwardness.

A further disadvantage that modern people have to endure (although the difficulty is again one of our own making) is that we treat the words of the psalter too lightly. Not everyone, of course, has the opportunity or the skill to explore them as discursively as Augustine himself did, but we cheapen them when we will not take trouble with them. We cannot expect the psalms to act as a vehicle of prayer if we do not take much notice of what they are saying. Both discipline and intelligence have to be harnessed to the heart.[12]

UNITY AND CORPORATE PRAYER

If heart, mind, and soul are to be bound together in unity, so also must it be with words, voice, and meaning. And it is the phrase "psalms and hymns" in the text that points to the deeper level of what Augustine is saying at this point. There are two New Testament passages in which these same words occur (Col 3:14-16 and Eph 5:18-20), and although the context to which they refer is different from that of the *Rule*, it is possible to see from other writings of Augustine that their underlying function is the same.

The first-century passages refer to gatherings of Christians (social gatherings, according to Armitage Robinson)[13] at which songs were sung to express the vivid enthusiasm[14] which characterized the lives of the first Christians. In the fourth-century passage, the context is formal worship with an ordered pattern. What binds the experience of the two centuries together is the fact that the undertaking is Christ-centered, both for each individual and for the group as a whole. If the uttering of psalms and hymns is to be a living thing that expresses what is in a man's heart, then it must be done in *love, which binds everything together in perfect harmony* (Col 3:14). This passage continues: *And let the peace of Christ rule in your hearts, to which indeed you are called in the one body. And be thankful. Let the word of God dwell in you richly . . . as you sing psalms and hymns and spiritual songs with thanksgiving in your hearts to God.* The Ephesian verses take the matter still further by showing how this same activity can take a group into the depth of God himself: *Be filled with the Spirit, addressing one another in psalms and hymns and spiritual songs, singing and making melody to the Lord with all your heart, always and for everything giving thanks in the name of our Lord Jesus Christ to God the Father.*

We should notice here the words *addressing one another*, for they remind us that corporate religious activity, whether of the first- or the fourth-century pattern, is always both vertical and horizontal. Some of what goes on in a monastic church may tend to lose sight of this double character: we may concentrate (if we concentrate at all!) on God, and beyond being careful to sing in time and in tune we may ignore those who are worshiping with us — even custody of the eyes can be a shutting out of other people. Yet although the length of each individual's vertical and horizontal lines of approach will vary considerably, without some awareness of all our sisters and brothers as persons sharing a common vocation our personal worship can be something of a mockery. But even this is not saying enough, for even awareness can be an antagonistic activity: the awareness that we extend to others as we worship must be informed with real love (which, as Paul says, *binds together in perfect harmony*), it must be open to the peace of Christ which through us can then extend beyond us, it must desire to make real the fact that in Christ we are one body and not a collection of individuals who have got to do something together. Our awareness must be open to the word of Christ, teaching and prompting us, so that a real thankfulness is at work within us. That is to say, we must be open to the Spirit (*filled with the Spirit* is how Ephesians 5:18 describes it) to be led by him in whom all are sons of God (Rom 8:14). Our very relationship with God makes us all siblings, and this dimension of our life must find expression in our corporate worship.

It takes many years and many failures to learn how to harness ability to listen to the heart's cry of our fellow-worshipers with the depth of inner concentration that is necessary if each one of us is to direct our listening also toward the still, small voice of the Spirit within us. In one sense, this is life's work within the common life.

Unity, fellowship, and a common understanding will only emerge to the degree that each one desires it, and as true companions we owe it to each other to make this a possibility according to our ability. But alone we cannot do this, human nature being what it is. In one of the later sermons Augustine explored all of this and said:

> Who can doubt that cries unto the Lord made in prayer, if uttered only from the mouth of the body, and not with the heart fixed upon God, sound in vain? But if they proceed from the heart, though the voice of the body be silent they may escape any other man whomsoever, but not God. Whether then we cry unto the Lord, when we pray, with our fleshly voices, when there is occasion for them, or in silence, we must cry from the heart. Now the cry of the heart is a solemn earnestness of thought which when vented in prayer doth express a deep longing and affection of him that prayeth, so that he despaireth not of success. Then also we cry with the heart, when we have no thoughts elsewhere. Such prayers are rare among the many, frequent among the few; whether all are such with any one person, I know not (*Expositions of the Psalms* 118, 29, 1).

So once again we are driven back to the truth that it is only in Christ that these things are possible. Once more the *Rule* makes us aware that our experience in community is the experience of the whole Church, of the living, suffering, loving and enduring body of Christ whose members we are. At the end of chapter I, the *Rule* showed the brothers that they are temples of God, the place of his presence. Now, in chapter II, a further implication is made: within us, God in Christ is more than merely present, he is active, he is our life. And when we open ourselves in prayer, it is not we alone who pray but Christ himself who is active in us. At the beginning of his Christian and monastic life, Augustine had thought that it was possible to pursue holiness and be made God (*deificare*) by a life of withdrawal,[15] but experience taught him that God had other ways of making deification possible.

DEIFICATION

Although there is no use of the word *deificare* in the *Rule*, its spirit permeates Augustine's understanding of monastic life; and for that reason it will be useful to discover what manner of

meaning he gives to this concept. The idea itself stems from
Platonism and was incorporated into Christian thinking during
the late second and early third centuries. It was possible for a
Christian to think in these terms if he spoke Greek because, as W.
R. Inge has pointed out,[16] for a Greek the word God had a fluid
meaning (which the Latin *deus* has never borne). The first known
Christian writers to use the word *deificare* or its Greek equivalent
were Theophilus, Clement, and Hippolytus, and they were followed by Athanasius, the Cappadocians, and others in the third
and fourth centuries. Thus the concept was taken over into the
thinking of the West, and deification became part of the Latin
Christian vocabulary. When Augustine took hold of the word and
attempted to set it within his own Christian thinking, he found
that its meaning lay within the fact of the incarnation. For him, the
notion could only make sense when one remembered that God in
Christ had made himself a partaker of human nature; and, as he
put it in the *City of God* IX, 15, "the blessed and glorious God, made
a partaker of our humanity, provides the means for us to partake
in his divinity." For him, the Christian's deification means his·
participation in the life and working of God.[17] Deification means
our transformation, and it is always God's work, not ours. Deification is a process, not a state; it is the interaction of Christ in his
nature with us in ours, and its effect is the restoration of wholeness
to men "perverted and distorted by sin" (Letter 140, 4, 10). Deification in its complete form can never occur in this life — but it
remains the Christians' aim, even though many of them might
never use that word to describe their sharing in Christ's life.

Augustine's appreciation of the term came early, as his letter to
Nebridius shows, but his deep understanding of it did not come
until many years later. His experience of monastic life soon taught
him that it was not (as he had naively hoped) a life of withdrawal
that brought about an interaction between Christ and his members, but that what was needed for that to be possible was an
ever-renewed attention to his creative presence within.

When, then, we meditate with the heart on the psalms and
hymns that our voice is uttering we are in fact opening ourselves
to the whole cry of humanity and also to the loving response of
Christ to the human condition. Psalms and hymns, as it were,
come to life as representatives of human need — a need into which
Christ himself has entered and with which he has identified

himself. But here it is best to let Augustine express the immensity of this dimension of prayer in his own words:

> No greater gift could God have given to men than in making his Word, by which he created all things, their head, and joining them to him as his members: that the Son of God might become also the Son of man, one God with the Father, one Man with men; so that when we speak to God in prayer for mercy we do not separate the Son from him: and when the body of the Son prays, it separates not its head from itself: and it is one Savior of his body, our Lord Jesus Christ, the Son of God, who both prays for us, and prays in us, and is prayed to by us. He prays for us as our priest; he prays in us, as our head; he is prayed to by us, as our God. Let us therefore recognize in him our words, and his words in us. . . . It was his will to make the words of the psalm his own words, as he hung upon the cross, and said *My God, my God, why have you forsaken me*? He is prayed to in the form of God, in the form of a servant he prays; there the creator, here created, assuming unchanged the creature, that it might be changed, and making us with himself one man, head and body. Therefore we pray to him, through him, in him; and we speak with him, and he speaks with us; we speak in him, he speaks in us the prayer of this Psalm, which is entitled "A Prayer of David" (*Expositions of the Psalms* 86[85], 1).

Rule, Chapter II, 4

And sing only what is set down for you to sing.
What is not written to be sung
is not to be sung.

A COMMON PATTERN

"Making us with himself one man, head and body." With those words of Augustine's in mind, at first sight the restrictive prescription of this paragraph of the *Rule* looks almost harmfully inadequate, but what it is attempting to safeguard and to foster is the very unity of the community in its common worship. The acceptance of a common pattern, once it is agreed upon by a consensus of opinion, is one aspect of the acceptance of the togetherness of the whole group. The willingness to adhere to the common practice of the group is a sign of consent to the life of the brotherhood. Conversely, deliberately to adopt a different mode of expression is destructive of the integrity of the group as well as an indication of a lesion in the individual concerned.

As we shall see in later contexts — chapters IV, 8 (twice) and VI, 2 — the healing of a wound must always be the community's endeavor, and as a monk grows in maturity he comes to learn how he himself can wound his brothers. Much of the *Rule* has as an underlying motif the need for healing and the community as a place of healing. And thus it has to be part of the community's office (in both senses of that word) to accept defiance with compassion if it cannot be thawed, provided it is not completely destructive of the group's unity, even though there may be little understanding of the causes of such behavior. Involuntary idiosyncrasies are another matter; but they, too, are to be borne if they cannot be cured. In both cases, there has to be room for every member. To crush is to destroy and thus to be afflicted with the very condition that one desires to remove.

WORDS AND MUSIC

In terms of formal instructions, it is impossible to know exactly what Augustine had in mind. But one thing is sure, and it must be pointed out as for centuries there has been misunderstanding of this paragraph of the *Rule*. He could not have been referring to written music because musical notation had not been invented in his day; singers relied on memory.[18] So in mentioning "what is set down" he must have meant words and not melody. This reflects the variety of versions of the scriptures that were available in the late fourth century as well as the problems that differing tastes give rise to. This set of difficulties is one that we can readily understand today. Augustine's answer lies in the realm of striving for unity with one another in God.

In the matter of singing itself, there has to be unanimity if what is sung is to express the common mind and heart of the group. Indeed, the act of attention to the music that is being made around him and of making his own contribution to the sound demands of each monk a deep capacity to listen and to be aware of his brothers. Singing together is an exercise in charity that challenges the integrity of each member of the group and it demands an acceptance of each other in a spirit of understanding. Obviously, it is not the quality of the music that truly expresses the heart's prayer; but the quality does to a considerable extent express the heart's intention. And if the intention excludes the intention of others, then both music and words will be an unworthy offering to God.

So the music of the worship which the community gives to God is an expression of its unity in him; and it is for this reason that the *Rule*'s forthright restrictions in this matter are to be seen not as limiting factors but as designed to express the gathering of all the thoughts, hopes, and aspirations of each member into a wholeness.

In the fourth century, music in Christian worship was going through a period of change. We know from the *Confessions* that while he was in Milan he was greatly impressed by the innovations which Ambrose had introduced; these were based partly on the model of monastic practice in the East and partly on the bishop's own creative talent. We know, too, from a number of passages that Augustine was constantly concerned for the eradication from Christian practice of customs associated with pagan festivals. It seems reasonable, then, to deduce that what is at stake here is the purity and clarity of the monastic witness, and in this the teaching of Paul would provide him with a valuable precedent. There is the carefully thought out passage in 1 Corinthians 14, in which the apostle discusses the variety of participation in public worship that may hinder as much as help the prayer of the congregation. There are the problems of spontaneity, understanding and tongues; and the conclusion that the apostle reaches is that whatever is done *must always be for the common good* (verse 26) and *with propriety and in order* (verse 40). We have noticed already how, in chapter I, concern for the common good is regarded as the touchstone of the community's integrity. And this integrity must find its supreme expression in its worship. (In fact, one of the painful experiences of community life is that the distresses and diseases of each individual often become most fully laid bare to the group within the context of its worship.)

The monks' worship together must express their common life in God — their adoration, praise, thanksgiving, and supplication; but this is not all. If it is to be whole, their worship will also express their common life in one another — their attention to each other and their concern for each other, their desire that what is done corporately shall be a vehicle of each man's unuttered cry. In practice, this requires of each man a great deal of goodwill and give-and-take. It means the setting aside of personal prejudices and a willingness to enter into the thoughts and the feelings of others to a profound and costing extent.

If the *Rule* says so little about the nature of prayer in theoretical terms, it postulates a life of prayer that draws from God the charity and the compassion that every individual needs if we are to live in true unity with our companions; it postulates also the prayer of desire which is the common bond of all the members of the group.

NOTES

1. A valuable study of Augustine's understanding of prayer is to be found in Thomas A. Hand, *Augustine on Prayer*, Catholic Book Publishing Co., New York, 1986.

2. This point is well made in Adolar Zumkeller, *Augustine's Ideal of the Religious Life*, Fordham University Press, 1986, pages 184-187.

3. See Zumkeller, *op. cit.*, page 181.

4. For example, the *Peregrinatio ad loca sancta* which the nun Etheria/Egeria made during the 380s (the most recent study and translation of this is John Wilkinson, *Egeria's Travels*, SPCK, 1971); and also Augustine in *Confessions* IX, 6, where he writes sensitively and enthusiastically about the liturgical music that he heard in Milan within the same decade. A summary of the early sources is given in Willi Apel; *Gregorian Chant*, Burns & Oates (no date, but the author's preface is dated 1958); and the musical history for the early centuries is given in chapters 1-4 of the *New Oxford History of Music*, Volume II, edited by Anselm Hughes, Oxford University Press, 1954.

5. See Johannes Quasten, *Patrology*, Volume III: *The Golden Age of Greek and Patristic Literature*, Utrecht/Antwerp: Spectrum Publishers, 1960, page 226.

6. See *The Ascetic Works of St. Basil*, ed. W. K. Lowther Clarke, SPCK, 1925, page 11, where it is stated that the translation was made in 397 by Rufinus of Aquileia.

7. *The Origins of the Christian Doctrine of Sacrifice*, Darton, Longman & Todd, 1978, page 69.

8. See Zumkeller, *op. cit.*, pages 182-183.

9. See Robert J. O'Connell, *Art and the Christian Intelligence in St. Augustine*, Blackwell, 1978, especially chapters 1-4.

10. *Expositions of the Psalms* 147, 2.

11. *Expositions of the Psalms* 148, 2.

12. There is a very valuable chapter on "praying the psalms" in André Louf, *Teach Us to Pray*, Darton, Longman & Todd, 1974, pages 50-58.

13. J. Armitage Robinson, *St. Paul's Epistle to the Ephesians*, Macmillan, 1903, page 122.

14. *Ibid.*, page 121. Reference is here made also to the rejoicing of the apostles at being able to suffer for the name of Christ, after they had been brought before the Council (Acts 5:41), and to Paul and Silas in the Philippi prison spending the night singing and praying (Acts 16:25).

15. Letter 10, 2 to Nebridius.

16. *Christian Mysticism*, Methuen, 3rd edition 1913, pages 356-368 and especially pages 356-357.

17. See the important article of Gerald Bonner, "The Spirituality of St. Augustine and Its Influence on Western Mysticism", in *Sobornost* 4, 2 (1982) 143-162 and especially the section headed "Deification," 157-159.

18. See Giulio Cattin, *Music of the Middle Ages*, I, Cambridge University Press, 1984, page 55.

3

Asceticism through Poverty and the Common Life

Rule, Chapter III, 1
Discipline your flesh
by fasting and abstinence from food and drink
as far as your health allows.
When anyone is unable to remain fasting until the afternoon
he should nevertheless not have any food until midday
unless he is ill.

TRUE COMMUNITY

In the first volume of his study of the works of William Faulkner, Cleanth Brooks explores the author's understanding of a "true community which is . . . a community of values as well as an organic society."[1] Such a phrase is an apt description of the sort of community that is evoked by the precepts of the *Rule* of Saint Augustine. Chapters I and II of the *Rule* are concerned with the community of values which emerges in terms of unity of heart and mind, in terms of a place where God is worshiped and in terms of the deep and continual prayer which is the cry of the search for God as well as the song of adoration and thanksgiving as God makes himself known. These are the values that infuse the whole life of the monastery — strengthening, challenging, teaching and directing it. It is with these values in mind that Augustine in chapter III of the *Rule* turns attention to the group as an organic society.

The emphasis continues to be on the place of the individual within the group and the precepts of this chapter are concerned not only with describing and defending its customs but also in helping the people to adapt themselves happily to them. The value of the observance of customs lies in the fact that they are designed to safeguard the ideals of the community. In the process of assimilation within the group, each individual will to a greater or lesser degree call in question the accepted customs and also be tested by them. Not everything comes easily to everyone, and it is necessary always to bear compassionately the struggles of one's companions

— and we may hope that our own efforts will be accepted with equal charity by the community.

The ideal that is being discussed in this chapter is that of poverty and its expression in the common life of the group. The self-denial that is explored in chapter I of the *Rule* in terms of values is now, in chapter III, looked at from the point of view of practice. And here we come to an important development of monasticism which has had a lasting influence. Two of the primary factors that led to the emergence of this way of life within the Church are: the search for God, and work in God's service. The third factor is asceticism, and that in a form far different from its earlier manifestations within monastic tradition.

In the collections of sayings and stories about the early monks, the simplicity of life that is described — in matters of living conditions, diet, and work — finds only slight echoes in Augustine's *Rule*. Felt needs are always related to environment, and the desert itself safeguards the simplicity and austerity that was the monks' ideal; it did not provide any alternative to a very simple life. Asceticism, the training needed for combat with the powers of darkness, was inherent in the way of life of anyone who chose to live far from "civilization."

For Augustine, monastic asceticism takes different forms from those of the fathers of the desert. For one thing, it is to be lived out in a busy seaport and not in any arid hinterland. It will always involve other people and will be visible to others, simply because they are there.

FASTING AND ABSTINENCE

But first of all Augustine treats the matter as it affects each individual, and the verb that he uses occurs only once in the whole *Rule*. "Discipline your flesh," he says. This is certainly one of the first lessons that the monks of the desert had to learn to do. Augustine stands in the same tradition. But the word which he chooses to describe what he means has no harshness in it. The Latin word *domare* is used primarily of breaking in an animal in order to enable it to serve and cooperate with its rider, and later it is used figuratively of persons and of the body's passions. It implies understanding, moderation, courage, perseverance, and, above all, a striving for unity and harmony.

"Discipline your flesh by fasting and abstinence from food and drink." This is another aspect of the self-giving which Augustine was at pains to probe in chapter I, and one which flowed naturally from prayer which is the subject of chapter II. To enjoin his readers to stretch their physical capacity as far as it can go in the matter of food and drink is to lead them to a form of real poverty that cannot be reached in any other way. To dispossess ourselves of rank, money, goods, and the like is one thing; but dispossession of nourishment above a basic minimum is to place ourselves entirely at God's disposal. As Augustine says, it is not for us to go beyond the degree of tolerance that our body has, but voluntarily to live on the borderline is an act of great courage. It is in this area that the asceticism of the eastern monastic tradition finds expression in the West. And Augustine can be completely realistic about the cost of disciplined fasting. A few years after the composition of *The Rule*, he reflected on his current experience when he was writing the *Confessions*:

> We repair the daily deteriorations of the body by eating and drinking, until the day when You will "destroy both the belly and the meats," for You will kill our emptiness with a marvelous fullness, and You will clothe this corruptible with eternal incorruption. But for the present time the necessity is sweet to me, and I fight against that sweetness lest I be taken captive by it. I wage daily war on it by fasting, bringing my body again and again into subjection: but the pain this gives me is driven away by the pleasure (of eating and drinking). For hunger and thirst really are painful: they burn and kill, like fever, unless food comes as medicine for our healing . . . This You taught me, that I should learn to take my food as a kind of medicine . . . While we eat and drink for the sake of health, yet a perilous enjoyment runs at the heels of health and often enough tries to run ahead of it: so that what I say I am doing and really desire to do for my health's sake, I do in fact for the sake of the enjoyment. For there happens not to be the same measure for both: what suffices for health is too little for enjoyment: so that often it is not at all clear whether it is necessary care of my body calling for more nourishment, or the deceiving indulgence of greed wanting be served. Because of this uncertainty my wretched soul is glad, and uses it as a cover and an excuse, rejoicing that it does not clearly appear what is sufficient for the needs of health, so that under the cloak of health it may shelter the business of pleasure (X, 31).

Fasting, then, is a testing practice which both needs and is needed by the practice of prayer, and this is the link in the chain of thought that holds the *Rule* together at this point. At this level, fasting had to be considered in relation to prayer, and also in relation to the ascetical practices of monastic life, for no monasticism could be valid without its asceticism in some form, just as there must always be a place for the search and the service. But the striking newness of the *Rule*'s approach to monasticism lies in the sort of asceticism that it postulates.

What each member of the community can do will vary from time to time, and here once more the challenge to the group is to allow room for each individual. Food, being a basic need, is also one of the commonest causes of dissension and disturbance; and the discipline which each one is to exercise in the personal use of food and drink has also to be exercised by every other member in charity, forbearance, and understanding. Concern for the health of others is referred to in a number of passages: in chapters IV, 8 (twice) and 9; V, 5, 6 and 8; and VII, 3. Concern for one's own health, as a matter of responsibility, is treated in this paragraph as a discipline and one's body is regarded as an object of discipline.

This approach, which is based on the Pauline example of fitting the body to be an instrument of God's work, is quite different from that of the earlier monks who in treating the body despicably had sought thereby their own salvation. What the *Rule* enjoins is respect for the body which is created by God and entrusted to us, and which becomes through Christ the place where he is to be praised and served. And there is the further fact that the body's endurance is not itself redemptive. Humankind's salvation is, like its creation, always a gift of God and, as the Christian sees it, this is only wrought in Christ and through Christ.

Two things are emerging, as we try to discover the interior meaning of the present precept, and both are explored in the remainder of chapter III. The first is that the asceticism of the religious is to be such that it directs attention away from self and toward other people, that is to say, the self-denial, discipline, and endurance of weakness or vulnerability are to be expressed within the personal relationships of the common life. The second point is that none of this is possible except in dependence on the enabling of God, and this is the underlying meaning of monastic poverty.

However, before we turn to these matters we must try to unravel the meaning of the remainder of this first paragraph, because it has long been misunderstood and consequently has had a curious effect on monastic customs through the centuries. The real unraveling has been done by Luc Verheijen in an article first published in 1971, and in my translation I have, as it were, expressed the fruits of his research.

The Latin is: *quando autem aliquis non potest ieiunare*, and in the past it has been customary to translate the verb simply as "fast." But that begs the question by assuming that the meaning of "to fast" is obvious, while in fact it has meant different things in different epochs. Verheijen has demonstrated what in practice it meant in the fourth century and therefore what is implied in this passage of the *Rule*. "To fast" meant to go without food until the *cena*,[2] the main meal of the day among both Greeks and Romans. This was common monastic custom.[3] Now the *cena* was normally taken at about three o'clock in the afternoon,[4] and for that reason I have translated *non potest ieiunare* as "is unable to remain fasting until the afternoon." This has seemed necessary in order to bring out the force of the next words in the Latin sentence which goes on to say that the monk who cannot fast should nevertheless not take food *extra horam prandii*. It has been customary to translate this in such words as "outside/except at the meal times,"[5] but this overlooks the precise meaning of *prandium* which was not a general word meaning "a meal" but the name of one particular meal. *Prandium* was the light midday meal "intended merely to stay the stomach from long fasting," and according to my dictionary of antiquities this meal consisted of bread and cheese, without wine, and not set out formally at table.[6] Thus what the *Rule* is providing is light nourishment at midday for those who cannot carry on without food for another three hours. The word used for food is *alimentum* (nourishment/sustenance), not *iuctus* (which implies all the ingredients of a meal). In colloquial English, probably the words snack and victuals best indicate the nature of *prandium* and *cena* respectively. We shall see again in chapter III, 4 how *alimentum* and not *iuctus* is used to describe the extra food that is needed by those who are weak. In the present passage, it has seemed best (as a parallel to the spelling-out of *ieiunare*) to translate the Latin here as "not have any food until midday."

Augustine's stress is on discipline according to each one's capacity. The practice in the Hippo monastery is no different from the common pattern, and the precept of "abstinence" points to simplicity rather than frugality at meals. Fortunately for posterity, no specific injunctions are given in the *Rule* concerning food. But we know from Possidius that in the monastery where Augustine spent his life after he became bishop meals were very simple; they were generally vegetarian, though meat was sometimes served for those in poor health and for visitors, and wine was served.[7]

Rule, Chapter III, 2

When you are at table, and until you rise,
you should listen without interruption or discussion
to what is read according to your custom.
Your throats alone should not receive food,
but ears, too, should hunger for the word of God.

MANNERS AND DECORUM

At first glance it might seem that this paragraph is a parenthesis in the chapter's discussion of a new monastic asceticism, but in fact this precept is concerned with the deep levels of life on which the community's customs are founded.

There is, obviously, an injunction here regarding table manners, insofar as orderliness and decorum are concerned; and in terms of the community's underlying unity there has to be a commonly accepted pattern of behavior. But even here each member's personal integrity has to be made room for, so that it is not possible for one individual or another to force his or her own pattern on the whole group. This is less of a problem when all the members are products of the same environment, but when a group is composed of people of different nationalities with different customs there has to be a wide measure of tolerance. There seem to be two attitudes to living abroad. One can be called colonialism, and this consists of maintaining one's heritage of customs and behavior in the new setting; the other may be called amalgamation, which consists of a deliberate break with one's past and a striving to conform to the new pattern as quickly as possible. There is good and bad in both attitudes, but pressed too far each is destructive of the unity of the group. As in every other aspect of community life, there has to be a large measure of acceptance and of give-and-take which is informed by the constant reflection of all the members on the fundamentals that hold the group together. That is why the transition of thought in this paragraph can move so easily from orderly behavior to attention to the word of God.

READING AT MEALS

Throughout the Church's history, the secret writings have been regarded as a way of God's communication with men and women, and within monastic tradition the habit of reading biblical texts during meals was already established by the time the *Rule* was written.[8] So in this passage the custom evoked is that of reading the word of God. But holy scripture is not always easy to understand, and the perfect will of God enshrined in it is not always acceptable to imperfect and struggling people. In the twentieth century one is normally accustomed to keeping one's problems and disagreements under control when one hears the Bible read aloud, but there is plenty of evidence in Augustine's sermons[9] that vocal interjection and a good deal of clamor were in his time normal occurrences. If hearers contended with the scriptures in church, then it is reasonable to assume that they felt free to do so also in a monastic refectory. It is not the words of scripture that reach into one's heart, but its demands. Failure to understand what is being read may still leave the heart open to the will of God. What is at stake here is the attitude to what is heard. There are several passages in Augustine's writings[10] in which he tries to uncover the reasons why the biblical texts draw out resentment and not acceptance from their hearers, and he concludes that it is because they are too challenging: those who hear the words cannot receive them into the heart because of their own pride and willfulness. It is those described by the Lord as the *meek* (Mt 5:5) who are able to accept the word of God and enter the kingdom.

Chapter I of the *Rule* is concerned with the way in which God looks out of the eyes of other members of the community, from his dwelling-place within each individual, so that everyone's integrity is challenged by all his or her companions. Here in this paragraph of chapter III, within the context of a search for true ascetic poverty, the group has to submit to the fathoming of God through the text of the Bible. I write "fathoming of God" deliberately because there is a two-way movement in the reading of scripture, as there has to be in any communication. The Bible can be both the means of deepening one's understanding of self and also the way of coming to a fuller knowledge of God. Yet the fact has to be faced that it can easily happen that the very opposite occurs when the word of God is being read. If we are self-regarding, or if we do not want to be challenged, we simply refuse to listen; if our public manner or our secret self is felt to be attacked by what we hear, we may reject the message then and there; if what is read is beyond our understanding and our experience we will either dismiss the whole as irrelevant or will set our mind to pursue meaning until we find it, accepting the challenge that it contains. This last is the attitude of the meek, and it is this that the *Rule* presents as the means that can bring fulfillment to us as we listen.

The use of the word "hunger" in the text is an even more direct evocation of the beatitudes that we have already uncovered in Augustine's phrases: *Blessed are those who hunger and thirst for righteousness, for they shall be satisfied* (Mt 5:6). The beatitude and the *Rule*'s phrase, "hunger for the word of God," both relate to a longing that is satisfied by him, and there is a striking contrast here with the slight vulgarity of the *Rule*'s previous phrase. "Throats" (*fauces* in Latin, which could equally well be translated "gullets") has ill-mannered overtones when used in relation to food.

In the refectory, as everywhere else, awareness of all dimensions of life have to be given full play. The reflectiveness in the recital of the psalms which is the important feature of chapter II has also to inform the hearing of other parts of the Bible. When that is the level at which each member's attention is held during a meal, then bad manners in oneself or the observation of them in others has little place. In theory, that holds good. But in practice, the downward drag (which is especially strong where food is concerned) is constantly exercising its influence, and that is what is examined in the next paragraph.

Rule, Chapter III, 3

If special treatment in the way of diet
is given to those who are not strong as a result of their former way of life
others who are stronger because they have had a different manner of life
must not be aggrieved
or think it unfair.
Nor should they think the former luckier
in getting something that they themselves do not get.
Rather, they should be thankful
that they are strong enough to do what others cannot.

ENVY

Again there is a precept concerning the presence of jealousy, though this time the background is not the establishment of unity within the group, but the striving for a true ascetic poverty. At a merely superficial level it is obvious how fruitless it is to be frugal and self-denying if one is at the same time envious of the less restricted diet of others: the object of the exercise is then unattainable, for if jealousy is present purification is not. So it looks as if within this area there is bound to be a long struggle before we can achieve real indifference to what others eat and drink. It seems to be somewhat easier to reach indifference as to what one actually eats oneself.

But to return to the diet of others: two words in the text serve to bring out the real considerations that will help us to do battle with this particular temptation. The first is "aggrieved" (*molestum*), and the second is "unfair" (*iniustum*). The first concerns the emotions, the second the reason — and one has to admit that in relation to food emotion often runs riot and reason is distorted. True poverty of spirit does not know how to be aggrieved and envious. Having a grievance seems to be the surest way of clouding the reason; it also prevents the purification of the self which is the main purpose of asceticism. Even if ascetic practices in general also serve to strengthen a person for inner or outer conflicts in the name of the Lord, the harboring of a grievance can distort a whole life, as it did with Absalom (2 Sm 13:22). Similarly, to make a false judgment in the realm of justice is the way to disaster not only for oneself but also for the other person. So long as justice is kept within legal and penal categories it can never bring wholeness to any situation, for so much of life lies outside these boundaries. The very presence of the varied needs of individuals within a community is itself conducive to asceticism; in this way there is less danger of self-satisfaction. Those who are weaker have the greater need if they are to fulfill the normal demands of the group, and these supranormal needs must be met.

It may well be that those who are committed to a way of life that includes the limitation of food are placed in a particularly vulnerable situation, for lack of physical sustenance makes life itself seem insecure. So what began in this chapter as a precept on external ascetic practices within the monastery leads inevitably to the vastly deeper subject of monastic poverty itself.

The voluntary poverty which a religious assumes operates at two levels: it engages us in an ethical struggle, and it supports our continuous search for God. To take the second point first: the absence or restriction of things forces us from undue concern in getting and maintaining them. Yet the very fact that the religious life has a purpose beyond itself means that our store of resources of all kinds must be well stocked. The concept of poverty which such a life is to make explicit is itself very well stocked in biblical tradition, and to this we must now turn if we are to reach the deeper level of understanding which this and the next paragraphs of the *Rule* attempt to disclose.

The insights of the Old Testament thinkers, poets, and prophets were given heightened meaning by Jesus himself.[11] "Poor" was an omnibus word used to describe people who were in any sense deprived. The poor were the afflicted, indigent, oppressed. They were the meek, those with no desire or intention to fight for their rights. They were the helpless, those difficult to meet and to help. They were the needy, those with less than the basic necessities of life. Relief from any form of poverty was not primarily a "social" issue because poverty was for long regarded as a normal condition and only later did it come to be thought of as a curse. It was against this background that the "religious" biblical thinkers strove to find ways out of the widespread misery that poverty produced. Thus there emerged an underlying philosophy of life which encouraged the poor to count their blessings, and from this there developed a new attitude to poverty. Then the word "poor" came to denote the pious and devout, that is, those who counted on God for everything. In a later addition to the book of Zephaniah the problem is considered against a background of moral and social disintegration, and the conclusion is reached that further reintegration could come about through the humble and lowly who sought refuge in the name of the Lord (3:12). The poets of the psalter pointed the way forward in a number of songs.[12] Relief from moral and social distress could come only from God: *Turn to me, and be gracious to me, for I am lonely and afflicted. Relieve the troubles of my heart and bring me out of my distresses. Consider my affliction and my trouble, and forgive all my sins* (Ps 25:16-18). Psalm 69 looks at the poor and afflicted from many sides and in verse 32 draws an interesting parallel (which does not come out very satisfactorily in any of the English translations) between the humble (= the afflicted) and those who seek God. Similarly, there are several passages in the Wisdom literature where poverty is not regarded as the greatest evil but as a pathway to God (Prv 18:12; 28:6; Eccl 4:13). All of this is summed up in the words of the Jewish writer, L. Baeck: "The word 'poor' is a word which the Bible pronounces with devoutness and with reverence, as if in holy awe."[13]

In the gospels, the dominant idea concerning poverty comes not only from the words of Jesus but also from his life. He was one of the poor and made no attempt to alter his station in life. In fact he regarded wealth as a hindrance to entry into the kingdom of God (Mk 10:23). His counsel to the rich young man to renounce all was a necessary condition for following him, in the sense of becoming one of the group that lived as he did and went everywhere with him. When Jesus said (Lk 6:20) that God's kingdom belongs to the poor, or (Mt 5:3) that the poor in spirit have the kingdom of heaven, the word "poor" is not used in a social sense, and not simply to describe a "spiritual" attitude in those who have few possessions; rather, the word carries the many-branched ontological sense which it bore among the later Old Testament writers. The poor are those who know their own lack and who are always open to receive from God, who dare to depend on him in the very condition of their neediness. Those who are poor in this way, says Jesus, are those who have the kingdom of God. This teaching brings out two facts: that the kingdom is worth discovering and also that it can be overlooked. The kingdom of God is the sphere of God's activity. That is why it was possible for the Lord to say that the poor have the kingdom. Those who live in dependence on God are those in whom he can work his work. And it is this attitude that lies at the heart of monastic ascetic poverty.

DEPENDENCE AND GRATITUDE

This approach is a challenge to exterior asceticism and also to interior weakness in the form of envy and jealousy. It is the attitudes of the poor which we have just described that enable a religious to win the ethical struggle which our commitment necessarily involves. The tendency to envy is bound to crop up as the process of interior purification is continued. But not having and not needing the things on which others have to depend is itself a gift of God which is continually given to us. Through dependence on God's sustaining we are enabled to live out our vocation, while for the community's weaker members God's sustenance is mediated through the extra things that they need to be allowed. Thus what a deep acceptance of poverty does within the community, whose members vary greatly in their actual needs, is to increase the bonds that hold them in unity, for all good things come from God. Poverty in the biblical and monastic sense lies near to the source of all fullness. So the thankfulness that the last sentence of this paragraph evokes is the gratitude of a humble person aware of need, not the blind and unreal thankfulness of the Pharisee who could not see what manner of man he was (Lk 18:11). The false values which we in our weak moments may adopt are brought out in the *Rule* by the use of the word *felix*, with its rather cheap overtones, and it is only after alluding to such cheap superficiality that Augustine points the way forward to the real happiness that can come from complete dependence on God.

The last sentence of this paragraph is deceptively simple: "they should be thankful that they are strong enough to do what others cannot." This makes concrete our faith in God's enabling gifts. Faith, gifts, and thankfulness are an encirclement that provides us with our one and only security. Faith in the certainties that Christ has revealed and humble acknowledgement that of ourselves we can do nothing: these are the characteristics of a life that is truly poor. God is not merely within us; he is also active, giving strength and ability for the sustaining of our life. There is no cause for pride in what we can achieve through the gifts that are in us, for all are the possession of God.

But this struggle toward a true dependence on God and a true ascetic poverty is long and hard. It is not only food that stirs up resentment, and the *Rule* goes on to probe other aspects of community life which put each member's disposition to the test. God's transforming power cannot be fully effective until all the dark corners of our life are illuminated and cleansed.[14]

Rule, Chapter III, 4

When those who have entered the monastery
from a more luxurious way of life
are given any food, clothing, bedding or covering
that is not given to others who are stronger and so more fortunate,
these last (to whom it is not given) should consider
how far the former have come down from their previous way of life in the
    world

even though they cannot reach the simplicity of living
which is possible for those who are stronger in body.
All should not desire to receive the extra things
which they see are given to a few —
such things are a concession not an honor.
Otherwise a detestable disorder would arise in the monastery
if the rich work there as hard as ever they can
while the poor who have greater strength
become weakened.

SAFEGUARDING THE INDIVIDUAL

In this paragraph also, it is the needs of each individual that are being safeguarded; and what these lines do in depth is to make more explicit the way of life which poverty of spirit makes possible with the group.

But first we should note the details of the common life that are briefly referred to here. The text gives no specific information of what any of these items consisted of — there was no need to do so, because they lay within the experience of all the *Rule's* intended readers.

"Food" (*alimentum*) and "clothing" (*uestimentum*) have been considered in an earlier context. We must look at the next two items on Augustine's list, which we have translated as "bedding" and "covering." As Luc Verheijen has demonstrated,[15] although *stramentum* originally meant straw for sleeping on or in, by Augustine's time the word had come to be used not only for the most frugal way of making a bed (by spreading out straw) and for straw in the more convenient form of a palliasse, but also for something filled with wool or feathers; the word was also used for pillows and cushions which, again, could have either kind of stuffing. Augustine gives no further indication as to what the monastery could supply in the way of extra help for anyone who is ill, so it seems best to use the imprecise word "bedding." The fact that he uses the word in the plural may indicate that pillows rather than a mattress were intended. It cannot be deduced from the text that in the Hippo monastery everyone slept on a palliasse.

Operimentum was the word generally used for any covering of any sort; it always went on top. Augustine uses the word in the plural, so there is no indication of the number; nor do we know what the coverings were made of. The monks for whom he wrote knew precisely what he was referring to; his later readers must be content with the fact that he was talking about the coverings of a bed.

The *Rule* contains no specific description of the general pattern of life in the monastery — again, because there was no need to do so. The monks probably already had the prescriptive document known as the *Ordo Monasterii*. In fact, the whole of the *Rule* can be described as a spiritual counterpart to that earlier text.[16] "Simplicity of living" (*frugalitas*) applies not only to food but also to the other basic necessities of life, clothing, and warmth; it applies too to the daily physical work which all should share according to their capacity. The obvious need for selflessness and self-denial runs through all of these things. The kingdom of God which is available to the poor in spirit is incompatible with self-love and self-interest.

Regret at not receiving what is given to others is the stuff from which renunciation is continually renewed. To be indifferent to what others have may be, during the whole long period of the ethical struggle, something of an indication that one has rather more than one actually needs oneself. On the other hand, the thought that others are being favored is an indication of at the very least an unfulfilled subconscious need in oneself. And what is implied in this penetrating paragraph is that the ascetic way to the resolution of one's own problems lies in an acceptance of the problems of others. In fact as religious face the complexities of who has what, they are coming to grips with the problems and temptations that beset human society as a whole; and in finding the way through them in a spirit that is rooted in a true asceticism they are making a valuable contribution to humanity. Experience and understanding in these matters is something that can be shared with all with whom we have to do. We have to struggle against covetousness and against self-interest as well as against ungenerosity; such things effectively stop the flow of whatever goodness ought to come from each member into the common life.

As the *Rule* states, it is thoughtful consideration that takes a vulnerable and needy person into a wider dimension than that of the self; witness the strong "should consider" (*debent cogitare*). The word *cogitare* is never lightly used in the text and occurs only three times: here in chapter III, 4, in IV, 5 where it is used to help the monk who is tempted to unchastity ("he should ponder the fact that God sees all") and in chapter VII, 3 where the prior is reminded that "he should . . . always [have] in mind" his accountability for the happiness and well-being of all the members. *Cogitare* implies deep reflection that results in clear understanding, and in the present context it carries its full weight of meaning. The troubled monk, Augustine says, must consider his brothers against their former background, against the present conditions and against their future goal. If he does that, he comes to see that there is no favoritism or particularity in the giving of special treatment; the weak member of the group is being excused from the hardest physical demands of the common life simply because he cannot support them and for no other reason. When it is recognized that the weakness is real, and when it is labeled by no other name, then one's whole attitude changes from that of judgment and jealousy to that of sympathy and admiration. Those who have been used to a high standard of living are in fact called upon to make a far greater renunciation than those who have been used to living more strenuously with less material benefits. For the former, the impulse to asceticism will have to take more material forms than it does for those who have never had much. For the former, entry into the religious life touches a level of costliness that is unknown to those less privileged.

It is clear from the *Rule* that in the actual group for which it was written this preferential treatment was only needed by a small minority. "All should not desire to receive" what they see is "given to a few." This is what one expects to be the case. But whenever it happens, as it sometimes does, that a majority needs a mitigation of the simplicity of life that has been customary in the community, then obviously there must be a change in the common practice. The very fact that the needs of the majority must establish the norm means that there will always be a pattern of change, and such a pattern demands flexibility of outlook among all the members.

Flexibility implies a willingness to give something up, whether this be a material thing or an idea, and for that reason we have used the noun-form "concession" in translating the Latin *tolerantur*. Concession implies a recognition of the worth of the other, and in this present context in the *Rule* it means the high value of the need of those who are weak through lack of training in hard living. It is not a matter of the high value of a privileged way of life and of kith and kin. By being helped in their weakness such members of the community are not being honored but conceded to. Asceticism implies more than a reversal of ordinary social standards; it involves for each individual a reversal of all that as a human being we have thought to be necessary for order and stability. The fruit of true ascetic poverty is not endurance but unhindered attention to the things of God.

POVERTY AND UNITY

How, then, are religious — living with people and with things — to be freed for this unhindered exchange? How are the ideals of poverty and unity of spirit to be brought into play within the group while it still remains (as it always will) a sheer necessity that for some there must be a mitigation of common standards? How can religious be converted, not once but many times, from human grasping, defenses, resentments, and distorted judgments which vitiate acceptance of the weaknesses of others and destroy the will-to-unity within the common life?

The answer lies in openness of heart, not in attention to detail. Self-regarding, mark-scoring, so-called acts of denial cannot take us close to God who is within each of our companions and every situation. Only willing readiness to respond can bring this about. This is true renunciation and also true acceptance of each other. The words of Augustine's Letter 243, 2 come to mind: "Your life does not belong to yourself but to all the brethren, just as their life belongs to you; or better, your life and the lives of your confreres are no longer separate lives but only one life in Christ."

The stress on recognizing the maximum resources of each member of the group is important, as seen in relation to unity within the common life. It is also important in relation to the order of that life, as the last sentence of this paragraph wryly points out: "A detestable disorder would arise in the monastery if the rich work there as hard as ever they can while the poor who have greater strength become weakened." We may note in passing the lightness of touch with which the resources of the poor and of the rich are mentioned here, and it is the poor/strong who are in the weaker position. A way of life that strains some participants almost beyond endurance (and the position of the word *quantum* in the original sentence is emphatic) exceeds justice just as much as it exceeds sensitivity. Such a way of life makes for moral, spiritual, and mental chaos, for it denies to some members of the group the right to be what they are. At the same time, a way of life that provides particularly easy and favorable working conditions for some members and not for others is an affront to their dignity.

It is, Augustine tells the Hippo monks, a *detestenda peruersitas*, an appalling perversion of all that the community stands for. Sometimes there may be a need for some members, for a particular purpose and for a limited time, to work almost beyond their capacity; but this is only possible to sustain when there is sensitive and appreciative support from the rest of the group. In such a case there is order and the lack of tension that goes with the well-ordering of things. But when the heavily-burdened are seen without compassion, then there is real disorder in the community and stresses inevitably follow, and there is no unity of heart, no peace. Augustine's later words are relevant here. Though they range far beyond a single group, they must be quoted in full because he regards the experience of one group as a paradigm for the whole of experience in this field:

> The peace of the household is ordered agreement of those who dwell together, whether they command or whether they obey; the peace of the city is ordered agreement of its citizens, whether they command or whether they obey; the peace of the heavenly city is the fellowship of enjoying God and enjoying one another in God, a fellowship held closely together by order and in harmony; the peace of all created things is the tranquility bestowed by order; order is the arrangement of equal and unequal which assigns to each its proper place (*City of God* XIX, 13).

When Augustine discusses peace in the *City of God*, he means a quality that can be experienced both individually and corporately as stillness, quiet, composure, equanimity. Augustine's tranquility is brought about by a willingness to be controlled. The last words of the above quotation are of special importance for our understanding of the *Rule*, and they are worth repeating: "order is the arrangement of equal and unequal which assigns to each its proper place." When Augustine came to write that passage he had much first-hand experience to go on.

WORK AND THE COMMON LIFE

One last — and most important — aspect of ascetic poverty in this paragraph is the emphasis that is laid on work and its place within the common life. By reading between the lines of the text, one gains the impression that hard work found a large place in the monks' life, and this is confirmed by the *Ordo Monasterii* referred to above. In that document it is laid down that the monks should work in the mornings until Sext; and in the afternoon during the interval between their meal — the *cena* presumably — and Vespers they are to work in the garden or wherever else is necessary. This with its counterpart of fasting, liturgical prayer, and the opportunities for private prayer provided by the oratory makes for a very full day that over a long period would make great demands on all the members. Within the framework of Augustine's precepts this costing way of life is to be seen as an aspect of asceticism. Hard work as a road to God is not so easy to see, but in uncovering the layers of meaning here a community will discover how deeply the directive to work hard penetrates into each member's being so that each individual becomes more open to God.

Augustine adopted the practice of the pioneer monks of the East as well as the theory of work that is reflected, for instance, in Basil and John Cassian. The Longer Rules of the former stressed the spiritual value of manual work,[17] while Cassian in both of his monastic writings urged the importance of physical work as a way to growth in purification and in dependence on God.[18] But for Augustine, work and the asceticism of work were set against a wider background and could include non-manual activity if necessary for those with other gifts that could be of service to the Church (*The Work of Monks* 29, 37). It will be noticed that in the previous sentence the words "necessary" and "service" have both been used; in Augustine's monastic thinking both are of great importance. Work of some sort has an essential part in the community's life because the members are servants.[19]

WORK IN THE ROMAN WORLD

In order to understand the contribution of Augustine's precepts to a deeper appreciation of work, it is necessary to look briefly at how work was experienced in the fourth century and the centuries preceding it within the Roman empire. Then we may be able to see how it became possible to place it within the setting of an ascetic life. It is not enough merely to state that work is a human activity obviously related to the role of the monk as servant.

Throughout the Roman world,[20] work was despised. This attitude was derived from the Greeks, though it differed in its rationale. For Plato, the body-soul dichotomy resulted in a contempt for any undertaking that was other than intellectual. And since so much of life depended on non-intellectual pursuits the whole structure of society came to depend on slavery. The Romans did not cling so closely to the superiority of intellectual activity as such but to the high value of public life and of the right and ability to participate in that. Those who were not so privileged were the despised ones, and if they were despised, so was the work that they did. Thus work itself was servile.

Because physical work was servile it involved uncertainty and loss of freedom. Most laborers were slaves, tied to one master from whom levies could be demanded by the government; the rest were poor dispossessed peasants whose strength and skill could be hired. For public works — the construction of buildings, roads, bridges, or granaries, and the maintenance of post stations — levies were usually employed. For church building or private undertakings, labor was usually hired. Agricultural labor on estates was done by hereditary slaves and by free tenants, and at harvest time a casual labor force was recruited from among peasant freeholders (though in Egypt townspeople as well as monks and hermits would also do such work: not the best monks, be it noted, but the restless and dissatisfied among them). Factory work was largely in the hands of private owners. But iron and metal works, as well as most mines, weaving mills and dye-works, were owned by the state. Those employed were usually local people, and factories were large, so that an establishment that provided work for a high proportion of inhabitants of an area had considerable local influence — for good or for ill. Factory workers ranked with soldiers and were subjected to the same conditions of service: they received rations, were tied to their work, and were branded. The work of craftsmen and merchants was largely hereditary, and they were obliged to join guilds according to their skills. These guilds served the double purpose of protecting the interests of the men themselves and also of providing a channel for the supply of indentured labor for public undertakings. Guildsmen worked for a city by rotation. Convoying animals was one of their duties (this had obvious advantages for both craftsmen and merchants, who could pursue their own line of business while traveling with the animals). Guildmen were not permitted to enlist in the army or to move to the country and take up agriculture. There was some mitigation of these restrictions in Constantine's time, in that the more skilled craftsmen (including doctors, architects, and artists) were exempted. But later, from 395 onward, Christian guildsmen were put at a disadvantage: they were not allowed to be ordained — to become a priest would be to rise above one's station. In other areas of life, however, guildsmen could become persons of considerable importance within the social structure. Enterprising silversmiths developed into bankers; merchants extended the animal-convoy work from land to sea so that they became shipping magnates. But still, for all their wealth and influence, they were not *arrivés*; their work was despised work. In general senators, *honorati* and even decurions considered industry and trade beneath them.

One final aspect needs to be mentioned, as it points to a perpetual threat to every poor man: the heavy taxes whose burden fell on all workers. Default was punished by flogging and torture.[21]

For most people, then, to be a worker meant to live in dread and to be without freedom. And the effect of this conditioned not only daily life but also aesthetic and spiritual attitudes to the whole business of living; it inhibited spiritual freedom.[22]

This was the *saeculum* from which men turned when they entered the Hippo monastery. And it is now possible for us to understand a little more clearly the conditions and attitudes of the erstwhile rich and poor alike. We can also appreciate more fully the tremendous conversion that was asked of the underprivileged monk if he was to live in unity with brothers who represented oppression and degradation. We have only to translate this into twentieth-century situations to be able to understand the fears, tensions, and confusion that Augustine's monks were struggling to overcome.

But of course the important thing is that they were Christians with behind them a nearly four centuries' attempt to bring an altogether different set of ideas to bear on the business of living.[23] Paul pointed to the value and duty of work (2 Thes 3:6-12; Col 3:23-24) and to good work by Christians as a witness to outsiders; moreover, good work gave a measure of freedom (1 Thes 4:11-12). A little later, Clement of Rome in his *Letter to the Corinthians* (34, 1) observed that zeal and care were the marks of a good workman. In the next century, the author of the *Didache* (12, 1-5) warned Christians against idleness and sycophancy. Not much later, Hermas, the author of *The Shepherd* and himself a former slave, regarded work for wages as making almsgiving possible.[24] Tertullian, in the third century, took the matter further: involvement by Christians in public life and in trading, he wrote, was a witness to their integrity.[25] And in another book he discussed the nature of the work in which Christians could rightly engage, concluding that for them all work was permissible provided that it did not involve sin.[26] Early in the fourth century Athanasius, in his life of Antony, interiorized the value of work for Christians, stating that it was a useful armament against demons — a point of view which, when separated from its imagery, is close to the idea of work as therapeutic.[27] Even nearer to Augustine's time, Ambrose perceived the interior-exterior dimensions of work in more general terms: for him, there is no virtue without labor, for labor is the genesis of virtue.[28]

AUGUSTINE AND WORK

In the fourth century a monk adopted manual work as part of his pattern of life, and in taking upon himself the work of a servant he was but following his Master who had spent all his life in exactly that condition. Within working conditions, then, and not by escaping from them, it was possible to redeem the time — and more than that, redeem one's soul. The most startling conversion to work is probably that of Augustine himself. In Milan, when Ponticianus told him and Alypius about Antony, his reaction was steeped in a superior attitude toward the lower orders: "What is wrong with us? . . . The unlearned arise and take heaven by force, and here are we with all our learning, stuck fast in flesh and blood" (*Confessions* VIII, 8). And even though after his baptism he spent some months getting to know the new monastic settlements in Italy, when he began to settle down with his group at Thagaste he still hoped to find his way to God by means of withdrawal from practical affairs (if we may attempt an English form of that untranslatable *deificare in otio* of Letter 10, 2, addressed to Nebridius). A life of *otium* in the ancient world was "one which, not lazily, but in the contemplation and examination of the truth is leisured" (so Augustine described it in *The City of God* XIX, 2).

He soon found, however, that the way for him lay not only in withdrawal but also in involvement in the ordinary affairs of the world. The opposite of *otium* was the negative *negotium* which in a later chapter of *The City of God* (XIX, 19) means *employment*. The implied negative and condescending attitude of ancient society to the necessity of employment, business, and work was one that could not measure up to Christian ideals of service, and it was Augustine above all who showed the way in which the search for truth can be married to a life of engagement in affairs. In the chapter just referred to he describes these two strands and adds a third:

> People may love a leisured life, as those who have desired and have been able to give themselves up only to the pursuit of doctrine; or a busied life, as those who, though they cultivated intellectual things, were greatly occupied in administering and directing affairs; or one combined of both, as those who gave up the alternating times of their life partly to learned leisure and partly to necessary business (XIX, 19).

For the Christian, what gives validity to "employment" is the "necessity of charity, the law, and the need of charity," and it is this that makes possible the leap of the mind that was essential for any Christian who voluntarily came to regard himself as a working servant. The deep transformation that had to take place within any such person involved the acceptance of work as a positive good and not as a negative degradation. Augustine found the way to God in a *via media* that combined *otium* and *negotium*.

WORK AND SERVICE

Christian ethos has turned servant/service into respectable words, but it was not always so. To speak to Gentiles about the Lord taking the form of a servant was to outrage conventional thought. To transform attitudes takes a long time, and for the majority of Christians in the early centuries there must have been a long and deep interior struggle between the two conflicting notions of work and service as they were held by themselves and by pagans. The servant songs of Isaiah — with their references to vicarious suffering, ransom-price, expiation, and voluntary sacrifice — were applied to the life of Jesus in a number of New Testament passages,[29] although it remains an open question whether he himself or the early Christian communities were the first to do so. Paul was the first to perceive that a similar role as servant must be adopted by Jesus' followers. To shoulder the work of a servant meant more than to assume a way of life that to all intents and purposes was socially degrading, though this itself must have been challenging. It meant also the kind of interior struggle which Augustine described so clearly in relation to fasting.

Early monasticism had discovered the necessity of restricting the types of manual work open to a monk because obviously not all were compatible with his life of prayer and silence. Hence the mat-making and the like. But there was a risk in this, because it is always easy for self-supporting work to become in-turned and thus destructive of any deeper values than those of ensuring the supply of daily sustenance. For this reason the instinct of the first monks was right in adopting the Pauline image of servant/slave as a characteristic of their commitment. Their work, to some extent at least, implied involvement in the affairs of the world and an outward-directed attitude to the work in hand. The Christian servant was the property of his Master; all that he did was in the interests of his Master's own business.

Thus while the monk in his work took into himself and aligned himself with the attitudes of his time, he was also involved in a gradually developing process of transformation of the whole concept of work/service/freedom. The process is still going on, but it would be mistaken to think that the feeling and thoughts that Augustine was assuming when he wrote of work among the monks of Hippo were identical with the attitudes of members of religious orders and congregations in the late twentieth century.

Perhaps even more than in the fourth century we can now see labor as an ascetic practice. Few who enter the religious life today, and this applies particularly in the technologically advanced countries, have had much experience of doing physical work for most of their working hours. Few have many manual skills, or the habit of thought that goes to the making of a good workman. And few come with the physical strength of one who has been at it since leaving school. Whoever places himself or herself in this situation is obliged to renew acts of self-sacrifice and self-denial frequently. If this renewal is to continue to hold meaning, it must be done with increasing depth as the years go by; and that involves a constant search for the meaning of what we are doing and a desire to find God who is dynamically present within each activity.

At the heart of all ascetic poverty there must be hard work, for it is through struggle and testing that we can find God and open ourselves and our world to him. And for this reason the full capacity of each one needs to be recognized and safeguarded. More than that: the full capacity of work itself must be tested. The community's undertakings in each day and generation must make room for the full humanity of each member and also the develop-

ing powers of creativity and participating responsibility for all
that its members do.

Rule, Chapter III, 5

As for the sick, they need to eat little
so that they do not become worse.
Thus after illness they must certainly be given special care
to help them to get strong as soon as possible,
even if they came from conditions of extreme poverty in the world.
In fact, recent illness has made necessary for them
what a former way of life has made necessary for the rich.
But when they have recovered their strength
they should resume their own more fortunate way of life,
since the less God's servants need
the more fitting it is.
In other words,
when they are stirring again
they should not desire to linger
in the state of luxury to which necessity has brought them
when they were ill.
They should esteem themselves the richer
who are stronger in enduring privations.
It is better to need less than to have more.

ILLNESS AND THE COMMON LIFE

There are many strands in this final paragraph on asceticism
through poverty and the common life: some of them are echoes of
previous motifs and others are a new contribution to the discussion. The general theme is the place of illness within the common
life, which was first mentioned incidentally in chapter III, 1.
Periods of illness have to be taken for granted in the life of any
individual and any group, and they are a testing time for both the
stricken and those who look after them. Because they are a demanding experience, a community must look seriously at these
demands every time they occur. Some aspects of this are not
discussed until chapter V, 5-8, and there the discussion centers on
the group's responsibility toward the sick person. Here, the chief
concern is with the latter.

The argument of this paragraph runs as follows: the sick should
not be expected to keep to the community's normal diet and in the
first stages of illness they will need little; each one is to be treated
according to his present necessity and previous conditions of life
must not influence the care that is given, since illness has a leveling

effect and within it the needs of rich and poor are alike; on recovery, special dispensations must be set aside, since simplicity of living is the way for those with normal strength and the less one can do with the nearer one is to the community's ideal in this matter; however, there are malingerers who luxuriate in dispensations and are reluctant to give them up. Such people strike a false note in the community's harmony, for in fact the well-endowed are those who have the strength to endure a limited diet.

In one way the experience of illness takes us away from the common life because of our necessary isolation and special treatment. In another way it gives us a particular place within the community. For the time being our role is that of a sick person, and a role is never a negative function. Our illness establishes a solidarity with all illness and brings it within the life of the community. The experience of illness is not — or should not be — static, for it gives us the opportunity to discover the depths of our humanness and of the activity of God within such a condition. In one way illness may require passivity, but much more does it demand participation and activity. It can be a richly creative experience, but not at a superficial level; and it is one of those instances where time itself is not clock-time. While the body is fighting its battles, the mind and spirit may be largely passive. But when the body has controlled the disease and is on the way to eliminating it then mind and spirit come into their own once more and the process of reflection begins to create a new level of being within the person.

People differ widely in their way of adapting to their own illnesses. The onset in a normally-well person can be bewildering at many levels. At one stage, all exterior pressures — of work and responsibility — are removed just because there is no room for them alongside the phenomenon of disease. At another stage, anxiety concerning these responsibilities is absorbed into the illness-experience. At first one can do nothing but receive — critically or uncritically, according to temperament and habit. Later a kind of dialogue is established between the sufferer and the illness. In space, the worst experience of illness centers on pain and weakness; in time, the stress comes from ignorance as to how long the condition will last and from the fact that all experience becomes narrowed to the present. Within the centered point of illness, the only link with the encircling reality of things and persons, time and space, is established through those who are caring for the sick person — a matter which the *Rule* probes more deeply in chapter V. What is enjoined here is that the sufferer is to be met in the situation of the illness and is to be given whatever food is needed: that is the responsibility of the infirmarian. The responsibility of the sufferer is to cooperate. Both have only one objective: restoration to health and strength. Other considerations, such as the previous living conditions of the sick person, have no place in the assessment of present needs — except, of course, insofar as they are a factor in the illness. One who has never before had access to delicate dishes and gentle treatment is not to be denied them on that account. What is now needed is what the privileged have always found necessary. In fact, when weakness is equated with the need for gentle and delicate treatment then the *Rule*'s logic is clear: those who have been ill and those who have been wealthy are on a par, for their needs are the same.

So something creative can at this point begin to come into play, once the crisis of the illness is over and mending has begun. One begins to relate one's experience to that of others — not simply in terms of others who have had the same symptoms, but more especially the many others who for any reason have been reduced to the same necessities as one's own. With the gradual return of strength, feelings expand; then imagination is kindled so that one can embrace many more sufferers within one's own experience. And finally sympathy is kindled, and in sharing one's own experience both actively and passively with others, one not only sets weakness in a wider dimension but also shares the strength of the experience with them.

In community life, all of this means that those who are ill have a vital part to play. Illness and infirmity should not cut a member off from the common life; rather, the common life should have room for those who are less strong and able. These conditions should not exclude from the group but should be a part of its whole structure. This will need to be discussed again later, but it is mentioned here because it does affect the attitude of members of the group when illness or old age overtakes them. What goes on in the sick-room and what goes on in the rest of the house are all of a piece.

But there are temptations in this situation, as in any other. Augustine, who knew his monks, singled out one in particular for consideration. For some people it is only too easy to cling to the cossetting conditions that illness has made necessary. The Latin sentence is striking and sensitive. The word that I have translated as "stirring" is *uegetos*, which means anything that has life in it; and "desire to linger in the state of luxury" is a rendering of *nec . . . ibi eos teneat uoluptas* (literally, let not luxury hold on to them). The state of relative luxury is an active ingredient in the healing process, but it must not be allowed to cling to those whom it has helped back to health. The state of being a passive recipient of food, warmth, cleanliness, and care is the state of infancy, and it is only too easy to regress into infantile dependence on them when they have again been given to an adult because of illness. They come to be regarded as the sole source of security and for a religious this represents a denial of our complete dependence on God for all sustaining. Further, it makes a mockery of our commitment to a life of simple living and service, which the *Rule* calls our "more fortunate way of life" (*feliciorem consuetudinem*).

The centrality of service in the life of each member of the community is stressed by the words that follow in the text: "since the less God's servants need. . . ." Here, the word translated servants is not *serui* but *famulos*. *Famulus* means a household slave, one who is intimately concerned with the family's affairs but whose relation to his owners is always one of service. The word is used only in one other place in the *Rule* (chapter V, 6), and there again it is in the context of ill health: if one of the "servants of God" reports a hidden pain, he is to be believed and given the help he needs. The contrast between these two passages is interesting, and it is revealing of the care which the community must have for all its members. The matter can be put this way: in the monastery one of God's servants has become ill and has been given every attention until his health is fully restored, after which he will want to resume his habitual way of life (chapter III, 5); but if, later on, he discovers fresh symptoms in himself and reports them (chapter V, 6) his word is to be accepted even if there is at that stage no external evidence of the fact. In a group where all are servants, roles will continually be changing as circumstances alter. Inevitably, sooner or later all will be recipients of the service of others.

What is given to the sufferer is not to be accepted as luxury but as service. It is not the provision of privileged treatment that constitutes the assets of a religious but an ability when in good health to live very simply indeed: "It is better to need less than to have more." It is better to serve than to be served, following the example of the Master (Mt 20:25-28).

As religious, human and subject to disease as much as anyone else, we are committed to use all our resources of spirit and body with but one end in view: the search for and the service of God. The whole of our ascetic discipline is a paring down of unessentials so that the God whose temple we are may be revealed. Our discipline of poverty is a giving-away of one good for the sake of another. Asceticism is not a stripping away of evil; it is refining of what is good. There is always a paradox in asceticism, as there is in the processes of producing anything fine and good. Much has to be removed and abandoned. Without this abandonment there can be no development. For the religious, abandonment is continuous and it touches every part of our being. That is why Augustine can with such succinctness undercut the cravings and temptations to give up both search and service: "They should esteem themselves the richer who are stronger in enduring privations."

This last paragraph of chapter III contains Augustine's last reference to differences of background among the members of the community, and it is interesting to discover that for him the field within which the problem can be solved is the ascetic poverty to which all are committed within the common life. The stresses and burdens which each member bears are vast and varied, but the sharing of them is common to all. Augustine's ideal of bridging a gulf in his monasteries through a truly Christian communication of love was one of heroic proportions. For him, ascetic poverty is a path leading to unity. But unity can never be a closed circuit system; it must always move outward. So, inevitably, the *Rule* goes on immediately to consider the monk outside his monastery.

NOTES

1. Cleanth Brooks, *William Faulkner: The Yoknapatawpha Country*, Yale University Press, 1963, page 107.

2. See Luc Verheijen, *Nouvelle Approche de la Règle de Saint Augustin*, Abbaye de Bellefontaine, 1980, page 306 (hereafter *Nouvelle Approche*).

3. *Ibid.*, page 306.

4. See Anthony Rich, *A Dictionary of Roman and Greek Antiquities*, Longmans, Green, 1874, art. *coena*.

5. As Fr. Verheijen writes in *Nouvelle Approche*, page 305: "Nous n'aurions pas la mauvaise grâce de citer ici les traductions de la Règle qui trahissent quelque ignorance dans ce domaine."

6. Anthony Rich, *op. cit.*, art. *prandium*.

7. *Life of Augustine* 22.

8. See Cassian, *Institutes* IV, 17.

9. For example, *The Lord's Sermon on the Mount* I, 11, 32; *Sermons 84, 2; 101, 9; 319, 8; 131, 5; Expositions of the Psalms* 88, 10. See Trevor Row, *St. Augustine Pastoral Theologian* (Epworth Press, 1974), page 33 and notes; also Van der Meer, *Augustine the Bishop*, Sheed & Ward, 1961, pages 427-432 and notes.

10. On all of this, see the article of Luc Verheijen in *Nouvelle Approche*, pages 387-394.

11. See the valuable study of Albert Gelin, *The Poor of Yahweh*, The Liturgical Press, Collegeville, 1964 and also Karl Rahner, "The Theology of Poverty" in *Theological Investigations VIII*, Darton, Longman & Todd, 1971, pages 168-214.

12. Pss 22:26; 25:16-18; 35:10; 37:11; 40:17.69; 86:1; 109:21-22.

13. *The Essence of Judaism*, quoted in A. Cohen, *The Psalms*, Soncino Press, 1945, page 23.

14. See the essay of M. Michael Labourdette, "The Theology of Religious Poverty" in *Religious Life, IV — Poverty*, Blackfriars Publications, 1954, pages 115-125.

15. See *Nouvelle Approche*, pages 352-374.

16. See Verheijen, *Les Maîtres de la Vie Religieuse dans l'Antiquité Chrétienne VI: Saint Augustin*, Forma Gregis, Number 6, Mars 1956, page 299.

17. See Gerhart B. Ladner, *The Idea of Reform*, Harvard University Press, 1959, page 78, citing *Regulae fusius tractatae* XXXVIII.

18. *Institutes* V, 39; X, 8-14; *Conferences* 24, 3-4.11-12.

19. See Gerhart B. Ladner, *op. cit.*, page 362.

20. See P. D. Anthony, *The Ideology of Work*, Tavistock Publications, 1977, pages 15-22, 24-25.

21. A. M. H. Jones, *The Later Roman Empire, 284-602* (3 volumes, Blackwell, 1964, reprinted in 2 volumes, 1973) Volume 1, pages 65-66, 462 and Volume 2, chapters XX and XXI, pages 769-872. See also the essay by Professor Hilary Armstrong, "Work in Ancient Greece and Rome" in John M. Todd (editor), *Work/Christian Thought and Practice*, Darton, Longman & Todd, 1960, pages 5-12.

22. In this connection, see the interesting observations of Jacques Maritain in *Creative Intuition in Art and Poetry*, Harvill Press, 1954, page 63.

23. See R. A. Markus, "Work and Worker in Early Christianity" in John M. Todd, *op. cit.*, pages 13-26.

24. *Mandates* 2, 4.

25. *Apology* 42.

26. *Concerning Idolatry* 5, 8, 12.

27. *The Life of Saint Antony* 3, 50.53.

28. *Cain and Abel* 2, 2.8.

29. For example, Mt 8:17; 12:18-21; Lk 2:32; 22:34; Acts 3:13.26; 4:27.30; Rom 4:25; 15:21.

4

Asceticism through Chastity and Mutual Concern

Rule, Chapter IV, 1

Your clothing should not be conspicuous.
You should not try to please by your clothes
but by your behavior.

TOWARD GROUP RESPONSIBILITY

In chapter IV asceticism and unity within the common life continue to be an important consideration. But here, more is at stake than the life of the monks as they affect one another — now relationships with people outside the monastery have to be taken into account. And there is more still. Up till now, interpersonal relationships have been probed and guidelines laid down insofar as the morally neutral but nonetheless disturbing characteristics of each one are concerned; within this chapter the effect of moral ill itself has to be discussed.

Moreover, within this chapter — which is by far the longest, occupying nearly a quarter of the whole text — there is also another significant shift of emphasis. Chapters I-III were dealing primarily with the situation of the individual monk in relation to the group; here, although the discussion begins with this in view it moves on to explore the corporate responsibility of the group for the individual. What is implicit in the analysis of community life which the *Rule* gradually unfolds is that group responsibility can only be effective when the depth of humanness has been taken fully into account, as it is in chapters I-III and finally in chapter IV.

The discussion goes backward and forward, the emphases shift and conclusions seem almost to slip from one's grasp — until the moment of vision at the end of paragraph 10. Thereafter, the *Rule* moves at a far deeper level of experience, even though the matters discussed may appear to be more trivial.

The present chapter follows on logically from what has gone before. Mention of food leads naturally to the matter of clothing. Two different words are used for what is worn, which I have distinguished by clothing (*habitus*) and clothes (*uestes*). I have not used the word habit in translation because in monastic parlance its meaning is too sharply defined to represent what Augustine meant.

PERSONAL APPEARANCE AND BEHAVIOR

Habitus occurs also in VI, 1 (twice) where it is used to contrast the clothing of the mind with that of the body. While it is used of what people wear it also implies what they look like in their clothes; it refers to customary appearance, and it goes further by being used also for deportment. So the *habitus* of a monk expresses what he stands for — which is why it has been narrowed down within monastic tradition to describe distinctive monastic dress. (Outside these circles it has been divorced from objects and has come to be used only of characteristics — an interesting development that lies outside our present concern.)

Uestes, on the other hand, simply means articles of clothing; as such it occurs also in chapter V, 1.3.4 and 9.

Augustine considered that a monk's general appearance should not give him a bad name. Many made themselves very conspicuous indeed — and not only monks but nuns too. Not everyone considered this a disadvantage. Jerome, for instance, in his famous letter to Eustochium, advised her to have as companions those who were thin and pallid through fasting.[1] And in a letter to Sulpicius Severus, Paulinus of Nola in his complaint about the unsatisfactory monk-courier Marracinus wrote:

> I pray that only poor fellow servants, pale of face like ourselves, will come on first or subsequent visits — not proud men in embroidered garments but humble ones in bristly clothes of goat's hair; not bodyguards in fine mantles, but men draped in rough cloaks, fastened up not with a military belt but with a length of rope; men with hair not long and trimmed over a shapeless brow, but cut close to the skin in chaste ugliness, half-shorn irregularly, shaved off in front, leaving the brow naked. Let them be unadorned, with the adornment of chastity, and let their appearance be suitably uncultivated, honorably contemptible. Spurning their natural physical attraction for inner adornment, they should even be eager to look disreputable, so that they may be chastely mean in appearance as long as they become honorable at heart and fit for salvation ... The appearance, disposition, and smell of such monks cause nausea

in people for whom the odor of death is as the odor of life, who regard the bitter as sweet, the chaste as foul, the holy as hateful.[2]

Augustine and Paulinus admired each other, but in this they could not have agreed — not that the subject is ever mentioned in their correspondence (and they never met). What Augustine thought fitting is as a real breath of fresh air: "Your clothing should not be conspicuous." From what follows — "You should not try to please by your clothes but by your behavior" — it could be that, if anything, the monks of Hippo tended to err on the side of the monk Marracinus rather than on that of monks acceptable to Paulinus. To some extent the problem of what the monks looked like still presented difficulties to Augustine very many years later; and the views of the faithful outside the monastery did not make a solution easy to reach. In a sermon preached after Epiphany in the year 426, in which he was obliged to discuss the life and witness of the cleric-monks who lived with him (not the lay monks for whom the *Rule* was written almost thirty years earlier) he said that all wore the same sort of garment which he called a *byrrhus* or *byrrhum* (no one knows exactly what this was; a modern writer has called it a duffle coat).[3] Whatever it was, it could be ornamented, and Augustine felt compelled to plead with his hearers not to make him presents of elaborate ones because he would not wear them and simply sold them. Then follows a heartfelt plea which many monks must have uttered in later generations: "If someone wants to give me something, let him give me something at which I shall not blush" (Sermon 356, 13).

No argument can justifiably be drawn from the present paragraph of the *Rule* to establish the unreasonableness of wearing what is now known as a religious habit, because the underlying issue in what Augustine wrote is not the monk's appearance as such but his purpose in wearing what he does. He is not, says the *Rule*, "to try to please" (*affectetis . . . placere*) by what he wears. If a distinctive garment is worn as a symbol of all that he is, that is another matter. To wear this or that in order to appear attractive and acceptable is clearly inconsistent with the life of a monk. There is, however, a legitimate way of appearing attractive to others if that is for the purpose of bearing witness to the Lord within, and that is done through pleasing behavior (*moribus*).

Behavior, then, is the aspect of asceticism that relates what the monk is aiming at in his heart of hearts to the many people whom he encounters in his ordinary daily life. Until now, the *Rule* has been concerned with behavior among the brethren; now it turns to behavior in the presence of others who are outside the monastery.

Rule, Chapter IV, 2

When you go out,
walk together;
and when you come to your destination,
stay together.

BEHAVIOR INSIDE THE MONASTERY

A reason for going out from the monastery could be that indicated in the *Ordo Monasterii* 8:

> If it is necessary to do any business outside the monastery, for the sake of the community, two people should go together. No one may eat or drink outside the monastery, except with permission, because that does not accord with monastic discipline. When brothers are sent to sell the work of the monastery, they should faithfully observe their instructions.

The necessary practice of going out to buy supplies and to sell produce was observed by eastern monks. Saint Basil reflects this in the *Longer Rules* 39 and 44, and its adoption in the West was clearly essential. The *Rule*, in paragraph 6 of this chapter, indicates a further reason for being outside on occasion: a monk will sometimes be *in ecclesia* (in church). Indeed, there is evidence that Augustine's sermons preached in the Hippo church were sometimes listened to by his monks as well as by other people.[4]

Augustine's injunction merely expressed common practice: two monks together had significance, one monk out alone was an ambiguity. Togetherness, moreover, gave support in whatever had to be done. To part by mutual consent, or to abandon one another, rendered each one vulnerable. It laid each one open to his own lacks — in ability, in confidence, in integrity, in strength and endurance. When two were together they could complement each other.

Such close association can be a valuable point of growth in community life. Within the unity of the group most things become predictable, because they are mentally and physically circumscribed; but when members of the group find themselves part of another group — in market, office, church, baths, or elsewhere —

new and unaccustomed factors are involved. Loss of nerve is a frequent response, and such loss is a disarming experience. The fact of being with a brother in such a situation is a real strength for both. Through the experience of meeting the weakness of his brother, each monk is forced to a deeper response — if he has goodwill. (He can, of course, fail his brother by being censorious or by withholding support.) In such situations it is possible to accept one's brother in a new way.

But this different way of getting to know a companion can present other difficulties beyond those of adaptation, self-giving, and support. What if one's companion's weakness is such that one cannot in conscience acquiesce in his or her conduct? What if it is a denial of what we both stand for as religious? The ethical struggle in which asceticism inevitably involves us is not contained within the monastery: it goes wherever we go. How will we conduct ourselves when we have gone out? And how will our companion react when the struggle is abandoned and there is capitulation? These are the problems that are explored in the remainder of this chapter. But first Augustine states what G. R. Dunstan has called "first-order principles" before going on to propose "second-order rules."[5]

Rule, Chapter IV, 3

In walking, in standing and in all your movements,
nothing should be done that might give offense to anyone who sees you:
everything should be in keeping with your holy state.

BEHAVIOR AND INTEGRITY

The principle, then, is that in all that a monk does his behavior must commend him to those who see him. But his behavior is not to be commendable merely in terms of the observer's own standards; it must always be consistent with the way of life to which the monk is committed. In the words "in keeping with your holy state" (*quod uestram decet sanctitatem*) Augustine is epitomizing all that has gone before; and as it is departure from these ideals that causes the pain and distress of the rest of this chapter, it will be as well to recapitulate briefly.

A monk in response to God's beckoning has withdrawn from ordinary life to go in search of him; he has bound himself to a way of life that strips him of all securities except God himself; having nothing, he commits himself to the building up of a community life that in its demands will penetrate to every part of his being. His simplicity of life, his exemption from family and business responsibilities, and the unifying shared ideals of the group are the conditions in which his search for God can continually be made; and from within these supportive conditions he becomes a witness to and a mediator of the riches of God. The singleness of heart and mind which are the characteristics of the group are also the marks of each individual. Perhaps the words which Saint Ambrose attributed to Saint Agnes are the simplest summary of this complete commitment: "He that first chose me, his will I be."[6]

If anyone were asked to identify the context of this paragraph of Augustine's *Rule* he might gain some sympathy if he placed it in a Victorian manual for godly damsels. But in fact it goes much deeper than that, for it requires not only outward deportment but an inner integrity if each monk is to be identified with what he has undertaken. He may be aware of his unholiness, but all the same the state that he has accepted is a holy one and it requires holiness in him. And observers may also be aware of his areas of unholiness and yet still recognize his striving to become a vehicle of holiness.

It is what happens on the way that is important: how a monk strives to overcome obstacles in himself and encounters weakness in others, and also how he responds to those who care enough to want to counter his weakness. The "second-order rules," to use Professor Dunstan's phrase, are what are worked out in the remainder of this chapter; but they are without value and validity unless the "first-order principle" of this paragraph is kept in mind. A clue to what is really at stake in this part of the *Rule* may lie in the use of the verb *offendere* which has been translated here as to "give offense." It occurs in only one other place in the text — in chapter VII, 1 where it is used with God as its object. It is always an aggressive, attacking word. And what is implied in the present context is an attitude that deliberately flouts conventions and accepted standards. Occasional lapses are not what is being discussed. This partly explains the severe note of much of what Augustine wrote in this chapter. Much more is at stake than guarded behavior. Augustine is concerned here with the monk's attitude to an important part of the whole being of each member.

Rule, Chapter IV, 4

Even if your gaze chances to fall on a woman
you should not stare at her.
There is no rule forbidding you to see women when you go out,
but to attract or encourage their attention is blameworthy.
It is not only touch and the heart's movement
but also glances
that excite and express desire for women.
You cannot claim to have pure minds
if you have impure eyes,
for an impure eye is the messenger of an impure heart.
When impure hearts exchange messages by their glances,
even though the tongue remains silent,
and when through wrong desire
they take pleasure in each other's ardor,
then chastity takes flight from their behavior
even though there has been no despoiling of the body.

INTEGRITY, CELEBACY, AND SEXUALITY

The first impression that this paragraph makes is one of shock. To move from the first three chapters into this paragraph of the fourth is to enter another world. It is precisely a world whose values, thinking, and customs are not those of the monastery. As we have seen in previous paragraphs, the monk abandons these attitudes and modes of behavior, and he spends his life being converted from the demands and pressures that they make upon him.

In another way, too, this paragraph makes an entry into another world — a confused world where edges are blurred, ideas and ideals are not fully worked out, and where convention itself is hard to establish because so many antecedent premises have pulled in different directions. The problems associated with sexuality seem to be inherent in the human condition, and down the centuries attempts to solve them have colored the society of each period.

It would take us too far from our purpose to make a thorough investigation of the social and religious attitudes to sexuality, love, and marriage in the era of antiquity. Recent studies have shown the fluctuations in *mores* among both Christians and non-Christians in the early centuries.[7] What concerns us in our study of Augustine's *Rule* is the significance of celibacy as a *modus vivendi* within the Christian community and the effect of committed celibacy on the thinking and behavior of monks. The first matter has been examined in chapter 2 of the book; now we must consider the second.

The one overriding factor that celibacy has to take seriously is each individual celibate's own sexuality. The Bible gives warnings about failure to guard personal integrity in this area of personality.[8] What each writer warns against is not the fact of sexual drives but a cheapening of their uses. That holds good for the vast majority of people who use these gifts in "normal" sexual relations; it holds good also for the small minority who as celibates must make other use of these impulses. Thus, what Augustine is saying in the present precept is that it is not legitimate for a monk to act as if he were free to enter into customary sexual relationships with another person (I write "another person" deliberately, because we now realize that such relationships may not always cross the male-female boundary). There is in principle nothing to deter a member of the majority group from seeking to attract and encourage the sexual interest of someone else, provided he is not already bound to other commitments and sanctions which in a wholly good way prohibit his freedom in this matter. Indeed, it is precisely a prior commitment that prohibits the monk from behaving in an otherwise "normal" way. For both the committed celibate and everyone else there is the possibility of sexuality being dominated by the sheer selfishness of lust and members neither of the one group nor of the other have an in-built immunity to it.

All the problems concerning sexuality have been encountered in the Church from the very beginning. The studies which we have referred to above provide the evidence. What concerns us in our exploration in the *Rule* is the climate of opinion among celibates in clerical and monastic circles during Augustine's lifetime. The very fact that monasticism had attracted such large numbers, in the East, was itself a source of weakness. In the fourth century the problem of monks and nuns leaving their monasteries was a serious one. In spite of the introduction of such a life to the West at this time, monasticism was beginning to go down into its first trough. The first Council of Carthage, for instance, meeting in 348, laid down that monks were to remain *separate and solitary* in their monasteries.[9] But as yet no deep thinking had been done on the subject of monastic celibacy which, as we have tried to show, fused all preceding attitudes into a synthesis. This had happened, as it were, of its own accord. In spite of the earlier treatises of Tertullian, Origen, and Cyprian, no theology of monastic celibacy had yet been developed. In one sense, monks and nuns lived out their single state in a spiritual void. Hence it is not surprising that many fell away. As early as 305, the Council of Elvira ordered perpetual excommunication for consecrated virgins who took to a life of licentiousness, though those who had lapsed only once were to be restored to communion on their deathbed if after the lapse they had lived in continual penance.[10] The Council of Ancyra, in 314, forbade ordination to those who had broken their vows of celibacy.[11] In 374 the Council of Valence laid down a canon which stated that former monks and nuns who married were not to be pardoned after too short a penance.[12] From all parts of the Christian world, then, the problems of being fully human, being married, being celibate, being acceptable, being unacceptable were living issues for very many people within and outside the monasteries. Many would have echoed Jerome's words written to Eustochium from Bethlehem: "I cannot bring myself to speak of the many virgins who daily fall";[13] and if nuns, then monks also. Celibacy requires of those who undertake it total faith, unbreakable hope, and sincere love.

This was the situation in which Augustine wrote his precept. That he should do so was entirely consistent with his office for, as Dr. Sherwin Bailey has shown,[14] after marriage changed from being a secular to a religious institution, it became normal practice for bishops and other leaders to issue directives on sexual matters. That Augustine should write without inhibition was consistent with contemporary practice.[15] That he should have attempted to codify his conclusions stemmed from the fact that he was a Latin through and through, with all the conservative and moral attitudes that that implies. There is no "theology of celibacy" in what he wrote, just as there is no developed treatment of prayer in chapter II. Like prayer, chastity and celibacy are subsumed in the very fact that monks are monks. The same lack of treatment is notable in other early monastic rules, and it is not until much later that monasticism came to examine itself at this deep level. This would seem to be right. Celibacy, being closely related to marriage, is so near to the fluctuations of social custom and thought that it has to be considered afresh in every generation. And, as Luc Verheijen has pointed out,[16] Augustine did not do his thinking on this subject until some years later when he wrote *Holy Virginity*.

With all the foregoing in mind, we must now examine what Augustine put into the *Rule*. But before doing so there is one point that needs to be emphasized: he is not writing about celibacy, he is writing to celibates about behavior that befits their calling.

ENCOUNTERING TEMPTATION

Augustine's previous words in the text were that everything that the monks did when they were outside the monastery must "be in keeping with (their) holy state." Then he continues: "Even if your gaze chances to fall on a woman you should not stare at her." When men are out and about, they cannot avoid seeing women; and, as Augustine says, no prohibition of the sight of women has been part of the custom of the monks. For men, the sight of a woman may be disturbing. Within the monastery, among the brothers, this difficulty would not arise; but when he goes out a monk may sometimes be immediately vulnerable. He will have to struggle to control his weakness. If he does not attempt to do so, or if he fails in the attempt, then his chastity begins to be assailed and he will look at women sexually. Women know when a man is behaving provokingly. For the most part they are annoyed or angered by such behavior; in any case, they generally ignore the offender. Occasionally, however, the man's attention is welcomed by a woman with a complementary weakness and she will by look or gesture acknowledge the intention of his regard. Such an exchange, the *Rule* states, is "blameworthy" (*criminosum*). The monk's weakness is not in itself incompatible with his "holy state," but the meaning of his life begins to be called in question if he gives way to it and lets his eyes also acknowledge a response; and in the following words of this paragraph Augustine spells out what are the consequences of allowing eyes to reflect urges.

Augustine is writing to men whom he knew, whom he had gathered round him and lived with for three years and more; they were men of goodwill who had adopted celibacy as part of their monastic way of life. He himself had faced the challenge at Cassiciacum, in terms of the search for truth or acceptance of the responsibilities of marriage. He knew, as he wrote in the *Confessions* (VI, 11), that "Many great men, well worthy of our imitation, have given themselves to the pursuit of wisdom even though they had wives." But he had found that that was not the way for him, and it was those who were like-minded who joined themselves to him in a monastic venture. It seems fair to presume, then, that he wrote as he did because he had to do so. This was not merely theorizing, it was a matter of sheer necessity for the unity and well-being of the whole group. It could be that among the monks there was, say, one individual with this sort of tendency to contend with. Augustine writes of attracting (*adpetere*) and encouraging a response (*adpeti uelle*), of glances (*aspectu*), touch (*tactu*), the heart's movement (*affectu*) and desire for women (*concupiscentia feminarum*). Between the fourth century and the twentieth there is not much difference in the understanding of these things at this level, but in the intervening centuries a conspiracy of silence, for which Augustine's later theorizing is partly responsible (though in all of this he was but taking to their logical conclusion the thought of his predecessors),[17] has left inhibiting marks on our present-day willingness to face these issues. For those in monasteries today it may be providential that in Hippo Augustine had to write of them openly, because, as we now know, very few people are entirely free from some inadequacy in the acceptance of their own sexual nature, as a result either of in-built weakness or of inherited taboos and mistaken teaching. Augustine does not deny this nature but advocates a proper attitude toward it, drawing a contrast between *pudicus* and *inpudicus* (pure, impure), and he concludes this part of his discussion by saying that if illicit exchange is established between a weak monk and a woman whom he meets when he goes out, then "chastity takes flight" (*fugit castitas*). For everyone who undertakes a life of chaste celibacy the process of interiorizing this commitment takes a long time. Its fulfillment is to be found in what Charles V. Heris has called "virginity of the heart."[18]

This whole chapter seems to be an example of the theory which William Lynch propounded in his book *Christ and Apollo*[19] that an upward movement toward illumination and insight is only possible if there is first a plunging down into the hard, soiling experience of living. Augustine does have to go down to the depths in these paragraphs before real insight emerges. Writing to his monks, he faces possible disaster in the community. And in the face of disaster strong measures have to be taken. But strong measures and hard words are unlikely to be just unless they are rooted in mercy and compassion. Augustine had both. A modern reader cannot get into the depths of these paragraphs without the same attitudes. It may be right, therefore, to look ahead at this point and to note how throughout paragraphs 7-9 sexual weakness is regarded as a malady that is in need of healing. As we have seen already in chapter III and will see again in chapter V, much emphasis is laid on the community as a place of healing. And members of a community cannot be channels of healing unless they have compassion.

The basic fact of the weakness that is considered in this paragraph is common enough: what begins as a weakness which in itself may be morally neutral although undesirable can become a sinful habit involving others in its course. If disaster is not to occur, there has to be plain speaking; the likely train of events has to be spelled out. For a monk who is already committed to a life of celibacy the whole continuum of sexual exchange is a contradiction of his undertaking. Even if he is only a short distance along the road away from his true meaning, he is nevertheless astray: his way of life, Augustine says, has already become unchaste in desire if not in act, even if there has been no "despoiling of the body" (*uiolatione corporibus*) — or, more accurately, no despoiling of the bodies. He was not alone in his thinking; Jerome said in his letter to Eustochium that "virginity may be lost by thinking" (XXII, 5.3). Everything possible must be done to avoid such a tragic breakdown in the fulfilling of each monk's vocation and in the unity of the group. So Augustine goes on to warn a poor weak monk of the risks that he is running.

Rule, Chapter IV, 5

Whoever lets his eye rest on a woman
and takes pleasure in having hers rest on him
should not imagine that he is not seen by others
when he does so.
He is bound to be noticed,
and that by those he does not think have seen him.
But even supposing that he does conceal it
and is seen by no human eye,
what will he do about him who looks down from heaven
and from whom nothing can be concealed?
Or are we to think
that he does not see,
because his patience is as great as his wisdom?
A man consecrated to holiness, then, should fear to displease him;
and then he will not want to please a woman in a wrong way.
He should ponder the fact that God sees all things,
and then he will not want to look at a woman in a wrong way.

For it is fear of God that is commended to us in this connection
when it is written:
He who stares fixedly is an abomination to the Lord.

FAULTS THAT CANNOT BE HIDDEN

Poor weak monk! How is he to be helped? In this paragraph
help is offered in the form of several warnings. As previously in
the case of social status and of fasting Augustine could write as
he did because of his own experience. In this present matter he
was well aware that his own struggle was not over. This is borne
out by the open and humble passage in the *Confessions* (X, 41),
written a few years later: "There yet live in my memory the images
of such things as my ill custom there fixed; which haunt me,
strengthless when I am awake; but in sleep, not only so as to give
pleasure, but even to attain assent, and what is very like reality."
Because the struggle was still going on, and because it concerned
the depths of his humanness, it was inevitable that Augustine's
approach and his conclusions are throughout this chapter incom-
plete. And perhaps it is as well that this is so apparent, for attitudes
to the existence and use of human sexuality must vary as humankind develops its own self-knowledge. For instance, there is in his
thinking — and equally in that of his predecessors in the faith and
in his successors for many hundreds of years — no recognition of
a metaphysical and eternal character in a developed man/woman
relationship which engages the full person.[20] The relation between
sex and love in its metaphysical sense is a later discovery.[21]
Therefore, if we are to enter into the terms of reference which
provide the framework for Augustine's warnings against the
misuse of sexuality by a monk we must attempt to set aside our
present understanding in these matters. What is important in this
and the following paragraphs of the *Rule* is not the particular
social preconceptions that all its contemporary readers would
take for granted, but the theological and spiritual insights which
Augustine brings to bear on the problems involved. These insights
have a validity that is durable, while the immediate occasion of
their appearance has disappeared. Perhaps an analogy with music
may help to get the matter into better perspective. You can listen
to and appreciate Handel's Water Music in a concert hall, in a car,
in the jungle, anywhere — you do not have to be in a barge or on
the embankment of the River Thames to enjoy it, in fact you might
find it distracting to your listening if you were by the river. With

Augustine and Handel the value of what they wrote transcends its occasion, even though it was formed by that occasion.

Having said all that, we must now go back to the monk who is beginning to run into difficulties. It may be that the relationship that he is beginning to establish is immediately so satisfying that it gives him no trouble; but it is more likely that the incongruity of his monk's commitment and his new attraction will cause him great pain. Guilt will make him want to conceal what he most enjoys — and that adds a further strain on his resources. So, by way of self-assurance, he will hope that his behavior goes unobserved. But, says Augustine, in the nature of the case his feelings cannot remain hidden, although he will not know who has observed his exchanges because their absorbing character blinds him to other areas of awareness. It may not be his brethren who are the first to notice what is taking place; out of doors, anyone could see. The falseness of his actions is an offense to the outsider who, however little he understands and values the monks' way of life, will at least expect it to be thoroughly consistent. Thus a positive deterrent is the fact that what he is doing is unlikely to remain undisclosed.

GOD SEES EVERYTHING

Augustine at this point again invokes scripture, for his next attempt at dissuasion lies in the fact that even if the ill behavior remains undetected and elicits no disapprobation by others, with God it is not so. In the nature of things, he cannot but see what is happening[22] — that the fabric of the monk's life is being torn apart. God knows that the singleness of heart which bound the brother's life to himself is being fragmented by conflicting claims. Yet, says Augustine, God does not apply force or interfere. That he does not act in restraint does not imply that he does not know; his withholding action is the result of his wisdom and his patience. God's very knowledge and understanding underlie his patience with the waywardness of humankind. And even in a grave matter that threatens the disintegration of all that the monk's life stands for, God will not intervene to prevent him from doing what he is minded to do. "Are we to think that he does not see because his patience is as great as his wisdom?" (*An ideo putandus est non uidere, quia tanto uidet patientius, quanto sapientius?*). These words echo Augustine's thought of a few years earlier when he treated of the Lord's words of Matthew 5:28 in his book *The Lord's Sermon on the Mount* (I, 12, 34). In that passage he was discussing adultery of the heart, relating it to the temptation narrative of Genesis 3, and there we find: "He [God] who put forth suasion will not compel." And he continues: "And all natures are beautiful in their order." What Augustine is concerned with in the *Rule* is the strengthening of the goodness that in the first place has made the man the monk that he is.

GOD'S PATIENCE AND WISDOM

This is the first time in the *Rule* that attributes of God are mentioned. Up till now, God has been thought of as the One beyond, the object of man's search, and as the One within. That is to say, up till now his being and his presence have been evoked. Now, at this point, it is his activity that is called into play, and the striking thing is that Augustine does this in relation to man's sinfulness — it is within the sinful human condition that God encounters men. The words of Jesus come to mind: *I came not to call the righteous, but sinners* (Mt 9:13). But the passage that the *Rule*'s words actually echo is Romans 2:4 where Paul, after asking whether his readers thought they could escape God's judgment, continues with the question: *Or do you presume upon the riches of his kindness and forbearance and patience? Do you not know that God's kindness is meant to lead you to repentance?* Thus once more the *Rule*'s call is to conversion. Forbearance and patience are tender qualities, rooted in wisdom. In calling to mind the compassionate nature of God which characterizes his dealings with the waywardness of men, Augustine is appealing to the monk's deep goodness of heart and his inner God-directedness. That he should be able to contemplate acting contrary to his commitment is still unthinkable. But thinking, when the heart is catching fire, is almost impossible. So the plea here, before it is too late and before events have gone too far, is for recollection and recognition of all that is at stake. Every monk's way of life, from his observable behavior to his innermost thoughts and desires, can have but one true concern: his givenness to God and his movement toward God. He is, says Augustine, *uir sanctus*, that is to say, he is someone who has been set apart for holy use. We have translated this as "consecrated to holiness," in order to express both the present and the future aspects of a monk's undertaking. Present and future are in some sense bound together in some moments of time and in some experiences. And sometimes the future is at war with the present, because the present is also bound to the past. In each present moment, the future either reaffirms or denies the past.

For the monk, in the situation of this paragraph, the past of his givenness uniquely to God is in conflict with the future of a commitment to a woman who attracts him and whom he attracts. From that point of view, his delight in her is a denial of his delight in God. As we have said above, there is no metaphysical level in the relationship which is discussed in this chapter, no possibility of the monk's relationship with the woman becoming an enriching experience of divine things, and we must keep this in mind as we explore the rest of the chapter. *Diligit*, the word which I have here translated as "takes pleasure in," is used by Augustine with a very full meaning — indeed a metaphysical one — by the time he has worked through the labyrinth of his thoughts in this chapter; but at this point it can carry no more than its lowest meaning, given the self-centered context in which it is used. We have to accept the notion that what gives delight to the wayward monk is displeasing to God. But we should also notice the twice-repeated phrase, "in a wrong way" (*male*), for this underlines the point that was made at the beginning of paragraph 4: Seeing a woman, even pleasing her, is not wrong in itself. It only becomes so when its motive is physical gratification (the *concupiscentia carnis* of paragraph 4). Such an attitude in a man who has already given himself to a life of holiness in celibacy cannot please God whom he has set out to seek.

At this point, all that Augustine can do, within the limitations of the outlook to which he was heir, is to evoke the dread of displeasing God in whose judgment the wayward monk must know himself to be failing. All that Augustine can do explicitly is once more to appeal to scripture and quote the sentence: *He who stares fixedly is an abomination to the Lord.* These words occur in the Septuagint but not in the Hebrew version of Prv 27:20, coming after *so also are the eyes of men insatiable.*[23] The tragedy of this insatiable monk is that his thirst for God is in danger of accepting a substitute.

It is the recognition of this substitution that takes Augustine to a deeper level in his thinking, for such an attitude is that of idolatry. And idolatry, as we have seen earlier, is one of the characteristics of the *saeculum* from which the monk's entry into the monastery had separated him. This is the level at which the monk is really falling into sin, and this is the reason why the way in which Augustine attempts to recall him must be taken seriously. However much the monk may be exhilarated by his new experience, he now has in him the seeds of moral disease and death.

One of the interesting facts of chapter IV of the *Rule* is the way in which no line of thought is pursued to a neat conclusion, whereas in all the other chapters without exception there is a clear sequence of thought. Here, however, some thoughts break off and are taken up again in later paragraphs while others are left inconclusively. This is an indication of the very complexity of the issues, as well as of the fact that there can be no cut-and-dried answers to the problems that are being considered. In paragraph 11 the possibility of the monk's voluntary confession and repentance is discussed. But much more space is given to a consideration of the community's responsibility for and toward the wrongdoer. A deeply personal difficulty can arise within any community, and the way it is handled affects both the present moment and the future of all those who are living in the monastery; the resources that the members have to draw on are those that are embedded in the whole tradition of their life. For those who are to be guided by Augustine's precepts, this tradition means a common life of mutual trust and interdependence which expresses a unity in heart and mind of seekers and servants. These resources are dynamic, living, and at work within the group because each one is the dwelling-place of God, and he is in the midst speaking to the heart of every individual. Therefore the perplexities and pain that a distressing situation must cause within a community are to be accepted and worked through with the same wisdom that God displays in his dealings with all his wayward children; and the same qualities of kindness, forbearance, and patience must characterize the actions and decisions of all those who become involved in a difficult situation such as the one envisaged in this chapter. Therefore — but the next paragraph begins with "Therefore," and so we will turn to that.

Rule, Chapter IV, 6

Therefore when you are in company together
in church or elsewhere
where women are also present,
you should protect one another's modesty,

for in this way God who dwells within you
will protect you from within yourselves.

MUTUAL RESPONSIBILITY

The discussion now moves away from the prurient behavior of
one wrongdoer to a consideration of the high value of mutual
responsibility.

Such responsibility is embedded in Augustine's understanding
of the monastic way of life. The singleness and separation of each
monk can never be an in-turned isolation. (The sort of conduct
that the previous two paragraphs have described is itself based
on a self-concern that blocks any awareness of responsibility
toward the group.) Mutual responsibility is at the heart of Christian living. *Am I my brother's keeper?* (Gen 4:9). The isolation of
Cain's defiant and self-regarding question finds its antithesis in
the New Testament, in the experience of those who committed
themselves to living in Christ. These people found a manner of
kinship in a caring community which in the Latin Bible is translated *caritas fraternitatis* and which the English Authorized Version gives as *brotherly love* (Rom 12:10; 1 Thes 4:9; Heb 13:1). This
is the level at which every part of a monk's being is to be engaged
in his relationships, and it is from this depth that each member of
the group can act for the building-up of the whole community.

The reason for assuming responsibility for one another is
founded on God's care for each one. The protection that one monk
affords to another is an embodiment of the protection that God is
bringing to each one, and the men are simply his instruments and
his servants. This is the level at which true responsibility operates.
Supervision and ensuring that customs and acceptable behavior
are observed are only peripheral. It has sometimes been thought
that the advice which Augustine gives in the following paragraphs is unacceptable because it smacks of the evils of a police-
state. But, as Luc Verheijen points out, Augustine's underlying
reason is solicitude.[24] There is no sense of pressure on either of
two brothers who are outside the monastery together, if there is
unanimity between them. Their objective and their terms of reference are identical, and each will experience the presence of the
other as a strength and a real companionship. Pressure is felt when
there is antipathy between them and a diffusion of motives. We
need not at this point discuss this particular problem in terms of
temperament and differences of personality; we have to limit our

horizon to a situation where there is no concord because there is no common aim — because one monk is on a course that is a denial of his commitment. If he is only beginning to take a wrong direction, then the presence of another member of his community may keep him from going astray; he may, because his brother is with him, be able to keep his integrity.

PROTECTING ONE ANOTHER

The goodwill and singleness of mind which each man brings with him into community life is tested, strengthened, and developed by his relationships within the group. At all points his whole being is challenged; and also at all points, with the testing comes strengthening. That is to say, it is in the presence and through the presence of others that each one may be made whole. But it is not the other monk who can actually effect any change in his companion; his presence may be a social deterrent to unfitting outward behavior, but it is God alone who can bring about whatever change of heart is needed. The same verb *custodire* is used by Augustine for the activity of monks in relation to each other and of the work of God in relation to each one: "You should protect one another's modesty" (*inuicem uestram pudicitiam custodite*) and God will protect you (*Deus . . . uos custodiet*). *Custodire* is primarily a caring word, having regard to the well-being and preservation of people and things ("custody" in the sense of imprisonment is a derivative meaning). It is an inevitable word to use in discussing the mutual care that each should have for all. Every monk must be concerned with the welfare of his brothers, in general and in particular, just because they are all one body in Christ, knit together in all their thought and activity. Thus the well-doing of one is the well-doing of all, and the failure of one is a corporate failure. All do good and all do ill; and it is this fact that makes it possible for each to bear responsibility for others, since each one knows what it is to fail more than he is aware of what it is to do well. "My brother is my life," as the Staretz Silouan said,[25] and the more we see our self in our struggling sister or brother the nearer we are to seeing that person with the eyes of God, for we are seeing him or her with knowledge and compassion.

For God, seeing is knowing. More than that, God's knowing is always a knowing in truth. So for him there can be no knowledge without judgment; and at the same time, he cannot judge without compassion and mercy, for his knowledge is always complete understanding. This is one of the meanings of the life of Jesus, and it is a revelation which the resurrection and the gift of the Spirit have incarnated within the continuum of the life of humanity.[26] New life, a new way of living, reaches men through their experience of both the judgment and the compassion of God. Encountering God, in whatever way this happens, is always a purifying experience. For the monk, it is his inner and outer purity of God-directedness that authenticates his way of life. This is what is held within Augustine's use here and previously in paragraph 4 of the words *pudicitia* and *pudicus* (purity, pure). *Pudicitia* implies habitual modesty and decorous behavior and it implies also a deep inner integrity that knows the boundaries that may not be passed.

GOD'S PROTECTION

The protection that is implied in this paragraph has, we might say, a forked root. Part of it draws its life from the very being of God who knows and cares and understands; and the other part is sustained by the fact of his presence within and between men. *Where two or three are gathered together in my name, there am I in the midst of them.* These words which Matthew 18:20 ascribes to Jesus express an experience of him that has molded Christian belief down the centuries, and it may be providential that their meaning is inexplicit for in that way they are open to a richness of interpretation that is informed not only by the head but also by the heart. The Lord may be present because he is present in each one; he may be present as an additional, though unseen, member of the group. He may speak to one from within the others who are present; he may speak to all from the growing understanding that comes from their presence to each other. So in this passage of the *Rule* we do well not to be rigid and limited in our attempts to discover what exactly Augustine was saying: the meaning transcends words. It is Christ's presence that saves, not any theory of what his words mean.

However, we do need to pay attention to the preposition that occurs at the end of the paragraph. Augustine tells the monks that God will protect them *ex uobis.* I have translated this phrase: "from within yourselves." Augustine is not saying that God will protect them from themselves. This point has sometimes not been noticed and the thought of the last part of the sentence has then been based on the fact that men are often their own worst enemies and need to be protected from their own selves. This may be true, but if that had been what Augustine meant he would have used another prepositional phrase — *ab uobis*. *Ex* evokes the inwardness of God's activity: he is living and at work within each one. He is in each one, and he is the ground of the response of the one to the other. When their hearts and minds meet in consent, it is the unity of God that is expressed; when their mutual consent leads to action his unity is, as it were, humanized; and when God is thus active in a human situation, then the participants are on the way to being divinized. It is in this way that deification finds its outlet — that deification which is so central to the Fathers of the East and which from the beginning at Thagaste was taken by Augustine into the heart of his monastic ideal.[27] Deification is the consequence of the double fact of the indwelling of God in a person and of his or her openness to the power and influence of the One who dwells within him.

Thus once more the theme of the end of chapter I proves to be central to the life of the monks: they are the temples of God, the holy place of his presence, expressions of his presence, and the place where his presence is to be honored.

But, as Paul warned when he used the temple-image in 1 Corinthians 3:16-17, it is possible to defile the temple. That phrase sounds slightly remote and today it fails to express the real impact of its meaning, so perhaps we ought to attempt a paraphrase in order to bring out the horror of what St. Paul was saying. Today, the desecration of sacred places is still regarded as an appalling act, both by its perpetrators and by those who come to know of it — it is recognized as a terrible thing to have happen. This is the force of what Paul wrote: *You are the temple of God . . . and you need to be on your guard lest you desecrate the place where he is.* And this is the force of what Augustine is saying in this paragraph of the *Rule*: You could, if you gave way to your weaknesses, desecrate the sacred dwelling-place of God which you yourself are. But, his reasoning continues, if you remain attentive to him who is within you then he himself can protect you from the effect of the downward drag of your nature. Each monk is primarily responsible for safeguarding his own integrity with the help of God; when there are two together, by the very fact of their unity in him each of them does more than maintain his own probity for he also strengthens that of his brother. Each is to the other not an inquisitor but a sustainer. Every one, going about, carries along his or her own perils; the presence of another with whom much of life, but not all of it, is shared (and no one can fully share another's life) — this presence is a means and a place of safety.

In the two preceding paragraphs of the *Rule*, the monks' experience has been explored beyond the difficulties of social antagonisms and personal characteristics such as were discussed from various viewpoints in chapters I-III. Chapter IV has brought the monks to the point where the presence of sin has to be taken seriously. This Augustine proceeds to do, not in treatise-fashion but by probing possible situations that might occur among the group for whom he is writing. Each monk bears his own sin and some sin is shared by many; but at the same time each one who is in his innermost heart centered on God has it in him to be an instrument of forgiveness and reconciliation for the sinner. Each can be both sinner and redeemed, and it is in this movement that the way to wholeness is opened up. The presence of each monk to his brother means far more than his presence with his brother, for it points to the awareness and attention which each may possess at a deep level if he is pursuing his God-directed way with sincerity, however dark and dangerous that way may be. And sometimes, probably more often than has at times been realized, a companion must inevitably enter into the darkness of another. His ability to do this depends on his own integrity and his own rootedness in God.

So we find that throughout the back-and-forth discussions of the next paragraphs there are always two areas of decision and action that are being explored: that of the man who is being dragged away from his monastic commitment by his own weak nature and who is moving toward what in marriage terminology would be considered as the sin of adultery, and on the other hand the area in which his fellow monks have to move in consequence of the discovery of his wrongdoing. The necessity of entering these areas when considering the monastic way of life should not shock us. Monks as persons are as ordinarily disorientated as any other person; each one has to work through his own areas of conflict and for some tragic failure may be inevitable. But God is greater than monasticism, and he can reach each one even when the community cannot; and sometimes this can only happen beyond the monastery.

Rule, Chapter IV, 7

And if you should notice in any one of you
such indiscreet looks as I am speaking of,
you should warn him at once
so that what has begun may go no further
and may be immediately corrected.

DISCOVERING INFIDELITY IN ANOTHER

Augustine now leads his readers into a consideration of one of the most difficult problems that can face a member of a community: how to act when one discovers deviance from the accepted norms to which the members are pledged. We shall need to look at this matter from several angles, and it may be best to follow the course of experience and begin with the beholder's immediate and spontaneous reaction.

In so serious a matter as that with which paragraphs 4-9 are concerned, the first reaction is most probably that of shock: recoil, fear or outrage may predominate, according to the persons concerned. The important thing to note is that it is the emotions that are primarily affected, and it takes time before reason can be brought to bear on the matter. Only a vicious person rejoices at the discovery of wrong in another. Yet it may be that every man is capable of some viciousness, and in exploring one's involvement in difficult situations precipitated by the failure of another it is well to be aware of the possibility of a contrary vice in oneself. But having entered that warning, we may set it aside for the present as in fact Augustine does not presuppose a vicious response in the brother who encounters another's failure.

One thing is certain: it would be morally wrong to ignore the fault — a matter which is considered again in the following paragraph. The very fact of being part of a community involves a responsibility not only for the well-being but also for the well-doing of one another, but this is a responsibility that many people would prefer not to have to exercise, for it is very costing. Those who are happy to do so are those who are naturally officious, and it is these who are least likely to be able to bring about any significant change in the wrongdoer. (It always comes as a surprise when one discovers how deeply the failure of another challenges one's own integrity.)

But all of that is theory, and there remains the problem of how to act responsibly: this is the problem with which Augustine is concerned in the remainder of this chapter. When the community's life is threatened by the failure of one member, how is well-being to be restored? What is responsible behavior in the face of irresponsibility? Augustine echoes the Lord's precept of Matthew 18:15-17: *If your brother does something wrong, go and have it out with him alone, between your two selves.* Although this is to be a personal encounter, the matter between the two is in some sense imperso-nal (the editors of the JB and NEB both point out that the addition of the words *against you/to you* is absent in some sources).[28] The attempt must be made to detach the wrongdoer from commitment to the wrong. Personal feelings have to be controlled, if the en-counter is to be fruitful; they cannot be eliminated, of course, for they are an essential component in each person's being, but if the other person is to be reached, one's own feelings that are in any way opposed to his or hers must be held in check. The fear or outrage that one has experienced will only reproduce itself in the brother or sister whom one is trying to win back. Fear and outrage are both rejecting forces, incapable of reconciling. Thus the first person to be challenged in the sort of distressing situation that this chapter explores is the innocent party. And this, of course, forces one to admit that no one is entirely innocent, no one's integrity is entirely perfected. The chief strength that anyone really has for entering into an encounter such as this is humility: there, but for the grace of God, go I. The other strength, arising from this, is compassion — the ability to enter into the dilemma of the wrong-doer, to let his mind and heart hold in tension all the conflicting claims that have brought the offender to his present state.

All the same, even when strengthened with humility and com-passion, the undertaking is never easy and one shrinks from it. As the Matthean passage goes on to show, such a singular attempt at correction often fails — the conflict in the other person is too complex to be resolved by one individual: *If he listens to you, you have won back your brother. If he does not listen . . .* (verses 15b-16a). Nevertheless, in justice to the offender, the situation must be dealt with in the first place by the eyewitness; there is no one else to do it. Two words in Augustine's text indicate the spirit in which the dialogue is to be approached by the brother who has to undertake the correcting. In the first place, the wrongdoing, which in the preceding paragraphs is described with considerably more force and disapproval, is here simply referred to as "indiscreet looks" (*oculi petulantiam*). *Petulantia* is a fairly light word within the category of sexual misdemeanor; perhaps one could say that it is a cheap word. The very least that could be said of a monk's initial deviance from the sexual standards that his commitment requires of him is that his behavior is cheap. To label a person's conduct as cheap is not to pass a heavy judgment on him; it is to invoke an accepted pattern and to express disapproval at a failure to observe it. This is not severe censure and there are no penal overtones. Thus Augustine's precept in the face of such a situation is that the eyewitness has the duty of warning the offender immediately (*statim admonete*), in order that "what has begun may go no further." "Look out!" is what one brother has to say to the other: you are making a false move, step back quickly lest you fall. The responsible way to give correction is to appeal to the sense of responsibility of the offender. One has no right to assume depravity in another, simply on the evidence of one's own eyes and the reaction of one's own reason and emotions. The only way to reach into one's brother is to assume that there is goodness within him; and so there is, for (to go back to the key thought of the end of chapter I), he is the temple of God. Wrongdoing, as it were, immobilizes the work of God and blocks the channels of his operations within us. Minor failures do this temporarily, major and continuous failure may imprison us almost totally. That is why we have to be concerned for the safety and well-being of each other. The whole of this chapter is about healing, and healers must have a light touch. It needs great skill to give correction effectively and one has to learn by one's mistakes. Moreover one cannot bring about the healing of another without being drained oneself — an experience which Jesus himself knew and which Mark and Luke both record: *I felt that power had gone out from me* (Lk 8:46). One has to be willing for this to happen and neither resent it nor seek to prevent it. And further, one has to be prepared for failure; the acceptance of another may involve the inefficacy of one's endeavor. The channel that at all costs has to be kept open is that of a relationship between the two brothers, and that means that in spite of the event the wrongdoer must be treated as a person and not as a malfunctioning machine — he cannot be relegated to the scrap heap where all meaning and identity are lost. So whenever a wrong is perpetrated within the community, agony and sorrow must follow as night follows day. Sometimes the very awareness of the distress he is causing is sufficient to deter the brother who is at fault; but when his whole person becomes committed to the course that he is pursuing then he becomes incapable of responding to the cry of pain of those whom he is wounding.

It is because the whole person is involved in the sort of misconduct that this chapter envisages that it is so difficult to accept warning and advice when one has embarked on an unwise course. Anyone who has had the misfortune to have to appeal for caution in another who appears to be trapped in an undesirable relationship knows that the reaction he is most likely to get is complete and outraged rejection: we warned him or her, but it was no good, one says with sorrow, admitting one's failure. Yet not to have warned would have been an even greater failure. Such an awareness of failure can be a positive good in a situation of this sort, for it keeps alive one's sense of responsibility. A negative attitude to the rejection is destructive anger, a desire to tear down what one cannot build up. The very real struggle between continuing concern and the desire to destroy which the rejected well-wisher must go through if he is to keep his own integrity is itself a means of entering into the contest that the erring brother is himself engaged in.

There is real agony in all of this, and the more intractable the problem the less likely it is that the well-wisher can handle the situation alone. Others may have to take this pain and suffering into themselves. Where one doctor and the local health visitor cannot bring healing, a team of doctors and nurses may be able to do so. It is the teamwork of healing that Augustine goes on to discuss.

Rule, Chapter IV, 8

However, if after this warning you should see him do the same thing again,
then or on another day
he who has noticed it should report him
as one who is hurt and in need of healing.
First, however, it should be pointed out
to a second or a third person,
so that he can be proved wrong
by the mouth of two or three witnesses
and can be restrained with whatever firmness seems suitable.
Do not think that you are being a mischief-maker
when you draw attention to this.
On the contrary,

you would be no more innocent yourselves
if by silence you let your brothers be lost,
when by reporting the matter
you could have corrected them.
If your brother had a wound in his body
which he wished to keep secret
for fear of medical treatment,
would it not be cruel to keep silent
and compassionate to make it known?
How much more, then,
ought you to report him
so that he shall not suffer from a more terrible festering,
that of the heart.

ENCOUNTERING SIN WITH COMPASSION

The key word in this long paragraph comes near the end, and many suggestions have been made by Augustine before he penetrates to a full understanding of what is required if the wrongdoer is to be helped and healed. This is common experience: one has to work through the superficial reactions that have followed one's shocked recoil at discovering a grave weakness in a member of one's community before one becomes purified oneself and in any sense able to bring about a cure. The only remedies that can be effective are those which are administered with compassion (*misericorditer*). This is the first time that the notion of compassion occurs in these precepts; it is repeated within the same frame of reference in the following paragraph and again in chapter VII, 4 when the question of the relationship between the prior and his monks is being discussed.

For Augustine, compassion was an attitude that deeply influenced his understanding of sinfulness in man. The word he uses, *misericordia*, means the ability to take another's misery into one's heart. In relation to sexual failure this seems to be one of the hardest things for humankind to achieve because customs and attitudes to this aspect of living are so deeply entrenched. That is why the story of Jesus and the adulteress is important.[29] This passage came to mean much to Augustine and in his commentary on John's gospel he explored the nature of sin, love, and forgiveness with great sensitivity. Jesus' role in the situation, says Augustine, was threefold: "As a teacher, he brought truth; as a deliverer, he brought gentleness; as a protector, he brought righteousness" (*Homilies on the Gospel of John* 33:46). In dealing with the woman, Jesus dealt also with those who brought her to him, and he showed truth, gentleness, and righteousness to accusers as well as to the accused. Truth has to be established and falsehood eliminated: Jesus challenged the accusers while accepting their challenge to the accused. Gentleness, which Augustine also calls clemency, is given full play because the Lord refuses to condemn while at the same time he requires a change of heart in the woman. And righteousness/justice ensured protection for her by challenging the accusers in their hearts also. These three facets of compassion are discovered by Augustine as he looks in turn at each of the actors in this drama; but it is when the Lord is alone with the woman that the complete meaning of compassion is expressed — and this Augustine can most forcibly describe by a play on words, with the woman herself portraying wretchedness personified: (*miseria*) the two left alone, *miseria* and *misericordia*. And he goes on to show that it was only within the Lord's complete acceptance of the adulteress' sin that he could talk to her of it and release her from it.

The commentary on John's gospel was not begun until several years after the writing of the *Rule*; but Augustine's understanding of compassion was already on its way to being worked out when he wrote chapter IV of his precepts. There are those who deplore the fact that in his monastic *Rule* he should have given so much space to a discussion of what is in itself an extreme example of failure within a community, and one that does not occur very often (but that it can occur is a fact that all should be aware of). What matters supremely is not the nature of the offense but the reaction of the offender's fellow monks. In chapters I and III the attitudes to offending through intrinsically innocent characteristics were explored to a great depth, and Augustine reached the point when he could show the brothers that their true unity lay in honoring God in one another. Now, in the painful discussions of chapter IV, he reaches the further point when he can show that mutual unity and acceptance require not only the finding of God in one another but also the discovery of evil, sin, and failure. At first, as we have already said, one recoils from this and one rushes to the barricades. From such a defensive position one can achieve nothing of permanent and constructive value; it is only when a man can open himself to the temptations and conflicts that assail another that he can help that one back to wholeness. Compassion means a willingness to enter the hell of another.

Entering the hell of another is a thing impossible to do alone, unless one is trained and experienced in that particular tightrope walking skill — which most people are not. It is therefore significant that Augustine does not reach this point of understanding until he has already developed the fact that it is often necessary for the first discoverer of wrong to take others of the group into his confidence. In this paragraph, the succession of events is set in two stages. Augustine begins by saying that if the unsatisfactory behavior continues the matter must be made known (*prodere*). But it is a serious matter to make known a suspicion concerning another member of one's community. Just because of the basic pattern of group-structures, once a matter is referred to the leader it immediately becomes an official concern; and a brother is reluctant to express his suspicions for fear of being in error or acting unjustly. The very fact that what he has witnessed has revolted him is a threat to his objectivity, and he needs the corroboration of others before it is judicious for him to lay the matter open to his prior. He will, says Augustine, be wise to share the matter with one or two trustworthy brothers; if they, too, notice the same undesirable behavior then there is no error in fact.

Throughout the whole course of the affair, the first responsibility must be concern for the offender. He is not primarily a wrongdoer who has to be restrained and punished; rather, he is to be seen as a wounded person (*uulneratum*) who needs to be healed (*sanandum*). The second or third brother to whom the fault becomes evident is in an easier position than the monk who made the initial discovery, because for the former the element of shock is less. Their appraisal of the situation will be calmer and less likely to be at fault. If the primary evidence is confirmed and a joint report is made to the prior, he again is in a still stronger position for dealing wisely with the offender than he would be if he accepted the evidence of one brother alone or had himself asked for the collaboration of some others in detecting the fault. If two or three brothers together lay the matter before the prior, he is then on the safest ground for undertaking the painful and necessary work of approaching the wrongdoer.

Within a community, the whole business of uncovering a grave fault is as unpleasant as the fault itself: that is to say, however individual the offense may be it will affect the group and cause great distress. And that is another reason for sharing the burden with a few members. The offense wounds the group, not simply by damaging its unanimity but by causing pain and agony to those who are called to bring healing to the offender. Because all are hurt, they need each other's support.

The observation that one witness alone cannot provide fully trustworthy evidence and the corresponding injunction that the corroboration of two or three is essential are embedded in biblical spirituality and social custom. The Deuteronomic passages (17:6 and 19:15) were echoed by Jesus (Mt 9:16) and by Paul (2 Cor 13:1 and 1 Tm 5:19). In each case it is both the offender and his accusers who are safeguarded by the numbers involved. Thus when Augustine advocates the same procedure within the monastery he is simply adopting a practice that was already proven as effective and that carried its own authenticity. The two or three witnesses are for the benefit of the offender. They also check and balance the evidence as it appears to a single individual: there is less likelihood of ill motives clouding judgment. A second or a third brother will be able to detect whether there is any spite influencing the discoverer. A spiteful attitude to the wrong of another is particularly unjust because it frequently masks a related wrong in the one who condemns. Thus Augustine's presumption that the discoverers will look into themselves to see whether they are being "mischief-makers" (*maleuolos*) is an important factor in bringing about the healing of the wrongdoer.

The two or three witnesses are not themselves the principal healers. Their function is like that of the friends who carried the paralyzed man to Jesus.[30] They see the need, they are instrumental in laying that need before the one who has the power and authority to bring healing, and the weak and erring brother is placed within the sphere not only of correction but of forgiveness. It is important to hold on to this point because often a witness' outrage makes him demand a kind of compensation for damage by being given a share in passing judgment. But once the matter has been reported it must be let go of, as far as taking initiative is concerned: if the prior asks for the further help of any of the witnesses, that is another matter. There is no reward for the witnesses. Rather, they are likely to suffer much in distress and self-questioning. He would be an insensitive man who did not ask himself whether he was right to report the matter. Yes, says Augustine, it is entirely right to do so.

Augustine justifies the reporting on two grounds: the relation of the discoverer to the discovery, and the relation of the discovering to the life of the community as a whole.

"You would be no more innocent yourselves" (*magis quippe innocentes non estis*) if you kept silent. If the erring monk's ways are to be mended, he must be spoken about. At whatever cost to the discoverers, the ill must be made known — for their sake, for the community's sake, and for the sake of the one who is at fault. It would have been morally wrong for the friends not to have carried the paralyzed man to Jesus for healing; it would be morally wrong to let an ill continue in the community because one chose to ignore it. Probably the paralytic did not at all like the experience of being carried up to the roof and then being let down through it, any more than a monk with a serious ailment likes the thought of treatment for it; but if he cannot and does not take steps to obtain a cure then those who know of his predicament have an obvious responsibility to override his reluctance and to report his condition. Similarly, says the *Rule*, a moral ill must be reported so that the disease may be arrested. Augustine does not draw a parallel with the healing of the paralytic; his analogy is with infectious disease. If a wrong is allowed free play in a community it will inevitably bring about a slackening of standards if not the disintegration of the group. That wrongs of all kinds do exist within a community is part of the human condition; but that they should continue without check is unthinkable. Were that to happen, the monks would be living in despair and not in hope. Augustine sensitively explored both despair and hope among Christians in his commentary on John's gospel, and he put these words into the Lord's mouth: "I have blotted out what you have done; keep what I have commanded you, that you may find what I have promised" (*Homilies on the Gospel of John* 33, 8).

FRATERNAL CORRECTION

It is the presence of hope, and of God within as the ground of hope, that makes it possible for fraternal correction to be undertaken effectively. The desire of the four friends in the gospel and the desire of the two or three brothers in the monastery are carried over into action because of the conviction that healing is possible once the healer is reached. The hope is twofold: that the ailing one may be cured, and that the illness may not spread.

The word that Augustine uses to describe the primary task of the one to whom the misdoing is reported does carry this double meaning of containment and of antidote: *coherceri*, which we have translated as "be restrained," is not limited to the meaning of the English word coerce. It means, in the first place, "to enclose" or "to keep in"; its derived meaning is "to correct." The word "restrain" has been used in the translation above, in an attempt to express both strands of thought.

We have also tried not to read too much into the text in translating what Augustine has to say about the attitude of the person or persons who have to attempt to dissuade the wrongdoer from his course. The restraining of the brother is to be done with what *seueritas* seems suitable. The Latin word has provided English with both "severity" and "seriousness"; its opposite is *lenitas* which means smoothness or mildness. Augustine does not say that the action taken must be characterized by mildness; he considers that the matter is serious enough to require serious measures. The word severity, when used in connection with correction, has strident and vindictive overtones which are out of keeping with the compassion which, Augustine insists, must inform every step that may have to be taken by those who are responsible for the community's well-being. For this reason I have translated *seueritas* as "firmness." Firm and confident measures need to be taken if there is to be no spread of the wrongdoing which one brother is pursuing.

One of the important underlying aspects of this paragraph is the way in which Augustine makes all the brothers aware of their own vulnerability and the danger of sin which is near to one. Superficially it seems unsatisfactory that the argument should go backward and forward over the same ground; but beneath this there is the fact of ambivalence in most of humankind. The bad is not wholly in some men and the good in others. *All have sinned and fall short of the glory of God* (Rom 3:23). The catalogue that Augustine enumerates in these few sentences is one that members of a community are very prone to: mischief-making, drawing attention to the faults of another, irresponsible silence, collusion, indifference. In any matter that concerns the well-being of another, each one has to examine his own motives for whatever part he plays in their common engagement, whether they are in collaboration or have different objectives. It is doubtful if all of the two or three witnesses would be completely guiltless on every count, and there is a challenge to the sincerity and truth of each one. And the more people who are involved in attempting to bring about the reformation of the wayward monk, the more there will be cross-currents of good and bad intentions. In justice to the man who is to be judged by others, it is essential that the integrity of the witnesses should be assured as far as may be. It is for this reason that the provisions of the following paragraph are so apt and right.

Rule, Chapter IV, 9

But before pointing it out to others
by whom he could be proved in the wrong,
if he denies it,
you should first report him to the prior,
if after a warning he has still neglected to reform.
This is in the hope
that he may be corrected more privately
without anyone else needing to know about it.
But if he denies it,
then without his knowing
other witnesses must be brought in;
from then on
he will not be accused by one witness alone
but will be shown to be culpable by two or three.
If, indeed, he is actually proved guilty,
he must accept such correction
as will help him to amend,
according to the judgment of the prior
or of the priest
who has power to give direction and make judgments.
If he refuses to accept this,
and yet does not withdraw of his own accord,
he must be expelled from your fellowship.
And moreover this is not cruelty
but compassion,
lest he should bring about the destruction of many
by poisonous infection.

REFERRAL TO THE PRIOR

You must do all in your power to prevent real corruption from overcoming the wayward brother — so Augustine ends his previous paragraph. Then he continues: "But" (and the conjunction is very important) "before pointing it out to others . . . you should first report him to the prior." It does not help a serious wrongdoer

to have his ways discussed here, there and everywhere; reformation can most easily take place if few people know about the
wrong. Augustine's compassion for the wrongdoer is, again in
this paragraph, his overriding consideration. As in the previous
one, the word does not occur until near the end; and this time it
is the safety and well-being of the whole community that has to
be safeguarded. His insight into the nature of compassion is very
important indeed, for it challenges the weak and false sentimen-
tality that often masquerades as genuine caring for an offender.
To take a person's misery into one's heart is not the same thing as
to take that wretchedness into one's feeling. The heart, in this
sense, is the compound of reason, understanding, and feeling; and
to fail in the coordination of all three factors is to approach a needy
one with a partiality that can never lead to wholeness. If one is
influenced by reason alone one can see but not share the sufferer's
agony; if one only understands that agony, one can reach it in
imagination but not in fact; if one simply feels the distress, one is
helpless to alleviate it. In each case, intervention in the name of a
spurious compassion may be destructive and lead to prolonged
agony for the one who is in distress.

In the sort of situation that Augustine is considering in this
chapter, the actual forms of distress experienced by the wayward
monk and those who seek to correct him are of a different sort
although they stem from the one set of circumstances. For the
wrongdoer, the distress may be that he is torn by conflicting
loyalties; or if he has reached the point of deciding not to mend
his ways then his distress will be of the nobody-understands-me
sort. For his brothers in the community who are aware of his
attitudes, the distress will be first that there is this sickness in the
community, second that this involves the well-being of the whole
group, and finally that the wrongdoer cannot be healed because
he does not want to be.

SAFEGUARDING THE WRONGDOER

But in all his thinking Augustine is concerned that the erring
monk shall have every opportunity to mend his ways and find
himself within the fellowship of the community; so at this point
we must look at the *Rule*'s advice as it is thought out, step by step.

Just because the issue is such as to touch the deep vulnerability
of every person who comes to be involved in it — rousing emotions, clouding judgment, and deflecting objectivity — if justice is

to be done the matter must be handled with the utmost delicacy. If the whole community is immediately informed a whole cacophony of reactions is likely to ensue which will reflect the inherent weakness of each individual rather than a concern for the weakness of the wrongdoer himself. Therefore it is not appropriate at this stage to make the matter generally known. First it should be referred to the prior, if the warning of two or three brothers has gone unheeded and there has been no amendment. The charism of the prior (which is here taken for granted and is not analyzed until chapter VII, when it is viewed against the whole background of the community's life) is such that he may be able to reach into the depth of the wrongdoer's wretchedness and touch his reason, understanding, and feeling with his own. If that happens — if deep calls to deep — and there is a true response, then from within the privacy of their exchange a reformation may come about. Reproof there must be — and this falls within the province of the prior, while warning is all that is proper to the intervention of the witnesses.

The witnesses' warning may have been ignored and the wrongdoer may have failed to "reform/correct" his ways (*corrigi*). It is then that the prior's intervention, which takes place in private, may produce a reformation by the way he signifies reproof. The word that is used here, referring to the wrongdoer, is *correptus* whose figurative meanings are "reproved/rebuked" with the intention of bringing about a change of attitude; or, more strongly, it can mean "accused" with the same end in view. As we have said, a frontal accusation of one brother by another is inappropriate. This is because, although each is his brother's keeper, none has the right to judge another (though this is one of the most easily forgotten factors in community life). But the monk who, as prior, is entrusted with preserving and furthering the well-being of the whole community must make judgments on the obligations and culpabilities of each member, and if reformation is to be achieved there must be a confrontation and, in some sense, reproof. The important point is that the rebuke is something that is done in the privacy of a one-to-one conversation, without witnesses, without assessors, and the result of such an exchange will depend in very large measure on the nature of the relationship that already exists between the monk and his prior. If a brother finds himself vulnerable in the ways envisaged in this chapter, it does not necessarily imply that he has a bad relationship with his prior, and if there is

mutual understanding and trust the present disorders could probably be corrected. If the relationship is unsatisfactory at the best
of times, then it is less likely that the prior's reproof will have
satisfactory results in this instance. In that case it is probable, as
Augustine foresees, that the charge will be denied.

Yet even so, the reasons for the denial have to be investigated.
In such a distressing interview, the accused monk might make a
denial because he considered himself innocent of the charge; or
he might deny through shame; or he might deny because of a bad
relationship with his prior, or even because of a bad relationship
with the original witnesses if their identity had to be revealed to
him. Whatever the reason for the denial, clearly the report needs
to be investigated more fully — for the sake of the man himself,
for the sake of the first witness or witnesses, as well as for the sake
of the well-being and reputation of the whole community. Thus
at this point Augustine advises the prior to engage the cooperation
of other members of the group.

An interesting fact emerges here. The advice is that "other
witnesses must be brought in" without the wrongdoer knowing
about it. But since, as we find in chapter VIII, 2, every bit of the
Rule is to be read aloud to the community once a week then it can
be assumed that each monk knows the precepts very well indeed,
in which case the injunction to secrecy that is found in the present
paragraph loses some of its meaning. It could hardly be that the
offending monk did not know of the provision of an investigation
if he had denied the charge when confronted with it by his prior.
So there is a curious anomaly, and one wonders whether there is
here a careless ineptitude on Augustine's part, or whether the
situation envisaged here is so little likely to arise that the provision
made for dealing with it may be so seldom invoked that it does
sink into the background for each member who hears it read (but
against this surmise, there is the important injunction of paragraph 10 that the same procedures are to be followed whenever a
serious fault is discovered in a brother).

The reasons behind this particular precept must therefore remain something of a puzzle, and we must turn rather to the advice
itself. As we have already said, the purpose of the investigation is
to safeguard the accused from slander and false judgment. Even
if he is aware, from knowledge of the *Rule*, that he is being
carefully watched by some of his brothers he will not know who
they are. It is for those entrusted with the task, a task which

requires the greatest integrity and self-scrutiny, to assess both the report and the evidence as they find it. At each stage of the affair, every person who is involved is himself being challenged, whether he be the wrongdoer or a witness. Each witness must, in justice, achieve a high degree of impartiality — and impartiality in any matter that touches the heart of the community's life is something that is very hard to come by. In fact, the whole of this procedure within a close-knit group would be impossible were it not for the further dimension of their life which is based on the indwelling activity of God. The investigators have to give over all their powers and all their weakness to him so that, using both their powers and their weaknesses, he may disclose the truth.

CORRECTION AND AMENDMENT

Then Augustine goes on to advise what should happen if the accused man is proved to be guilty of the charge. In that case, the wrongdoer will have to accept/bear (*sustinere*) such form of correction/punishment (*uindictam*) as will persuade him to mend his ways (*emendatoriam*). The obligation to attempt reform through correction and punishment was, of course, not simply a monastic device; it had its roots deep in scripture — which means, in effect, deep in the experience of the developing community of the children of God. The New Testament echoed the Old in seeing the activity of God in the putting right of what was wrong; indeed, both correction and punishment are seen to be his work which was sometimes effected through the instrumentality of men, sometimes through that of circumstances and sometimes through that of natural forces. The sole purpose of whatever action is taken is to bring about amendment. To this day, there is no consensus of opinion as to effective means of bringing about the reformation of character and a reordering of life at any level of society or in any size of group. Each age has attempted to deal with the problem according to its own insights and customs. And it is as well that Augustine provides no specific precept as to how the wrongdoer in the Hippo monastery is to be helped.

The important point in this present passage is that the responsibility for the decision lies with the prior and the priest. The investigators have no part in the means of correcting, just as the earlier witnesses had no part in the passing of judgment. Only those with a very particular charism within the monastery are to be entrusted with so serious a decision as this painful situation requires. Within the life of the community, these two are the most likely to be able to bring about a change of heart in the offender, and for each of them their standing and their experience will enable them to act with compassion, wisdom, tolerance, and courage.

THE ROLE OF THE COMMUNITY'S PRIEST

What each brings to the situation differs according to his relationship to the community. It is in this paragraph that the priest (*presbyter*) is mentioned for the first time, and there has only been one previous reference to the prior, in chapter I, 3. There are three subsequent references to the priest (chapters IV, 11; VII, 1 and 2); and seven to the prior (chapters IV, 11; V, 3.4.5 and 7; VII, 1 and 2). The text contains no job-description for either monk; such was not necessary because everyone in the monastery knew from experience what lay within the province and powers of each. The text assumes that although the prior has the widest sphere of activity in terms of responsibility for the ordering of the life within the monastery, the priest has primacy in certain defined areas.

Before we consider the place of the priest in the monastic community, we need to understand his position in relation to the Christian community as a whole.[31] It was only in the fourth century, that is, in the period immediately antecedent to the writing of the *Rule*, that the nature and function of the priestly office began to be analyzed and formulated. The divergent and wide-ranging views that became formative in the East and in the West need not concern us here. What does matter is the fact that the notions that underlie modern procedures should not be read back into the situation of the Church in the early centuries. Today, the sequence is generally that of a sense of vocation, testing, training, ordination, and appointment to a sphere of work (frequently in a place previously unknown to the man). In Augustine's time, the sequence was the local community's need, the choice by the people of someone fitted to fill it, his ordination by a bishop, and his commitment to his duties. In both East and West, ordination was sometimes accepted reluctantly (as, for instance, in the case of Gregory of Nyssa,[32] Ambrose,[33] Jerome,[34] John Chrysostom,[35] Paulinus of Nola,[36] and Augustine himself).[37] Sometimes the choice was made by an individual bishop: Gregory Nazianzen was ordained by his father against his will. Sometimes, as for Ambrose, Augustine, and Paulinus, it happened (as the last-mentioned put it), "through the sudden compulsion of the crowd."[38]

Several important facts emerge from this evidence. The acceptance of priesthood was an act of obedience, and one that was often undertaken contrary to a man's natural inclination. Priesthood required in many cases a deep and wide self-denial which brought it into close relation with the ascetics when their movement emerged in the third century. Again, a man's priesthood was closely related to the local congregation, the little Church in the place where he was known. He was the chosen priest of the Christians in any given place; he both knew them and was known by them. His authority in the Christian community stemmed both from his intimacy with its members and from his commissioning within the order of the Church. The close relation between the priest and his people in any place — the fact that he was known, trusted and chosen — must have laid a special burden on him. Being a member of a community in which he already had an identifiable role (whatever his previous way of life may have been), he was now invested with an additional function as teacher, mediator, and presider of the mysteries. As such, he was accepted by the community; as such, he had to learn to accept himself. As von Campenhausen has pointed out, such a demand on a man's integrity would weigh very heavily on the priest "who believes in the greatness of his task as mediating salvation, but equally knows what tremendous demands it makes on him, both religiously and morally."[39]

We must now look briefly at the place of a priest within a monastic community, particularly in relation to the group for which the *Rule* was written.[40] The first thing to keep in mind is that the monastic movement was principally a lay movement, and the presence of a priest in a community was of the same pattern as the presence of a priest in a congregation. The priest in a congregation was concerned with the deep things in the lives of the laity, while much of their energy and activity came under the authority of the local civic leader. The priest in a monastery had a similar responsibility among the brothers, while much of their life was coordinated by the prior. The priest's role kept him more in the background, although his authority surpassed that of the prior (as the present paragraph of the *Rule* states); and it is to the priest that obedience is due even more than it is to the prior (chapter VII, 1 and 2). The prior is mentioned first in three of the four passages where he and the priest are both named, because he had the primary task of seeing to the day-to-day affairs of the brothers. The exception occurs in chapter IV.11 where it is the priest who must make a decision in the case of a monk who is receiving clandestine letters and presents.

Not every matter that fell within the jurisdiction of the prior had to be referred to the priest, as if he were the ultimate authority and the prior were his delegate. The prior in his own field was autonomous, as was the priest in his; but clearly there was close collaboration between them. In the sequence in which the situation is disclosed in the *Rule*, the first thing that must be referred to the priest is an exceptionally grave transgression on the part of a member of the community; and this is, as the *Rule* states, in virtue of his "power" to "give direction and make judgments." The member to whom the power to dispense pertained was not, as in modern "monastic" English, the one with authority to dispense from obligations; rather, he was the steward of the household and the one who could allocate its resources. (This last, limited meaning has been retained in English in reference to a pharmaceutical dispenser.) Such a function, in terms of a priestly ministry, implies a responsibility for maintaining and diffusing the ideals of the group according to the need and capacity of each member. For this reason I have, in translation, used the phrase "has power to give direction" (remembering the importance that spiritual direction has had in monasticism from the beginning). The corollary of priestly stewardship in this sense is the ability to make a judgment (*arbitrium*). Perhaps it is as well to point out that to make judgments is not the same thing as to convict or to give sentence. The priest, in virtue of his other gifts, has this one also: he is recognized as the one who can make right judgments. He has a moral authority within the group. In the later passages, Augustine refers to further functions of the priest in a monastic community. In general a man was chosen as priest because of his ability to understand and hand on the meaning of the scriptures and to relate them to all the circumstances of life.[41] This meant that in addition to his ministry as a reconciler he was also the group's teacher on religious matters. And beside being teachers, priests were also the principal formulators of doctrine. It is these further priestly functions that lie behind the injunction at the end of chapter VII, 2, where it is assumed that the prior will refer to the priest whatever lies beyond his own competence.

The presence of a priest in the lay monastery at Hippo was not an innovation; the same pattern is to be found in the monasteries of the East.[42] But it is Augustine who probes the relevance of the priest to the group, though he had not done so at the time when the *Rule* was written. Perhaps the experience of the years between 397 and 404 helped him to be clear about the issues involved when his friend Aurelius, bishop of Carthage, asked for his advice in certain monastic matters: his response was *The Work of Monks*. Here the presence of a priest-monk is not specifically mentioned, but the priestly office is assumed in the work that such a monk had to do. The priest in a monastery is no less a monk than the lay brothers; and a lay brother is no less a monk than the priest. Their work within the monastery is different. While manual work is the normal accompaniment of worship, prayer, and study, some monks, says Augustine, may have to set it aside in order to give time to ecclesiastical obligations and to teaching the doctrine of salvation.[43] A monk with the necessary education may be called upon to use this in a service for his brothers which takes him away from the common work of the group but which is nonetheless an expression of the monastery's ethos. His role is one that must keep him at the heart of the community's life; in interpreting the scriptures he not only opens up to the brothers the treasures of God, but he also opens up the common life and the life of each individual to the searching light of God's revelation. His function is both moral and religious. But this does not mean that he is the group's leader. The qualities of the leader are somewhat different; Augustine discusses them chiefly in chapter VII, 3.

Here in chapter IV, 9 the aspect of the priest's responsibility that is evoked is his power to direct in accordance with sound judgment.

This is not an arbitrary precept on Augustine's part. The priest's role in the situation belongs to his office. The verb used is *pertineo*, which implies whatever is wholly consistent with a way of life. The same word is used with a negative in chapter V, 1 where Augustine says that it is unfitting for a monk to complain about the clothing given to him; in chapter V, 3 it is used of anyone who has links — a belongingness — with a member of the community; and in chapter VII, 2 it refers to the responsibility inherent in the office of the prior.

In the monastery, the priest need not have been concerned with the earliest stages of the misdoing of the erring brother, but when all the other persons involved have failed to bring about a change of heart the matter must be referred to him. It is because of his power to discern and his knowledge of the ways of salvation that he is the one who must make the decision as to how best to help the wayward one.

The priest has a key function in maintaining the unity of the group. So many factors can disturb that unity. Where the discord stems from inherent diverse human tendencies which it is well-nigh impossible to eradicate, unity of heart can usually only be restored by an acceptance of the one by the other, by living and letting live. But when these tendencies have spilled over into deliberate wrongdoing, then unity is fractured. The matter has passed beyond the point where patience and tolerance have the power to reform, for when the will is set against reformation, unity is broken (and it does not need an open scandal to bring home this truth to generation after generation within monasteries, for this is a common enough experience). A hasty reading of the text might give the impression, based simply on the sequence of statements, that it is the priest who must take the final, irrevocable step of dismissing the unrepentant malefactor. But it is not he who effects the expulsion: his part is to use his particular charism in order to bring about repentance and a change of heart. If he fails, then the wrongdoer must be separated from the community.

WRONGDOING AND THE WELL-BEING OF THE GROUP

The reason why this particular wrongdoing may have a severely damaging effect on the whole community — it could, says Augustine, cause destruction (*perdere*) — is that it is a denial of the asceticism which forms the bedrock of monastic life. The whole matter of the relationships within the life of a monk as an individual is very complex, but the touchstone by which these may be tested is whether they tend to the building up of the whole community or to its destruction — and today we realize that this need not be across the male-female boundaries. What the fourth-century monk is doing when he begins to derive meaning and satisfaction from his encounters with a woman is to give ground against the temptations which from the beginning beset the ascetics of the desert. In the twentieth century, when the understanding of the meaning of persons and the place of sexuality in human living has shifted considerably from that of the earlier period, it is not easy to grasp precisely the terms of reference which Augustine brings to bear on the case of a lapse by one monk in Hippo; but the demons that the ascetics were bound to combat were the irrational impulses of their own nature which had to be brought under control and disarmed. If one soldier defects the whole sector is in danger; or, to use Augustine's analogy, if one monk gets an infectious disease, all in the monastery are in danger of catching it. If one ascetic abandons the struggle that his way of life necessarily involves, then he is weakening the work and witness of the whole group. That is why Augustine insists that it is a merciful act when those responsible for averting disaster are obliged to take drastic measures in relation to the defaulter — drastic, too, in relation to the whole community for they involve a rending of the fabric of the common life in a deeply hurting way.

EXCLUSION — THE LAST RESORT

In advising that the incorrigible wrongdoer should, for the sake of the community, be expelled Augustine was following St. Paul's counsel in 1 Corinthians 5.[44] Paul himself was evoking Deuteronomy 13:5, and his doing so indicates the category in which he set the sexual irregularity that he was condemning: idolatry. What lies at the heart of the evil is the turning to an object of worship other than God. *If your eye causes you to sin, pluck it out and throw it away*, Jesus said (Mt 18:9); and here, too, it is entrance or non-entrance into close communion with God that is at the heart of the situation. If one member of the group persists in withdrawing his primary assent from God, if he no longer lives in unity of heart and mind with his brothers but pours his energy, interest and devotion into an external relationship, then his membership in the group is broken *de facto* if not *de jure*. As Roger Schutz pointed out in the statement that he made at Taizé on Easter Day, 1970, when announcing the plans for the inauguration of the Council of Youth, what happened in the early Church when the unanimity described in Acts 4 was broken was that "tensions became divisions."[45]

By persisting in his uncharacteristic behavior the monk has divided himself from his brothers, and in taking the drastic step of expulsion the community is making explicit the intention of the wrongdoer even if he himself has declined to leave of his own accord. In advising this expedient in extreme cases, Augustine not only had plenty of precedent within the general Christian tradition; more specifically, it had had a place in monastic tradition for a long time. Pachomius had sought to protect his community in the same way;[46] and so had Basil. Basil (in the Shorter *Rules* 281) even says that a nun who will not sing the psalms is a corrupting influence and for that reason she should be expelled. His statement on the attitude of the community toward a disobedient brother is in many respects what Augustine advised:

> As for one who shows hesitation in obeying the commandments of the Lord, in the first instance all should sympathize with him as a sick member of the body and the superior should try to cure his infirmity by his private admonition; but if he perseveres in disobedience and will not amend, then the superior must correct him sharply before all the brethren and apply methods of healing by every method of exhortation. But if after much admonition he is still unabashed, and shows no improvement in his conduct, he becomes his own destroyer, as the saying is, and with many tears and lamentations, but nevertheless firmly, as a corrupted and utterly useless member, we must cut him away from the body after the practice of doctors. For they too, whenever they find one member affected by an incurable disease, are accustomed to remove it by surgery and cauterization, so that the harm may not spread further, corrupting the neighboring parts by its continuity with them. We too must of necessity adopt this course in the case of those who hate or oppose the commandments of the Lord. . . . For kindness in such cases resembles the uninstructed complacence of Eli, which he showed toward his sons . . . such spurious kindness toward the wicked is a betrayal of the truth, a plot against the common good, an accustoming of men to sin lightly.[47]

For both Basil and Augustine, there is the double obligation to protect the wrongdoer and also the community, and the same medical analogy occurs. But it is Augustine who goes the further in prescribing ways of safeguarding the one who is at fault; and it is he who lays down the series of protective measures that are designed to give the defaulter the maximum opportunity to mend his ways without becoming an object of censure for the whole community. If paragraphs 4-7 are confused, they do but reflect vividly the complexities which result from willful wrongdoing that has no regard for the well-being of the community and which has to be met with great compassion.

THE BROKEN FELLOWSHIP

There is a deep hurt in all of this — hurt to each individual including the wrongdoer himself, and hurt to the group as a whole. The brother has broken the fellowship of the group, fractured its togetherness, placed himself beyond its reach in the orientation of his relationships; and it is because of this that, in consideration of the well-being of the whole community, "he must be expelled from [its] fellowship" (*de [uestra] societate proiciatur*). We have already seen the richness of Augustine's understanding of *societas*. Fellowship is the flowering of unity; and unity is rooted in the willingness of each one to live in accord with his brothers at every level as and when it is uncovered. Thus incorrigibility — which creates tensions in any case — will inevitably itself create division, if it is not overcome. We cannot pretend that this precept of Augustine's is not a hard saying, but it merely reflects the hardness of heart that is in the wrongdoer. Expulsion from the monastery will clearly free such a man from a painful and ambiguous situation and as such it may make him a happier man; but the damage that his behavior and its corollary have done to the community is such that the expulsion cannot give happiness to the rest of the members; they are the ones who suffer from the breaking of the fellowship. Assent to the separation is for each one a very costing act of compassion that is wrung out of him by the overriding necessity to protect his brothers and all who know the monastery from the harm that a flagrant breach of its ideals inevitably creates.

What began, in paragraph 4, as an unpleasant example of misdemeanor by a member of the community has by the time Augustine reaches this point at the end of paragraph 9 become a matter of real suffering and challenge for the whole group. Compared with the distresses that differences of temperament and character create, the situation that is unraveled in chapter IV is vastly more painful. But it is through this shared experience that the deepest meaning of community life comes to the surface. In the following paragraph Augustine reaches the very heart of his understanding of monastic life.

Rule, Chapter IV, 10

And what I have said about not staring unbecomingly
should be applied carefully and faithfully

to the discovery, warning, reporting, proving and punishing
in the field of other sins too,
and that with love of the persons
and hatred of the offenses.

It seems inevitable to ask whether the circumstances that have been explored in the preceding six paragraphs refer entirely to an actual series of events within the community, or whether Augustine has used an hypothesis in order to consider the matter of sin among the brothers. It is only in this present paragraph that the word sin (*peccatum*) is used; in all of the foregoing it only gradually emerges that what the monk had begun to do has hardened into sinning. But there is no indication in the text as to whether the occurrences alluded to are fact or fiction. They may at the beginning refer to an established fact and then lead on fictionally to a discussion of persistent sinning by a brother; or perhaps the whole plot of the story was spun from Augustine's imagination; or the community of Hippo may have had to suffer in the whole miserable sequence of events. There is perhaps a faint indication that the first of these possibilities is nearest to the truth, for when referring here to the subject matter of the preceding paragraphs, all that he says is "about not staring unbecomingly" (*de oculo non figendo*). We cannot be sure, and that does not matter. That such a course could occur has been demonstrated many times down the centuries.

The chief importance of all that Augustine has been working out in paragraphs 4-9 is not the events created by one monk but the conduct of the community in the face of it. Augustine meant his readers to take his writing seriously, and he stresses this by the use of the word *obseruetur* (should be applied). It was pointed out earlier that this word is used solely in emphatic places in the *Rule*. In chapter I, 1 it introduces all that Augustine has to say about the struggling striving for unity within the group; here in chapter IV, 10 as also in chapter VIII, 1 it is used in relation to his fundamental notion of love (*dilectio*).

However, before we go on to explore this, his supreme characteristic of monastic life, we must first examine what he has to say about the matter of correcting one another, for it is from within situations of disturbance, sin, and suffering that the deep and the challenging meaning of love emerges.

Augustine says that what he has written should provide the normal pattern for any brother or group of brothers who are constrained by circumstances to correct one of their number whose behavior is overtly sinful. Once the discovery has been made a warning should be given; if this is ignored, the matter should be reported; following on the report, its truth must be investigated; and if the report is confirmed, then the wrongdoer must expect some form of censure or punishment (*inueniendis, prohibendis, indicandis, conuincendis uindicandisque peccatis*). At whatever point reformation and repentance occur, at that point the sequence is broken. Augustine worked out the sequence in relation to a monk's sexual misbehavior, but he realized that other grave offenses can be committed within a monastery. An unchecked roving eye can lead to the rest of the sorry story; a filching of food can lead to theft; a complaining attitude can lead to destructive subversion. If a brother begins to show these or any other weaknesses that could destroy the unity of the group, then members of the community have the responsibility to point them out to the offender.

What Augustine has to say about corporate responsibility will find echoes in twentieth-century minds that are conditioned by our present understanding of mutual responsibility, even though the sequence of correction may now not need to be taken as seriously as he meant it to be when he wrote it. This is the only part of the *Rule* where exact procedures are laid down, and this may indicate the exceptional circumstances which evoked them. What is far more important is the spirit in which correction is given and received. Today, the notion of men's accountability to and for one another is in tune with Augustine's.

RESPONSE TO SIN IN THE CHURCH — FORGIVENESS

However, his precept in this matter is rooted in a set of circumstances that no longer obtain. Christian moral law was still barely formulated, and the relation of wrongdoing to correction and of a wrongdoer to those with the power to correct him was still undefined. Crime and punishment were regulated by civil law, but the relation of the doer to his deed had other than civic dimensions and particularly so for Christians.

In the early Christian period there was no system of sacramental confession, with its provisions for privacy and secrecy, such as was developed later. If sin was open and manifest, so was its cure; if the sinner was publicly identified, so was his corrector. The distinction which moralists now make between a misdeed as a crime and a misdeed as a sin was unknown to Augustine and his contemporaries as well as to his predecessors. The conception of the public nature of crime and the private nature of sin lay many centuries ahead. For Augustine and his world, if crime was manifest, so was its sinfulness; if the one required open and direct intervention, so did the other. All Christians were in some way responsible for the suppression of wrongdoing and the reformation of the offender, but the means at the disposal of those who would cure him of his malady were limited.

The problem was: What symbols could represent the fact that the forgiveness of God could reach the sinner? Or, to put it another way: What symbols could show that the sinner could be reconciled with God and with his fellows? Or again: What could symbolize the forgiveness of sin? Man, made in the image of God, must be a forgiver as God is; or rather, he must reflect God's forgiveness in thought, word, and deed. That is the meaning of the symbolic acts of the Old Testament that are echoed in the New. If God's forgiveness is to meet men's sinfulness, then men must be ready and able to think and act in terms of reconciliation. Luc Verheijen has pointed out[48] that in addition to what the wrongdoer said to God in his private prayer, and in addition to his reparation of fasting and almsgiving, there was by Augustine's time a well-established custom of using the Lord's Prayer at the eucharist as an important rite of reconciliation within the Church. Christians whose life had any depth were in the habit of saying meaningfully and with all their heart, "Forgive us our offenses as we forgive those who offend us."

The publicity of both an offense and its correction could be taken for granted; but what Augustine was striving to do in the *Rule*, which concerned the close-knit and more-than-usually public life of the monks, was to ensure that what was done toward an erring brother was done with the utmost integrity, purified of meanness, vindictiveness, vengeance, and all the rest. Reconciliation could not be effected if the correctors themselves had motives and methods that were worldly (indeed, of the *saeculum*) and self-regarding, and if they had anything in them that was not capable of being used for the restoration of the wayward one.

At the end of paragraph 9, Augustine used two words which pointed to the depths in which he was trying to root all that he had been saying in the preceding discussion: fellowship (*societas*) and compassionately (*misericorditer*). Here, in paragraph 10 which is marked by the almost solemn word *obseruetur* (should be applied), he adds further dimensions: all that he is enjoining is to be fulfilled "carefully and faithfully" (*diligenter et fideliter*). Faithfulness demands the utmost integrity. It is not a matter of meticulous, detail-observing procedures that regard Augustine's "discovery, warning, reporting, proving, and punishing" as a series of steps that lead from crime to punishment. Fidelity cannot exist without a sensitive awareness of the real nature of the sin that is involved in the wrong, of the areas of temptation that are experienced by both the wrongdoer and his corrector, and of the over-arching fact that it is God who alone can heal, cure and re-establish a man however broken he may be. One man can only reach out to another forgivingly if he is aware that he too lives only because of God's mercy, because he too needs forgiveness. In the *Rule*, Augustine seems to be striving, in a somewhat labored way, to express the overwhelming nature of true reconciliation, the extremes to which a man must be prepared to go if he is to mingle compassion with justice. It was not until later that he came to express this, almost literally, unrestrainedly:

> If Christ has forgiven your sins seventy seven times only, and has refused to pardon beyond that, then you also may fix that limit and refuse to go beyond it. But if Christ has found thousands of sins on top of sins and has nevertheless forgiven them all, then do not you withdraw your mercy but grant the forgiveness of that great number (Sermon 83, 3).

Augustine's other adverb is *diligenter* which I have translated as "carefully." The force of its meaning lies in its verb-form; *diligere* means to love and to cherish. The verb occurs twice in the *Rule*: in chapter IV, 5 where Augustine writes about the wayward monk who attracts a girl's attention delighting (*diligit*) in her response, and in chapter VI, 3 where he describes the real concern (*beneuolentia*) with which a monk loves (*diligatis*) the brother whom he has had to call to task. *Diligenter* is a beneficent word, implying here not only care for the righting of wrong but also care for the restoration of the wrongdoer if that is possible. And even when there is no softening of obduracy and no desire for reconciliation so that expulsion is inevitable, even here all must be done from within a heart that cares and cherishes.

In other words, all the painful precepts of the preceding paragraphs can safely be pursued by the brothers if they have the capacity to love. Augustine's use of the adverb leads him straight on to use for the first time the word that is central to his understanding of monastic life, and indeed to all Christian living: *dilectio* (love). There has to be love of the person we are encountering, whatever the circumstances of the encounter.

THE CHALLENGE OF LOVE

"With love of the person/with love of the man" (*dilectione hominum*), says Augustine. The nature and meaning of the experience of this very human capacity was for him an integral factor in the search for God which engaged his whole life. His explorations took him beyond the togetherness of friendship at Cassiciacum and Thagaste, into the diversified group at Hippo for whose benefit the *Rule* was written. And here, as we have seen in the preceding paragraphs of chapter IV, he finds that love must face the agony of sin, betrayal, and the breakdown of relationships. Luc Verheijen has suggested[49] that the reason for the stringency of Augustine's precepts in the face of a monk's failure to accept the demands of celibacy is that he himself had not at that time considered deeply the meaning of either virginity or marriage (*Holy Virginity* and *The Excellence of Marriage* were written at the beginning of the fifth century). For him, at the beginning — as for almost every other man or woman at the beginning of his or her life in a monastery — to adopt that way of life merely implied not marrying.[50] The meaning of celibacy can only be discovered and appropriated into one's own being as one continues in this life. It seems that in 397 Augustine had not yet unraveled the knots of experience that were later to find expression in his understanding of marriage as a sacred sign (*sacramentum*),[51] a symbol of the transforming power of God's grace within human situations. And it was not until later that he came to see in deliberately-undertaken virginity the sign of a person's total gift of himself to God. In *Holy Virginity* 8 he says that virginity is "held in honor, not because it is virginity, but because it is consecrated to God"; and later in the same treatise he shows how that consecrated life is essentially Christocentric, opening every layer of being to the deepness of a relationship with him that is shown in the "joy of the virgins of Christ, in Christ, with Christ, after Christ, through Christ, for Christ" (*Holy Virginity* 27).

But, as we have said, that clarity of understanding had not emerged when the *Rule* was written. Yet it is evident that Augustine is already on the way to making that discovery. Already the centrality of love was fundamental to his thinking. Neither marriage nor celibacy can be deeply understood unless there is a concomitant understanding of love; and love cannot be understood unless and until it is discovered in adverse circumstances. Love is not a theory.

For all Christians, love is a focal word, rooted in the life of Christ, explored in the Bible and made explicit in the lives of individuals. It is Christ who provides the terms of reference by which love may be recognized. It is in the Bible that the meaning of love is searched for and drawn out, and what the New Testament writers were doing in their evocation of love was to relate what they found in Christ to what they found in the lives of their fellow-Christians.

The contribution of the evangelists to the understanding of love lies in their portraits of Christ. In the synoptic gospels the pictures are left without title, but John describes the Lord's activity in terms of God's love. Commentators have supplied titles for the other three gospels, but it is only in the fourth that there is explicit mention of divine love as the motivating power in the life of Christ and in the relationship between him and his followers (chapter 3, 16 and chapters 14-15 *passim*).

In the letters the phenomenon of love and man's response to it is more deeply explored. Paul's first references to the exercise of love[52] are in Philippians where he says that growing love leads to growing knowledge and discernment (1:9) and that love makes for unity of heart and mind (2:1-2). In 1 Corinthians he takes the next step, in 8:3, when he writes that love, as a response to God, means that the believer is open to be known by him. Later, in 13:12, he says that being known (and who does not long to be known?) will in the end be complemented by knowing God oneself: understanding will be complete in the light of love. Galatians 5:14 provides an insight which relates the work of love to the character of the Christian: *through love be servants of one another*. In Romans 5:5 he refers to the source of love: it is God's love that is poured into the hearts of Christians through the gift of the Holy Spirit. In 8:28 this thought is developed further and God's outgoing love is perceived as eliciting a response of love in believers who in the light of their experience of him can detect his purpose and activity in all things; this experience gives confidence and security to the Christian who, as the previous verses show, is well aware of his own inadequacy: *We know that in everything God works for good with those who love him.* The manifestation of a love-relationship between the Christian and God begins to appear as cooperation. Then in verses 35-39 fullness of response, the unifying potency of the two-way movement of love between God and those who believe in him, is described as something that can hold within its compass all disaster and strain and can resist all deterrents, whatever their power and their source:

> Who shall separate us from the love of Christ? Shall tribulation, or distress, or persecution, or famine, or nakedness, or peril, or sword? . . . No, in all these things we are more than conquerors through him who loved us. For I am sure that neither death, nor life, nor angels, nor principalities, nor things present, nor things to come, nor powers, nor height, nor depth, nor anything else in all creation, will be able to separate us from the love of God in Christ Jesus our Lord.

Further on, in chapter 12, this security lies behind the exhortation to extend love to one another, recognizing each one's great worth that is due to the fact that he is beloved of God (verse 10). In 13:8-10, the exchange of love between Christians is described as the height of self-giving. It is love alone that is able to release the power of goodness into any set of circumstances however distressing they may be. True love can never wrong another person. Finally, at the end of chapter 15, when Paul commends himself — fears, needs, and all — to the prayers of his readers, he takes deeper still the thought that he had first expressed in 5:5; such love is the love of the Spirit himself. And this love of the Spirit is inextricably related to Christ: *I appeal to you, brethren, by our Lord Jesus Christ and by the love of the Spirit* . . . (verse 30).

The letter to the Ephesians explores the working of this love, beginning — as in Romans — with the thought that it is God's love that is active in those who believe in him, making them his sons: *He has destined us in love to be his sons through Jesus Christ according to the purpose of his will, to the praise of his glorious grace which he freely bestowed on us in the beloved* (1:5). Here we find an intimation — not a fully worked out image or a developed sketch — of the movement of love. It is in chapter 3 that the hinted-at dynamism of love is fully articulated in the prayer to the Father *that according to the riches of his glory he may grant you to be strengthened with might through his Spirit in the inner man, and that Christ may dwell in your hearts through faith; that you, being rooted and grounded in love, may be able to comprehend with all the saints what is the breadth and length and height and depth, and to know the love of Christ which surpasses knowledge, that you may be filled with all the fullness of God* (verses 16-19). The challenge of love lies in the fact that it is a mystery, that it remains indefinable, that it can embrace contradictions without being false, because of its knowledge that what is known is less than all. Love can dare to accept what it cannot grasp: this is the *forbearing one another in love* which is asked for in 4:2. Later in this chapter the discovery is made that love makes possible the exchange of differing opinions and outlooks. Love of its nature is constructive, not destructive: *Speaking the truth in love, we are to grow up in every way into him who is the head, Christ, from whom the whole body, joined and knit together by every joint by which it is supplied, when each part is working properly, makes bodily growth and upbuilds itself in love* (verses 15-16). But this readiness to accept and absorb others who are different from ourselves is always costly. However much love unifies and constructs, a part of it is always experienced as a denial of what it proclaims. Love is always sacrificial, in the sense of a giving away of oneself and an abandonment of one's own self-interest. *Be imitators of God as beloved children, and walk in love, as Christ loved us and gave himself up for us, a fragrant offering and sacrifice to God* (5:1). God's love is sacrificial.

The insight of this passage brings us close to the most extensive treatment of love in the New Testament, that of the first letter of St. John; and it is this letter which has the greatest bearing on our understanding of the *Rule.* The letter begins with an evocation of fellowship and joy that is made possible for those who, even though they are sinners, accept the revelation of God in Christ. The remedy for sin is one aspect of God's gift of love to men; his love calls forth obedience in its recipients, an obedience which in the nature of things must result in counteracting the downward drag of sin. The search for the truth of God is frequently hindered by men's sinfulness, and it is only obedience to his commands that can unblock the way for the effective working of the power of his love. It is in the man who keeps (*observes*) God's word that love for him is perfected (1 Jn 2:5). Chapters 2-4 seek in various ways to describe the ontology of love — its source in God and its characteristics manifested in human beings are always considered in conjunction. The themes interweave.

Here we need to note the close relationship between obedience, knowledge, understanding, action, and faith which together and severally express the three-way movement of love from God to humankind, from men and women to God and from individuals to each other. The trials and the temptations that assail Christians are felt with their full weight throughout the letter — they are a matter of experience, but an equally potent experience is the prevalence of love in all circumstances. Love is not an abstract but a power that transforms. Love is expressed in obedience, and obedience means keeping God's commandments: *And his commandments are not burdensome* (1 Jn 5:3). The fulfilling of God's commandments goes on all the time, yet it remains a spontaneous act that is renewed in each fresh situation; there is no compulsion in the love that Christians must exercise.

Saint John's penetration into the meaning of love has a direct bearing on what Augustine has to say in the *Rule*. Over the twenty-year period following its composition he found himself thinking more and more deeply about the nature of love, and this finally bore fruit in his commentary on 1 John. In this work the word that is habitually used for love is *dilectio*, the same word that is used in the *Rule* and in the Latin version of the Bible that was available to him. Although he uses the word sparingly in the *Rule*, its meaning which is explored so deeply in the commentary is in fact integrated into the monastic precepts. It is therefore legitimate to relate the explicit discussions of the former to the implicit evocations of the latter.

The first chapter of the *Rule* is concerned with the ways in which true unity is to be formed within the community. At that stage Augustine is not prepared to evoke love as the motivating force in unity, for to do so at that point would be to over-simplify the issues and to evade the problems involved. Yet, at the heart of the matter and when many deep deterrents have been faced in a spirit of humility, it becomes clear that the one single factor that is able to embrace contradictions, fears, and tensions is love itself. It is love that creates unity; or, as Augustine put it in his commentary, "Christian love is altogether of one piece, and as itself is compacted into a unity, so it makes into one all that are linked to it, like a flame fusing them together" (*Homilies on the First Letter of John* X, 3). Now we can go further and say that what makes diversity possible within unity is the operation of love which alone is able to fuse together disparate elements. For what love brings to situations where there are many points of view and modes of behavior is the power to bear all for the sake of that unity which lies at the heart of community living. "The lover of his brothers," Augustine wrote, "endures all things for unity's sake" (*Homilies on the First Letter of John* I, 12). This aspect of the work of love becomes very evident whenever a monastery goes through a time of great strain because of diversely held views on many of the major issues that confront the Church at any time. Not all members of a present-day group think alike on, for example, racial matters, or the ordination of women, or even the community's role in society; but while a few may leave or retire to the fringes of the common life, the great majority of members willingly remain within the group because the community itself is what supremely expresses the wide-openness of the unity in God into which all Christians are called. True tolerance is only positive and constructive when it is based on love for other people. Intolerance destroys love.[53] Love as a living factor within the relationships of a community is what makes explicit the fact that God is at the heart of the monastery's life. But behind that shared love is the fact that each member is himself enabled to love, to reach out from his own self into the self of others. For Augustine, personal loving and the indwelling of God are themselves a unity: "If you begin to love, God has begun to dwell in you. Love him who has begun to dwell in you, so that by a more perfect indwelling he may make you perfect" (*Homilies on the First Letter of John* VIII, 12). Taken out of context, this sentence might be thought to refer to a Christian's love toward God; but it is Augustine's comment on 1 John 4:12: *No one has ever seen God; if we love one another, God abides in us and his love is perfected in us.* The indwelling of God, which forms so important a part in Augustine's understanding of monastic life, is what makes possible the completeness, the perfecting of men and women. But such a process of perfecting requires a winnowing and sifting of the good from the bad. It is not enough to be able to see and note words or behavior, for they are conditioned by many factors. The ability to discern truly what is going on in oneself and in others, and to assess its origins and effects, is something that is only possible in a person who looks outward with the eyes of love and speaks in the tones of love: "it is love alone that discerns the sons of God from the sons of the devil" (*Homilies on the First Letter of John* V, 7). If love can discern, love also is the way of healing. In chapter IV, 5 of the commentary Augustine says that Christ took the form of a servant in order that he might bestow form and comeliness on those who have been deformed, distorted, and stained; and the wholeness and beauty given by God is, he says in chapter IX, 9, the "love of charity" (*dilectionem charitatis*).[54]

THE CENTRALITY OF LOVE IN THE *RULE*

This brings us to the point when we must try to interpret what Augustine means when he uses the word *dilectio* in the *Rule* and also in all the passages that we have given from the commentary on 1 John. It is the noun-form of *diligo* which means to select, to make a choice, hence to value or esteem highly, to love, to be fond of doing. So the noun *dilectio* describes the kind of love that values what it loves for the very lovableness of its object, that can weigh up and hold in balance all the stirrings of men's hearts and minds, thoughts, and deeds, as they live in relationships — with themselves, with other people and with God. John Burnaby, in his study of Augustine's understanding of love in all its aspects,[55] defines *dilectio* as "the love of conscious preference,"[56] the love that enables a man or woman not only to discern between values but to choose the best. This is what Augustine explores in *Homilies on the First Letter of John* II, 11. Choosing is always a qualitative function, and when love is the motive for choice it must involve a deep sharing and releasing of what is good and beautiful in the other. This bringing-alive applies equally whether the self or another or God is the object of love.

While "the love of conscious preference" may stand as a definition of *dilectio*, a vivid description of it is to be found in an essay by Peter Brown: "Dilectio . . . for Augustine, stands for the orientation of the whole personality, its deepest wishes and its basic capacity to love. . . . It is dynamic: it is a criterion of quality that can change from generation to generation."[57] The basic capacity to love is the mystery that is so profoundly explored in John's first letter and its meaning may come alive for the reader who, as an exercise, substitutes *dilectio* or "loving concern/care" for every occurrence of the noun "love" in the text, for that is the word and the meaning that presented itself to Augustine when he read it. The capacity to love is also the theme that is explored with so much discernment and realism in the remainder of the *Rule*. All that is encountered within the fabric of the community's common life is to be seen with the eyes of the whole person who desires above all to accept others, in the continuing stream of changing situations, as those in whom God wills to create form and comeliness.

It would have been untimely if Augustine had begun his *Rule* with the key notion of love, for then it would have been very difficult to draw out all the sad and soiling aspects of the struggle to create true unity within the monastery. All the weaknesses and sins of ourselves and of our brothers and sisters are part of the material from which the community is made; equally, all the ideals and aspirations which each one holds are the ground in which the common life is rooted. The deep acceptance of these two strands in community life is only possible when love is paramount. The kind of love that Augustine says must lie at the heart of the life of the monastery necessarily involves a deep caring for all one's brothers, and caring itself must involve the exposing of all one's own weaknesses if one is to reach into the weaknesses of others. As Henri J. M. Nouwen has put it, "To care one must offer one's own vulnerable self to others as a source of healing."[58]

"With love of the persons and hatred of the offenses. . . ." It is within the context of laying open one's own weakness that the full meaning of Augustine's precept is to be found. In relation to the self it is comparatively easy to distinguish between the self and the self's faults, and one does know what it means to love one's self and hate one's ever-present sins. In relation to other people, the edges get blurred and there is a strong tendency to equate the sinner with his sins and to direct toward him as a person a justifiable rejection of his offense. And it becomes all too easy to hide behind abhorrence of another's faults and to refuse to accept him as the same sort of weak and sinful person as oneself. *Look to yourself, lest you too be tempted* is the advice of Galatians 6:1 to those who have to act against a brother who is overtaken in any trespass. In the commentary on 1 John Augustine reminds his readers that one does not love a wrongdoer for what he is as a wrongdoer but for what he may become, for that is how God loves sinners.[59] For those members of a community who have responsibility for maintaining the common well-being (a responsibility which in some measure falls on each one) and who must on occasion take strong measures against a wrongdoer, there must always be great watchfulness on motives and on reactions. It is possible to err in two ways. One can confuse the offense with the offender and reject the person as well as his wrongdoing. And one can be so identified with the person in a spurious relationship that his offense is accepted and condoned. Both these weaknesses lay strain on the unity of the group as a whole. Augustine's admonition about keeping the distinctions clear is very important indeed for the healing and health of each member of the community as well as for the group as a whole. The conscious preference which lies at the heart of the sort of love that Augustine is talking about is compounded of affection, happiness in fellowship, caring concern, discernment, respect for truth, faith, obedience, and reverence. It takes most of us a lifetime to learn how to love with such love; and that is why it is so right that it should be set at the center of the precepts of the *Rule*. Living together in a monastery, we inevitably find ourselves discovering the faults of our brothers and sisters; unless we can meet these offenses and their perpetuation with an over-arching love there can be no unity, no justice, no growth, no peace. Such love is the one factor that can hold a community together, for only love can reach into the depths of others and not be repelled by what is to be found there.

When love is at work, then true unity, true togetherness, is to be found. Up to this point, the *Rule* has been primarily concerned with the ways in which individuals are to be helped to live the common life of the monastery; from here onward, it is the community as a whole whose ways are discussed. The working-together of a wrongdoer and the community forms the basis of the considerations of the last paragraph of chapter IV.

Rule, Chapter IV, 11

Someone may have gone so far wrong
as to receive letters or little gifts secretly
from a woman.
Then, if he confesses of his own accord,
he should be dealt with gently
and prayer should be made for him.
But if he should be found out and proved guilty
he should be corrected more strictly
at the discretion of the priest or the prior.

AGAINST SECRECY

As throughout the *Rule*, a general problem of behavior is set in a concrete situation, whether hypothetical or actual it is impossible to tell. If one of the brothers has established prohibited relations with a woman it would be natural (even if unwise in the circumstances) for her to write to him and to send him gifts. And in all probability he would keep this to himself. And there is another aspect of the matter which T. Van Bavel has pointed out: "In antiquity, a letter was in its nature something public; where secrecy was involved in an exchange of letters it was always a matter of love letters."[60]

In any case, to retain something for oneself is a singularly un-monkish thing to do since the handing over of possessions and having all things in common is one of the hallmarks of monastic life. Previously the monk was faced with a temptation against his commitment to chastity; the corollary of this is an abandonment of commitment to poverty and total sharing. Augustine here makes no attempt to uncover motives, nor does he labor his point in this short paragraph which stands in marked contrast to the analyses of the preceding ones of this chapter. It suffices that the contingency he has just described is an offense against the common life, whatever its motive.

CARING LOVE

The chief concern here is how the matter is to be dealt with in a spirit of caring love. He first postulates that the wrongdoer make a clean breast of his offense against the community. There is no indication as to whether this happens publicly or in private; but whether the one or the other is the case, he is treated gently. *Parcere*, which I have translated as to deal gently, means to spare, to avoid inflicting injury. Thus Augustine is urging the brothers to accept the offender as Jesus accepted sinners, with care and concern. And the wrongdoer is to be prayed for (*oretur*). We noted in chapter 2 that in the *Rule* Augustine's treatment of prayer is discursive and not concentrated. There is something very tender in the way he introduces it at this point: he simply says *oretur* (let him be prayed for). There is no rhetoric and no analysis of different facets of the prayer that is to be offered for the offender. He is simply to be surrounded with prayer, and that means surrounded also by love. He is to be given open love in exchange for the little things that he had kept hidden; he is to be accepted as one of themselves by those whose way of life he had come near to rejecting; he is to be treated with a gentleness which can build upon the humility of his own confession. The confession itself shows that the process of healing has already begun in him and it is through the prayer of the group (which includes the wrongdoer himself) that integrity and wholeness can be restored, for it is through prayer that the risen Lord makes his power available to those in need of it. Here the *Rule* echoes James 5:16: *Confess your sins to one another, and pray for one another, that you may be healed. The prayer of a righteous man has great power in its effects.* When a man is very battered in spirit, his prayer is a cry for help; it is then that the prayer of others on his behalf must carry him as the friends of the paralytic carried that man and laid him at Jesus' feet for healing. There is no place for judgment here, no necessity to stand at a distance; what the penitent needs is forgiveness which is mediated to him through his brothers. When he knows he is being held in the prayer of his brothers he can have the courage to face himself and the consequences of his failure. Thus a real fellowship begins to be formed between himself, his brothers and God. This is real community. Augustine has brought his monks to the point where the common life is subsumed in true community. Their patterns of life and their strivings to accept one another have acquired a new dimension: the brothers can now experience the fellowship of love.

Common life and common prayer are the fruit of love, not the means of attaining it.

Yet in the day-to-day and the generation-to-generation development of a community's life no reached position ever becomes static. The fellowship of love is at once experienced as present and as not yet. What is being healed in one member may still be concealed in another, and the realism of Augustine will not leave his readers in a false utopia.

It can happen that the recipient of letters and gifts is impenitent and that the exposure of his offense is not of his doing. Here again there is moderation in the precept. He must not be allowed to continue in his misdeeds, but neither must he be subjected to a strictly-laid-down form of correction, nor subjected to the judgment of the whole community. Whatever approach is made to him in his need, it is to be decided by one of the two people who are principally responsible for the good of the community — the priest or the prior. It is not the business of each and every brother to set about reforming a wayward one — if that were so, there could be little room for the free movement of love within the group. Fraternal care, fraternal concern, and fraternal warning are the expressions of responsible love in the community; but for the sake of unity in freedom correction is rightly limited to the two

members whose office gives them particular insight and authority.

The members' freedom, and therefore their development toward maturity, is safeguarded by the discretion of the priest and
the prior for in the nature of things they have the widest horizon
in which the life of each individual is to be seen. In paragraph 9
when the community's priest is first mentioned, he is placed after
the prior; here in paragraph 11 his role appears to be the leading
one. In the situation discussed in paragraph 9, his help was needed
when a monk's weakness was placing him at risk at a stage when
Augustine considered it to be primarily within the competence of
the prior to steer the waverer and the community through that
particular crisis. Here, Augustine is concerned with a state of
affairs where a monk's chief impetus has moved from within the
group to outside it, where a part of his being is removed from the
demands and the concerns of the common life. Such a one is
becoming a divided person and only a part of him is, as it were,
now in an ontological relationship with his community and so
with its prior. But the community's priest, because of his priesthood, is always set against a wider background: he speaks in the
name of the whole body and for that reason he has a greater means
of access to the wrongdoer. He can speak in the name of all
Christians, not simply in the name of the community. In the early
centuries (though this is not necessarily true today) the priest, as
we have already seen, was the one who had studied the scriptures
deeply and thought through their application to the lives of men
to a degree that was not possible to the laity. He was both leader
and teacher. He was the one who could set the wrongdoing in a
wider perspective than was possible for the group of monks living
together. He was the shepherd skilled in caring for the flock and
bringing back the sheep that strayed. For Augustine, the shep-
herd-image of the priest was a very important one.[61]

And here, at the end of this long and often troubling-chapter —
which, after all, reflects the troubles and the pain and the bewil-
derment that can beset a community in any generation — Augustine leaves the wrongdoer and his wrong, the sinner and his sin,
with the priest who in the name of the Church and in the name of
the community will seek to correct him and bring him back to the
full life to which he first committed himself. The priest would be
powerless without the love of the brothers, sinners, and wrongdoers also; there would be no community for the strayed one to

be restored to unless all the members were loving and accepting and also very humble; there would be no reality against which failure could be seen, without the fidelity of prayer which carries each member into the oneness in Christ to which they are all called.

This short paragraph 11 forms the firm bridge between the two parts of the *Rule*. Until now, the main emphasis has been on each individual monk's adaptation to the demands of the common life. This life itself is to be characterized by a deep unity which binds together the disparate members of the group. It demands recognition of the positive and negative aspects of each personality, of each one's strengths as well as his weaknesses and sins. This life cannot exist unless it is vitalized by a dynamic love which is strong and courageous as well as tender and compassionate. In this paragraph the approach to a monk's failure is positive and accepting. There is no suggestion of his being rejected because of his actions even though they do in fact represent a more advanced stage in an undesirable relationship than that of the eye-contact that gave rise to the *Rule*'s whole discussion of this sort of difficulty. The wrongdoer, however his wrong comes to light, is to be dealt with gently, surrounded with prayer and helped toward healing. Such an attitude is love in action.

It is with love in action that the next chapter of the *Rule* is concerned.

NOTES

1. See *Letters of St. Jerome* XXII, 16, 3, volume I, translated by Charles Christopher Mierow, *Ancient Christian Writers*, Newman Press/Longmans, Green, 1963.

2. St. Paulinus of Nola, *Letters* 22, translated by P. G. Walsh, *ACW*, Newman Press/Longmans Green, 1967, pages 197-198.

3. Peter Salway, *Roman Britain*, Clarendon Press, 1981, page 655.

4. *Life of Augustine* 15.

5. *The Artifice of Ethics*, SCM Press, 1974, page 27.

6. *Virgins* I, 2.

7. See Derrick Sherwin Bailey, *The Man-Woman Relation in Christian Thought*, Longmans, 1959; Ruth Tiffany Barnhouse and Urban T. Holmes, *Male and Female: Christian Approaches to Sexuality*, Seabury Press, 1976; Peter Brown, *The Body and Society: Men, Women, and Sexual Renunciation in Early Christianity*, Columbia

University Press, 1988; Dorothea Krook, *Three Traditions of Moral Thought,* Cambridge University Press, 1959; Lucien Legrand, *The Biblical Doctrine of Virginity,* Geoffrey Chapman, 1963; James B. Nelson, *Embodiment: An Approach to Sexuality and Christian Theology,* Westminster Press, 1971; Philip Sherrard, *Christianity and Eros,* SPCK, 1976.

8. Job 31:1; Sir 9:5.8; Mt 5:28.

9. Henry C. Lea: *History of Sacerdotal Celibacy in the Christian Church,* Williams & Norgate (4rd revised edition), 1907, Volume I, pages 109.

10. Canon 33. See Henry C. Lea, *op. cit.,* page 108, note 2.

11. Henry C. Lea, *op. cit.,* page 105, note 1.

12. *Ibid.,* page 110.

13. Letter 22, 13, 1.

14. Derrick Sherwin Bailey, *op. cit.,* pages 19-102. The whole chapter contains a full account of the texts.

15. *Ibid.,* page 70-72, citing the literary evidence of the "canonical letters" of Basil of Caesarea, and the conciliar evidence for the fourth century and beyond. Augustine's own writing showed the same characteristic, for example, *Soliloquies* I, 25, and, later than the *Rule, Confessions* X, 41.

16. Luc Verheijen, *Nouvelle Approche de la Règle de Saint Augustin,* Abbaye de Bellefontaine, 1980, pages 124-125 (hereafter *Nouvelle Approche*).

17. See the whole of chapter III in Bailey, *op. cit.*

18. *Spirituality and Love,* Herder, 1965, page 226. For a general study see Paul M. Conner, *Celibate Love,* Sheed & Ward, 1979.

19. I have used the 1975 edition published by the University of Notre Dame Press. Chapter 1 explains Lynch's thesis which the rest of the book attempts to substantiate. His book is concerned primarily with the literary imagination but he also shows, in chapters 7 and 8, that the same may be true for what he calls the theological and the Christian imagination.

20. See Sherrard, *op. cit.,* page 14.

21. Nelson, *op. cit.,* page 106, and see the whole section, pages 106-109.

22. For example, Job 11:11; 23:10; Ps 32(33):13-14; Wis 1:8; Eccl 15:18-19; 23:19; Mt 6:4; Heb 4:13. I am indebted to Luc Verheijen for these references, and here and in much of what follows I have been guided by his essay on chapter IV of the *Rule* which appears in *Nouvelle Approche*, pages 107-150.

23. See Verheijen, *op. cit.,* pages 118-120, where similar passages are discussed: Eccl 9:5.8; Job 31:1.

24. See *Nouvelle Approche*, pages 112-113.

25. See above, chapter I, note 2.

26. For example, Mt 9:13; 10:34; 20:28; Mk 2:17; Lk 12:50; Jn 1:17; 9:1.39 (here the Lord's compassion in healing the man born blind and the controversy that this aroused are immediately followed by his statement: *For judgment I am come*); 10:10; 12:27.44-50.

27. See Letter 10:2.

28. AV, RV, and RSV have retained these words, so weakening the force of the sentence.

29. Despite its wrong placement in Jn 8:3-11, there seems no reason to doubt its historicity — see the editors' note U in JB.

30. Mk 2:3-5.

31. See Hans von Campenhausen, "The Origin of the Idea of the Priesthood in the Early Church" in *Tradition and Life in the Church*, Collins, 1968, page 217.

32. Johannes Quasten, *Patrology*, Volume III: *The Golden Age of Greek and Patristic Literature*, Utrecht/Antwerp: Spectrum Publishers, 1960, page 237.

33. Paulinus, *Vita Sancti Ambrosii* 6-9. See F. Homes Dudden, *The Life and Times of St. Ambrose*, Clarendon Press, 1935, pages 64-74.

34. J. N. D. Kelly, *Jerome: His Life, Writings, and Controversies*, Duckworth, 1975, page 58 and note 3.

35. Johannes Quasten, *op. cit.*, page 425.

36. Letter I, 10, to Sulpicius Severus (*Letters*, trans. P. G. Walsh, ACW series, Newman Press/Longmans Green, 1967), Volume I, page 37.

37. *Life of Augustine* 4; Sermon 355, 2.

38. *Sermon* 2, 2, to Amandus.

39. Hans von Campenhausen, *op. cit.*, pages 227-228.

40. In what follows I have drawn on Verheijen, *Nouvelle Approche*, pages 394-401.

41. Incidentally, this was Augustine's own reason for asking his bishop for time off for study immediately after his ordination (see *Nouvelle Approche*, page 266).

42. See Saint Basil, *Shorter Rules* 64 and 231.

43. *The Work of Monks* 19.

44. See *Nouvelle Approche*, pages 110-114; also pages 322-346 for a full treatment of Augustine's thought on necessary rejection.

45. I have only seen a duplicated copy of this statement.

46. See Philip Rousseau, *Ascetics, Authority and the Church*, Oxford University Press, 1978, pages 53-54.

47. *Longer Rules* 28 (W. K. Lowther Clarke, *op. cit.*, pages 193-194).

48. *Nouvelle Approche*, page 115 and note 15.

49. *Nouvelle Approche*, page 149.

50. The same undeveloped attitude to celibacy is to be found a century later in the *Rule* of Saint Benedict. See Daniel Rees and others, *Consider Your Call*, SPCK, 1978, page 157.

51. See Bailey, *op. cit.*, page 89, note 4: "Augustine . . . expressly describes marriage as a sacrament," referring to *The Excellence of Marriage* VII, 6; XXIV, 32, and *Marriage and Desire* 1, 17.21.

52. Here as earlier I follow the dating of the canon as given in the Jerusalem Bible.

53. There is a fuller discussion of this matter in John Burnaby, *Amor Dei*, Hodder & Stoughton, 1947, reprint, pages 102-103.

54. See the Maurist edition of the works of Saint Augustine, Volume III, columns 2576-2578.

55. Burnaby, *Amor Dei*, Hodder & Stoughton, 1947, reprint, note 140.

56. The same phrase occurs also in Hand, *op. cit.*, page 51.

57. *Religion and Society in the Age of St. Augustine*, Faber, 1972, page 42.

58. Henri J. M. Nouwen and Walter J. Gaffney, *Aging*, Doubleday Image Books, 1976, page 97.

59. *Homilies on the First Letter of John* VIII, 10.

60. "The Evangelical Inspiration of the Rule of St. Augustine," *Downside Review*, (1975) 84.

61. This appears succinctly in a later writing, Sermon 46.

5

Love in Action

Rule, Chapter V, 1

You should keep your clothes in one place
under the care of one or two persons, or as many as are needed
to keep them shaken out and free from moths.
Just as you are fed from a single storeroom
so you should be clothed from a single wardrobe.
As far as possible,
it should be a matter of indifference to you
what is supplied for clothing
according to the season — whether you receive what you left off
or another garment which someone else has had before —
so long as no one is denied what he needs.
But if quarrels and murmurings arise among you on this account,
and someone complains that he has received something that is not as good
    as what he had before,
and he considers that it is beneath his dignity
to wear what another brother has worn,
this shows how far you are lacking in holiness
in the interior clothing of the heart
since you dispute about the clothing of the body.
But even if concession is made to your weakness
and you do receive what you left off,
what you put aside must still be kept in one place
by those who are responsible for all those things.

LOVE IN THE COMMUNITY

We said above that the final paragraph of Chapter IV formed a bridge, and certainly there is a great contrast between the territory of the first part of the *Rule* and the area in which its readers and hearers now find themselves. Augustine has moved right inside the monastery which is the place where all the searching, commitment, and love of the brothers is to find expression.

Each man brings into monastic life all the formative influences that have made him what he is, and in the discussions of chapters I-IV each man's background plays an important part in the process of discovering what this new way of living is all about. All the varying stimuli that prompt thought and action inevitably create tensions. And tension is in some aspects a good and necessary element in creative situations; tension is not the same as stress. The art of living consists largely of holding tensions in balance. This is the function of caring love.

The whole of the second part of the *Rule*, in which the corporate life of the community is explored, is based on the fact that there is love among the brethren and that they love one another. Love exists as a factor that is common to all the members, creating their unity; it exists also as that which enables caring and accepting relationships between person and person. When love is alive, it holds diversity in unity, and it also welds all disparateness into a whole. In the ancient world and for many centuries after that time, all those who evoked love — above all Jesus, Paul, and Augustine — were primarily aware of it as ministering to need in a collective form;[1] and this is an important fact to bear in mind throughout the remainder of the *Rule*. In the first four chapters, which were principally concerned with the building up of unity among the brothers, there was comparatively little reference to the rules and customs that were observed in the monastery. In the second part of the *Rule*, when love is the dominant feature, many more of the community's rules come under scrutiny. On the surface, this seems odd; but I do not think it is, because it is only when love is paramount that constancy has any real value. Rules without love are tyranny, but rules that express love ensure freedom. That is why rules have to be flexible and even need to be changed from time to time. There is a valuable analysis of the place of rules in communal life in a book by James B. Nelson.[2] If love is taken to be what he calls the central moral norm for each person, then rules can be seen as illuminative maxims that may or may not give appropriate guidance in a given situation and may be disregarded if not serving a person's best interests; or they may be regarded as always relevant but not necessarily decisive. To regard rules as a moral absolute, binding in all circumstances, is to disregard the needs of individuals and also the well-being of the group. This theme is exemplified in all that Augustine has to say in his explorations of community life, from small matters to great.

THE SHARING OF GOODS

Having brought the monks to the discovery of the central place of love in their lives, Augustine — in chapter V — goes on to describe love in action, and here in this first paragraph he looks at its working in the ordinary little things of daily life.

Throughout chapters V-VIII there is a recapitulation of the main themes of chapters I-IV, and in fact this return to the primary themes does take place in the bridge-paragraph, chapter IV, 11. We pointed out earlier that the monk who keeps his friend's gifts to himself is reneging from his commitment to the demands of the common life; he is failing to hand over his possessions so that they may be held in common (chapter I, 3 and 4). Now, in chapter V, 1, the subject of having all things in common is discussed in terms of domestic details — the sort of details that in an institutional setting become regulations but in a group of friends living together are just the-way-things-are-done. The details require the cooperation of all the members, not merely their observance of them. In fact, love in action as it is described in these precepts could also be described as cooperation among brothers.

First Augustine is concerned with the monks' clothing which was first mentioned in chapter I, 3; like everything else, it is to be kept in common. There are two methods of keeping a common supply of goods. One is to put them all together and leave every member free to use what he wants when he wants it, and the other is to put them in one place under the care of someone who is responsible for keeping them in good condition and distributing them when they are needed. The former way may be practicable for some goods; but for clothing, one has only to think of a dusty little old shop with piles of unsold stock and of a clothing bargain counter in a big store to realize that in neither case are the articles responsibly handled. Failure to take good care of the community's goods is a failure in voluntarily accepted poverty. And, as the practical Augustine points out, there are always the depredations of moths to be guarded against. So it seems that his precept of giving some particular brothers responsibility for looking after the supply of clothes is the wisest course.

Being put in charge of any part of the community's work is a challenge. It will bring out the best or the worst in a person, or both. Such people may approach the job with a zeal that conceals and then reveals latent aggression. They may respond to their own fears with the tyranny of a perfectionist, they may be insensitive to the needs of others to such an extent that laziness and neglect are the result, or they may so identify themselves with their work that for them it assumes paramount importance.

Responsibility[3] operates on two fronts: it controls the doer's relationship with his task, and also his relationships with the community for whose sake the task is done. Thus the primary problem that has to be recognized and solved (although this may in some instances take a long time) is how to create unity on this double front. When a brother is put in charge of a certain sphere of work he tends to see either the task or its beneficiaries as his chief concern; in fact there is a more fundamental necessity, namely his ability to see what he has to do within the context of the whole life of his community. Responsibility requires a high degree of flexibility and self-sacrifice that is not capable of achievement without deeply caring love. And it is impossible to love without sometimes being hurt, disappointed, and frustrated. A brother who is accountable for any detail of work (and from this point of view everyone in the monastery has a position of responsibility) must be prepared to face distressing claims that may come to him from many directions.

The physical, nervous, and mental energy required for the job is an obvious claim; so is the actual set of circumstances under which the work has to be done (how one would like to know the amount of space that was available for the community's clothing at Hippo, and what precautions were taken against moths!); so is the time that can be given to the job, in relation to all the other obligations of the monk's life; so is the fact that his assistants, if he has any, are also experiencing the pressure of these claims; but the most important claim comes from the varying needs of each individual whom he has to serve. It is at this point that the *Rule* goes deeper.

ATTITUDES TO WORK

From the mechanics of having a common stock of clothing for all the monks, Augustine goes on to discuss the attitude of each one to what he wears. There is a sensitive realism here that expresses a caring attitude: "as far as possible" (*si fieri potest*) — a phrase that accepts the fact that even the following of the coming precept is sometimes beyond the bounds of possibility. "As far as possible, it should be a matter of indifference to you" (*non ad uos pertineat* — which implies that no rights are involved) "what is supplied for clothing." The ability not to mind what one wears is something that varies in people. Some seem to have an impersonal attitude to clothes when they are young but become more conscious of specific tastes and needs as they grow older; others take a personal interest in their attire in their early years but care less later. A consistent indifference in this matter is as rare as sanctity itself, hence Augustine's "as far as possible." For most people, clothing is an expression of their person, and their attitude to it is an expression of both strength and weakness. In spite of the strong stress on the criterion of need throughout the *Rule*[4] and in spite of Augustine's exhortation here that those in the monastery must try to be indifferent about what is given them to wear, for most members of the group the factor of taste is almost ineradicable since taste itself is an expression of personality.

What Augustine is driving at here is a simplicity of outlook that comes from trust in God. *Do not be anxious about your life . . . nor about your body, what you shall put on. . . . Why are you anxious about clothing? . . . If God so clothes the grass of the field . . . will he not much more clothe you, O man of little faith. Therefore do not be anxious . . .* (Mt 6:25.28.30-31). Jesus' words are an amplification of his command to seek first the Father's kingdom and his righteousness, and he adds that for those who do that the Father's response will be the fulfilling of their needs. Thus what Augustine is evoking in this passage of the *Rule* is his earlier discussion of the trust that arises from true poverty of spirit in chapter I, 7. The man who knows that he is entirely dependent on God knows that what he receives comes to him as a gift and not as a right. (We should note in passing that at this point there is little exploration of the part of the distributor in the allocation of the common stock; that does not come until chapter V, 9-11.)

MIXED MOTIVES

It is the recognition of the motive for asking for things within the common life that provides the touchstone. A genuine need does not have to be pressed; it can be simply stated. Similarly, the motive for dissatisfaction with what is issued has to be looked at carefully. The reaction of the receiver is conditioned by the person that he has become. There will be willing acceptance by the monk who has reached the point of being truly dependent on the bounty of God; there will be undifferentiated acceptance on the part of the man who is striving to set aside his own foibles; acceptance will be grudging where there is much inner insecurity; there will be jealous comparisons where this insecurity spills over into discordant relationships; and there will be outright rejection when no attempt at all is made to come to terms with one's own inadequacies — they will be projected on to the supplier and the thing supplied.

QUARRELS AND COMPLAINTS

It is the projection of inadequacies that leads to downright quarreling and grumbling, though at this stage Augustine does not explore this aspect of community life; he does that in chapter VI, 1-2. He is not yet prepared to unravel the tangled motives that lie behind resentment and rejection, and all he does here is to point to the obvious fact that this can occur among the members.

Although there is little unraveling of the attitude of those who have to give out the clothing, at this point Augustine's choice of words does indicate what he expects of them. In my translation I have used "is supplied" for Augustine's word *proferatur*. The verb is literally an expressive one, implying not only a bringing forward but also a concern with the one to whom the gesture is made. It occurs three times in the text, and each instance is a telling one. In chapter II, 3 it is found in the phrase: "Meditate in the heart on what is expressed (*proferatur*) with the voice" and in chapter VI, 2 we find "let that mouth which caused the wound provide (*proferre*) the cure." In each case it implies a thoughtful and responsible awareness of the recipient as he is in himself, whether this be God or a fellow-monk. Where clothing is concerned, it is not only climatic conditions that influence judgment, but the prevailing conditions of each monk. When it can be assumed by all that personal needs are taken into consideration, then the tensions and fears that spring from each one's area of uncertainty are diminished and controlled.

There is a sensitive lightness of touch in Augustine's description of how disaffected members do express their disapproval — after all, he knew the men he was addressing and they would be able to put a name to the one given to complaining because he is issued something previously worn by someone else, or because its quality is inferior to the garment he used to have, or because he thinks he is too grand to be wearing things not made for him. It all sounds very silly, when it is set out like this; and this makes it easy for Augustine to make his chief point in this paragraph — that frightened or greedy concern over what a monk wears is at variance with the true purpose of his life. The link between holiness of living and acceptance of one's fellow monks was made in chapter I, 7. In chapter IV, 3 it was related to the witness of one's behavior in the presence of people outside the monastery, while in chapter IV, 5 Augustine was writing about behavior in the presence of God. Here in chapter V, 1 it is the holiness or otherwise of the monk's attitude to his own self and his own needs that the *Rule* brings to the fore. Attitudes to the provisions of the common life are, fundamentally, attitudes to one's own self. In being aware of the nature of his own rejection of this or that aspect of the common life, a monk is in fact beginning to open the door of his closed heart so that holiness may enter and assume control; or, to use Augustine's own metaphor, by attempting to discard the foibles and particularities that jeopardize happy relationships within the community a monk is allowing himself to be clothed with holiness which not only will ensure his own well-being but will also make him attractive to others.

BE CLOTHED WITH HOLINESS

Explicit reference to holiness is, then, comparatively rare in the *Rule*; and that is right, because it is always a gift given by God in response to men's striving. Holiness is always a result of something else; it is neither a means nor an end. *Be holy, for I am holy*, we find in 1 Peter 1:16, echoing and summarizing the Jewish law of holiness given in Leviticus 17-27. But, as the previous verse of the letter and the Levitical passages show, holiness is always reflected in conduct. And, as the letter goes on to say, for Christians holiness means more than conformity to a pattern. Becoming holy as God is holy implies the transformation of human nature in the power of the cross (1 Pt 1:17-21).[5]

Holiness comes to the Christian who seeks to be conformed to Christ, and in this way he is transformed by the renewing of his mind[6] so that by the love that is poured into his heart[7] he can give himself to and for others even to the point of extreme personal suffering. By evoking holiness at this moment in his discussion, Augustine deftly shows the absurdity of fussing and fretting about what one wears.

THE EXPERIENCE OF NEED

But then he goes on to concede that infirmity does create special needs and if the desire for particular clothing is genuinely based on that, then it must be fulfilled. This is in line with what he had said earlier about special food in chapter III, 3-5, and we can now see that the *dilectio* which was not mentioned then was at any rate governing his thought even if at that stage he did not find it appropriate to express it explicitly. And just as chapter III warned against the temptation to cling to dispensations, so here there is advice designed to reduce it as far as possible: garments not in use are to be put into the common stock and not held by individual monks. When a person is constantly aware of his need the ability to trust others becomes diminished; and it is in acute situations that a monk is most tested as to his willingness to leave himself entirely in the hands of God.

Real need is a real experience of poverty for all religious, and our whole life is a training in trustful self-abandonment. The way in which this training is incorporated into the pattern of the common life that is based on caring concern for one another is the subject of the following paragraph.

Rule, Chapter V, 2

So, then, no one should work at anything for himself.
All your work should be shared together,
with greater care and more ready eagerness
than if you were doing things for yourself alone.
For when it is written of love that it "does not seek its own" (1 Cor 13:5)
it means that it puts the common good before its own
and not personal advantage before the common good.
Thus the more you are concerned about the common good rather than your
    own,
the more progress you will know that you have made.
And thus the love which abides for ever will reign
in all matters of passing necessity.

UNITY AND SERVICE

It is in this paragraph that the togetherness of the community is most fully expressed, and we may note that such expression is described not in connection with acts of worship or of witness but in the shared ordinary things that make up the routine of those living in the monastery.

Augustine begins negatively: "No one should work at anything for himself" (*nullus sibi aliquid operetur*). This follows naturally from what was said at the end of the previous paragraph about having the trust to hand things over to the common stock where they will be looked after by those who are responsible for them.

Within the monastic pattern that Augustine has established among the brothers, to do things for oneself is a denial of one's total givenness to God within the community. This pattern is not one that now finds universal acceptance, since it can result in irresponsibility, opportunism, and immaturity; and it may well be that today common service in most things has to be offset by personal work in a few. But in all circumstances the spirit of Augustine's precept holds good; trustful sharing and concern for the well-being of others are the marks of love.

In this short paragraph, the antithesis between self-concern and the welfare of the community is stressed: both *communis/in commune* (that is, things that make up the common life) and *proprius* (one's own) occur four times. Self-concern is a strong factor in human life, and it can work either for a man's undoing or for his upbuilding. If it operates alone (and when Augustine is writing about this point he uses an isolating word — *singuli*, alone) then it turns back on itself and forms a circle which is an effective barrier between the individual and other people. But it can operate within a group and become a strength to others; this is possible when self-concern is balanced by concern for others. This requires effective coordination, and monastic life can provide a setting for the working out of togetherness, whether the group is large or small. In any teamwork, the first requirement is proficiency on the part of each individual. Sometimes a particular function is fulfilled by more than one person, yet each one has his own specific role. At the same time, there has to be as keen an awareness of the functions and capacities of the others as there is of one's own. The making of television programs has enabled us today to see the high degree of common awareness that has to operate in any joint undertaking, the quick reaction to the movements of another, the awareness of sudden stress and the ability to counteract it, the sheer concentration on a common objective. We have learned the importance of working together in any undertaking, and what this togetherness enables is the high value set on both the operation and the operators. All of this is what Augustine is describing when he says that work done in common should bear the marks of "greater care and more ready eagerness" (*maiore studio et frequentiori alacritate*). His use of *studium* is evocative of single-minded concentration on the matter in hand and an attachment between the doer and the deed; for that reason it seemed best to translate it by a word that implies relationship, and "care" seemed the most appropriate.

Such single-minded care, says Augustine, may not be used in one's own interest but — like goods themselves — is to be placed at the disposal of all: even a monk's skills are to be used according to the needs of the community. In theory it is easy to see the force of this, but to put it into practice is costing. The handing over of material possessions for the common good is a bagatelle compared with the problems that arise over placing one's abilities entirely at the disposal of others. There are those who force their expertise on the rest of the community, and in so doing cause resentment and insecurity; and there are those who never seem to be aware that their help might be useful. When it comes to asking a brother or sister to do something, the gospel itself points to the fact that some find it easier to undertake than to fulfill while others do fulfill what they are reluctant to undertake.[8] And, to confuse the issue even further, there is the uncomfortable fact that even the person who is always and at all times willing to be used may be motivated by masked self-indulgence.

Willingness to be used, then, is an attitude that challenges the integrity of each person. Augustine looked for a resolution of the tensions that work creates, by assessing it in relation to God; for him, a person's availability was the way of cooperating with God as creator, of honoring him as Lord and of serving him with a devotion that involves every part of one's being. Within the human condition, work usually contains an element of alienation and a part of the person remains withdrawn from commitment to the undertakings. This is always evidence of a lack of some sort. The lack may lie in a man's skill for the work, or his interest in it, or its place in his scale of values; it may lie in his inability to identify with the work's aim in either personal or material terms. Work for work's sake can never fully satisfy, for its sake lies beyond.

AUGUSTINE AND WORK

In expecting the monks to work for each other's good with eager readiness (*frequentiori alacritate*) Augustine was introducing a scale of values that was fundamental for him and which he later explored at length.[9] For God, work is not laborious and his creative work is entirely free in its spontaneity.[10] In him "the gulf between the seriousness of work and the fun of play is closed."[11]

For men, work has a penal aspect,[12] yet because work is primarily an activity of God it is also a way of return to him from alienation. Work itself establishes a creative relationship with God. Because work is capable of producing results that serve, enlighten, and enrich, it has great dignity. Yet the trivia of work do have the effect of belittling men if they are separated from their meaning in God, inside monasteries as well as anywhere else. Work, Augustine comes to learn, is man's way to the fullness of being. As R. A. Markus has put it:

> Labor belongs only to man's growth in maturity. It belongs neither to his archetypal childhood innocence, nor to his fully human eschatological stature. It is a discipline, an *askesis*; but a discipline not of purgation and purification so much as of growth. But from the primal state of innocence, through the growing pains of the restoration of wholeness, to the final achievement of mature manhood, the dignity of work is man's privilege. It is a far cry from Adam's work, work "without the affliction of labor but with exhilaration of will" (*The Literal Meaning of Genesis* VIII, 8, 15), to the work of toiling and sinful man. But in their essence, the two things remain the same: the worker "so to speak, lends his skill and ministry to God the creator in the service of nature" (*ibid.*, IV, 16, 29). . . . To the natural order as constituted by God man brings his rational powers and voluntary activity to exploit, to preserve and to enhance that power (*ibid.*). In this is to be found the excellence and dignity of human work . . . *magna haec et omnino humano* (*The Magnitude of the Soul* 33, 72) . . . "great and wholly human" — that is his verdict on human work and its achievement.[13]

Work relates to more than its environment, it relates also to the people who are in the environment; and in this respect it is to be seen principally as service. The work entrusted to human beings through the first Adam gave them domination over nature (Gn 1:28); the work entrusted to Christians through the second Adam gave them the power to serve others in a creative way (Mt 20:28; 25:44, 1 Pt 4:8-11). Service based on deeply caring and sensitive concern for others is liberating; it frees the receiver to be himself, to be open to others and open to God. It is the very opposite of forcing one's good will and good deeds on others, for it has to be closely attentive to the other. We have already found attention emerging as a necessary ingredient when we were considering the way to true unity within the group.

When Augustine came to set down his theories on the work that monks ought to engage in, he used another set of terms of reference: monks undertake work because they are soldiers of Christ.[14] This makes little sense today; but in the fourth century it said a lot for, as we saw earlier, a low-grade toiler and a soldier had the same social standing. Augustine did not write simply about warriors for Christ — conjuring up battles and heroic deeds in a holy war. Rather he meant that monks were — like soldiers — marked, controlled, having nothing of their own. For him, monks lived like soldiers in military service. Yet what for the factory worker and the soldier was degrading and depersonalizing became in the monastery a way of releasing love into every act done for the sake of another. It is in the two letters of Timothy that the soldier-image is evoked. In the first passage (1 Tm 1:18), courageous integrity is being discussed. In 2 Timothy 2:3-10 there is an interweaving of endurance and the work of a soldier which is likened to the toil of a husbandman (verse 6); but the reason for endurance is that deliverance will come — *salvation which is in Christ Jesus with eternal glory* (verse 10): the end of the campaign brings a glorious reward bestowed by Christ. As Augustine sees it, when he is writing to the monks of Carthage, the work of the soldier-monk is a sharing in the saving work of Christ and a sharing in his glory. And glory, as we saw earlier, was what Jesus perceived to be a vital fruit of his own oneness with the Father.

So there are two ways in which the work of a religious — any Christian's work, for that matter — is to be regarded as a partnership in the work of creation and also in the work of redemption. The work done is the same toil that occupies every other man, but the reason for doing it is different. For God's sake and for people's sake: that is the motive of work for the Christian. We are united with Christ the Son who was sent because God loved the world so much that he desired its salvation at all costs (Jn 3:16-17); and the cost of the release of love into the world was the lifting up of the Son in a life of love that endured through death.

DAILY WORK AND THE SPIRIT OF LOVE

In the monastery, all the ordinary labor of daily life has to be seen as a way of placing love at the center of living. To give primary importance to work as a means of providing food and clothing for one's brothers and sisters, or as a means of identification with all humanity, or as a means of justifying one's existence by earning one's living — all of this leaves out of account the true spirit in which it is to be undertaken in the monastery. Work is an expression of love.

In any group, a common undertaking creates a sense of belonging (and so, in the nature of things, it pertains to both creation and redemption). Belonging[15] gives meaning to activity and a sense of purpose; it also carries us beyond ourselves. Building, repairing, gardening, sewing, cooking, cleaning, studying, praying, playing — all of these are acts of service to one's fellow members forging links with each other in wholly individual ways. When a sense of belonging develops to the point where committed identity with the community is an existential fact, then the unity of heart and mind which were seen from the beginning to be the monastery's ideal takes flesh.

But the feeling of belonging can be ambiguous and stem not from fact but from desire, and for some people it may be an evasion of personal responsibility. It is possible to hide behind the group and use it as a shield. There are others who automatically talk about "we" when they mean "I," in an attempt to acquire an unrecognized need for security. Others again tend to use "we" as a path out of loneliness. In all such cases, what follows the plural word is a singular idea related primarily to the speaker. The person who really belongs to the group is concerned above all with his fellow-members at every level of their being. For such a one greater care and more ready eagerness do express outgoing love and nothing else.

In this context, where co-inherence is the matrix from which activity derives, action and service are acts of love. And it is significant that in this deeply revealing paragraph of the *Rule* Augustine twice uses the word *caritas*, using it for the first time (the only other use of it is in chapter VII, 3). Here both instances refer to 1 Corinthians 13: *love (caritas) . . . does not seek its own* and later *love . . . abides for ever*. Deeds of love which express the deep concern of *dilectio* cannot, in the nature of things, be self-seeking. The ordinary service that fills up much of a monk's time cannot be an end in itself, neither can its primary concern be directed toward the doer. It must always have the rest of the community in focus — an imperative that is far easier to talk about than to practice, because the self in each person must be satisfied if we are not to become diminished. This means that in calling for unselfishness within the community Augustine is doing something else as well: he is challenging the members to seek their own good in the good of others, to be willing to set aside their own interests for the sake of the well-being of everyone else. Thus once more the theme of the search comes to the fore, and the path that has led each monk away from the *saeculum* into the monastery, and into the discovery of God within himself, now leads him by a more obscure way. For in the early stages of abandoning all for the sake of God, the issues are comparatively easy to identify, and one of the means of identification is — as it were — a reciprocity of understanding: what comes to the monk from outside himself corresponds with what he already experiences within himself. In this way, the journey of discovery is authenticated. But now, Augustine says forcefully that from this point onward authenticity is to be sought within the unknown territory of the personality of every other member. The search which caring love makes possible does not bring reassurance and validity to the seeker but to those whom he encounters on the way. It is when he finds himself more concerned with those whom he meets than he is with the journey he is on that he will know that he is on the right track and going in the right direction.

Augustine's neat play on words is so tightly packed here that in translation it is necessary to spread it out if it is to have the force that he gives to it: Love "puts the common good before its own and not personal advantage before the common good" (*communia propriis, non propria communibus anteponit*). Care for others is, he says, a sure indication of the presence of love in the heart, "and the more you are concerned about the common good rather than your own, the more progress you will know that you have made" (*quanto amplius profecisse noueritis*). The use of *proficio* is telling, because it means more than progress in the sense of gaining ground; it also carries the meaning of rendering service and making a contribution. Love upbuilds both the giver and the receivers. And it is because this is so that it is capable of abiding for ever — it is a continuing activity, working for God through persons toward persons, using what is at hand and transforming it into something of far greater value. Creation and redemption are one.

This is the quality of life that Augustine is setting before the Hippo monks in this paragraph of the *Rule*. Its landscape is the whole of experience within the monastery, and its horizon is the glory of God; but the position from which the whole is to be seen is the "matters of passing necessity" (*transitura necessitas*) which make up the daily life of the community.

Augustine turns next to look at these passing necessities in more detail — but always as one for whom *dilectio*, deeply caring love, is the primary concern. Throughout the *Rule*, as we have seen right from the beginning, the needs of the brothers have a very marked significance for the whole community. The experience of need can itself be an experience of unity. One is reminded of the prayer of Eric Milner-White: O Savior of the world, in need we are all one, needing thee.[16]

Rule, Chapter V, 3

It follows
that should anyone bring anything to his sons who are in the monastery,
or to others there with whom he has a particular link,
whatever the gift —
be it clothing or any other article that is considered a necessity —
it should not be received secretly
but should be given to the prior for him to put into the common stock
so as to be able to give it to anyone who needs it.

SEEING THE UNIQUENESS OF OTHERS

For Augustine, the consequence of recognized need is the desire to fill it. Because acts of love must predominate in the day-to-day demands of life in the monastery "it follows" (*consequens ergo est*) — one might almost say it obviously follows — that the means of filling needs must be available, and the material for this lies in the alms and gifts that come to the community. So the *Rule* turns back to the point that was made in chapter IV, 11: Whatever is given must not be privately retained.

In the previous chapter, the reason for this was the safeguarding of a member who might be establishing an undesirable relationship outside the monastery; here, the concern is for the building up of relationships within the common life. It is possible to interpret the theme of this present paragraph thus strongly because of what has gone before — the placing of loving care and selfless service at the center of the group's activities.

Earlier, we saw how the distribution and sharing of goods contributed to the unity of the monks; here, sharing is an expression of love that can look at others not only with compassion, but also with understanding. All people in need know well whether the person who relieves it is aware of him as another person or only as an individual in need. To give and to love are not the same thing: in fact, it may often not be appropriate to speak of a giver at all — a supplier is more accurate. So it is significant that in this paragraph Augustine emphasizes the monks' "necessity" (the word in different forms occurs three times). We showed earlier that while Latin has two words that English expresses by need/necessity, only *necessitas* has personal overtones while *opus* applies to administration.

There are no purely administrative overtones in the present paragraph. The original donor gives because this monk or that is his son or his friend. Here, the fact of belonging, which emerged in our consideration of the previous paragraph, now becomes explicit — and that not only in relation to the members of the group but also in their ties with family and friends. The monks are in the monastery but their relationships extend beyond it. Gifts are made because people belong to each other (*ad se pertinentibus*) and it is in this sense that all needs are to be filled within the group — not because there is a hole to be filled but because there is a person to be appreciated and loved. Giving to other persons establishes relationships and so contributes to the well-being of the group (in contrast with the destructive relationship which was expressed in terms of gifts in chapter IV, 11).

The deep experience of belonging has to undergo radical transformation when a person enters a monastery, and strained relationships with those from whom we are separated are a common experience. All the uncertainties and weaknesses that are concealed before separation come to the surface on both sides when one enters, and it often takes years of painful misunderstanding before a true set of relationships can be established. Sometimes the tensions are never removed: that happens when there is, somewhere along the line (and it need not be the family-and-friends' line), an absence of desire for understanding of the other and only the presence of a desire to be understood. Belongingness is something that is always in need of purification. It can go on expressing itself in terms of encounters and gifts, but it falls short of completeness until it loses itself in an attitude that transcends belonging and which I would describe as the appreciation of significance. The significance of each person is a crucial factor in the development of all relationships. It means seeing other people in their uniqueness, and being able to love them as they are.

Significance, however, has two parts. First there is the fact of identity itself, and then there is the fact — or conglomeration of facts — of the meaning of what is identified. But it is not possible to identify other people until one has begun to accept one's own identity. And this only becomes possible when one knows one is cared for, and there is always a series of movements — or rather, one movement which weaves together a number of themes, the themes of each person's being — in accepting and giving, being loved and loving. It is this movement which, as it were, attracts light and brings about illumination, making it possible to see into others.

Seeing into another with the eyes of love makes it possible to go beyond identifying him or her as a person; it enables the seer to give meaning to the one he or she sees. There is a vast difference between thinking *about* people and thinking *of* them. To be concerned about people's needs is a possible but limited way of reaching them as persons — limited because it operates from outside. To be concerned for people's needs means knowing them from within through an empathy in which one accepts the other's selfhood.

Seeing into others with the eyes of love enables one to accept them with judgment but without destructive criticism; it means using one's critical faculties, but using them toward the persons concerned and also toward all the circumstances that surround them. Then one begins to understand the significance of others — and to be recognized as significant is one of the liberating factors in human living. Within the monastery the distribution of the community's goods is an important way of giving each member a sense of his own significance, and the more that can be done in a personal way the easier it is for individuals to become themselves — and this is a process in which all members share because all are to some extent the channel through which goods become available. Every member of the community is called to give to the others, and every giving is a gift of one's self. As Noel Dermot O'Donoghue has said in another context: "The gift is the giving that is given. What is shared is itself a sharing. To love is to give the power to love."[17] This gives an added dimension to the precept of handing over one's possessions (chapter I, 4). The common good involves far more than daily work for the sake of others; it asks for the active concern of each one for the well-being of all, a *wanting* each to have what his need requires. Giving becomes sharing, and sharing becomes loving. And it is in the light of this sublimity that selfish holding on to goods of any kind can be seen for what it is: a sad undermining of the community's fellowship. When members seek by any means to have a prior claim on what comes into their hands by way of a gift, they give a higher significance to their own self than to the self of others.

At one level there is a problem here. How far is the desire of the original donor to be fulfilled? Ties of family, friendship, and gratitude precipitate the giving of presents by one person to another. And in community life it is not always easy to honor the intention of the giver. This is a difficulty with no cut-and-dried solution and probably it is best to accept the fact that there will frequently be pain for someone or other — for the one outside the monastery, for the one who receives the gift, or for the community as a whole. But the very acceptance of this pain should make each member more, and not less, sensitive to the feelings of others. All that is received needs to be regarded by the recipient as a gift to the whole community, and the disposal of it must rest with the person who is in the best position to understand the significance of each member — namely, the prior; and it may well be that sometimes he will know that the recipient is in fact the one most in need of the gift. Judgment must rest with him, for otherwise unity of heart and mind are impossible and not merely hard to achieve.

It was pointed out earlier that it is not until chapter VII that the relational aspect of the prior's office is considered deeply, while all the preceding references to him can be described as administrative. This present reference to him is the point at which administration (attention to the *opus* of others) begins to give way to personal caring (attention to *necessitas*). But his personal caring should always have implicit in it the personal caring of the whole community whose representative he is in relation to each member.

The important point which this seemingly superficial paragraph is making is that love needs to be able to give; and the material of the gift is an expression of the community's deep interdependence. Unity of heart and mind is truly created when the significance of each member is appreciated at its full worth. So much for the ideal; in the next paragraph Augustine singles out one basic area of difficulty and through it points the way to a deeper self-giving.

Rule, Chapter V, 4
Your clothes are to be washed
at the discretion of the prior,
either by yourselves or at the cleaners,
so that too great a desire for clean clothing
may not cause interior uncleanness of the mind.

ATTITUDES

No person is without significance. In community life no matter is so insignificant as not to merit attention, for the simple reason that the togetherness of the group has to be expressed in material ways that affect every aspect of living. There is a distinctly Monday-morning feel about this paragraph of the *Rule* and there is no dignity about its opening word: *indumenta* (clothes). Two other words were used earlier in the text. *Tegumentum* (clothing) occurs in chapter I, 3 and 5, in company with *uictus* (food) and here the meaning is generalized; *tegumentum* just means what covers a body. In chapter IV, 1 the word *uestis* is used when Augustine warns the monks to commend themselves by their behavior and not by their attire. It is a dignified word, meaning a robe, and it occurs four times in chapter V — first in paragraph 1, clothes are to be kept "in one place," then in 3 (when it may be a present from a relative or friend), later in this present paragraph (where its overtones are similar to those of chapter IV, 1) and finally in paragraph 9, "Those who have charge of the storeroom . . . should serve their brothers without murmuring."

But in the present passage a humbler word appears, signifying just garments, the things-you-wear. It is nearer to *tegumentum* than to *uestis*. Wearing apparel is too formal a translation, but the generalized notion that those words carry does cover the meaning of the Latin. For want of a better word and in order to express the Monday-morning atmosphere of the sentence, "Your clothes are to be washed" (*indumenta uestra . . . lauentur*) seems the most adequate translation.

The prior is not only the distributor of such clothing as is needed; he is also the one who must be ultimately responsible for its condition. It would be interesting to know such domestic details of the Hippo monastery as the laundry facilities and the service they fulfilled; but that cannot be. All that we can be sure of is that the community's washing could be done by the members or by "fullers" (*fullonibus*). That word has no exact modern equivalent as it concerns a particular method of cleaning cloth materials;[18] its meaning is wider than that of ordinary launderers because it is concerned as much with texture as with cleanliness. It seems best to translate it by the weightier word that is normally used in English: "cleaners" (but not dry cleaners, because the fulling process was a very wet one). Perhaps one may hazard a guess that the lighter articles of clothing were washed by the brothers and that the heavier things were sent to the cleaners. And one might hazard a further guess that what was sent and what was not sent was sometimes a matter of contention; so, says Augustine, the prior must decide what is to be cleaned by whom. Very probably the professionals made a better job of it, and it is not difficult to imagine the sort of criticism that might be made when clothing was redistributed.

Augustine had already shown his awareness of the demoralized attitude to clothes that a monk may have, and he had reminded his readers that they ought to be indifferent to what they have to wear (chapter V, 1). Here he goes further and warns about the results of being over-concerned with the condition of what is given to them. Those who complain about the actual garment that they receive are reminded that holiness is lacking in them. To those who grumble about the condition of what is given to them he now says that they possess an "interior uncleanness of the mind" — or, more accurately, interior uncleannesses of mind (*interiores animae sordes*). The play on words holds the readers' attention: but the seriousness of the fault of complaining, fussiness, and over-concern about clothing is stressed by the word desire that occurs at the end of the sentence. The Latin word is *adpetitus,* and this is the word which Augustine had used twice in verb form in chapter IV, 4 — to attract and encourage the attention of women is blameworthy. In each case, what Augustine is doing is to underscore the ultimate question which every monk has to ask himself in countless numbers of contexts: What is my main objective? Where is my mind set? To the extent that it is not set on a direct Godward course but turns into byways of self-concern, Augustine would say that it was unclean; and in this he was echoing the words of the Lord given in Matthew 15:10-20: *What comes out of the mouth proceeds from the heart and this defiles a man* (verse 18). A man's thoughts can completely defile his personality and disorder his whole life. This would seem to be how Augustine views the wrong seeking implied in his use of *adpetitus/adpeto* in this and the previous chapter.

The possibility of a monk's setting his sights on the wrong target is a recurring theme in the *Rule* and it has already occurred in chapters I, 5-7, III, 2-5, IV, 1.3-5.9.11 and V, 1-2 — for the downward drag of humanity's insecurity is no light thing. To live with God always in view is to live the life of eternity, or, to use Paul's phraseology, it is to live the resurrection life. Colossians 3 may be regarded by those in a monastery as a description of the whole trend of their life, and it touches on many of the themes that characterize Augustine's *Rule*. *If then you have been raised with Christ, seek the things that are above, where Christ is, seated at the right hand of God. Set your minds on things that are above, not on things that are on earth* (verses 1-2, which are evoked in chapter I, 6 of the *Rule*). *For you have died, and your life is hid with Christ in God* (verse 3, a theme which lies at the heart of a monk's response to his vocation). *When Christ who is our life appears, then you also will appear with him in glory* (verse 4 — we saw earlier the close relation in the mind of Jesus, in the high priestly prayer, between glory and unity). *Put to death therefore what is earthly in you: immorality, impurity, passion, evil desire, and covetousness, which is idolatry . . . anger, wrath, malice, slander* (verses 5-8), which express Augustine's thought that we have already discovered in chapters I, III, and IV and which he develops further in chapters VI and VII). *Do not lie to one another, seeing that you have put off the old nature with all its practices and have put on the new nature, which is being renewed in knowledge after the image of its creator . . . Christ is all and in all* (verses 9 and 11b, which embrace Augustine's understanding of the recreating indwelling of God that finds expression in chapter I, 8). *Put on then, as God's chosen ones, holy and beloved, compassion, kindness, lowliness, meekness, and patience, forbearing one another and, if anyone has a complaint against another, forgiving each other; as the Lord has forgiven you, so you also must forgive* (verses 12-13, which in the *Rule* finds expression in every single chapter). *And above all these put on love, which binds everything together in perfect harmony* (verse 14: Augustine in the *Rule* evokes harmony — in chapter I — before he evokes love — in chapter IV, 10 — but both writers' primary concern is with the close relationship between the two). *And let the peace of Christ rule in your hearts, to which indeed you were called in ihe one body. And be thankful* (verse 15, and within the context of monastic life as in every other expression of Christian living, it is love that is deeply concerned for the welfare of others which, as it were, disinfects all the defiling thoughts that come to the surface in day-to-day living — from the irksomeness of one's clothing to the irksomeness of one's companions). Inordinate dissatisfaction with what one is given to wear is symptomatic of a discontent with life in general that destroys any awareness of the utter dependence on the providence of God which is fundamental to monastic poverty. Augustine singles out clothing when he wishes to make his point, but every other object or set of circumstances within the monastery would have done equally well: we are all challenged by everything that comes to us, as to whether we will accept it in simplicity and thankfulness, utilize it with rebellion or reject it outright. Augustine's warning is a reminder to be aware of one's motives.

For of course in the matter of the condition of one's clothing there can be no hard and fast rule, since some people have a higher threshold of tolerance than others. This is one of the factors that the prior has to take into account when he establishes the community's practice about clothing and everything else — and in chapter III, 3-5 Augustine has already discussed this subject from the point of view of the brethren. The prior is bound to take into consideration the many levels of need of each individual and to balance these with the needs of others and with the total practicabilities of life within the monastery. And it is only when there is unity in love that the disunities of singular needs can be held in tension. It would be stupid to expect that all tensions can be overcome, because they are an expression of the human condition; and, indeed, if that were possible the result would be a dehumanized man or woman and sterile monotony. The value of learning to live in tension is that it leads to a rich creativity because then every occurrence is a field for invention and for the discovery of new aspects of living.

It is with unusual, or comparatively rare, aspects of living that Augustine is concerned in the next paragraph.

Rule, Chapter V, 5

Regarding the use of the public baths,
if someone is ill and this is necessary
he must not refuse it;
it should be done without murmuring, on the advice of a doctor.
Even if he does not want it
he must, at the command of the prior,

do what has to be done for his health's sake.
On the other hand, if he wants it and it is perhaps not expedient,
he should not yield to his craving
for sometimes he thinks that something he likes will be good for him
when in fact it is harmful.

THE PUBLIC BATHS

Many tensions are reflected in this paragraph, some of which are not as apparent in the twentieth century as they were in the fourth.

Illness itself inevitably creates tension: in the sufferer himself, in those who care for him, and in those who care about him. Cross-currents of conflict can so easily arise and it is all too easy for each person involved to consider his point of view as decisive; but this is never entirely so.

It is interesting, and surprising, to discover that it is in such a situation (and not at any earlier point in the *Rule*) that Augustine introduces obedience for the first time (the word occurs twice later, in chapter VII, 1 and 4). This is the first occasion, also, when the authority to command is mentioned (*iubente praeposito*) — and it is only referred to in one other passage, paragraph 7 of the present chapter, where it occurs again in connection with visits to the public baths. Clearly this was a matter that required firm decisions, and for that reason we must next seek to discover the acute difficulties which provoke the introduction of these related themes at this stage in the *Rule*'s evolution.

The experience of illness is in some measure an experience of being lost: one's world is the same but different, one's person is the same yet different, and the same is true of relationships. This is true of the patient as well as of those who are concerned for him or her. The interpretation of explicit requests, stated or unstated needs, apparent and hidden motives and the advisability or otherwise of acceding to them demands a listening heart and a loving ear. The skill of doctors can only penetrate into the experience of illness itself through the mediation of those in attendance. "What did the doctor say?" is a common first remark after he has gone away. Caring for the sick is an interpretative ministry, demanding many levels of cooperation. It often happens, as Augustine points out, that what the patient wants will only make his condition worse; and when that is so the task of persuading him to change his mind and drop the request requires patience, understanding, and love. But the patient's point of view is distorted by his illness, and it sometimes happens that no further discussion is possible. When that point is reached, then a firm decision has to be made and a direct order given by the one who has primary responsibility for the sufferer — and in the monastery this is the prior.

The question of making use of the public baths would be one that added to the ordinary tensions of illness, especially for Christians. Every city had its baths which, with public games, A. H. M. Jones has placed in the category of "essential luxuries";[19] their maintenance was a civic responsibility that was sometimes placed in the hands of contractors, and the amenities — waiting rooms, changing rooms, cold, warm, and hot baths — provided a place that surpassed mere utility and moved into the sphere of relaxing social exchange, rather like that of a crowded beach at a modern seaside resort. To read the description of the Pompeii bath in Rich's dictionary[20] and/or that of the illustrated guide, The Roman Baths, produced by the Bath Archaeological Trust,[21] is to discover something of the atmosphere of the public baths. Warmth, cleanliness, relaxation, freedom, excitement, camaraderie together contributed to an experience that could never be entered into in one's own home; yet at the same time the baths were a common factor in most people's lives. For Christians, though, with their awareness of separation from the world and their ambivalent attitude to the human body, the use of public baths did present problems in both East and West.

There had been no unequivocal resolution of the difficulty more than a century later, when the Palestinian hermit Barsanuphius was asked for counsel on the very issue that Augustine confronts in the Rule. Someone asked: "Since I am ill, and my doctor has ordered me to take baths, is it a sin?" To this he replied: "Bathing is not absolutely forbidden to a man in the world, when need demands it. So if you are ill and need it, it is not a sin. But if a man is healthy, it cossets and relaxes his body and conduces to lust."[22] Augustine does not consider the use of the baths by monks in good health, but the rest of his judgment is the same as that of Barsanuphius. Jerome, on the other hand and quite predictably, showed no such tolerance when he accused Jovinian of being particular about his clothing, liking good food, mixing freely with women, and also frequenting the public baths.[23] Thus there were bound to be arguments in favor of whatever point of view an individual Christian adopted. For the monks, Augustine says, the criterion must be necessity and expedience. The sole purpose of visiting such a place is the patient's health; and the sole reason for not doing so is the same.

THE RISK OF COMPROMISE

Translated into general terms — and it is in these that Augustine's precept is relevant in succeeding monastic generations — the problem is this: to what extent is a monk justified in running risks or seeming to compromise his standards by the things that he does and is seen to do? To what extent is it desirable to conform to either ecclesial or secular conventions? Once these questions are posed, it is easy to see that the area concerned is always variable, and that what is legitimate in one generation may be illegitimate in another. And that fact alone is a strong reminder that in all such matters there needs to be considerable flexibility in attitudes. Jerome's stringent criticism of Jovinian was for a long time upheld as valid, but in the twentieth century his assumptions find less acceptance. To his list of undesirable behavior one might today add the use of alcohol, tobacco, confectionery, radio, television, the theater, and much else. There are those both inside and outside monasteries who would consider these things unfitting for monks; but equally there are those, in and out, who find them acceptable. Augustine's insistence on need and expedience places all such problems within a limited, individual context. One cannot talk about what religious in general may or should do in these matters, but only about what one religious (or perhaps a group of religious) may or should do in a specific situation. What is done must not be motivated by personal craving or indulgence (*cupiditate*) but must be deemed to be of value for the person's well-being.

But the discernment of what is in one's own best interests is a very difficult thing, and for that reason there is value in the possibility of questioning and censure by others. While in many areas there can be a fairly objective stance, for most people there remains a certain field of self-knowledge and sensitivity that is heavily clouded; it is here that a religious is to some extent safeguarded by his or her community.

AGAINST MURMURING

It is all too easy for an ill person to want things that will only make him worse; and it is equally easy to worsen the condition by refusing to accept prescribed treatment. Augustine uncovers another factor that can militate against restoration to health: If the doctor prescribes bathing, this should be done without murmuring. The destructiveness of murmuring was first discussed in chapter V, 1, where Augustine condemned an individual monk's complaining about the clothing allocated to him; and the censure appears again in paragraph 9 of this chapter where a grumbling attitude in those who look after the community's resources is mentioned. In the present paragraph, it is the grumbling of a patient that is alluded to, his discontent with what is prescribed for his healing. Disappointment with what is asked of one is potentially a creative experience, for it enables a person to enter into an area that lies outside the limits of his or her own expectations; the acceptance of disappointment is possible in those who are in intention open to the movement and intervention of the Spirit in their lives. Disappointment is enriching when it is a partner to gratitude. But being disgruntled and complaining about one's lot is destructive, for it sets up limits to a person's ability to surrender to a situation as it is actually and as it may develop beyond the present moment. A murmuring patient worsens his or her own condition. Those who care for complaining patients have to learn to distinguish between habitual complaining which in the absence of illness would exist in some other form, and complaining that shows the inroads of disease into a person's character. The latter can be cured as the disease itself is cured; the former can, over the years, reach incurable proportions — and for this reason Augustine's repeated warnings are of great value. Murmurers — those whom Augustine later characterized as full of hatred, troublesome, turbulent, disturbers of others — are, he says, those "in whom the love of Christ is not perfected"; they are like the wheel of a cart that is forever creaking; but the one in whom the love of Christ is active is "quiet, peaceable, humble, submissive, pouring forth prayer in place of murmuring" (*Expositions of the Psalms* 132, 12). Murmuring is a sign of disunity.

If caring and giving are aspects of love, so also are acceptance and the absence of murmuring. Active love is always a two-way movement, requiring reciprocity for its effectiveness. Insecurity leading to craving (and this is true of both ill and well people) can be counteracted and assuaged by finding oneself in relationships that are founded on caring love. The problems that seem to lie below the surface of this paragraph about the use of the public

baths center on the ability to trust — whether one can trust oneself
and others in a potentially compromising situation, whether one
can trust the judgment of others as to their wisdom or their
integrity, whether one can trust oneself to the care of others. Only
the two-way movement of love makes such trust possible, and it
is trust that is discussed in the following paragraph.

Rule, Chapter V, 6
Finally,
if one of the servants of God has a hidden pain and reports it
he is to be believed without hesitation;
but if it is uncertain whether what he asks for can cure his pain
the doctor should be consulted.

THE EXPERIENCE OF ILLNESS

Trust is doubly assumed in this paragraph, once in the brother
who is suffering and once in those to whom he reports his condition. The ailing monk is here called a "servant of God" (*famulus
dei*) which, as we noted in chapter III, 5, denotes a household
servant/slave who is closely associated with the affairs of his
masters. In the earlier passage also, the phrase occurs in connection with the health and well-being of the community, but there
Augustine makes a general observation which assumes that all
the members are servants of God. Here, the condition of a single
monk is brought into focus. His act of trust lies in reporting his
state of health when there is no evidence of illness which others
could already have discovered: it is hidden (*latens*) but nonetheless real, and he asks for specific treatment. People's attitude to
illness in themselves differs widely. Some are too frightened of
disease to be able to articulate its presence; others are too frightened of being wrong in their concern and keep silent for fear of
making an unnecessary fuss; others again fear or even mistrust
(justifiably or unjustifiably) the reaction of those to whom they
should report their misgivings; and there are those who fear
doctors and treatment more than they fear disease. All of these
will be slow to report an unobservable malady. On the other hand,
there are those who find nothing easier than to talk about their
health, and here again there are many motives. Some people are
fascinated by disease in itself and speak of it in and out of season;
others can keep silent where other people's ill health is concerned

but are absorbed in their own and talk about it endlessly, whether it is real or imaginary; others are dogged with poor health and need to speak of it, either voluntarily or involuntarily. From the sufferer's angle, then, there are innumerable stresses and distortions which complicate the treatment of disease as well as the attitude of those who have to administer it. It is easier to overcome these very real obstacles in a community that is consciously striving for unity in love than it is among people whose fear encounters not love but another fear.

So Augustine shows a sure instinct when he counsels that reports of illness must be "believed without hesitation" (*sine dubitatione credatur*). *Sine dubitatione* does not simply mean without doubt, neither does it go to the other extreme and mean without skepticism; *dubitatio* allows for the possibility of uncertainty, and Augustine says that a monk's report of pain (*dolor*) must be received with the possibility of certainty. For that reason I have in translation avoided the strong word doubt and used "hesitation" instead: the brother is to be "believed without hesitation." That does not mean that what he says is to be believed explicitly but that his condition, real or imagined, is to be considered seriously — which is not the same thing as to say that it is to be considered serious. The monk to whom health reports have to be made must be someone who not only has skill but also has an accepting attitude to others and at the same time the ability to discern what lies behind the spoken words of his brothers. What he hears may or may not be a true description; and there is the further point that if specific treatment is asked for it may not be the most effective.

Thus, on the part of the monk who has care of the sick there has to be trust and the possibility of mistrust; and these contradictory attitudes, both essential, have to be yoked together so that each can move easily within its rightful track. To develop this skill challenges a monk (or anyone else, for that matter) to the depth of his being, and it would obviously be unrealistic for any group to expect of its infirmarians unerring judgment in every case. The patients (and everyone is a potential patient) have to accept this as a part of the human condition and as a factor in their own healing. But the involvement of relationships, especially when there is an inevitable element of mistrust, does need a neutral intermediary; and so Augustine suggests that when there is uncertainty a doctor should be consulted. His profession gives confidence to patient and to nurse, and to the extent that he is uncommitted in his relations with the members of the community his service goes beyond that of healing and extends to keeping open the channels of trust and communication between the sufferer and those who have the care of him. The truth that he speaks reaches toward each person involved and their common acceptance of it creates a bond between them, and such a bond is an extension of love.

The extension of mutual trust and love is explored still further in the next paragraph.

Rule, Chapter V, 7

If you should go to the baths,
or anywhere else where it is necessary for you to go,
there should be not less than two or three of you.
A brother who has to go out should not choose his own companions
but should go with those whom the prior appoints.

THE PUBLIC BATHS AGAIN

Again Augustine refers to the question of the use of the public baths; clearly this was a burning issue among the brothers and one in which flexibility itself was not always a sufficient safeguard against abuse. Paragraph 5 made it clear that such visits were permissible when they were necessary. Here the concern is with the safeguards that ought to surround the risks. The risks involved the vulnerability of the individual monk and the offense that his presence might give to observers. Since it was commonly known that Christians were not supposed to visit the baths, the sight of so obvious a Christian as a monk entering the place did lay itself open to adverse comment. If he were alone, his being there would almost certainly be illicit. If there were more than one monk going in, their presence could be presumed to be licit, and then both the brothers and their observers might gain reassurance.

But the paragraph reads as if Augustine was trying not to isolate this particular aspect of the monks' emergence from the monastery: the same general precept covers "anywhere else where it is necessary" (*siue quocumque ire necesse fuerit*) for the monks to go. And the reasons of caution and protection behind Augustine's insistence on companions were given earlier in chapter IV, 2-3.6.8-10. A new slant on his general precept is now to be found in his "not less than two or three" (*Nec eant . . . minus quam duo uel tres*). In chapter IV, 2, when he wrote that monks should not go out of the monastery unaccompanied, he was simply stating traditional practice. His specific references to two or three occur in chapter IV, 8-9, when he is describing different phases in establishing the fact of a monk's misdemeanors out of doors. And the mention of two or three again here in chapter V, 7 seems to point to their double function: the sight of monks together was to be seen by others as an apostolic gesture — they were behaving in a "monkly" manner, however compromising might be the place where they were seen, and the companionship of a group of monks was a safeguard against illicit behavior initiated by one of them or by anyone else whom they might happen to meet. Companions were in a very real sense guardians. Companions in any enterprise do generally act unconsciously as both protector and assessor — the very fact of sharing an activity makes us more aware of the factors governing the situation we are in and of our companion's strengths and weaknesses (as well as our own); both possibilities and impossibilities are perceived instinctively, and word or gesture can prevent disaster or indicate a disadvantage ("Look out — you'll get knocked down" — "Is that fruit really fresh?"). But two people are enough for that sort of valuable interplay. When Augustine mentions two or three, the note of caution is unmistakable. At a social level with no moral or ethical overtones, this sort of protection is obvious. If two monks enter any concourse of people, the probability is that very soon someone or other will have engaged one of them in conversation and in next to no time the pair will have been split up. But if a group of monks, even a small group, enters into a gathering it is much more likely that their cohesion and integrity will remain intact. If their group does become split up, it is very likely to be a result of their own initiative. Thus from the social point of view Augustine's protective advice is sensible.

But it seems clear that he was not confining himself to social protection. His insistence that a brother who has to go out should not choose his own companions has an air of suspicion about it, distasteful as it may be. Very difficult situations seem to be involved here. A particular monk needs to go out, for reasons of work, worship, or health (there is no indication that he would ever go solely for pleasure); and that means that he needs companions. It is common experience that each monk is happier and more at ease with some of his brethren than with others: some are a strain on his resources, others support him. Where his health and well-being are concerned, it is better that his companions should be people with whom he feels at ease, and for their part the companions will be of more use to one who accepts them than to a brother whose instinct is to reject them. So, once again, it is the office of the prior that is the decisive factor: he must appoint the companions. And this he will do, taking all the factors into account. When reasons of health are paramount, if the monks who are closest to the patient were among the more irresponsible members of the community, then they would not be chosen. If there were a deep-seated antipathy between the patient and the most reliable and level-headed brothers, then it might not be advisable for the prior to send them as companions. If either the patient or the companions were instinctive manipulators, then there would be hazards. The same is true when the expedition is a business errand; and there is the added factor that the companions should not be those who might antagonize the people whom they have to visit. On the face of it, it would seem that when the little group is going to church the choice of companions could be wider: but from the evidence of chapter IV, 6, the place of worship is a danger spot.

Thus the prior has no easy task in making provisions for the well-being of the monks when they have to go out, and the difficulty is one that Augustine appears to be fully aware of. Nonetheless — and this is characteristic of the breadth of the whole *Rule* — he makes no attempt to lay down a formula for conduct outside the monastery. The monks are "temples" of God, he reminded them at the end of chapter I; their behavior out of doors must always be in keeping with their holy state, he wrote in chapter IV, 3; and through their companionship with one another in an ever-increasing unity of heart the indwelling God can protect each one of them, he told them in chapter IV, 6. Having said all that, he leaves them entirely free to translate it into practice as they will; how they fulfill it is their own responsibility. The absence of prescriptions throughout the *Rule* and Augustine's trust in his readers to accept his general precepts leaves the doors wide open for great freedom within community life. For all the subterranean fears that are evident in this paragraph and in a large part of chapter IV, he knows that fear is not cast out by rules and regulations but by the power of love. But love is both strong and fragile. Its strength lies in the fact that it can bind what is broken, including the very fabric of relationships. Thus we may say that the prior's power to command is primarily the ability to judge and to act in a spirit of love; and it is this same love — the love that chooses to act and to think in accordance with all that is best in the community, in one's companions, and in oneself — that will carry each monk through all the challenges that he encounters as he fulfills the prior's command to go out with others. From chapter I onward, throughout the *Rule*, consideration for others is the twin foundation of the community's life coupled with the direction of their lives that is always God-centered. Care for others is to be a dominant quality in the lives of the monks, and Augustine proceeds to look at special situations where this care is needed.

Rule, Chapter V, 8

The care of the sick —
whether they are convalescent
or suffering from any bodily weakness
even if there is no fever —
should be entrusted to a particular person
so that he may obtain from the storeroom
what he sees each one needs.

THE LOVE OF THE SICK

If nothing is to be left to chance when an ill monk has to be taken to the baths, in the same way the welfare of the sick in the monastery must be safeguarded. An ill person, confined to his room or to his bed, can feel isolated, lonely, and neglected because each of the other members of the group thinks that someone else is caring for him — and whether the group is large or small this is indeed likely to happen if everyone has a full timetable anyway. Augustine, himself a busy man, yet has the sensitivity to ensure that in the monastery there is no neglect of an ill brother. Whenever anyone is ill, whatever the stage of weakness and incapacity he has reached, his care is to be made the responsibility of one particular person. The word which in that last sentence is paraphrased as "made the responsibility of" is *iniungi*, and it is difficult to find an adequate English word to translate it. "Enjoined" is accurate but sounds mannered in ordinary speech. "Imposed" is too formal to reflect the flexibility that characterizes the *Rule* as a whole; and the same applies to "charged with." All of these meanings are in a sense taken for granted when a monk is given a particular work assignment by his prior, but in his acceptance of the task a reciprocal element enters in just because of the unity of heart and the dimension of love which is a vital factor in all relationships within the community. For that reason, *iniungi* is here translated as "entrusted to." That does reflect the spirit of the community's life. All tasks given are given in trust; and trust is the underlying theme of this paragraph. So many people are involved in trusting relationships here. The prior must trust the monk he chooses to look after those who are ill; there needs to be trust between patient and helper; and there has to be trust between the latter and those who are in charge of the storeroom if the patient is to get the nourishment that he needs; then, if food has to be prepared, the monks working in the kitchen and scullery are also involved.

There are many links in this chain, human links each with its own share of weakness and susceptibility. And it sometimes happens that an interior mistrust or sheer pressure of work or anxiety does strain the links. The primary cause of mistrust is fear; and fear is always very near the surface where the care of the sick is concerned and it will break through to the surface even in those whose responsibility for the patients is the remotest, if there is any provocation. One brother may fear to ask; one may fear he is being imposed on; one may fear that he will not get his work done — the catalogue could be extended.

We have noticed earlier, in chapter IV, how Augustine both experienced and expressed fear in face of the problems he was handling with the monks. And here again, and in a quite different context, there is latent fear which can so easily inhibit trust. What he perceived when he was struggling with fear in the difficult situation of chapter IV was that the only quality which could break through all tensions was *dilectio*. In the daily life of a monastery, as each one experiences it, it is only love that can overcome fear.

It is common experience in any close-knit family or monastic community that it is often easier to be fearless and to love spontaneously in relation to people outside the group than it is toward one's own brothers or sisters. This is because the farther one person is from another the less he is experienced as a threat. In a setting that requires total commitment there can be no evasion of the darkness that lies in each member; it has to be taken into account in all dealings, at whatever level the encounter takes place. Only a deeply caring love can dare to do this and so make trust possible. What love creates is a growing sensitivity.

From beginning to end, this short paragraph evokes sensitivity in those who have the care of the sick. This comes out first in the words "even if there is no fever" (*etiam sine febribus*), for what Augustine is saying is that a man does not have to be extremely ill with a high temperature to need help and attention in his sickness. During most of his convalescence, the time when he is recovering from illness (*post aegritudine reficiendorum*), and also when he is suffering from any sort of incapacity, he will need the watching eye and the listening ear of a helper. What the helper must exercise is the perception that can sum up and appreciate the totality of the experience of the ill one. He needs to be in tune with the patients. This is a skill which professional nurses must acquire if they are to continue in their work; but in communities it may well happen that there is no professional, just as there is often no trained helper within a family when a member is ill. For such as these, the development of perception is the chief criterion of fitness for the work. Pity is not enough, for it operates within the parameters of the beholder's own resources. Compassion, the ability to identify with the patient in his suffering, is here inadequate because again its expression is limited to personal experience. There is also a subtle weakness evoked by compassion: a tendency to identify the patient's needs with one's own and to provide him with the amelioration that suits oneself but not the sufferer. People who are happiest when looking after the sick can sometimes be happier than the patient who may feel helpless and dominated by their attentions. And a protective attitude, which may mask anxiety or possessiveness, likewise belittles the sufferer.

Because of all these factors, it is often very difficult for a patient to trust the people who care for him, and similarly the helpers, however remote their help, may find it difficult to trust the patient. The very fact of latent or overt mistrust, in oneself or in others, is an additional factor that the perceptive helper has to take into account — and this is a deep challenge to his own integrity. It is also a signpost on the road to his own sanctification. The way one accedes to the requests of others is a reflection of the truth about oneself.

In the next paragraph Augustine considers service to others in a number of contexts.

Rule, Chapter V, 9

Those who have charge of the storeroom,
or the clothes,
or the library,
should serve their brothers without murmuring.

RESPONSIBLE SERVICE

This sentence is rather like a medieval miniature. One could almost paint it: all the business of food supplies coming in and being stored, the work of cooks and scullions — then in another part the workroom with shelves, racks, and drawers, where the monks are at work on fabrics or leather — and somewhere else the studious ones among the community's manuscripts — and in the face of each figure one could read his character and his attitude to his work and to his brothers.

Life in a monastery is very busy (it has to be, because of the double nature of the monastic vocation, the search and the service). Each part of our life could alone occupy the whole of our waking moments, but it is of the very stuff of that life that we are committed to both. And it is this double activity that makes us sometimes feel threatened: both people and things are the stuff of our fear.

People react so differently to fear. Some are paralyzed so that in an acute situation they can neither act nor speak; in the long term this paralysis shows itself as inertia. Others are made aggressive by fear, attacking both work and fellow workers as if they were an enemy to be overcome. In yet others, fear shows itself as cowardice, and for such as these the only reaction to stress is to remove oneself from it as effectively as possible — by absenteeism, indisposition, or simply by finding something else to do. I have given these examples in their extreme form; but I think that the characteristics are such that anyone who has lived in a group will recognize the symptoms when they appear in a more attenuated form.

Augustine's approach is far more delicate than that of the above paragraph where some of the harsh possibilities have been touched upon. He assumes, as far as one can tell, that all requests made by the monks are necessary. And service is what they all owe to one another. Their activity as servants of God lies in their continual striving for unity of heart and mind, in fidelity to their life of prayer and worship, and in their continuing choices prompted by love in acceding to the demands that are made on them in the day-to-day business of their lives. Here in chapter V, 9 we find the first explicit reference to the service of the brothers — and it is seen to extend to every part of their lives. Their service is their responsibility for specific undertakings. Augustine sees service as an actualization of a monk's office — though it is not until chapter VII, 3 that he states this explicitly, when he is discussing the place of the prior within the community. In the present passage, service is an aspect of fraternity.

Brother (*frater*) is one of the key words in the *Rule*, evoking the quality of the relationships that are to be part and parcel of life in the monastery. When Augustine used it twice in chapter I, 8 he was penetrating the divisive attitudes of the privileged toward the underprivileged; when he used it twice again in chapter IV, 8 he referred to the physical and moral weaknesses of the members, pointing out that all should feel responsible for giving help to those in trouble; in the first paragraph of the present chapter there is a touch of irony when he shows disapproval of the monk who complains when he is given any clothing that another brother (*alius frater*) has already been wearing. In a family one is sometimes glad to have the use of something that belongs to another member, provided that there is no obligation to do so. But in chapter V, 1 Augustine does not stress the fact that the former wearer was a brother. By way of contrast, in the present paragraph the fact of brotherhood is important, for it provides the setting for every act of service.

Among Christians, it seems from the evidence that from the beginning the word brother was used to denote a complex of facts: their faith in and allegiance to Christ whose risen life gave them power and whose earthly ministry gave them an example, their cohesion with others of like mind, their responsibility for each other which such fellowship both facilitated and required.[24] Although Acts 22:5 and 23:5 indicate that the extended use of brother/brothers obtained in Jewish custom, in Christian circles the use of the word carried overtones which were readily recognizable. So when in the present passage of the *Rule* Augustine uses this same word he is appealing to an awareness, in each member of the community, of an obligation and responsibility as well as an awareness of fellowship. Thus every encounter, every request, and every felt need are a personal matter — a fact which tests most of us and finds us wanting.

Yet the fact of failure is not necessarily a bad thing, if what it shows up in the way of weakness (in the sense of inability to adapt) and sin (in the sense of unwillingness to do so) is humbly accepted for what it is. Such a revelation can be critical in the sense of evoking judgment and amendment.

What Augustine is warning against in his injunction to serve without murmuring is sinful failure, not weak failure: the rejection of the asker when the request itself is acceded to. Such a rejection may be due to a felt lack in the other person or to a felt lack in oneself: one can have nothing whatever against the asker but still treat him abominably because one feels abominable oneself. In any case, the rejection of another is always a projection of oneself — and of one's worst self. Rowan Williams, in *Resurrection*, speaks of "myself as crucifier."[25]

The area of being that is explored implicitly and at times almost imperceptibly in this whole chapter is far deeper than the personal and social characteristics that were seen to hinder true unanimity in chapter I. Here Augustine is moving nearer to the center of each man. This is a bold thing to do, and there is only one effective precondition for acting constructively in such a situation: the awareness that the controlling factor is the exercise of deeply caring, self-giving love. *Dilectio* requires the will to hold heart and mind steadfast in the pursuit of the common purpose that has drawn the monks together.

In the following two paragraphs Augustine sets certain aspects of the common pursuit over against the personal needs of individual monks.

Rule, Chapter V, 10

Books should be asked for at a definite time each day,
and anyone who asks for them outside the time
should not be given them.

BOOKS AND READING

The place of books and reading within the life of a monastery has come to be greater and greater over the centuries, even though the day has not grown beyond its twenty-four hours. The provision of reading material itself marks a step away from the foundation-pattern of the ascetic of the desert, and it underlines the fact that the ways to God are many and that their signposts are the fruit of experience on the part of those who are also explorers and pilgrims. If one is to absorb the Christian faith into heart, mind, and will there is need, except in rare cases, for awareness of the heart, mind, and will of others through whom God makes himself known.

The need for reading material, then, underlines the interdependence of people — each can be a source of learning and insight to others. Among monks, in whom the search for God is a primary undertaking, the degree of dependence on the thought and understanding of others is high. This appears in the fact that in the earliest period an ascetic would attract disciples; and not only that, but his teaching was treasured and eventually set down in a collection of such material. Chronologically, the writing and reading of stories of the Fathers of the desert came later than the reading of other material; for the high value set on literacy related primarily to the importance of the scriptures, and it was for this reason that Pachomius in the first half of the fourth century stated in his *Rule* that "no one at all is to be admitted to the monastery who cannot read."[26]

We know from Possidius' *Life of Augustine* that in the clerical monastery at Hippo there was much copying of manuscripts of the bishop's own works or of those of other writers.[27] But we do not know how codices came to be collected in the first monastery there — whether they were part of the monks' personal possessions that were placed in common on arrival, whether they were gifts, whether their authors were members of the community, or whether they were copied within the monastery walls. Codices would need careful handling, and this may have been the reason for Augustine's ruling that they could only be given out at certain times and not on instant demand, and clearly the monks were not allowed to help themselves to them.

It is interesting to find that the *Rule* refers to *codices* and not to *volumina*, though one can assume that Augustine's own writings were transcribed into volumes.[28] A codex was held together in the same format as books of today. In a volume the sheets were stuck together to form a long strip which was kept rolled up and then unrolled gradually when in use. Each main section of work was transcribed in one volume and referred to as a book (hence the many books into which Augustine's own works were divided).

The monks at Hippo had a collection of codices and Adolar Zumkeller, citing Possidius' *Life of Augustine* 31, has suggested that Augustine established a library in each of his monasteries.[29] The tradition of the care of books in monasteries has continued down the centuries, and the cupboards cut into the stone walls of medieval monastic buildings may be a link with such storage as Augustine was thinking of when he wrote the *Rule*. Since at least some of the monastery's foundation members were Augustine's personal friends with tastes and habits like his own, it can be safely assumed that study played a considerable part in the life of the first Hippo community. The Thagaste years were not all that remote, and it was there that the withdrawn life of *otium* had provided the material circumstances in which the search for truth could go forward through study and prayer.

There is not, and never has been, a hard and fast rule which ensures that prayer and study are yoked easily together — in most communities as well as in most individuals the space and time required for both of these activities tend to create demanding tensions. This should be no matter for surprise, for while most aspects of living are always in flux, expanding and contracting, the one thing that never changes is the twenty-four hour day. So long as heart and mind are set toward God, the ability to concentrate and become wholly absorbed in prayer will inevitably increase until age brings diminishment; and the same is true of reading and study — each person becomes mentally and spiritually capable of giving more time to these things. As he does so, and as they mold his personality, he will become someone with more to give to other people at many levels — he will become an open channel for God to use. But to be used in this way, whether inside the monastery or out of it, requires time — and so the pressure on time increases, and with it the need for still further time for recuperation from the ever-growing volume of demands that are made on such a person. The fact of pressure and tensions has to be admitted and accepted as a condition of living as liable to occur as hunger, cold, or pain. The ability to pray, to read, to sift, and to share experience is itself a gift; and it would seem that the attitude toward it which is most likely to hold the different components in harness is sheer gratitude for receiving them. Like the rest of God's gifts, they evoke responsibility in those who receive them, as Augustine himself found at Thagaste. Possidius said that "what God revealed to him during his contemplation and prayer he imparted to others, to those who were with him by discourse, and to those who were absent by writings."[30]

The exercise of responsibility involves self-discipline. Uncontrolled spontaneity can be overwhelmingly destructive and in community life it can do great harm to the group. Thus a responsible attitude which in the first place protects its possessor serves also for the strengthening of the group as a whole. One of the human activities that puts love most at risk is irresponsibility in the utilization of gifts — be they persons, time, natural resources, artifacts, or books. And irresponsibility in any of these areas does strain relationships in community life from the nursery onward. If we look at the beginnings of protest against despoiling irresponsibility in early childhood we can see that same pattern which is so destructive in adult relationships. There are the elements of disregarding the rights and interests of others, and of giving higher value to oneself; there is the desire to make one's own mark on things which is a way of seeking to possess them; there is also a projection of self-hatred onto something else. In all of this the child is father of the man and the same attitudes produce the same reactions on the part of their victims among both children and adults — with this difference, that adults can appraise what they are doing.

In all group living, there is a possibility of victimization unless the more compelling force of love is present. When Augustine places *dilectio*, a freely-chosen love, at the heart of monastic life he is ensuring that in every aspect it is possible for the downward drag of self-regard to be redirected into an outward reach toward others. But, as the whole of the *Rule* makes plain, such a redirection is not self-perpetuating. Loving must be consciously willed in each fresh situation; and, according to the nature of the demands made upon it, it will either acquiesce or deny what is asked for. In the present paragraph Augustine has shown that denial is sometimes necessary for the sake of the group. The following paragraph shows how acquiescence may be necessary for the sake of the individual.

Rule, Chapter V, 11

However, those who have charge of clothes and shoes
should give them without delay to those who have need of them.

CARE AND DISTRIBUTION OF CLOTHING

Chapter V ends as it begins: with a close-up view of the community's clothing room. The present paragraph is the fifth in the chapter that is concerned with wearing apparel, but here a different word is used. In paragraphs 1,3,4, and 9, Augustine used the word *uestis* which, in relation to people, simply means clothing in the sense of covering for the body. It can also be used of a carpet or a tapestry, meaning the covering for a floor or a wall.[31] *Vestimentum*, on the other hand, means any garment. One can imagine shelves and cupboards stored with every conceivable article that a monk might need from his head to his feet. Augustine's precept envisages order in the care and custody of clothing, but in the distribution and use of it there is no rigidity. Things are to be supplied when they are needed. The sole of a sandal wears through, a *birrus* gets soaked in the rain — immediate replacements must be provided.

This paragraph looks at the matter of care and distribution from the opposite direction from paragraph 1. There Augustine considered the varying attitudes of individual monks to what was given to them. Here, with much less need to point an admonitory finger, he addresses the monks who look after the community's goods and ensure that they are available for all the brothers.

We may note first of all that there is delegation of authority here. In chapters I, 3 and V, 3, it is the prior who is responsible for deciding how goods are to be allocated; here it is those who have the oversight of them who are charged with decision-making and action. Augustine sets the delegation of authority against the background of service to the whole community and as a means of ensuring that each member is supplied with what he needs when he needs it. The monk who has charge of clothing or, for that matter, any other portion of the community's goods is the servant of all — the household servant who is intimately involved with all the members of the group and knows their needs, tastes, and interests. A true servant is in the deepest sense attentive to others, aware of the uniqueness of each one even though the materials of the service that he can offer are in no sense unique.

Throughout this chapter, which orchestrates the theme of love at the level of the ordinary affairs of the monastery, Augustine has gradually moved his focus from the soloists who express their own particular theme to the full harmony in which each individual becomes an intrinsic part of the whole. In paragraph 1 there were those who fussed about their clothes. In paragraph 2 there was the sound of personal advantage. Paragraph 3 spoke to the monk who could deceive others, while paragraphs 4 and 5 sounded warnings against self-deceit. Paragraph 6 held the cry of the fearful. In paragraph 7 the theme is caution, and this carefulness is the bridge to the rest of the chapter where the emphasis is different. The precept in paragraph 8 gives guidance for the care of the sick and opens up the resources of the community to give help as it is needed, and the remaining three paragraphs indicate some of the many ways in which the whole community is engaged in the single enterprise of living the common life in love.

One last insight of Augustine needs to be mentioned. He has brought his readers away from the area of self-concern (paragraphs 1-7) into that of acceptance and sharing, where uniqueness has high value yet where togetherness is of paramount importance. The problems that were faced and discussed in chapter IV and the first paragraph of chapter V have their roots in self-love. And it is this which Augustine's understanding of *dilectio* challenges, for it involves a choice directed toward the good of others — a choice which denies room to self-love.

The good of others for the sake of God is a primary aspect of life within the monastery as Augustine sees it, and this has a direct bearing on a monk's attitude to the materials that he is responsible for. It is all too easy for an over-conscientious person to become identified with the goods in his charge, so that an outrage to them is experienced as an outrage to oneself. It is also possible to become possessive of them, regarding them as existing for one's own well-being and not for that of the group. It is also possible to hate them as an extension of oneself or of the community, in which case one ill-treats them or is grudging in making them available to others. In all of this one is governed by self-love. What Augustine has tried to show in the matters discussed in this present chapter is that love which reaches out to others, discerning their needs and striving to relieve them, is the supreme factor that makes true unity possible. When caring love is at work within any situation, however ordinary and unremarkable it may be, then one cannot be over-concerned for the good of material things, or cling to them as to a lifeline, or despise and misuse them. Love can identify with other people. It can let them be themselves. Caring love cannot misuse others for its own advantage.

Yet there is one sense in which there has to be an identification between the giver and what he gives. The paradox lies in the sense that this only has validity when there is also an identification with the recipient. Love must have a threefold dimension. And this is what Augustine implies when he says that "those who have charge of clothes and shoes should give them without delay to those who have need of them." The response of love to need must be instantaneous, there may be no holding back (*dare non different*). One has to be prepared to give away whatever one has command of, as an expression of one's love for the others.

One has also to be prepared to give away oneself. It is with this deeper aspect of love that Augustine is concerned in the next chapter of the *Rule*.

NOTES

1. The point is well made in an article by Dr. Jack Dominian, "The Capacity to Love, (1) Love of Self" in *The Tablet* (1981) 197.

2. *Moral Nexus*, Westminster Press, 1971, page 192.

3. There is a valuable discussion of responsibility in chapter 5 of Donald Nicholl's *Holiness*, Darton, Longman & Todd, 1981. The whole of this book is relevant to this chapter of the *Rule*.

4. Especially in chapters I, 3 and 5, and III, 5.

5. See E. G. Selwyn, *The First Epistle of St. Peter*, Macmillan, 1946, pages 141-142 and 146-147.

6. See Rom 12:2.

7. See Rom 5:5.

8. Mt 21:28.

9. In what follows I am indebted to the essay of R. A. Markus, "Work and Worker in Early Christianity" (see above, chapter III, notes 21 and 23).

10. *On Genesis: A Refutation of the Manicheans* IV, 8, 15; I, 6, 10.

11. R. A. Markus, "Work and Worker in Early Christianity" in *Work/Christian Thought and Practice*, Darton, Longman & Todd, 1960, page 23.

12. For example, *Expositions of the Psalms* 7, 16, *The Literal Meaning of Genesis* I, 6, 10.

13. R. A. Markus, *op. cit.*, page 26.

14. *The Work of Monks* 16; 19. See Adolar Zumkeller, *Augustine's Ideal of the Religious Life*, Fordham University Press, 1986, page 156.

15. Noel Dermot O'Donoghue has a perceptive chapter entitled "Belonging" in *Heaven in Ordinarie*, T. & T. Clark, 1979, pages 81-96.

16. *My God, My Glory*, SPCK, 1956, page 7.

17. *Op. cit.*, page 176.

18. A full description of the processes, with illustrations based on the excavations at Pompeii, is to be found in Rich's *Dictionary of Roman and Greek Antiquities*, under *fullo, fullonica*, and *fullonius*.

19. *Op. cit.*, page 705.

20. *Op. cit.*, under the article *balineae/balneae*.

21. Text by Barry Cunliffe, illustrations by Mike Rouillard, Bob Wilkins, and Roy Worskett, 1978.

22. Quoted in A. M. H. Jones, *The Later Roman Empire, 284-602* (3 volumes, Blackwell, 1964, reprinted in 2 volumes, 1973), volume II, page 977. Barsanuphius died about 540.

23. See J. N. D. Kelly (citing *Against Jovinian*, 1, 40; 2, 21. 36) in *Jerome: His Life, Writings and Controversies*, pages 180-181.

24. The letters provided the following evidence: 1 Thes 4:10; Phil 1:14; 1 Cor 8:11-13; 2 Cor 11:9; Rom 12:1.10; Jas 5:12; Eph 6:23; Col 1:2; Phlm 1.7.16; 1 Pt 3:8; 1 Tm 4:6; Heb 3:1; 2 Pt 1:7; 3 Jn 3:5; 1 Jn 3:13-16; 4:21. I have given these references in chronological order according to the editors of Jerusalem Bible, in order to show how the meaning of the word came to be broadened and deepened. In the gospels a few passages stand out, for example, Mt 23:8, 25:40, 28:10, and Jn 21:23. In Acts there are a number of passages: 6:3; 9:30; 10:23; 12:17; 14:2; 15:1-3.22-23.40; 16:2.40; 17:6.10.14; 18:18.27; 20:32; 21:7; 28:14-15.21.

25. *Resurrection*, Darton, Longman & Todd, 1982, page 80. The same theme runs through Sebastian Moore's *The Crucified Is No Stranger*, Darton, Longman & Todd, 1977.

26. See Quasten, *Patrology*, Volume III: *The Golden Age of Greek and Patristic Literature*, Utrecht/Antwerp: Spectrum Publishers, 1960, page 157.

27. *Life of Augustine* 18 and 21.

28. See the articles *Codex* and *Volume* in Rich's *Dictionary of Roman and Greek Antiquities*, pages 184 and 730.

29. Adolar Zumkeller, *op. cit.*, page 228.

30. *Life of Augustine* 3.

31. So Smith's dictionary tells me, citing Lucretius, Cicero, Ovid, and Horace.

6

Forgiveness

Rule, Chapter VI, 1

Do not have quarrels,
or at least bring them to an end as quickly as possible,
lest anger should grow into hatred — straw into a plank —
and produce a murderous heart.
You have read the words:
Anyone who hates his brother is a murderer.

QUARRELS

It is at this point that Augustine takes his courage in both hands, as he had done earlier in chapter I, and puts his finger into the deep wound of damage that people can inflict on one another, whether they are monks or not. In chapters I and III he explored the antagonisms that arise through social and cultural differences. Chapter IV provided guidelines to help the brothers when they were confronted by self-will and sin in each other, and chapter V pointed to the ways, so ordinary and unassuming in themselves, in which self-concern and inadequate self-awareness can be replaced by a love that cares deeply for others just as they are.

But it is impossible to think about love and people just as they are without looking also at the opposite of love and at the sheer unattractiveness of all people in some part of their being: one has got to be honest about the part of oneself that cannot love and is not lovable.

Quarreling is an inevitable aspect of being alive (I cannot say being human, as I hear the sparrows' rivalries outside my window as I write). Quarrels are concomitant with the existence of others who have as many needs and rights as one has oneself, and the art of survival is the art of mutual accommodation. There has to be willingness to accept the place of others in the world, in the home, in the monastery.

In this paragraph, Augustine provides no anatomy of quarreling; he simply assumes that his readers know what he is writing about. Within any group, reactions to a quarrel can differ widely among both participants and witnesses, and these are explored further in paragraphs 2 and 3. He is content to give a warning, for he is not so much concerned with the event of a quarrel as with its results. That is to say, he is pointing out the really serious danger of unresolved quarrels.

To avoid quarrels, we have either to ignore our companions or to know them very well. To ignore people for the sake of peace and quiet is to avoid responsibility and also to inflict deep wounds. To get to know others very well, to be able to relate to them, and to give oneself to them takes a long time and much patience — and also a measure of failure, for without the experience of failure it is rarely possible to reach the point of being able to accept the dark side either of oneself or of another. Quarrels arise from the inability to face conflict creatively; and the ability to accept conflict grows with experience, beginning at the nursery stage and continuing into maturity. It is because of this fact that the two opening phrases of chapter VI, 1 are a lightning sketch of the whole field of relationships and of man's attitude to them — first the ideal and then the common experience: "Do not have quarrels, or at least bring them to an end as quickly as possible." Sometimes quarrels erupt in a flash point of time when neither participant is expecting such a confrontation; sometimes they happen as a thunderclap that is the culmination of long rumbling. In both cases they emerge because neither party has fully accepted the inevitability of dissonance in human living. Conflict itself there must be, since time and space have to contain the always-extending variety of human lives, but conflict itself is not quarreling. What Karl Rahner has written of the Church as a whole is true of any one of its parts and applies completely to a monastic community: "Disputes and opposition, conducted on both sides in faith and love, justice and self-critical caution, are part of the life of the Church. Real conflicts and disputes cannot be solved by the exercise of authority. Conflicts arise in any living community: they are part of its life.[1]

We saw in the discussions of chapters I, 3, and 4 the many human factors that make unanimity among the brothers very hard to attain; yet nothing deters Augustine from making this the ideal of the monastery. In the second half of the *Rule* there is no mention of unanimity itself, because all is subsumed under the precept of mutual love. And the reason why unresolved quarrels are so destructive within the community is that they dam up the springs of love. It is possible to love and to quarrel; love in this life can never be perfect, and quarreling occurs when one or both persons are failing to understand the other. The way to avoid quarrels, or to bring them to an end as soon as possible, is to accept the fact of conflict.

Right rarely lies completely on one side, yet there are times when one participant is more sinned against than sinning. It is common experience that when a quarrel results in the breakdown of a relationship, the innocent or relatively more innocent party is the one to take the initiative toward reconciliation. The first move may be rejected by the chief wrongdoer, but without that first approach he may never begin to repent. But it is not possible for anyone to take the first step if we ourselves are controlled by anger. That is why Augustine finds himself constrained to use forceful hyperbole in his warning against the effects of unbridled rage: a mere "straw" (*festuca*) becomes "a plank" (*trabs*). Yet it can happen that the quarrel goes deeper in the more innocent member because he is outraged as a person and then sheer anger shows its ugliest face.

ANGER

Anger itself is so primary a reaction as to be capable of moral neutrality. The biblical writers took it so much for granted as to ascribe it to God,[2] though there were some who were keenly aware of his tenderness and who described him as slow to anger.[3] Anger in men, and as attributed by them to God, is clearly related to a sense of value — to the rightness and fitness of people and things; in this respect anger is justified, as the author of Ephesians perceived when he wrote, *Be angry but do not sin* (4:6). The sin occurs when the sun is allowed to go down on one's anger, that is to say, when reasoned judgment has failed to take control. The estimation of the value of others presupposes the ability to make judgments, and anger becomes morally offensive when the power of judgment is clouded and words and actions are motivated by outrage. Anger is roused when a person perceives that the world around him or her does not conform to his or her own norms, whether these are related to personal, social, or cosmic experience. Anger is a response to experience of negativity — injustice, unpopularity, expulsion, disagreement, abuse, controversy, defamation, misconduct, neglect. Protest against the pressures of negation is right and just, but it begins to become wrong and unjust when it takes the form of complementary negativities and it becomes totally wrong when the manifestations of protest surpass in intensity the evil which they are denouncing. That is what

Augustine is pointing to in his contrast between a straw and a plank. A sheer hardness and rigidity of outlook in the face of anything or anyone that gives offense — whether real or imaginary, self-induced or rooted in the offender — brings about a total breakdown in communication which can be completely destructive. And when the impulse to destroy gains the assent of mind and feelings the result is the malevolence of a murderer.

HATRED

The dynamism of hatred, a really destructive malevolence, is uncovered in 1 John, within the context of the author's attempt to penetrate the meaning of love. The fact or activity of hatred in the subject is accepted without discussion; but hatred in its subject-object aspect is what has to be examined, and the writer looks at this situation in its most extreme form (a form which is similarly treated in the *Rule*). What is really being brought into existence when a man hates his brother-in-Christ? (It is necessary to use that qualifying phrase, because from the context in 1 John it is clear that the discussion concerns relationships within the Christian community and not specifically within a natural family.) In the letter hatred is seen in three sets of contrasts. First, in 2:9-11, the man who hates is said to be in darkness, whereas *the darkness is passing away and the true light is already shining* (verse 8). Then in 3:15 there is the passage which Augustine quotes, in which a hater is a killer in whom eternal life does not abide. And in 4:20 hatred is linked with falsehood: *If anyone says "I love God," and hates his brother, he is a liar*. Light, life, and truth are the characteristics of one who loves; darkness, death, and untruth mark the one who hates. Quarreling and anger move in the middle area between these two extremes and their situation is always to some extent fluid. Hatred is rigid, hard, and static so that when another person encounters it he or she is inevitably injured even when not killed outright. Haters deny value to the life of another; even if they do not go so far as to end the life of the one they hate, they can wish that one dead.

The real tragedy in a hate-filled situation lies not with the object but with the subject, for our hatred reflects our own darkness and death and hence our inability to see the truth of another. Yet in one sense hatred is perceptive because it enables the hater to pinpoint the weaknesses of the victim and to use them as a tool. By contrast, it is love that is blind — and hence the lover is disarmed and disadvantaged. And that is why mutual hatred is so deadly, for both participants have the psychological weapons for doing the maximum damage.

Hatred of another has self-hatred as one of its powerful ingredients. If its proximate cause is jealousy, the remote cause lies in despising oneself for not possessing or attracting desired benefits. If deprivation is the proximate cause, the remote cause lies in self-distrust. If feeling threatened is the proximate cause, the remote cause is the experience of inadequacy. And it is the remote causes that are the decisive factors, for they lie beyond the control of reason; it is they that direct jealousy or deprivation or frustration away from the area where reason and common sense can enable us to see our hatred for what it is and our victim for what he or she is.

Hatred stirs up strife, love covers all offenses (Prv 10:12). There are very few people inside or outside a monastery who are totally incapable of hatred. Immunity from the temptation to let anger take control, after it has rightly or wrongly been roused, comes first of all from a willingness to acknowledge its presence. That is why Augustine's instinct is right in bringing it into the open when he is discussing the deepening of relationships among the brothers. When the presence of hatred is admitted, then it is already in process of dissolving — or, as 1 John 2:8 puts it, *the darkness is passing away* and light is already entering. Struggle on this front is no once-for-all matter; it has to be renewed again and again. As John Burnaby has written, interpreting Augustine, "Nothing dies so hard in the human heart as hate."[4]

Because of the stimulus of the sheer novelty of life in a monastery it often happens that this particular weakness does not emerge during our first years as a religious, though we may have been aware of it in our self before we entered. When it does appear, we may be appalled to find ourselves in its grip; but this is rarely sufficient to release us from it. Very often it is the victim, the one to whom our hatred is directed, who becomes the means of loosing us from it. We have already suggested that the first move toward reconciliation often comes from the victim. But he or she sometimes has another function. Christopher Bryant reached the heart of the matter when he wrote: "God addresses me through [those who repel me] in warning and judgment . . . through those who repel us. God . . . often challenges us to face and come to terms with rejected bits of ourselves which we have been repudiating."[5]

To recognize someone as your enemy may be your first step in recognizing that one and yourself as persons and, as persons, the sphere of God's activity. It is because of this that hatred among members of a community/Christians is so tragic an occurrence. When 1 John and chapter VI, 1 of the *Rule* call a brother-hater a murderer they are demanding recognition of the fact that hatred is utterly destructive — and the greatest tragedy of all is that it involves also the destruction of the hater. In his commentary on this verse of the letter Bishop Westcott wrote: "Such hatred is identical with murder not simply as being the first step toward it but as involving the same moral position. It is moreover in the man himself the destruction of that life which is love."[6] And Augustine stresses this same point when he says that the hater in a community has a murderous *anima*, one that would destroy the very life for which the community exists and of which the same hater is a part.

Augustine's use of the word *anima* in the *Rule* is instructive, for it shows his courageous realism as he looks at the total personality of the brothers to whom he is writing. In chapter I, 2, he set out the monastic ideal as *one soul (anima) and one heart entirely centered upon God.* But by chapter I, 7 he has had to take account of the fact that the soul/mind/heart is often in a wretched and contemptible state; later, in chapter V, 4, he speaks of its sordidness or uncleanness; while in the present paragraph he admits that it is capable of murder. There is no reason at all for any monk to adopt a holier-than-thou attitude to other people, for there is a capacity to hate in every man.

When later Augustine wrote his commentary on 1 John he faced this very issue: "Are you sure that you are not still hating your brothers — which is worse than failing to love enemies? If you loved your brothers only, you would not be perfect but if you hate your brothers, what and where are you? Look each one into his own heart; cherish no hate against a brother for some hard word: in a quarrel for earth, turn not to earth" (*Homilies on the First Letter of John* 1, 11). It is the man who recognizes and admits the hatred in his soul who is best able to control and overcome it. In the next paragraph Augustine turns his attention to ways and means of restoring good relationships.

Rule, Chapter VI, 2

If anyone hurts another by abuse or foul-speaking
or by serious accusations,
he should be careful to heal the wound he has made
by apologizing as soon as possible;
and the one who was hurt should himself be careful to forgive
without further discussion.
But if both have been hurtful they should forgive each other's offense,
remembering the prayers which, because you repeat them so often,
ought to be made with entire sincerity.
Nevertheless, it is better to be one who is often tempted to give way to anger
but is quick to ask forgiveness of the person he admits that he has injured,
than to be one who is more slowly roused to anger
but finds more difficulty in asking pardon.
Anyone who is never willing to ask pardon,
or who does not ask it from his heart,
is in the monastery without good reason
even if he is not expelled.
You should take care, then,
not to use harsh words;
but if they should have escaped from your mouth
then do not be ashamed
to let that mouth which caused the wound provide the cure.

HURTING ONE ANOTHER

In this paragraph Augustine takes his readers back to the state of affairs when blind hatred has not yet gained possession of one or more of the brothers. Here, he examines the more normal breakdowns in relationships, the ones that it is possible to restore provided one has the generosity and the goodwill to do so.

That people do hurt one another is as inevitable as daylight. Evoking daylight in this context is important, because it points to the fact that it is necessary to see what is happening if there is to be true reconciliation after things have gone wrong. It is possible to hurt others without knowing that one has done so, but in a group that is living together and sharing deep ideals this cannot be sustained indefinitely. Some people are more easily hurt than others and sometimes the experience is sheer self-indulgence and a cover for one's own weaknesses which one avoids bringing into the open. Sometimes people look for occasions of hurt and even imagine them: all of which stems from insecurity which one's spiritual and intellectual life has failed to transcend.

Again, some people for various reasons conceal their hurt, whether it is real or imagined. In some instances this is both wise and necessary. Parents, for instance, are often wounded by their children's aspirations, but to articulate the hurt would be destructive of the freedom of their offspring. Sometimes it takes a long time for reconciliation to become possible, since the process of healing has as a basic requirement a measure of understanding on both sides — an understanding which grows with experience and is the result of a high degree of synthesis between spirit, intellect, and emotions. Within a religious community it can be presumed that the common outlook on life is that of adults, though in all members there generally remains an element of childishness that has to be taken into account both by its possessors and by those who have to deal with them. And the degree of maturity attained by each adult is a variable factor.

Thus the need for sympathy and tolerance is of primary importance for the brothers whose monastic life is committed to the attainment of unanimity and concord. Occasions of hurt are not to be passed over lightly, as Augustine points out in the course of his discussion.

THE BREAKDOWN OF RELATIONSHIPS

The whole of this long paragraph is carefully worked out. It moves from specific instances of the breakdown of relationships in the community to a general consideration of the ways of reconciliation, and then it brings both of these aspects together in a final telling precept that is both particular and general.

First Augustine points out three common ways in which one person can hurt another: by abusive language, evil-speaking, and serious accusation. These are all positive failures and it is to be noticed that there is nowhere in the second part of the *Rule* any treatment of the negative weaknesses such as neglect and insensitivity which may be equally hurting or even more so since these things are more difficult to bring out into the open. It was in paragraphs 5-7 of chapter 1 that this form of misunderstanding was considered, and then it was not considered to be particularly culpable. An understanding of this level of interpretation belongs to a later era than the time of Augustine; indeed, it is only within the last century that men have become aware of the social dimensions of sin which can operate both positively and negatively. But however wide or narrow a person's awareness of sin and failure may be, the remedies are the same in principle though their application varies. Before we look at Augustine's way of bringing about reconciliation, we must consider the three ways of hurting another which he mentions at the beginning of the present discussion.

First there is the way that makes the most noise and therefore probably draws the most attention to itself. The word that Augustine uses is *conuicium* which means violent reproaching and abuses. One of the most insidious characteristics of ill-feeling toward another is that of giving tongue to it, for this frequently results in the magnitude of the offense increasing in the mind and the emotions: one word of abuse leads to another, and another, and another, until the original cause of the dispute is lost sight of altogether. At the same time, the articulation of a minor disapproval may release pent-up feelings that cover a wide field of grievances. In either case, the effect on the victim is wounding physically, mentally, and spiritually. The effect on the body of one who has plenty of adrenalin is to produce the ability to counter the attack, which means that there is a first-class row in which both participants may lose control; in one whose supply of adrenalin is low, the wound will be inflicted more on the mind and the likelihood is that the evil will be interiorized and become uncontrollable at that level. In both cases, the ability to be fully alive and accepting of others and of God at all levels is impaired by the vituperation of another. Augustine in this paragraph is more concerned with the interior hurt that does not erupt and become an open quarrel. Quarrels that imply mutual recrimination are what he talked about in the previous paragraph, and then without finding it necessary to examine them closely. Here, he does see fit to look at causes — because his chief concern is to find a cure.

His second word is *maledictum*, speaking ill of another, either to his face or behind his back. This is more serious than just swearing and shouting at him because it attempts to influence the judgment of others — after all, there is no point in denigrating a person if you know that what you say will be given no credit. Evil-speaking is a deliberate attempt to damage a person by taking away his character, and it is a temptation that comes frequently to members of a close-knit group with a common but limited purpose. If one monk thinks that another is not pulling his weight, or is becoming out of sympathy, or is in any way failing to show a reasonable degree of acceptance of the demands of the common life, then in rage and frustration and in an attempt to force the issue he may move to the attack by talking about the offender. Another reason for resorting to evil-speaking is an unreasoning sense of inadequacy and therefore of being threatened. One monk may, for reasons which he does not understand, feel disadvantaged by another, and on that account he may find it safe to blacken his brother's character both as a means of deliberately hurting him and also as a means of lessening his own feeling of vulnerability. If I can convince other people that X is a liar then I need not take so seriously what he says to me. The effect of evil-speaking on its victim is far more likely to be interior than exterior, and so the measure of defenselessness is greater. The discovery that one is being spoken against by a brother makes it very difficult to encounter him without constraint and to accept him with all his faults. Smear-tactics are underhanded and subversive and therefore very difficult to overcome.

Augustine's third way of harming a brother is not privy and subversive but public. The words he uses are *criminis obiectu*, which we have translated as "by serious accusations." The force of *obiecio* is to lay bare and so to publicize. It is good to have our foibles talked about in public and in our presence, because that helps us to recognize their absurdity. But when one brother publicly makes serious charges against another he is slashing at the very fabric of the community's life as well as at the person he is trying to injure. Sometimes a brother may do this in the heat of the moment, and this is not so serious; but when he seeks occasion to denounce another he is committing a very great wrong. In all forms of social grouping, the presence of suspicion and recrimination, whether justified or not, poisons the common life (which is one of the reasons why, in chapter IV, 8, Augustine stressed the importance of having two or three witnesses: one person may be prejudiced and suspicious, while a group is less likely to be).

In each of Augustine's three ways of expressing ill-will toward another, he seems to be assuming pent-up emotions which can destroy the happiness of both the victim and the community. And the person who is in a key position to bring about a change of heart is actually the victim for that is the one who not only knows but also experiences what is being done. Sometimes the hands are tied and one is not free either to act or to speak out immediately, and it may be necessary to wait upon events before doing so — but always one must remain attentive to the other in order to discern the moment when by word or deed we can break through the other's malevolence.

RECONCILIATION

The factor that makes this kind of suffering creative is the willingness to accept it. This is the way that Jesus chose in the face of the mounting animosity that was directed toward him. When 1 Peter 2:23 says of him that when he was reviled he did not revile in retaliation, it is pointing to the selflessness with which the Lord countered every attack made on his integrity and on his life; and in accepting all that was done to him he made himself available as a reconciler. If healing is to become possible, then the victim has to accept and not reject what is done to him or her, whether it is just or unjust. Nothing ever stays still and if a hurt is not accepted but only received, it in its turn will develop into a desire and a capacity to injure. There is a terrible sentence in Alan Paton's novel, *Cry the Beloved Country*, with its pleas for reconciliation before it is too late: "I have one great fear in my heart, that one day when they are turned to loving, they will find that we are turned to hating."[7] The victim has to be a willing sacrifice; one has to offer oneself, yet we may not choose the moment when our offering is to be made.

The victim's self-offering happens in two stages. The first is when one accepts the blow and the ill intentions behind it, without recrimination. The second is when the wrongdoer begins to show contrition. Augustine is writing to brothers who recognize when they hurt each other, and he urges them to apologize (*satisfactione curare*) as soon as possible. The words that he uses recognize the fact that the wrongdoer is in debt to his victim — literally, he owes an apology. And when that is given, the work of mutual reconciliation can begin. The apology is not the last word of healing but the first. The apology is prompted by an awareness of the fact that one has wounded another, and it expresses the fact that healing cannot begin until an admission of guilt has been made. The apology is a deliberate act of reaching out to the other. All of this is reflected in the words that Augustine chooses to use in the middle section of this sentence: "He should be careful to heal the wound he has made . . . and the one who was hurt should himself be careful to forgive." The word which I have translated as "be careful" is *meminerit* which implies "calling to/having in mind"; and the word for "to heal" is *curare* which means both to care and to cure. An apology is an attempt to release both parties from the static relationship of wrongdoer and wronged; it means to restore movement between the two. Tragedy is being made when two people cannot move away from the positions of their estrangement. It is therefore essential, as Augustine points out, for the wronged brother to move at once by extending forgiveness (it should be noticed that in this sentence *meminerit* applies to both parties).

FORGIVENESS

Forgiveness is to be extended "without further discussion" (*sine disceptatione*). On the face of it, such an attitude is not altogether acceptable to twentieth-century readers who are learning slowly and painfully to discuss their quarrels together as a means of creating understanding. But what Augustine is meaning is "without further argument" — do not let the dispute begin all over again. Even present-day experience shows that in the initial stages of reconciliation few words are better than many, and generally they are all that either party is capable of at that point. The time for talking through the problems that disagreements raise lies further ahead, but without the articulation of contrition and acceptance that time will never become present.

At this point Augustine begins to turn from a particular to a general discussion, and the actual words that he uses are very telling. He writes with a sureness of touch and an economy of words (in contrast to the prolix discussion of chapters 1 and 4 in particular). That he feels sure of himself is implied in his use of the words *debebunt* (they should), *debita* (debts, transgressions), and *debet* (ought) which occur within the one short sentence — whereas they are found only eleven times in the whole of the rest of the precepts. We should notice also that seeking or giving pardon (*ueniam petere, dimittere, relaxare*), occur, in different phrases, five times in this paragraph.

Consideration of these two sets of words cannot be kept entirely separate, because the Latin *debere/debitum*, which have to do with obligation and owing, run into the related factors of forgiving and remitting debts.

When a person wrongs another he devalues him, denying his worth. It is in that sense that he places himself in debt to his victim, for in heaping injuries on him he takes something very precious away from him; and what is worse, he damages the thing that he

has taken — namely, part of his brother's self. If you take something from another it is either because you appreciate it and want
it for yourself or because you despise it and want to destroy it.
Anger caused by jealousy of the other's possession of something
comes into the first category; anger caused by repulsion against
what the other person is or values comes into the second. The
effect on the wronged brother is the same in both cases.

The degree to which any individual is aware of the hurt that he
or she inflicts on another depends far more on one's own self-
awareness than it does on any sensitivity to the other, and it is
significant that Augustine uses one word (*dimittere*) when he is
writing of the forgiveness that a wronged person must extend to
his tormentor, and another (*relaxare*) to describe what must happen when each has wronged the other. *Dimittere* is the normal
Latin word meaning "to forgive" in the sense of to discharge
another from an obligation, and it is the one that Christians used
in the Lord's Prayer. *Relaxare* means "to release," to let go one's
hold on anything. If two people are held in acrimony each must
release the other from his clutches — but not strive to release
himself from the clutches of the other.

Augustine regarded the acts of forgiving as an aspect of almsgiving.[8] "Forgiveness is itself a sort of almsgiving, and no one is
too poor to do that" (Sermon 206, 2). Forgiveness is almsgiving in
the sense of showing mercy and giving to someone in need — and
this in itself is one aspect of prayer for a wrongdoer (Augustine
actually calls it one of the wings of prayer by which a person may
fly to God).[9] Thus to ask for pardon is to beg for alms, to ask for a
gift.

PRAYER AND FORGIVENESS

It is not possible to be precise about the reason given in the *Rule*
for mutual asking for and giving pardon, when each has injured
the other. Certainly Augustine challenges the integrity of the
contestants by pointing out that their acrimony is out of keeping
with their prayer; but what he means by their prayer is not
altogether clear. Nor is he clear when he describes the quality of
that prayer. His words are *propter orationes uestras, quae utique,
quanto crebriores habetis, tanto saniores habere debetis* (on account of
your prayers which, in the measure that you use them frequently,
you ought to that extent to keep/make them sane/whole/
healthy).

It may be that Augustine is saying "because you are committed to be men of prayer you must, by being readily forgiving, free yourselves for this prayer" — and here the underlying appeal is to each brother's presumed longing for holiness. It may be that he desires forgiveness to be extended because of the damage which acrimony causes in the life of prayer of the whole community. A further suggestion has been made by Luc Verheijen:[10] that the frequently-used prayers are specific — namely, the Lord's Prayer which includes the plea *Forgive us our sins, as we forgive those who sin against us* — in which case the frequent repetition would be seen to challenge the integrity of the brother who uses it. Tertullian calls the Lord's Prayer *oratio* (The Prayer),[11] and on the same pattern Augustine's *orationes* here in the *Rule* could perhaps be translated as Our Fathers, as if he were saying "You repeat many Our Fathers in the course of a day; therefore you ought. . . ." Elsewhere Verheijen quotes an article by A.-M. La Bonnardière, "Pénitence et réconciliation des pénitents d'après Saint Augustin," drawing attention to the author's thesis that in the fourth century, before the firm establishment of private sacramental confession, the public recitation of the Lord's Prayer at the eucharist was an expression of regret for sin and asking for pardon.[12] If this is indeed so, there is added meaning for Augustine's precept in the *Rule*: you say that you want to receive and give pardon every time you repeat the Lord's Prayer, but if you do not put this into practice your prayer is false.

The exact meaning that was in his mind need not be the only one that his words carry, and I have kept this fact in mind in translating the present precept. In general, he means that prayer challenges the integrity of those who pray, particularly when one has been involved in a quarrel. The word that he uses, *sanus*, refers to well-being, health (which is a recurring theme in the *Rule*).[13] The more frequently you repeat the prayer, or, the more frequently you pray, the healthier (*saniores*) the prayers/prayer should be. In the word *saniores* there is an echo of 1 Peter 4:7, where the Revised Standard Version translators keep closest to the Greek and have *keep sane and sober for your prayers* while the Jerusalem Bible has *to pray better, keep a calm and sober mind*. Augustine's words, *orationes . . . saniores*, reflect this same understanding of the close relationship between prayer, feeling, and thought — the prayers the brothers pray are to be an expression of their best intentions, and it is for this reason that in translation I have not used the word integrity with its strong intellectual and moral overtones, but the simpler word sincerity which also allows room for feeling: "prayers ought to be made with entire sincerity" — a statement which challenges most of us in our worship as well as in our daily living.

DISRUPTING CHARACTERISTICS

Augustine is now in a position where he can examine men's differing characteristics when broken relationships occur, and when he can assess their respective merits. There are some people, he says, who are often roused but also quick to recognize and apologize for any angry outburst; and there are others whom it takes more to upset but when they do give way to fury they have to live with it longer and therefore are incapable of attempting quickly to make amends. The *Rule's* expression here is a very sensitive and delicate one — it is more difficult (*difficilius*) for such a person to do so. Augustine says that it is better to be the first sort of person than the second.

It is hard for the fiery-tempered to realize the damage that their sudden outbursts inflict on others. They have less significance for the perpetrator than they do for their recipients. Whether it is better to be the victim of one frequently roused or of one less given to attacking others is an issue that is not touched on in the *Rule*; but this is not surprising because most of this chapter is addressed to the wrongdoer rather than to the wronged.

Augustine rightly has sterner things to say to the monk who is never able to begin seeing life from another person's angle and who therefore is incapable of even desiring to ask for pardon or does not ask it sincerely (*numquam uult petere ueniam . . . aut non ex animo petit*): there is, he says, really no justification for his being in the monastery at all. (We may notice in passing that nothing is said about a brother whose burden of guilt and inadequacy is so heavy that he is inhibited from acknowledging the harm that he does — understanding of this very real problem belongs to a later age, and it is one that modern people do have to take seriously.) The reason why an impenitent religious is out of place in a community is the very fact that he or she is not concerned with the well-being and the unity of heart and mind of all the members; his concern is self-concern. An unwillingness to take responsibility for one's bad temper and to apologize for it when necessary is symptomatic of an unwillingness to be responsible for oneself in general, and it is this attitude which calls in question a person's fitness for life in the monastery. But it is a characteristic that may not emerge clearly in the first years of the life of a religious. Being in the monastery expresses a desire which in its turn will cause him or her to conform to the common pattern. It is only later, when the community's life begins to be interiorized in a newcomer, that deep flaws of character will appear. If he or she refuses to admit to and attempt to mend them, then that person becomes alienated from the group and is solitary in the very worst sense. Such a one may live among the members but his or her life has no meaning in terms of the common life. There may be times of stress when any religious may be obliged to go through this experience — it would be surprising if we did not, since the whole of our being is in process of becoming open to the influence of God; but Augustine in this passage is dealing with a monk whose alienation is on the way to becoming paramount. Although such a person may be found in any generation of monks, it is unusual for him or her to be dismissed from the community — because the reason for dismissal, as Augustine stated in chapter IV, 9, is the danger of "poisonous infection." Only if other members are likely to be corrupted or if there has been public scandal over the behavior of a monk is a culprit likely to be sent away. In the present case there is no disintegrating danger to the community, because alienation is not an attitude that attracts other people. But certainly any kind of group does suffer very greatly if one member is alienated — there is hurt and frustration as well as a sense of loss. Hence there is true insight in Augustine's warning that the man who cannot bring himself to ask for forgiveness is an anomaly in community life. He is suffering from a sickness that inhibits both the free movement of love in the community and also his own prayers — the prayers that should be the more healthy and sincere, *saniores*, because they are frequently made.

Yet while it is true that alienation in one member does make it difficult for the others to love him, this is the very attitude which his fellow monks must show toward him. In such a situation the capacity to choose to love (*diligere*) faces a stringent test. Such a love will express itself principally in tolerance and forbearance. It is possible to be patient and lenient cynically and as taking the line of least resistance, but this will only harden already unsatisfactory relationships. The only firm foundation which love provides for creative tolerance in the face of alienation is pity. When a man genuinely pities another who is suffering, then he is always open to receive him just as he is. "The sense of pity," William Lynch has written, "comes closest to being the best of human instincts and, if we keep an eye on the Christian story, pity brings man very near to the divine action itself."[14] This is the quality which Augustine evoked in paragraphs 8 and 9 of chapter IV, when he used the word translated "with compassion" (*misericorditer*), and this brings us close to his notion of forgiveness as almsgiving which we have mentioned above.

Nevertheless it has to be recognized that a facility in apologizing may itself be a weakness. There are those whose begging pardon is pathological and disordered, and this is an indication of an insecurity which community life can aggravate. The falseness of this attitude lies in projecting hurt onto others and then feeling sorry for the imagined injury. Members of a community have to learn how to bear with this sort of inadequacy which creates as unreal a situation as does a case of alienation.

Augustine begins his summing up of this precept with a homely warning expressed in simple language: *uobis a uerbis durioribus parcite*, spare yourself from harsher words. Because that sounds stilted and forced in English, and because it is necessary to bring out the appeal to unaffectedness which is implicit in this chapter as a whole, I have translated it as "you should take care, then, not to use harsh words." Then follows the most telling phrase in the whole of this paragraph which, as we have discovered in our exploration of its themes, does go very deep into the being of the brothers: "do not be ashamed" (*non pigeat*). This takes us to the very heart of the experience of forgiveness. Often people are so ashamed of what they have done that they are even ashamed to apologize for it. But the expression of shame is the very factor that can bring about healing. If there is genuine regret at what one has done and also a genuine desire to make amends then one's proper sense of shame is the factor that is most likely to reach one's victim. If shame is repressed or if self-justification is superimposed on it, then there can be no real meeting.

From the moment when Augustine's understanding of the common life reached the stage when he found that love was pivotal, he has become more and more concerned with the necessity for real encounter and exchange between the brothers. This theme has been taken to deeper and deeper levels in the personal lives of the brothers, from chapter IV, 10 onward. At this point he turns to look at the realities of encounter against the corporate background of the community's life.

Rule, Chapter VI, 3

But if the necessity of good order compels you
to speak forcibly
in order to put in their place those who are younger than you are yourself,
even if you yourself feel that you have gone too far
it is not demanded of you that you should apologize to them.
For it is their duty to defer to you;
and your power to act should not be weakened
by a display of excessive humility.
All the same, you should ask pardon of the one who is Lord of all
and who knows with what real concern
even those whom you may have reproved with more than justice
are loved by you.
Moreover, even love among you
must not be based on the standards of the world
but on the standards of the Holy Spirit.

REPROOF AND CORRECTION

A certain discomfort is produced by the reading of this paragraph both in the fourth century and in the twentieth. But its challenge is met in different ways.

The passage reflects precise attitudes that a modern person cannot readily accept because their dynamics are outside today's experience, and it is therefore necessary to take particular care in disentangling the meaning and the assumptions that underlie the *Rule*'s packed sentences. Here there is an inescapable difficulty, because it is impossible to be certain what Augustine meant in one particular — his use of the word *minoribus*. We shall look at that problem later; for the moment there are other points to be noted.

In the first place, there is a contrast in language. The phrases at the end of the previous paragraph used homely words in making their appeal. Here the terms are more formal — and this may indicate an element of irony or mockery in Augustine's approach to what is, in fact, a matter that has to be taken seriously in community life (as he himself shows before he has finished dealing with the present subject). Or perhaps he as author is setting himself at a distance from what he is writing about — not because he needs to be more dispassionate than in other parts of the *Rule*, nor because his theme is remote from experience, but because he is aware of the rather thin ice that he is treading on. Whatever his reasons, he does use here some rather pompous words:

necessitas disciplinae — "the necessity of good order"

cohercendis — translated, "put in their place," with the implications of correction or restraint

conpellit — "compels"

non . . . exigitur — "it is not demanded"

ueniam postuletis — "apologize," with stress on asking forgiveness (the second Latin word, which means "to request," can have legal overtones: in the previous paragraph the simpler word *peto* was used three times in connection with forgiveness, and it is also used at the end of the present paragraph when the sting of its opening theme has been drawn)

subiectos — to be subject to, "to defer" (the formal aspect of this word has a place in Christian tradition from an early date)[15]

regendi auctoritas — which can be strongly expressed as "power to rule" or — as has been done in translation — "power to act" in any situation

Now the surprising thing to discover is that these words are not directed to the one who is in full charge, the prior; they are directed to all the members. The Latin "you" is in plural form (*uos*), not singular. This point is important, because it highlights the fact that in community life all have to recognize "the necessity of good order," all may in some circumstances have to put others in their place, all may be driven to do so whether they like it or not because "good order" requires it, all stand under the same precept that in these circumstances apology is not needed if the reprimand has been greater than the fault, all at times are in a position where others must defer to them, all exercise some authority over others. When we realize that all members of the community have a personal responsibility to take this precept seriously, some of its seeming arrogance disappears. Or perhaps this is the point that Augustine is trying to make with his stiff language: if a brother is not careful he will behave (and sometimes he surely will) in just such an arrogant way as the words imply.

THE NECESSITY OF GOOD ORDER

In community activity, either inside or outside a monastery, there has to be good order if any objective is to be reached; and there has to be deference to the one on whom responsibility ultimately falls. This in no way undermines the valuable principle of subsidiarity by which responsibility is placed as far from the center as it can be set without weakening the object in view. What good order meant for Augustine in practical terms has been described in chapters 3 and 4; what it meant in attitudes has been explored previously in chapter 1.

His most penetrating description of good order was written toward the end of his life, after years of experience within a monastery and within the whole Church in North Africa. We have quoted it earlier in connection with the ordinary details of life in the monastery, but it is worth quoting again now for the bearing it has on the attitudes of the brothers to one another. It begins where the *Rule* begins, with those who are members of a household (chapter I, 2):

> The peace of the household is ordered agreement of those who dwell together, whether they command or whether they obey; the peace of the city is ordered agreement of its citizens, whether they command or whether they obey . . . order is the arrangement of equal and unequal which assigns to each its proper place (*The City of God* XIX, 13).

This is the ideal, but it does sometimes happen that either consciously or unconsciously an attempt is made to usurp the position of another, either negatively by refusing to accede to a request or positively by doing something different from what is ordered. One does not have to resort to the use of imagination to realize the sort of situations that fall under Augustine's judgment in this matter.

PRESUMPTUOUS BEHAVIOR

Presumptuousness is a temptation that most people fall prey to, and by the same token it is also a disposition that everyone has to deal with in himself as well as in others. In the present context, Augustine is only concerned with the interpersonal aspect of the matter. Different ages will produce different manifestations of it, but that is for the most part irrelevant. In attending to what Augustine is saying at this point it is necessary to guard against a tendency which has been noted by W. B. Stanford in connection with an entirely different aspect of the writings of antiquity: "To allow current fashions to affect . . . judgment in matters of decorum."[16] Courtesy and good manners, as well as acceptance of the greater responsibility of others, are attitudes that take varying forms according to their social situation, for example, at home or at work. One of the early lessons that a child learns is the difference between formal and informal occasions. A common pattern of acceptable behavior is evolved in every society, both human and subhuman; and the common problem that Augustine is touching on — only touching on — here is the behavior that is precipitated when there is a breach of accepted norms.

At this point it will be best to look at the perpetrators of presumptuous behavior whom Augustine calls *minores*. As Luc Verheijen has pointed out,[17] the *Rule's* first readers or hearers will have known exactly what — who, in fact — was meant by this word, but for others it is ambiguous. It could mean social inferiors (in which case the precept given in chapter I, 7 would need to be borne in mind); or it could mean those who are less advanced in the monastic life, whether in terms of their spiritual maturity or of their relative sphere of responsibility; or it could mean those who are younger in age or in their number of years as a monk. Although it is impossible to be absolutely sure what was meant by the word *minores*, it is certain that those referred to were in some sense in a disadvantageous position. Unfortunately, a translator has to choose when there is no way of determining an author's exact meaning, but because of the use that Augustine makes of the same word in a sermon that echoes many of the ideas of the present paragraph, I have used the phrase "younger than you are yourself." In Sermon 211:4 we find him saying: "I say to everyone, men and women, *minores et maiores*, lay people and clerics, and I say to myself also that we must all hear and be on our guard lest we cause offense to our brothers." Here the meaning can only be "young and old." As such it is as acceptable as are the other pairs of words: men and women, lay people and clerics — all refer to a clearly defined status. And there is corroboration of this understanding of Augustine's text in the minutes of the Council of Carthage held in 348. At that meeting some of the older bishops complained of the proud and contumacious attitude of younger bishops toward them, and it was agreed that the *minores* should be called to task when they were rude.[18] Thus it seems a fair inference that in the monastic community to whom the *Rule* is directed the position of *minores* was one recognized by all the members, and the code of behavior expected of them would also be known to every brother.

REACTIONS TO PRESUMPTUOUSNESS

Sometimes an accepted code is ignored; and the *Rule* assumes, rightly, that there are occasions when a brother reacts forcibly against such presumptuousness — and that usually involves hard words. An uncontrolled reaction occurs when the victim is taken by surprise and is thrown off guard. Then he himself will overstep the bounds of discretion (*modum uos excessisse*) and say more than is needed and more than is just by way of correction (*plus iusto forte corripitis*). When that has happened there is no need, says Augustine, for apology from the one who has reproved too strongly. This unequivocal statement shocks modern readers, and yet it has to be admitted that what it advocates is precisely what does sometimes happen. As he has said in the previous paragraph, people vary in how easily they are roused and in how spontaneously they can apologize. Sometimes anger and reproof are justified; but, *be angry but do not sin*, wrote the author of Ephesians (4:26). However, in the *Rule* as it stands it is not easy to reconcile Augustine's precept with the words of scripture. But before we dismiss his injunction as either offensive or irrelevant outside its immediate context, it will be useful to look further at the sermon in which we have just found a similar line of thought. Augustine's theme is that while it is part of the human condition that people do hurt each other it rests with them whether the offense goes deep or not. "While we live," the sermon continues, "let us do what the Father commands (he who will be our judge), let us ask pardon of the brothers whom we may have offended and hurt by some provocation or other." Then Augustine stops to consider the effect that apology may have on those to whom it is offered — and it is here that he comes across a difficulty (whether it is still so in the twentieth-century is another matter). For, he says, there are some people who will only get overweeningly proud if you apologize to them.

> This is what I mean: sometimes a master does sin against his servant. Although one is master and one is servant, yet each is the servant of another because both have been redeemed by the blood of Christ. But it seems too inflexible to insist or advise that if a master does sin against his servant, by reviling him unjustly or by unjustly giving him a beating, he must say to him, "Forgive me, grant me pardon." Not because he ought to do so, but because there is the risk that the other will begin to get above himself. What, then, should he do? Before God he

should repent; before God he should punish his own heart. And although it may not be fitting that he should say to the servant "Give me pardon," yet he should speak to him soothingly. To speak to him with kindness, that is to beg his forgiveness (Sermon 211, 4).

Anyone who looks honestly into his own heart will need to admit to a certain degree of smug satisfaction if ever someone of higher rank does apologize to him. But who is to judge whether that sin of pride is greater than the sin of meting out more than justice to another in word and deed? Only God really knows, and anyone who attempted a judgment would soon be guilty of yet another sin. So perhaps the matter is best left unjudged but with these points kept in mind: (1) the twentieth-century revolution in the understanding of interpersonal relationships and the new social structures that this involves did not obtain in Augustine's day, but (2) the tendency to self-satisfied pride at signs of weakness in others is the same now as it has always been.

Augustine's next point is the obvious one that within any group consideration and good manners are incumbent on every member. We need not think in terms of master/servant in looking at this passage in the *Rule*. In any group there are written and unwritten standards and terms of reference which those exercising any responsibility must observe and should expect to find observed by those whom they encounter as they fulfill their own function. By acting outside the expected patterns of behavior one attracts scorn and suspicion — Michal's reaction to David's dancing before the Lord is an obvious instance.[19] Whether one is justified or not in breaking with convention, one must be prepared to take responsibility for doing so. The situation that Augustine is dealing with here is that two brothers have, in different but related ways, exceeded the bounds of decorum and recognized good order. One has been rude to another, and the second has then shown his disapproval in no uncertain terms. What Augustine is getting at in his rather studied language is that it does not help matters if the second steps even further from accepted norms by an "excessive" (*nimia*, which could also be translated as overmuch) display of abjection (*humilitas*): for to do so is only to make a fool of himself. He knows that he has said more than he should, but the precept's advice, as also the sermon which we have looked at above, is that gentle behavior and gentle words are more capable of erasing the first monk's error than any extraordinary efforts on the part of the *maior* (older). Gentle words which meet the other in his disordered state are of more value than forceful ones which attempt to express one's own lack of balance (though here in the precepts Augustine omits to mention gentle words — instead, as we shall see shortly, he describes an even better way).

Damaged relationships do more than block communication between brother and brother; they also often result in turning a wrongdoer away from God (many people do give up the practice of their religion because of unresolved problems of guilt). A person feels all the more important because he has been affronted and so has been forced into a false position. It is the falsity that creeps into a situation such as this one examined in the *Rule* which points to where the deep sin lies — namely in one's pride and little regard for the other person, even though he also is in the wrong. The place where sin can be removed is within God, and this points to the logic of Augustine's next words: "All the same, you should ask pardon of the one who is Lord of all" — although, he means, it would be absurd to grovel to the presumptuous brother whom one has more-than-firmly corrected it is not out of place, in fact it is truly right, to be very humble indeed about the whole episode before God. Augustine's choice of words here, as throughout this passage, is pointed and his use of the word *domino* (to the Lord) and not *deo* (to God) is very telling. The two monks, both of them, have been overweening, that is to say, they have been lordly in their attitudes. So in using the word *dominus* (which has only occurred once previously, in chapter IV, 5, in a quotation of scripture) instead of *deus* (which is used ten times altogether), Augustine is subtly reducing his offenders to size.

LOVE, THE CONTROLLING FACTOR

At this point he probes deeper into what has been going on within the outraged monk in the uncontrolled encounter. In his heart he sincerely loves the other man, accepts him, values him and gives him his worth: the Lord knows, Augustine says, "with what real concern" the offender or offenders are loved. But love can only be put into effect when one is feeling secure and safe. Whenever a person's security is threatened by the attitude of another, the capacity to give love and a sense of security to others is shattered. The intention is to love, but the capacity to do so is impaired. And there is nothing, humanly speaking, that one can do to heal oneself. The source of healing is God, and the path to that source is contrition, which is a healthy compound of a sense of responsibility and a sense of guilt. God knows the confusion and the struggles that go on within a person; he knows the disparities between rational intention and irrational behavior; he knows the degree of wrong we inflict on ourselves as well as the damage that we do to other people; he knows that our better nature wants to be loving and accepting, to be a vessel for the fruit of the Spirit which Paul names in Galatians 5:22 as *love, joy, peace, patience, kindness, goodness, faithfulness, gentleness, self-control.*

So Augustine goes on to point out that it is at a deep level that restoration of a person and between persons has to take place. Having introduced his key word, love, in its verbal form (*diligatis*) — "[the] Lord of all . . . knows with what real concern even those whom you may have reproved . . . are loved by you" — he goes on to make a distinction. The matter of "good order" and accepted standards, with which the first part of this paragraph was concerned, is largely one of social dimensions; and, by that token, it can be approached in a worldly, secular spirit. But, says Augustine, the monk's attitude even in ordinary everyday affairs must not remain at that level; loving care must be more than a social matter. "Moreover, even love among you must not be based on the standards of the world but on the standards of the Holy Spirit."

THE STANDARDS OF THE HOLY SPIRIT

This final sentence of chapter VI is important because it supplements the teaching of chapter IV, 10. We saw, in our exploration of that passage, the wide and embracing quality of the love that Augustine was evoking. At this present point, when his mind and heart have moved further into the processes of true forgiveness and reconciliation, he directs his readers to further aspects of that love. Ordinary standards, which in fact fluctuate like health and the seasons' temperatures, cannot in the nature of things express the depth of our loving; they remain superficial because they represent the lowest common measure of rapprochement between people. It is this contrast between fluctuation and transformation which is expressed in the Pauline passage on which Augustine bases this last precept on the subject of reconciliation. He says, "love among you must not be based on the standards of the world but on the standards of the Holy Spirit."

The phrase, "based on the standards of the world," is a paraphrase of Augustine's adjective *carnalis*. This word and its prepositional form, *secundum carnem*, is a recurring theme in the New Testament and it means ordinary standards that are orientated toward humanity, not toward God.[20] In the principal passages where the words occur, the Revised Standard Version gives *according to the flesh* in John 8:15 and Romans 8:4.5.12, *according to/of worldly things* in 1 Corinthians 1:26 and 2 Corinthians 11:18, and *earthly* in Ephesians 6:5 and Colossians 3:22. It has seemed best in translating the *Rule* to use the more innocuous phrase of the Corinthians passages, although it is the first two of the above passages which have a bearing on the *Rule*. In the Johannine verse, Jesus is in controversy with the Pharisees when he tells them that their judgments are made according to the flesh and he goes on to say, *I judge no one. Yet even if I do judge, my judgment is true, for it is not I alone that judge, but I and he who sent me* (verses 15b-16). The point that is being made is that Jesus' "judgment is performed on a different plane, and not subject to the same standards."[21] Because Christians are sons in the Son, living on a different plane from that of other people — though still living with them in common social conditions — their judgments and their actions are to be governed by different terms of reference. But because Christians as much as others find that humanness and the business of living impinge on them as they do on everyone else, they face a constant temptation to be guided by lower standards. These lower standards apply not only to the flagrantly bad things which Paul lists in Galatians 5:19-21 — *immorality, impurity, licentiousness, idolatry, sorcery, enmity, strife, jealousy, anger, selfishness, dissension, party spirit, envy, drunkenness, carousing, and the like*. Also included are the good things which are the obverse of these characteristics and which do enrich human life: the faculty of worship, awareness that the subconscious and the unconscious have a great bearing on human behavior, a capacity to love, a refusal to be submerged by people and circumstances, a sense of the value of things, an ability not to acquiesce uncritically in everything that is presented to one's consciousness, a power of self-protection, an ability to express disagreement as well as to relate to others who are like-minded, and finally a realization that good things are worth striving for. These are ordinary human abilities. But Christians know that they are called to a very profound way of putting them into practice.

In the particular context of the present chapter of the *Rule*, because it arises naturally from what Augustine has already said about the restoration of good relationships between the monks, he singles out one of these high human capacities for discussion — it is love which is to be exercised "according to the standards of the Holy Spirit" and not according to ordinary standards. This is a point which he needed to stress because the word that he uses for love (*dilectio*) is capable of both secular and religious meaning. As we have already seen, he himself uses it consistently when he discusses Christian love in his commentary on 1 John — he does so because this is the word to be found in his Latin Bible. But its primary meaning is pre-Christian, denoting a love that chooses to love, a love that is concerned with values. What Augustine is stressing when he tells the monks that the love that binds them to one another is to be based on the Spirit's standards and not on those of ordinary life is the fact that Christian life is life transformed. Christian life is no negative set of definitions and prohibitions; it is creative and dynamic because it is empowered by the Holy Spirit. Christian vocation involves living in the flesh according to the Spirit, and not living in the flesh according to the flesh.[22]

For the sake of clarity, it has seemed necessary in translation to add the word holy when dealing with Augustine's *spiritalis*. In the Pauline passage which he is echoing (Rom 8:1-2) it is clear that the Holy Spirit is being referred to; but in the passage of the *Rule* it would be possible to interpret the phrase as meaning merely "taking into account spiritual values." This is too weak a sense to carry much weight, and it would not prompt the transition of thought which occurs at the beginning of the next paragraph and chapter. *Spiritalis* refers to the activity of the Holy Spirit as Paul describes it in Romans 8.

What needs to be looked at more closely is the fact that Augustine has chosen to draw a distinction between "the standards of the world" and "the standards of the Holy Spirit" in regard to what is in any case considered to be the highest human capacity, the capacity to love. Loving concern for other people operates within the limits of any social structure — and that in itself is a merciful providence. In practice, few human beings either give or receive the same quality of love within every compartment of their lives. It is possible for a person who is unhappy and unloved at home to be entirely happy and loved (and to that extent to be a different person) at work, just as it is possible to be unloved at work (work being a necessity here) but to be loved and accepted in one's leisure activities which are of one's own choosing. Love can and often does encounter only a part of a person and it can be confined within the limits of specific areas of encounter — very few colleagues do meet outside the boundaries set by their work. But what fellowship in Christ demands is the transcending of limits — and this is very costing indeed, given the fragmentation of life which is characteristic of most societies. Christians are separated from others in the church-organized part of their lives; they are separated from each other as soon as they move away from whatever their church-center happens to be. Until very recently Christians seldom entered the home and family circle of fellow-Christians, though the appearance of neighborhood groups and the celebration of the eucharist in houses is now beginning to break down barriers in a significant way. Yet it still remains generally true that loving fellowship and loving service are experienced in relation to different groups, a painful fact which underlines a fundamental disunity in the body of Christ.

THE SPIRIT-DIRECTED QUALITY OF LOVE

Monastic life, which holds together every part of a monk's life, is an attempt to overcome such fragmentation. For a monk who is trying to live the life fully (though one has to admit that it is possible to opt out of its demands) it is impossible to split off his experience in, say, the kitchen from his encounters at recreation, or his relationships there from his experience in choir. Monastic life is all one — and that is why it is so costing and why "ordinary" standards of love and friendship are not sufficient to hold it together. Augustine himself came to see very clearly both the obstacles to the flowing of love and also the results that follow when love is poured out. When he was an older and more experienced man he put his insight succinctly when he wrote: "You are to love all people, even your enemies . . . not because they are your brothers and sisters, but in order that they may be" (*Homilies on the First Letter of John* 10, 7). Such love, he says, turned away from the self and toward another, is not inherent in men; it needs to be asked for from God. It is the awareness that the quality one is expressing transcends one's self that distinguishes love according to the standards of the Spirit from love according to the world's standards. In another place he describes the integration that this first kind of love implies: "It is love of God for the sake of God and of one's self and of one's neighbor for the sake of God" (*Teaching Christianity* III, 15, 23). Thus, for the Christian, love itself has one source and one object in whatever circumstances it operates. An early passage from the commentary on 1 John brings this out distinctly: "Christian love is altogether of one piece, and as itself is compacted into a unity, so it makes into one all that are linked to it, like a flame fusing them together" (*Homilies on the First Letter of John* 10, 7). Love lies in "not rending our unity, in maintaining charity" (*Homilies on the First Letter of John* 2, 3). Such love is God's love at work in his lovers and though it shows itself in quite ordinary circumstances it springs from the hidden depths of the Spirit that are within people. Augustine had grasped this fact very early in his Christian life, some years before he came to write the *Rule*, and he realized that this love which is so commonplace in its manifestations is itself an actualization of the search whose end is both present and future. In his first book against the Manichaeans, written before his return to Africa, he wrote of

> the pure and sincere love of God which manifests itself especially in one's way of life. Inspired by the Holy Spirit, this love leads to the Son, that is, to the wisdom of God through whom the Father himself is known. If wisdom or truth is not desired with all the powers of the soul, it shall not be found at all, but if it is sought after as it deserves to be it cannot withhold or hide itself from those who love it.

And after quoting Matthew 7:7 and 10:26 he continues:

> It is love that asks, love that seeks, love that knocks, love that discloses, and love, too, that abides in that which is disclosed (*The Catholic Way of Life* 31).

From these few passages it is possible to see that for Augustine love according to the standards of the Spirit comes from God and is always directed through people toward him. Yet though this love is potentially so wide and so deep it nevertheless has to be expressed in precise and concrete ways. That is to say, it can only be expressed in terms of individuals. Hans Urs von Balthasar has pointed out that although there is such a thing as brotherly love for people in general there is no such thing as a generalized love for one's neighbor — love for one's neighbor is always particular.[23] And Christians are bidden by their Lord to love their neighbors as themselves, with the same intensity and concern and with the same ability to overlook faults. This quality of love requires a continuing attempt to put oneself in the other's place, to search for his or her inner meaning as humbly as one searches for one's own.

It is possible, without this Spirit-directed quality of loving, to build up a viable community. Any community of necessity requires rules and structures to safeguard its life. Human nature tends to codify its ideals and to quantify their expression, but this is a danger to the very qualities that it is aiming to preserve. That is why Augustine's precept at this point in the *Rule* is so important: even the ideal of love can perish and it will do so unless its life-force is of the Spirit. In a monastery, beyond the structures and regulations that are always provisional and contingent, there is the added dimension of living which is created by the Spirit. While it is evident that Augustine has Romans 8:1-13 in mind in calling the monks to live according to "the standards of the Holy Spirit," the actual function of the Spirit is expressed more clearly in 1 Corinthians 2:12: *We have received not the spirit of the world, but the Spirit which is from God, that we might understand the gifts bestowed on us by God.* To recognize the gifts of God is itself a very great gift, and what differentiates the standards of the world from those of the Spirit is their objective. We have quoted above the passage from *The City of God* in which Augustine describes the nature of good order in a household and in a city. After mentioning the ordered agreement of citizens and before defining order as such, the passage continues: "the peace of the heavenly city is the fellowship of enjoying God and enjoying one another in God, a fellowship held closely together by order and in harmony; the peace of all created things is the tranquility bestowed by order" (*The City of God* XIX, 13).

Peace, tranquility, and order reflect the thought of Paul in Romans 8: *To set the mind on the flesh is death, but to set the mind on the Spirit is life and peace* (verse 6); *you are not in the flesh, you are in the Spirit, if the Spirit of God really dwells in you* (verse 9); *if you love according to the flesh you will die, but if by the Spirit you put to death the deeds of the body you will live* (verse 13). Thus when Augustine frames his short precept about the way in which love is to be lived, he is directing his monks away from self and toward their brothers who are their brothers in Christ. The love which all are to exchange with each other, whatever their rank or their role in the community, is a love that is seeking and finding God in all created things and not least in one another. Their fellowship (*societas* — the word that was used to describe the life of the community in chapters I, 7 and IV, 9) lies in "enjoying one another in God," not solely in each other (which is the quality of love according to the standards of the world). The household of the monks is to show the marks, here and now, of the heavenly city; and Augustine is right in stressing that such order and harmony are only possible when men's capacity to love is Spirit-filled. Rules, regulations, and diversified functions within the community cannot reach into the hearts of men; they remain exterior. It is each monk's interior attitude that can enable his exterior behavior to conform to the standards of the Spirit because the Spirit himself dwells within each one (chapter IV, 6), drawing all toward God and toward each other, enabling them to enjoy their growing knowledge of the workings of God and to enjoy their growing knowledge of one another.

From this point onward, when Augustine is writing to the whole community he is writing to a household of faith.

NOTES

1. *The Religious Life Today*, Burns & Oates, 1977, page 39.

2. For example, Nm 25:4; Jgs 2:14; 2 Chr 28:11; Ps 78:31; Jer 4:8, 23:20; Lam 4:16; Zep 2:2-3; Jn 3:36; Eph 5:6; Rv 14:10, 15:1, 16.1.

3. Neh 9:17; Ps 103:8; Jl 2:13; Jon 4:2; Na 1:3.

4. Burnaby, *Amor Dei*, Hodder & Stoughton, 1947, reprint, page 135.

5. *The River Within*, Darton, Longman & Todd, 1978, page 84.

6. *The Epistles of St. John*, Macmillan, 3rd edition, 1892, page 113.

7. *Cry the Beloved Country*, Jonathan Cape, 1948, page 46.

8. For a full discussion of Augustine's thinking on the meaning of forgiveness, see Luc Verheijen's study of Sermons 205-211 in his *Nouvelle Approche de la Règle de Saint Augustin*, Abbaye de Bellefontaine, 1980, pages 178-189 (hereafter *Nouvelle Approche*).

9. Sermon 205, 3.

10. *Nouvelle Approche*, pages 181-185.

11. Tertullian's treatise on the Lord's Prayer is entitled *De oratione*.

12. *Nouvelle Approche*, page 115. The article la Bonnardière appeared in *Revue des Études Augustiniennes* XIII (1967) 31-53.

13. In chapters III, 5; IV, 8; V, 6 and 8.

14. *Christ and Apollo*, page 126.

15. See, for example, the treatment in E. G. Selwyn's *The First Epistle of St. Peter*, pages 386-389, 402, 412, 415, 420, 422-439, 440 and 460ff.

16. *Enemies of Poetry*, Routledge & Kegan Paul, 1980, page 41.

17. *Nouvelle Approche*, page 187. And in what follows, see the whole section, pages 186-188.

18. The text is quoted in *Nouvelle Approche*, page 87.

19. 2 Sm 6:16.

20. See C. K. Barrett, *The Second Epistle to the Corinthians*, A. & C. Black, 1973, page 72 and *The Epistle to the Romans*, Black, 1957, page 157.

21. Barnabas Lindars, *The Gospel of John*, Oliphants, 1972, page 317.

22. See Hans-Ruedi Weber, *The Cross: Tradition and Interpretation*, SPCK, 1979, pages 93-94.

23. *Science, Religion and Christianity*, Burns & Oates, 1958, page 150.

7

Obedience

Rule, Chapter VII, 1

You should obey your prior as you would a father,
with respect for his office,
lest you offend God who is in him.
This applies still more to the priest who has responsibility for you all.

HOUSEHOLD OF FAITH

The first part of Romans 8, which we have found to underlie the final precept of chapter VI of the *Rule*, also sets the direction in which Augustine now moves. After discussing the difference between worldly standards and those based on the promptings of the Holy Spirit (as far as verse 13), Paul continues in verse 14: *For all who are led by the Spirit of God are sons of God*. The sequence in the *Rule* is: "Moreover, even love among you must not be based on the standards of the world but on the standards of the Holy Spirit. You should obey your prior as you would a father" (end of chapter VI, 3 and beginning of chapter VII, 1). In each case the sequence is the same: the inadequacy of worldly standards, the life-giving and enriching power of the Holy Spirit, and the experience of being part of a family.

From this point onward in the *Rule*, Augustine's thought is dominated by the idea of family relationships — an idea that is far wider than what in English we mean when we speak of family relationships. We shall need to look at this in a moment.

In general, Augustine has now said nearly all the important things that he has to say to the community as a whole; at this stage he turns the members' attention to the one among them who fulfills the office of prior. The prior is to be accepted as a father is accepted in a family.

THE *PRAEPOSITUS*

We need to be clear as to what the monks meant when they heard or used the word *praepositus* which for want of anything better is usually translated as "prior" in monastic texts (meaning, the one in the first place). The English word prior has ecclesiastical overtones which have been forced on it by history, but *praepositus* was in no sense a specialized word: it was "a civil title for any chief executive officer" — the head of a factory as well as the head of a monastery was its *praepositus*.[1] Throughout the *Rule*, it is principally an executive role that has been allotted to the prior, and it is only at this late stage, after the discussion at the end of the previous chapter, that Augustine gives him another sphere of duty and one that still belongs to ordinary society and not solely to a body of Christians. The prior is the head of a social entity, but that entity is a household, a family, not a workshop or a civil service unit or any such group. The prior is the father of the family and so, says Augustine, you should obey your prior as you would a father.

This sentence of the text contains the only use of the word father (*pater*) and the first important use of the word obey (*oboediatur*).[2] We will consider the second word first, because it is the other one to which Augustine gives his chief attention in this chapter.

OBEDIENCE

Obedience is a word that has contracted in meaning and become impoverished. In many languages even today it expresses both hearing and compliance, and that double meaning lies also in the Latin word's derivation (*ob audio*) although, as in English, the primary meaning soon dropped out of sight. To obey is to do more than fulfill a command; it is to accommodate oneself to another person — not only to his words but to the underlying currents of his thought. The fact that obedience is the last of the fundamental monastic obligations to be mentioned in the *Rule* has its counterpart in the later history of monasticism itself, particularly in the West, for its adoption by monks — in a large sense and also within individual experience — was and is preceded by that of poverty and chastity. At a personal level, first a man renounced all, then he undertook to remain unmarried, and eventually he accepted obedience as a way of life. In the fourth century, when a recognizable structure of monastic life came to be established, obedience became a basic norm together with simplicity of living and celibacy. Henry C. Lea suggested that its adoption may have been an antidote to the defection of many monks and nuns after the monastic "population explosion" of that century.[3] Whether this is so, or whether the concept arose of necessity simply because groups create the need for leadership, a monk's commitment to obedience was something that was inherent by the time Augustine embraced monasticism.

The tradition created by the monks of the East was described in a number of passages by Augustine's contemporary, Cassian (360-435). In his travels among the eastern monasteries he found that absolute obedience was a quality that had to be learned by young monks,[4] for obedience and subjection were an essential aspect of their common life;[5] and this extended throughout a community because everyone owed obedience to his senior.[6] In addition to obedience to persons, there was also obedience to the community's ancient and approved customs.[7] Cassian understood obedience as an aspect of humility. Yet the impression one gains from reading the *Institutes* and the *Conferences* is of impersonality in the structure of a community, with little interaction between person and person in practical affairs.

On the other hand, in matters of the spirit, humility and personal dependence on the wisdom and experience of another had a vital part to play in the development of each monk and in eastern monasticism as a whole. The supreme factor in this evolution was the perception that the wisdom and insight of a spiritual guide was not something that had been striven for and attained; it was itself a gift of the Holy Spirit — and that was the sole reason for spiritual leadership and the only reason for its acceptance by a learner.[8] Obedience, therefore, was fundamentally directed to God.

Even before Cassian began his monastic explorations, the structure of Saint Basil's monasteries reflected a more personal outlook and a fuller awareness of the deeper levels at which each monk lived. There is a sense of caring in his Rules. Nevertheless, when it came to describing the quality of the obedience which a monk should give to his superior Saint Basil said that it should resemble that of a servant/slave to his master.[9] The paramount obligation is the fulfilling of a master's will.

Thus the essence of the concept of obedience by Augustine's time was that of humble submission and deference. What seems to be lacking in it is warmth. One of Augustine's great contributions to the development of monasticism was that while accepting the notion of obedience as essential to the life, he set it against a different background from that of his predecessors — inevitably so, in view of his understanding of the primacy of love. When love is the way, and unity of heart entirely centered upon God is the goal, then obedience itself is above all concerned with personal relationships: "You should obey your prior as you would a father" (*praeposito tamquam patri oboediatur*).

The importance of this precept far outweighs the attention that its author actually gives to it in the *Rule*, for it places the life of a monastery on a quite different footing from any of its predecessors while at the same time it incorporates all that is best in the tradition as it had developed since the days of Pachomius and the beginning of cenobitic life. Not that the use of the word father was new. *Abba* was the common title for a spiritual guide in the East, and its derivative *abbatus* was an accepted title for the head of a monastery. Augustine had admired the monasticism he had met in Italy where he found that an abbot was obeyed because of his goodness and his powers of leadership. But his own ideal was that obedience should be a response to fatherliness, and what he is doing in the present sentence of the *Rule* is to break down exclusive and particular attitudes toward life in a monastery in order to provide an analogous pattern that is much nearer to ordinary life. For him, a monastery is home; it is where the monks belong.

A monk is in some senses separated from the world, but his life should never be entirely different from his previous experience of living. His way of life is to be a heightening of the values that he held before he entered and a way of penetrating more deeply into their meaning. Augustine, by using the analogy of fatherhood and of life in a family, stresses the mutuality of the relationship between the head of the monastery and those whom he serves. We have noticed in earlier passages how the prior's service was taken for granted: he was the one who decided how all the community's goods were to be distributed according to need (chapter I, 3 and V, 3), and it was he who had the final responsibility in matters of health and general well-being (chapters IV, 1.11 and V, 4.5 and 7). These duties are also those of a father of a family, and they are different from the responsibilities of a spiritual father, *abba* — responsibilities which Augustine assigns to the community's priest (chapter IV, 9.11).

THE FATHER IN ROMAN SOCIETY

Roman *patres* were more than parents with children to care for; they had a whole household to take care of, servants/slaves as well as kindred. In English the word family signifies a man's kin, but in Latin *familia* meant the total community that came under the care of the head of a home establishment; we noted earlier that one word for a household slave is *famulus*. So when Augustine uses the word *pater* he is thinking of a *paterfamilias*, a father of a family, with all the responsibilities that that implies.[10] In one sense, a Roman father operated on two fronts, with intimate personal responsibility for his wife and children and other relatives as well as with responsibility for the other members of his household. In another sense, the responsibility was one, since it was concerned with establishing good relationships and good conduct among all the members, and for this he needed to exercise love and attention.

In one way, a father can be taken for granted as head of a family, its provider and to a large extent its orderer. The function of the father is something to be responded to, and this response is conditioned by his character and attitudes. If the father is positive and encouraging, the response will be one of love; if he is negative and critical, fear will be the family's response. In outward appearance both responses may take the same form; there may be a conformity to the father's wishes, since behavior is largely imitative and an inborn sense of self-preservation prompts acquiescence. But a simulated obedience is false because it lacks a spirit of desire for the good of the one who gives the command, it is introverted and is more concerned with the self than with the other, and it lacks respect for him as a person as well as for his function within the family.

The sort of father whom Augustine has in mind in this precept is not a perfect one, for there is none such; the image that he evokes is of a good father, as he shows more specifically in paragraph 3. That means that the monks' response to the prior will be a response to his goodness and to all that he does for their welfare. As time goes on, they will each become more aware of his strengths and his weaknesses. He is continually developing, and so are they. As the rest of this chapter makes clear, Augustine is assuming an adult attitude to another adult; he is not evoking a childlike response by a monk to his prior. One of the ironies of history is that while the broad function of a *paterfamilias* (which lies at the root of medieval feudalism) has been diminished and dismissed as a viable model, its successor, the father of children, has been given a place in monastic thinking that it was never meant to have. The paternal model has resulted in the infantilism that has been the bane of monasticism in the West (I do not know about the East) from which we are now, in the second half of the twentieth century, becoming emancipated. We need to be freed from this image for two reasons: (1) because what Augustine is talking about in his *Rule* is consistently a relationship between adults, and (2) because many people today have no adequate model of fatherhood which they can use effectively if they enter a monastery — there are so many one-parent families nowadays, and when there is not this particular limitation there is often another one stemming from an unsatisfactory relationship with one's father which can vitiate one's attitudes within community life.

What needs to be kept in mind in considering the deepening of a monk's attitude to the head of his monastery is that it must of necessity be based on loyalty, appreciation, and trust.[11]

In community life an individual's relationship with the head of the house is one that is always in movement. For both, it is a learning process — a learning about oneself as well as about the other. No son or daughter, no monk or nun, no subordinate of any kind can ever accept the father, prior, or boss uncritically, but that does not, in a mature person, prevent one from receiving from that person whatever direction has to be issued. As Augustine puts it: "You should obey your prior as you would a father, with respect for his office."

The word that has been translated as "office" is "honor" which is the normal Latin word for a public function. Office is the English word that expresses a similar public function with overtones of bearing a burden as well as a responsibility. Later, as we shall see in paragraph 3, Augustine touches on these tensions in a telling way.

OBEDIENCE TO THE PRIOR, OBEDIENCE TO GOD

The word respect is a translation of the Latin *seruatum* which carries the double meaning of "to keep unharmed" and "to pay attention to." Augustine now takes the matter further. Obedience should be given to the prior because God is in him, and to reject him is to reject God: "Lest you offend God who is in him" (*ne in illo offendatur deus*). Two points are to be noticed here.

God is in this monk not because he is the prior, but because he is a Christian. *As you did it to one of the least of these my brethren, you did it to me* (Mt 25:40). The theme of the divine indwelling runs through the whole *Rule*. In chapter I, 8 we find that the indwelling of God is one of the factors that makes possible the unity of mind and heart that is the core of Augustine's understanding of monastic life. The Spirit within each one creates the holiness of the monks' lives, and for that reason their actions should be a reflection of their holy state (*sanctitatem*) — chapter IV, 3. The Spirit dwells within them and protects them from themselves (chapter IV, 6), and it is this that enables them to act in love in the events of their lives (chapter V, 2). For those with eyes to see, everything that they do can be a response to God whom they recognize in others, and it is this attitude which underlies the precept at the end of the previous chapter: the duty of deference to the one in charge of any sphere of work. The social aspect of monastic life is closely linked with the theocentric (the life is to be entirely centered on God, as chapter I, 2 has it) and if it is not, then the customs and behavior of the community need to be called in question and revised. Each monk in his sphere is the instrument of God to the extent that he is open to him, and in this present passage attention is focused on the prior.

Thus, secondly, if — Augustine now says — a monk rejects his prior's orders he is in fact rejecting the enabling Spirit of God who sustains and enlightens the prior as he fulfills his office. Augustine's verb is *offendere*. I have rendered this as "offend" in translation, but it is capable of being a stronger word than the English offend — it can mean to repel or to kick against. Its aggressive tones need to be borne in mind if we are to grasp Augustine's point: there is something outrageous happening when a monk refuses to obey the commands of the prior; his obedience and his disobedience really have God for their object.

There is no more about the nature of obedience at this point in the *Rule*; attention is now turned to the work of those who are to be obeyed, and it is only after that has been described that Augustine turns again, in paragraph 4, to the obedience that they should expect to receive.

OBEDIENCE TO THE PRIEST-BROTHER

Now Augustine looks at the other member of the group who should be given obedience by all: "This applies still more to the priest who has responsibility for you all." This final sentence of the paragraph evokes the established tradition of spiritual leadership which we have referred to above; and it also has its roots in the place and function of priesthood in the Church. Augustine has more to say about the priest's place in the community in the following paragraph. Here all that needs to be emphasized is the fact of his authority and the duty of all the monks to accept it.

In chapter IV, 9 the priest is said to have power to give direction and make judgments, and in chapter IV, 11 he and the prior together are required to find appropriate ways of correcting someone who has been receiving clandestine gifts. Here in VII, 1 we may note the implications of the words that Augustine uses. The word which we have translated as "responsibility" is *curam* which implies care, concern, and solicitude. It has been used three times previously in verb or noun form. In chapter V, 2 there is a reference to the care (*cura*) of the sick. In chapter V, 8 we find care for the common good rather than for one's own. And in chapter VI, 2 the same word is used for curing a wound inflicted on another's feelings. So when it is used again to describe the priest's task, it immediately stresses the fact that he is concerned with the well-being of persons and relationships. It is in this context that obedience has its part to play; obedience is a response to love by love.

Another significant phrase in Augustine's sentence is "still more" (*multo magis*, which bears the force of "very much more"): the injunction to obey "applies still more to the priest who has responsibility for you all." Augustine recognizes that the quality and the extent of obedience do in fact vary. Obedience itself, if it is to be constructive, must have a measure of elasticity and be able to adapt itself to persons and circumstances. Obedience must be yoked to freedom, and freedom is only possible if obedience is motivated by love and respect. When Augustine has thought further through the implications of obedience in the following three paragraphs he will add another ingredient; but we will wait for him to reveal it in his own time.

OBEDIENCE IN SCRIPTURE

The double theme of obedience and respect is characteristic of the Old and New Testaments, and so is the close relationship between obedience to God and obedience to specific people. In Exodus 20:2 the injunction to honor one's parents is a command from the Lord. The gospels quote Jesus as saying that whoever hears a disciple hears him also, and whoever receives him receives the one who sent him; and, similarly, whoever rejects a disciple rejects the Lord also.[12] Paul perceives that those in a position to command and to receive obedience have been instituted by God, and this is the reason why respect and honor are due to them.[13] In Ephesians 6:1-3, the Old Testament commandment is evoked, following an admonition to children to obey their parents, and Hebrews 12:9 relates filial obedience to obedience to God: *We have had earthly fathers to discipline us and we respected them. Shall we not much more be subject to the Father of spirits and live?*

Within a monastery, this interaction between man and man and the fact that they are instruments of God are of special importance, but they have their basis in the whole Christian understanding of the nature and place of obedience in human conduct. This is something that needs constant attention and appraisal if it is to avoid sterile rigidity. There needs to be a continual effort to relate norms to particular events, if the creating and redeeming work of God is to find expression in the lives of the monks. And this is why at this precise moment Augustine lays special emphasis on the existence of the priest within the life of the community. In doing so he is echoing the exhortation of 1 Timothy 5:17: *Let the elders who rule well be considered worthy of double honor, especially those who labor in preaching and teaching.*

So in the following paragraph he sets before the whole community his understanding of the functions of both prior and priest.

Rule, Chapter VII, 2

It is chiefly the responsibility of the prior
to see that all these instructions are complied with.
If anything is not complied with
he should not let it lapse through negligence
but should take care that the matter is corrected and put right.
It is taken for granted
that he will refer to the priest who has the greater authority among you
anything that exceeds his own province or powers.

THE DUTIES OF THE PRIOR

Until now Augustine has in various ways described the administrative role of the prior. Like the father of a family, he is the provider and the one who sees that things get done: that goods are distributed, health is maintained, and well-being is assured.

He cannot and should not do everything himself, and thus responsibility also is distributed among the members of the group. The
delegation of effective function always involves risks of
misunderstanding, incompetence, or downright self-seeking.

But most of the things that Augustine has been discussing in
the *Rule* involve something far deeper than administration. They
are concerned with the endeavor to achieve a unity that holds
together the uniqueness of each individual monk, and because of
this the bearing of responsibility challenges its holder in his innermost being. Augustine began his precepts by discussing the effort
that is required to overcome social differences and he went on to
oblige his readers to face the fact of temptation and sin in their
midst. Now, as it were, in the presence of all the monks he lays on
the prior the charge to keep the community aware of the precepts
which he has drawn up for them. Each member knows that the
prior carries this charge, and there can be no cause for resentment
when he discerns failure among them. Each one, Augustine implies with his carefully chosen words, is responsible for heeding and
fulfilling the precepts. But the responsibility belongs chiefly
(*praecipue pertinebit*) to the prior — as it does to the head of a family.
When a *paterfamilias* and his household work together in a common enterprise, the oversight normally rests with him because his
experience is wider than that of the others and he is in a position
to be more aware of antecedent traditions. Both father and prior
have a pastoral care and a ministry toward each of the household;
and it is they who are the most fully aware of the interaction of
persons and circumstances within the group. And such a position
is recognized by the members.

THE PRIOR AS INTERPRETER OF THE COMMUNITY'S LIFE

The prior, then, is to see that the precepts are complied with. In
the first place, he is their interpreter. The art of interpretation
involves many factors. Like the conductor of an orchestra, the
prior needs to be able to relate each part to the person who has to
perform it as well as to relate the sum of the parts to the group as
a whole. A conductor has to be aware not only of the music but
also of the players. More than that, he has to understand the
significance of each detail as it was in the mind of the composer,
as it is in his own mind and as it is in the mind of each performer
— and these last two must of necessity be in a state of movement
if the work is to continue to have relevance. The prior and the

conductor have to be able to take into account the capacity of each member, both to understand and to perform.

I stress the importance of understanding and interpretation because they are embedded in the word which Augustine uses and which I have translated as "complied with." The word in the text is *seruentur*. Its primary meaning is to save/deliver/protect, and from this a derivative meaning emerges: to pay attention/watch/ look into. The thing itself, whether it be an object or an idea, is regarded as something of value, something whose intrinsic worth is to be cherished — but cherished and preserved not covertly but openly. In the *Rule*, Augustine first used the word in chapter V, 3, in the phrase *dum nimia seruatur humilitas* which we translated as "by a display of excessive humility." He used it again (chapter VII, 1) when he reminded the monks to obey their prior as a father "with respect for his office" (*honore seruator*). Now we find him using it again, twice, in this next paragraph: the prior is to see that all the precepts that Augustine has drawn up for the community are to be displayed, respected, that is, as we have indicated in translation, they are to be "complied with"; and if they are not, the fact is not to be negligently ignored but steps are to be taken to put things right.

The most significant word here, however, is *negligenter* (through negligence). This is a challenging word because it questions motives. On superficial reading it might be thought that Augustine is condemning every non-intervention as a sign of neglect, but such an attitude is out of keeping with the sensitivity of the rest of the *Rule*. It is possible to pass by on the other side of wrongdoing with indifference;[14] this is common experience and it would be surprising if priors were exempt from it. The dynamics of such neglect may be fear, cowardice, laziness, contempt, or opportunism; and no one can attempt to fulfill the responsibilities of his office without discovering the things within himself which make it difficult for him to do so. But there are times when it is right and good to overlook faults — as God is having to do all the time in his dealings with men. If a prior were to set about correcting and putting right every fault that came to his notice he would have to work for twenty-four hours of every day. Some faults he will discover for himself, but some will be brought to his notice by the brothers; in either case, his means of dealing with them are his responsibility and not, for instance, that of a complainant.

Most people who present the wrongdoing of another to their superior are in fact projecting themselves, and this alone suggests that there should always be caution in acting. The complainant, of course, will label the misdemeanor as negligence. On the other hand, there may be justification in a complaint, but the prior may know that the wrongdoer is not yet spiritually or psychologically ready to be corrected and put right. Again, other issues beyond the immediate one may be involved, in which case it may be wiser to defer action.

In mentioning correction that has to be made on the basis of reports by a member of the community (a matter which was discussed very fully and carefully by Augustine in chapter IV) we have drawn attention to another aspect of this precept. The monks of Hippo have not been the only ones who need reminding that the responsibility for putting things right lies with the head of the house. There are always some members of a group who think that the burden lies with them, and they can make life burdensome for themselves and for the other members: they are the legalists, the perfectionists, the dominators, and it takes years of maturing before such people come to perceive what they are doing and why. The actual lodging of complaints is not the only course that stems from these dynamics; such people may even give themselves the task of bringing about a reformation without recourse to the prior. Whatever form this overzeal takes, its underlying characteristic is unawareness of other people as unique persons. That is why this provision in the *Rule* is so important for the well-being of the community, for it protects the group and ensures a just balance among the members. Some of the prior's responsibilities can be delegated, but those which depend on knowledge of and care for all the brothers, the things and the ideas which are the ingredients of problems, must remain with him. To be at the receiving end of the working of this ministry requires a deep trust on the part of all the members. The prior may not be able, in wisdom and charity, always to give his reasons for action or inaction; but his silence has to be trusted as well as his speaking. He will show his worthiness of such trust by the way that he deals with offenses and offenders.

The duty which falls to the prior can itself get dislodged from its context and be regarded as a mandate to deal with all the minutiae of happenings in the monastery. But what Augustine tells the brothers is that the prior is responsible for seeing that the precepts are observed, and these are wide-ranging and general-ized. There are, as Simon Tugwell has pointed out, "two modes of monastic life, one structured in such a way that giving orders is legitimate and proper, the other relying simply on the motiva-tion and zeal of the individual, supported by a context that could be formative."[15] Augustine's concept of monasticism lies at the heart of the second of these two modes, because his *Rule* is more concerned with the character of his monks than with how they are to fill their days; and he requires the prior to ensure that the wide-open spirit of the precepts is maintained. The monks of Hippo, as well as those of other times and places who have adopted this *Rule*, must not expect of their prior a detailed order-ing of their daily lives — what they can expect of him is that he will judge their way of life by the generosity, compassion, and love with which they accept whatever rules are necessary for the maintenance of the group's life.

The prior's perspective has to be all-embracing if he is to main-tain the community's well-being at this level. Matters of all kinds do go wrong in any group, in the way of administration and behavior as well as in relationships. But all the members, the prior and the brothers alike, need to see these things not as a matter of complaint which has to be put right (what must the other man do?) but as a problem to be solved (what must I do, given the circumstances?). Throughout the *Rule* Augustine has stressed the necessity of adjusting oneself to others,[16] and it is this that is at the heart of all correction in the monastery. This means that there must be time and space for talking things out — and in discussion one's own awareness grows. So it can often happen that what began as a superficial matter is seen to have far deeper implications — in the sphere of understanding as well as in practice; and sometimes the prior will perceive that the area of concern has moved beyond his sphere, let alone his competence. He will see what the real need is and know that his own resources cannot fill it.

THE PLACE OF THE PRIEST IN MONASTIC TRADITION

But he is not alone; there is always the community's priest to whom he can turn — "it is taken for granted that he will refer to the priest." The word which we have translated as "it is taken for granted" is, succinctly, *ita* which here means consequently in the sense of obviously. It stands first in the phrase, implying its importance, and because in English consequently or obviously can sound weak it has seemed best to use a forceful phrase to carry the point which Augustine is stressing here. Luc Verheijen has shown from a study of Augustine's *The Work of Monks*[17] that the function of the priest within a monastery was that of teacher of the faith, minister of the altar, and dispenser of the sacraments.

A large part of the teaching of the faith consisted in exegesis of the Bible, and within the monastery there would be great need for someone with the skill to do this. The other aspect of teaching the faith, evangelization, would not be needed as a ministry to the brothers who were already committed Christians; but ways of living a good life, of dealing with the temptations and tensions that Augustine has been considering within every part of the *Rule*, of relating intellectual and emotional understanding of the gospel (understandings that are always in a state of movement) to the events of their lives would be matters which the community's priest would need to be constantly exploring with his brothers. Often the necessity to pursue such matters would come first to the notice of the prior. Some of these would involve questions of conscience, but others would not. Some would fall outside the lay prior's province or powers (*modum uel uires*) because they required a priestly ministry, while others would be outside his ability to handle because of his lack of experience and training.

The priest's function in early monasticism is less conspicuous than that of the prior. Hans von Campenhausen expresses this more forcibly when he states that the first monks often judged the priesthood unfavorably and had no need of it themselves,[18] and this could explain the inconspicuousness of this role in a community. A further reason for the monk-priest's isolated status lies in the uniqueness of his situation. Every other brother has had to abandon his trade or profession on entering the monastery (even though he inevitably brings its acquired skills with him); but a cleric remains a cleric and is obliged to function as one even among the members of the community. But, as A. Mandouze has pointed out,[19] Augustine viewed the two vocations as fundamentally different. That would explain why, in the *Rule*, he saw no need to explore the role of the priest in any depth, as he does the role of the prior. There is no description of the functions of the community's priest; the phrases used of him are generalities which assume that the readers know exactly what is meant.

The isolated status of the priest would enable him to appreciate the inevitable isolation that is also inherent in the office of the prior. Their common yet differing experience of life in community (the one being in the foreground and the other in the background) would create a concord which would be a source of strength to the whole group as well as to each other. Luc Verheijen has shown how Augustine regarded the working of this concord, in which sometimes the prior and sometimes the priest would be in the dominant position.[20] Authority rested with the prior in matters of everyday life; the priest had the greater authority in what concerned the life of the community in relation to the Church as a whole (for example, in matters of faith and morals).

It is interesting to look at the implications of this structure. It could be thought that the prior, as the leader of a group of committed Christians, would be their principal link with the Church and that the priest, being concerned with the interior life of the brothers, would be concerned also with their day-to-day lives. But this is not so. In the later development of monasticism these two poles converged: more monks were priests, and the superior was always a priest. And when that had come about, the establishment of a viable way of life for the monks became the responsibility of the superior alone. Today there are signs of a return to the early pattern in some communities.

We may note also another aspect of the division of responsibility in the Hippo monastery, which indicates a divergence from the eastern pattern. Whereas Augustine implies in each of his four references to the priest that the spiritual welfare of the monks comes under his care, both Basil[21] and Cassian[22] show that the common practice in the East was for monks to turn to the older and more experienced members of the group for guidance, to men who were laymen like themselves. The provision in Augustine's *Rule* is a stage in the evolution that was completed in the middle ages. But here again, in modern times the charism of spiritual guidance is beginning to lie also with the laity both inside and outside monasteries (and among women as well as among men).

As we have seen, in the Hippo monastery the province of the prior and that of the priest are distinct although they have an important common boundary: for each of them, the sphere of their work is the community. Each of them is concerned with the life of the brothers in unity. While the priest is there to help them in the continuing search for God which is the basis of their life, the prior is the one who helps them in their life of service. This does not mean, however, that he must only safeguard and encourage their activities; he must also protect and support them as people.

It is in the next paragraph that Augustine expounds this last point further.

Rule, Chapter VII, 3

All the same,
he should consider himself lucky not in having power over you
but in being able to care for you with love.
Before you, he has to be at your head in honor;
before God, he should be prostrate at your feet in fear.
He should show himself to all around
as a model of good works.
He should restrain the restless,
encourage the fainthearted,
support the weak,
be patient toward all.
He himself should keep these instructions gladly
and so give them their due weight.
And, although both are necessary,
he should seek rather your love than your fear,
always having in mind
the account that he will have to render to God for you.

THE PRIOR'S WORK

Now, at last, Augustine addresses himself to the prior at a deep level; and in doing so he is, in fact, recapitulating many of the themes of the *Rule* as a whole.

First of all he warns against a common human temptation, and he does so by repeating a word that he had used in chapter I, 5. In that passage, addressed to the brothers whose former life had been underprivileged, he said that they were not to think themselves lucky (*felices*) if they now had better clothing than before. Now he tells the prior to consider himself lucky not in being in a privileged position but in being all the more able to serve others with love. The real privilege of the prior lies in having boundless opportunities for service. In coming to the community he had committed himself to living as a servant of the Lord, and during his years in the monastery he will have been learning what true service implies, and also what it costs. Augustine has used the verb "to serve" only once before in the *Rule*: that was when he charged the monks responsible for food, clothing and books "to serve" their brothers without murmuring[23] (implying, of course, that the temptation to murmur was a very real one and also that there was present the provocation that results in murmuring). The prior will be accustomed to facing this temptation, and he will have learned in some degree how to overcome it (otherwise it is unlikely that he would have become prior).

Monastic life consists to a large extent in doing the same sort of things for a great many years, and the challenge lies in accepting demands creatively, which means accepting them with love. We have already pointed out Augustine's careful use of words when writing about love; and we have shown how the whole of the second part of the *Rule* is an exploration of what love in action means. Here, in the present passage, the word used is *caritas*: the prior is to find his happiness and his fulfillment in serving the brothers by acts of love (*caritate seruientem felicem*). This, of course, is what is required of every monk in his own sphere, but the sphere of the prior is as large as the community itself. And in this lies the cost of what his office asks of him. He has to be available to all, to be prepared to give loving acceptance to all, to bear with their weaknesses, to encourage their strengths. But, poor man, he is only human with only one body to live in and only one spirit to absorb all the problems, tensions, and interactions that are brought to his notice. At that level, no prior could feel lucky in bearing his office — a point which Augustine goes into explicitly in the following paragraph, and which is only mentioned here in order to bring out the irony of the word *felix* which he has used in this context. (In all five occurrences of *felix/felicior*, Augustine points to the absurdity of the brother who may be thinking himself lucky.[24])

The real temptation, as Augustine says here, is to try to solve problems by dominating (*dominantem*) the people who cause them. Then if the brothers concerned fall in with whatever is proposed, the practical difficulty is overcome — but overcome also are the brothers. Such an abuse of authority is destructive of unanimity primarily because it has no regard for the value of each person. The exercise of authority has a social and a moral aspect,[25] and both of these aspects form part of Augustine's discussion of the work of the prior.

In point of fact, although at various places in the *Rule* it has been stated what the prior should be responsible for, the word authority (*auctoritas*) is never applied to him. The first use of the word, in chapter VI, 3, is directed to all the monks who are in any position of responsibility (which in practice includes everyone at some stage in his life); and in the only other passage, chapter VII, 2, we read that the prior is to refer some matters to the priest "who has the greater authority among you" (implying, nonetheless, that the prior does have some authority). Right from the beginning Augustine has shown how the prior's work is one of service to all (especially in chapters I, 5 and V, 3-5). This is not to be seen merely as a matter of convenient centralization; rather it is an expression of the loving concern that should be the hallmark of the whole community. For the authority that is exercised in the group — in any Christian group — is a derived authority coming from the Lord whom each member is seeking and serving. The gospels stress Jesus' repeated efforts to instill his meaning of authority into his followers.[26]

LOVING AND SERVING THE COMMUNITY

It is by serving one another in a caring way that a true community is established. For, as Hans von Balthasar has beautifully put it, "by the help we give we create meaning for others."[27] Seen in this way, the two strands of social and moral significance are intertwined, and it is only in discussion that they have to be separated.

The charge to care for the brothers in love means that the prior is always alongside them — neither above, nor below. Within the social structure of the group, however, he is above the members, for he is the first, the "prior" (*praepositus*): he is, as Augustine says, "at [their] head in honor." Morally, though, he will find himself prostrate at their feet, for like them he is a sinner and he will know himself to be no better than they. Augustine's word which I have translated as "at your head" is *praelatus* which has survived in English as an ecclesiastical term, prelate. Meaning "carried in front" or "carried in a prominent position," it was used to describe persons or regalia carried in religious or military processions, that is to say, it always denoted display in some form. Within the organized life of the community (before you/*coram uobis*), the prior's position is an exalted and revered one (*honore*). But morally (before God/*coram deo*) he should be "prostrate at [the] feet" of the members (*substratus . . . pedibus uestris*) in fear.

As Augustine himself knew very well, a Christian leader of any worth will always be acutely aware of his own unworthiness; and it is right that he should feel so, for of himself he has nothing and whatever talents he may have are entrusted to him by the Lord. Augustine's use of a subjunctive verb-form (*sit*, let him/he should) shows that he does not mean that the prior is to be under the feet of the brethren as if he were downtrodden: that could only describe an undesirable state of affairs which would require the indicative, *est*, whereas in the text the prior is admonished to be very humble. Nevertheless it is all too easy for a prior to feel trampled on by the members of the community with their conflicting needs and demands.

Augustine will shortly discuss the prior's ministry to the brothers in terms of his service to them. But before that there is a glance at the teaching function which falls to him, as distinct from that of the priest which we have examined earlier. The prior's instruction is to be given by way of example: "He should show himself as a model of good works to all around." *Let your light so shine before men, that they may see your good works and give glory to your Father who is in heaven*, Jesus said (Mt 5:16) but it is not this passage that prompts Augustine at this moment; rather he is concerned with deeds than with their doer, and his injunction is a quotation from Titus 2:7 but with one difference — where the letter had *Show yourself in all respects* (*in omnibus*) Augustine writes "He should show himself to all around" (*circa omnes*). The latter is less precise, but its nuances are more open and less formal, less self-conscious. The prior's attitude and behavior must exemplify the assumptions and the conduct that should be common to all the brothers who — like their Master, Jesus — are called to serve and to go about doing good. In contrast to whatever formality his office may seem to require of him, his manner to all around should be marked by informality. While the letter's emphasis is divided equally between the person, the doer, and his deeds (which in the Latin version is *in omnibus teipsum praebe exemplum bonorum operum*), Augustine's stress lies principally on the prior's approach to people. The prior's way of life, he says, must be characterized by goodness in all that he does. The emphasis is on good deeds, not on rectitude. The doing of good in the ordinary things of life means that there is always the possibility of an encounter with badness. But rectitude cannot face the badness that is in most of us, with the result that our dark side is repressed and not brought out into the open in order to be cured. A prior before whom a brother dare not display his anger or hatred or any of the other demeaning parts of his nature does his community little service. On the contrary, his doing good to all around means that he needs to be able to enter into all sorts of situations even to the extent of sharing the faults and failures of others. Repression may produce good behavior but it will never produce good people or good works, and this is why it is important for the prior to be seen to identify with the dark side of the personality while always pointing to the light.

We must now note a further divergence between Augustine and Titus 2:7. While Titus is incited to integrity, gravity, and sound speech in order that he and the whole body of Christians may not be put to shame by opponents (verses 7-8), Augustine's precept echoes a passage from another letter (a passage incidentally, which is not addressed to one person alone but describes what is incumbent on all the brethren for whom it is written). 1 Thessalonians 5:12-14 reads:

> We beseech you, brethren, to respect those who labor among you and are over you in the Lord and admonish you, and to esteem them very highly in love because of their work. Be at peace among yourselves; and we exhort you, brethren, admonish the idle, encourage the faint-hearted, help the weak, be patient with them all.

As we have seen throughout the second half of the *Rule*, the community's whole life is to be an expression of a desire for love and peace, and the function of each monk, including the prior, is set against that background. The warmth and confidence that pervade the whole of 1 Thessalonians 5 find their counterpart in the present precept of the *Rule*. Augustine assumes that the prior will be among the brothers, not at a distance from them, and the succession of verbs from verse 14 is very telling: *corripiat* (restrain) comes first, then *consoletur* (encourage), after that *suscipiat* (sustain/support) and finally *patiens sit* (be patient). To be effective in this way and at this level, the prior needs to be a person of insight and deep compassion, alert, courageous, and calm.

When an author quotes scripture in his text he often does so in order to reinforce his own statement. But here Augustine takes the biblical passage as it stands and uses it as the statement of his meaning. We therefore need to look closely at Paul's fourfold admonition which Augustine makes his own.

RESTRAIN THE RESTLESS

Corripite inquietos is translated in older English versions as "admonish the unruly," this being based on the Latin. But modern versions refer to "idlers" (JB) or "the idle" (RSV), this being nearer to the Greek. The underlying meaning of the Greek word, ατακτοσ, refers to a marching soldier who is not in battle order, who has quit the ranks — one, that is, who has failed in the performance of duty. Thus while Latin speakers were justified in interpreting such action as unruliness, which can equal willful disobedience, modern English biblical translators have regarded this dereliction of duty as slackness. A translator of Augustine's precept is thus faced with a problem: Is it best to feel behind the Latin words to their Greek counterparts and so produce something akin to or identical with modern English translations of 1 Thessalonians or to accept Augustine's Latin as it stands (knowing that this reflects what he read in his version of the Bible) and so produce something that differs from the Revised Standard Version, Jerusalem Bible, and other recent translations? The second course is the one that keeps closest to Augustine, which is where one ought to be; so I have looked at his words as they stand and tried to get near to the living impact which they would have had on their first hearers. *Inquietos* I have translated as "the restless" — those who cannot be still and conforming in any situation (this leaves aside the question of their motive). The word *corripiat* I have rendered as "restrain." What Augustine is indicating here is that the prior must be watchful of those who find it difficult to toe the line or to persevere in their undertakings, and he must be ready with a firm recall to duty when occasion demands. I have therefore translated this phrase as "he should restrain the restless." Restlessness always indicates unresolved conflict, and my chief reason for using this word for the Latin *inquietos* is that it is unspecific. The words unruliness and idleness both limit the manifestation of inner conflict and suggest judgment, but the word restlessness leaves all the options open. It would be surprising if any monk ever lived the whole of his life without suffering from restlessness in some form or other. The resolution of conflict is a process that must be at work in him all the time, and when he is faced with problems it would be surprising if this did not show itself in some form. The prior who knows his brothers well will know when it is right to intervene and when it is best to hold his hand. People vary so much as to how far they can work through their difficulties on their own. The prior may need to take action if the sufferer cannot manage alone; he will certainly need to do so if others become involved in the distress.

ENCOURAGE THE FAINTHEARTED

Encourage the fainthearted (*consoletur pusillianimes*) is more straightforward. The Latin matches the Greek, and English versions faithfully echo both of the earlier languages. Faintheartedness implies a lack of confidence and within any group there will be a number who suffer in this way. The symptoms vary widely — from overbearing brashness through gaucherie to inarticulate withdrawal; and skill must be combined with compassion if the prior is to reach into and encourage every sufferer, begin to build up self-trust and make it possible for each one to relate without fear to both the events and the persons who make up the daily common life within the community. Whereas the injunction to restrain the restless implied a readiness to act promptly, the task of encouraging the fainthearted may be a very slow one with little result appearing for a considerable time. There is a temptation to abandon the effort, but that means abandoning a sufferer, and the experience would throw him back into deeper self-distrust. The cost, therefore, to the prior in this part of his ministry is very great indeed; and it is one that Augustine intends all members of the community to be aware of (the *Rule*, including this passage, is to be read aloud once a week and so no one can fail to know its requirements). It will take much patience and tolerance on the part of all the brothers if the prior is to be supported in this slow and demanding work. Augustine's verb (and Paul's also) implies a readiness to be with the sufferer in his misery — otherwise *soletur* would have sufficed. It is possible to give limited encouragement, cheer, or comfort to a person from a distance and without becoming involved in his situation; but the *Rule*'s *consoletur* implies that the prior must go further than that: he must be prepared to enter into the misery of his fainthearted brothers.

SUPPORT THE WEAK

More than that, he is to "support the weak" (*suscipiat infirmos*): he is to take them up and hold them, to be their prop and stay. This, too, is a long-term ministry, for *infirmos* refers to those with little ability as well as to those with little strength. Throughout the

course of the *Rule* Augustine has been concerned with the fitness
or lack of fitness of the monks. Six times he refers to physical
illness by using *aegroto* and its related forms;[28] and once he uses
inbecillitas,[29] when he is describing a state of convalescence. The
words *infirmitas/infirmus* occur six times, and whenever they appear it is within the context of needs that go beyond those of the
body: the spirit's suffering, however tortuous it may be, has also
to be taken into account. In chapter I, 5 Augustine says that the
monks whose former way of life was a deprived one are to be
given all that they need when they are ill. In chapter III, 3 he refers
to those whose former life was exactly the opposite; they find life
in the monastery a real struggle because their erstwhile privileges
did not prepare them for it, and the weakness that they now suffer
from must be taken seriously in the community. In chapter III, 5
there is advice for those who are getting over an illness and
tending to malinger and to cling to special treatment longer than
is necessary. A precept in chapter V, 1 brings us nearer to the hurt
of what we are exploring in the present passage: in dealing with
the distribution of clothing, Augustine says that sometimes concession has to be made to a defect in a brother's attitude to what
he wears and his demand of a privilege has to be acceded to —
here, what goes on in the brother's mind is of more importance
than the obligation to keep him warm or cool as the case may be.
Then in chapter V, 5 there comes the discussion of the use of the
public baths, with an awareness of the varying attitudes that
Christians have to them. "If someone is ill and this is necessary he
must not refuse it; it should be done without murmuring, on the
advice of a doctor." And the passage goes on to describe the
tangles that the mind can get into when this sort of problem arises
for a person who is ill. It is difficult for anyone in the twentieth
century to feel the impact of this dilemma — perhaps its equivalent might be a proposal to try an unusual sort of treatment. The
infirmus, the ill one, is having to face more than the assault of
disease on his body; he is faced also with a tax on his mind and
emotions. And so we come to Augustine's last use of this word,
in the present paragraph, when he enjoins the prior to support the
waverers and the feeble in their weakness. In a literal sense he has
to be their strength.

For most people, weakness is a state that comes and goes. But
there are some for whom it is a chronic condition. There may be
a physical defect, or the deficiency may be emotional or intellec-

tual. In any case the sufferer will be aware of a deep sense of inadequacy. The person who is able to give real strength and support to those who are afflicted in this way requires great resources of wisdom and compassion as well as endurance. This does not mean that he must be one who has never himself lived with the weakness of illness or lack of ability; indeed these very experiences can be the background to his own ministry within the group. What the sufferer needs from him is the reassurance that defeat does not line the road he must travel nor stand at his journey's end. In fact, he needs something more than companionship on his way; he needs to feel the strength that his companion possesses — and this is embodied in the verb that Paul and Augustine use. *Suscipio* literally means to take hold of from below.[30] So the prior's support for the weak members of the community is the very reverse of offering help from above, from the chief position: it must come from underneath, from the ground of all personal experience of helplessness relieved. *I was hungry and you gave me food, I was thirsty and you gave me drink, I was a stranger and you welcomed me, I was naked and you clothed me, I was sick and you visited me, I was in prison and you came to me* (Mt 25:36-37). This is the measure of the loving service that the prior must offer to the brothers. He has to help them to acquire what is lacking to them, though he may not himself be the one who can actually provide whatever is needed; indeed, were he the sole resource that the monks could rely on he would be drained, exhausted and useless in next to no time. By giving support from below to people with a great diversity of needs he can make it possible for all manner of help to be available from a variety of sources both within and outside the community. It is significant that the Pauline passage which Augustine quotes in the present precept is set in the course of a discussion on the building up of the corporate life of Christians. This suggests the great importance of the community itself in the work of healing that needs to be done among the members. It is not the prior alone who is to be the channel of love, strength, confidence, or well-being for those who suffer from their own lack of these blessings; the support he gives them is directed toward enabling them to receive it from their fellow-monks and also from other people with whom they come in contact.[31] A support that consists solely of a relationship with the supporter can only cause damage, simply because there is always movement in life and if the support is for any reason not available then collapse is inevitable. A supportive role always needs to be a diminishing one, which is another safeguard for an always-busy prior.

BE PATIENT WITH ALL

The cost, then, to the prior is very high and he will inevitably suffer within his own person because of the demands that his office makes on him. And this factor gives point to Augustine's next precept. The prior is to be patient toward all (*patiens sit ad omnes*). Although both the Revised Standard Version and the Jerusalem Bible translate this last phrase of 1 Thessalonians 5:14 as *be patient with all*, I have retained the Authorized Version form, *be patient toward all*, because this brings out the force of the Latin *ad omnes* which are the words that Augustine has taken over straight from his Bible. Patience means more than endurance; it involves a willingness to suffer and to go on suffering at the hands of others. It means more than making allowances objectively for the feelings and behavior of those around one; it involves also the experience of what such dispositions and conduct do to oneself. Paul and Augustine do not enjoin anesthetized indifference but an increasingly high measure of tolerance of the impact of others on oneself. This requires, all the time, an enlarging of one's own self-awareness, of one's own vulnerability and also the realization of one's own ability to cause distress to others; it requires, too, tremendous courage if one is to accept oneself without despair. Only one who in truth is able to see his own capacity for a restless getting out of line, his own faintheartedness, and his own many signs of weakness and inefficacy can accept the failings that occur in others; and only when he does accept these can he resist the promptings of the disordered instincts which shriek along his nervous system and urge him to retaliate and to injure (Paul goes on to make this point in verse 15). Patience, then, is an acquired skill for humankind; and when people do possess it, it has come to them from God. Patience, says Paul (Gal 5:22), is part of the fruit of the Spirit as he brings about maturity in believers. Patience in relation to other people always involves a degree of suffering. The ability to feel injury and irritation is part of the human condition; what patience does is to enable the sufferer to set aside his feelings for the sake of the one who inflicts trouble on him; and everyone inevitably will cause him distress in some form of other, simply because there is only a limited amount of physical and psychological space in the world as we experience it.

Paul admonishes all his readers to be patient, to support the weak, to encourage the feeble, and to restrain the misfits; and against the wide background of everyday life this sounds demanding but not frightening. Augustine, however, lays this same fourfold charge on the shoulders of one particular member of a sharply-defined small group with a distinct corporate identity. In that setting, this injunction sounds very daunting indeed. And, we may ask, who is there who can fulfill it? Is he some special person with exceptional gifts? The answer must be both No and Yes. He is, above all, a member of the group. His roots are intertwined with those of his brothers in the monastery. He is chosen from among them to act as their prior because at a specific time in the life of the community his insights and his experience have reached a stage when they can be channeled into an effective ministry among the whole group. It will not always be so, for movement is constant, and in due course another leader with another set of insights and experience will be needed. The prior-for-the-time-being has gained his wisdom and his skills by the way and to the extent that he has lived his monastic life faithfully and realistically.

OBSERVE THE *RULE*

This is the point that Augustine goes on to make by continuing: "He himself should keep these instructions gladly and so give them their due weight" (*Disciplinam libens habeat, metum inponat*). The prior's monastic life has been formed by the community's spirit and practice which are embodied in the precepts that Augustine set about writing after he had to leave the group; and in order to safeguard their continuance as the norms of community life it was necessary that they should continue to be embodied and exemplified in the conduct of the prior. There is a temptation, within any leadership situation, for the normal demands of the group's life to be set aside, and in the long history of monasticism there are very many examples of such failure; there is no need to cite examples.

In referring to the precepts as *disciplinam* Augustine is striking a chord that harmonizes a body of teaching, a willingness to learn, a way of life, and an acceptance of discipline in the modern sense of that word. One or more of these terms can readily be applied to each aspect of the *Rule*. Human nature being what it is, it is doubtful if every detail of it is enough to prompt the prior to observe it gladly, for there are always some areas of struggle in our lives, and what at one time seems an obvious and commendable good will at others becomes a hard challenge. Yet Augustine boldly enjoins the prior to keep the precepts gladly/willingly/readily (*libens*). The Latin of the final phrase of this sentence is so compressed that it has been open to a number of amendments which have themselves been interpretations.[32] *Metum inponat* can be translated literally as "he should set respect/reverence (on them)"; but as this sounds clumsy I have, for the sake of exposition, placed a conjunctival clause "and so" before the phrase "give them their due weight." To give due weight to a statement means to recognize its implicit worth and to be willing to make its demands explicit. And this seems to be why Augustine enjoins the prior to be glad and ready in his observance of the precepts. At all levels the way of life and the ethos of the community have proved their value within the experience of the very group for whom Augustine is writing, and the continuing existence of the monastery will be rooted in this *Rule*. Therefore it is important that this experience should find expression in the life of the prior — indeed, unless it does, it will in time disappear from the community altogether. *Metum* can mean religious awe, and down the centuries this has tended to characterize attitudes to the great monastic rules. But there is danger here: *A written code kills; the Spirit gives life* (2 Cor 3:6). A written code needs the continuous movement of the Spirit among its followers if it is to have any effectiveness as a set of norms guiding succeeding generations. Insofar as the prior, or any other monk, conforms himself to the way of life of the community and to the common understanding of the *Rule*, to that extent the Spirit can move freely as revealer, interpreter, and director. If the prior is grudging in his own acceptance of the demands of the common life, then he is cutting the community off from the sources of its own life. The *Rule* is not an end in itself, nor is the life of the community; but together they have a single aim which Augustine set before the monks at the beginning of his precepts: they should have "one soul and one heart entirely centered upon God" (chapter I, 2). A traveler on a journey, or a member of an orchestra rehearsing a symphony, will gladly follow the directions of his map or his score in order to achieve his end. This is the meaning of Augustine's use of *libens* (gladly) in the present passage. The prior will have such deep respect for the traditions of the community that he will love them.

Augustine then goes on to say something about love and fear, and at first glance this may seem to be a strange mental leap. But in fact it takes his readers back to what he had written a few lines earlier. The link is provided by the nuances of language in the word *metum* which to his hearers would carry overtones of awe and fear as well as great reverence. The injunction addressed to the prior is: "And, although both are necessary, he should seek rather your love than your fear" (*Et quamuis utrumque sit necessarium, tamen plus a uobis amari adpetit quam timeri*).

The precepts of this paragraph are concerned first with the role of the prior and then with his position as teacher and guide. His example of service will be his means of instruction: the things he does and his manner of doing them will express the aspirations of the whole group. And further, this paragraph — indeed, the whole *Rule* — is concerned with the development of relationships within the common purpose which holds the members together. This is an issue which Augustine had given thought to some years previously, when he wrote *The Catholic Way of Life* 28, 35. The link between what is taught (*disciplina*), the teacher, and the taught is summed up thus:

> This discipline which is the medicine of the soul is, as far as we can gather from the sacred Scriptures, divided into two parts: coercion and instruction. Coercion implies fear, and instruction love, on the part of the one receiving the discipline; for he who offers assistance to another is not moved by fear, but only by love.

Augustine's insight in this passage supplies the dynamic for the precept that he now gives to the prior. His reading of Scripture has shown him two distinct ways of instructing others. Leviticus 25 and 26 are full of the threats of punishment which will be meted out to wrongdoers by the Lord. Psalm 25:7-9.12, whose theme is trust in the mercy of God, shows an intermediate stage. It is the prayer of a meek man:

> *Remember not the sins of my youth, or my transgressions; according to thy steadfast love remember me, for thy goodness' sake, O Lord. Good and upright is the Lord; therefore he instructs sinners in the way. He leads the humble in what is right, and teaches the humble his*

way. Who is the man that fears the Lord? Him will he instruct in the way that he should choose.

Here the man who is humble before God is the one who is able to receive instruction — and the instruction that he receives is to influence his freedom of choice. The humble man perceives that the Lord who is the teacher is prompted by steadfast love. Then in Psalm 51:10.12-13, where the power to instruct is in the hands of a man not in the hands of God, it is the one who in deep penitence knows his own dependence on God who can teach others the right way to live: *Create in me a clean heart, O God . . . Restore to me the joy of thy salvation, and uphold me with a willing spirit. Then I will teach transgressors thy ways, and sinners will return to thee.* The coercion of the Leviticus passage makes no demands on the inner being of those who carry it out; its aim is to ensure "right" action. The humble man of Psalm 25 is aware of his own short-comings but asks God to overlook them. He still has fear of what he deserves and he exposes his sinful condition as providing a way of appeal to a good and upright God; his trust is based not only on God's mercy but also on the fact that he is in awe of him. In the *Miserere*, by contrast, the penitent sinner cries out for renewal and the joyful experience of salvation, and he knows that if these are granted to him he will be enabled to lead other lost ones back to God.

Augustine, in *The Catholic Way of Life*, carries this insight over into his consideration of how men teach and are taught. He had been a professional teacher himself, and he knew what he was talking about. He knew that the desire of a teacher is for the good of his pupils, which means that his motive is one of love (a perception that, in the case of God, was present in the writers of the psalms we have just quoted but lacking in the authors of Leviticus). Anxiety for good results may prompt anyone with responsibility for teaching or training to methods of coercion which can range from laying down the law to threats and even punishment. And, quite rightly, such an approach elicits fear. The element of fear of repercussions as a deterrent from transgression is part of the human scene and it is used by all who are concerned for the good of others — eat up your porridge or you can't go out to play. And fear of the threat leads to fear of the threatener — even though, as Augustine implies, this is the very last thing that the threatener desires.

Therefore, the *Rule* continues, although inevitably there will be times when it is necessary to lay down the law the prior must be very careful to see that his manner and behavior provoke fear as little as possible. A major concern of the prior which touches on this teaching ministry is the correction of negligence and offenses, and it is chiefly in this sphere that he may tend to make himself feared. Even while Augustine was living in the monastery in the garden he had given much thought to this matter — not in connection with his fellow-monks but with the abuses that he considered to be rampant throughout the Church in North Africa. When he wrote to the bishop of Carthage on the subject, he said that one should not attempt to eliminate these wrongs in a harsh or hard way, but by "teaching rather than by commanding, by exhortation rather than by threatening" (Letter 22, 5). If threats had to be uttered, that should be done with sorrow.[33]

Sometimes the brothers' fear will be the result not of the prior's handling of community affairs but of his own personal reactions to people and events. So there are two dimensions to the challenge of this precept — corporate and personal; and because the life of the community is always moving, they are challenges that will never go away — just as they never go away from parents or teachers or union officials or executives. But although it is sometimes necessary to meet the challenge in its own area, which is negative and destructive, it is generally best to shift the ground altogether: "He should seek rather your love," that is, he should seek to elicit love, he should both make himself lovable and evoke love in others. Augustine uses the verb-form in speaking of love here, *amari*, and this is the only instance of this word and its cognates in the whole of the text.

ASPECTS OF LOVE AND FRIENDSHIP

In the *Rule*, three words are used for love. *Diligere/dilectio* occurs first and is the one most frequently used; then there is *caritas*; and now we find *amare*. Oliver O'Donovan, in his study of Augustine's understanding of self-love, considers that his usage is a matter of style rather than of theological content. Certainly Augustine's professional experience taught him how to use words, and to use them in relation to his specific hearers or readers. O'Donovan then suggests that:

> When we find ourselves distinguishing different strands of thought [in Augustine] about love-of-God and love-of- neighbor, it is not that there are several different loves, immanently distinguished, but that the loving subject stands in a complex and variable relation to the reality which his love confronts.[34]

He therefore sees Augustine's words as expressing different aspects of love rather than different kinds.[35] Thus when in the *Rule* we find *amare* used to describe the quality of the loving that should exist between the prior and the other monks, this is entirely appropriate because *amor* is the most generalized word for love such as would exist throughout any household where there was a good *paterfamilias*. By using the most homely word for love, Augustine stresses an aspect of community life which has had a fluctuating history down the centuries. His model of family affection counterbalances the importance that he placed on friendship at the beginning of his life as a monk.[36] At Thagaste, the community consisted of a close-knit group of his kindred spirits; and some new beginnings in monasticism have been brought about by a group of friends. But at Hippo, as time went on, the distance between the different members would inevitably have lengthened. In these circumstances, the cohesiveness of ordinary friendship came to have a diminishing role in the infra-structure of the monastery. Augustine sees the problem, which is an unavoidable one, and by his stress in the present admonition to the prior he is doing his best to mitigate it.

The difficulty lies in the demands of the group as a group. As we have seen throughout the *Rule*, Augustine emphasized the fact that each brother was to be served according to his need; indeed, this lies at the heart of the western cenobitic tradition. But a relationship centered on need felt and need fulfilled is not friendship, and whatever affection it arouses is not true affection for it is not fully reciprocal. The classical exploration of the meaning of friendship is contained in Cicero's *De amicitia*, and in a number of passages he makes this point:

> In friendship there is nothing false, nothing pretended; whatever there is is genuine and comes of its own accord. Wherefore it seems to me that friendship springs from nature rather than from need (VIII, 2).

And again:

It seems to me, at any rate, that those who falsely assume
expediency to be the basis of friendship take from friendship's
chain its loveliest link. For it is not so much the material gain
procured through a friend, as it is his love, and his love alone,
that gives us delight (XIV, 51).

Friendship, says Cicero, is natural — and Augustine would
have agreed, for with him the need for friendship was one of the
chief characteristics of his nature. But friendship, just because it
depends on persons-as-they-are, is in the nature of things selective. And that is why he is entirely right in laying stress, for his
monks, not on the friendship that was his early ideal but on the
importance of love which is wider and deeper. True, as Cicero
says, it is love between friends that holds them together; but as
O'Donovan has reminded us, this is only one aspect of love. The
love that Augustine is thinking about is one that can do what
Cicero's friends cannot; it can take into account not only the
natural affections but also the needs and the ugly side of other
people. This is important. However much Augustine knew his
own need for the love of friendship, he was also aware of many
other aspects of love. The love of friendship has to exist alongside
love of many other kinds — of compassion, of gratitude, of
identity of purpose, love that springs from the experience of being
part of a fellowship, *societas*. There are so many aspects of love,
and it is all of these that Augustine makes room for in his *Rule* by
suggesting family ties as the model for the love that he wishes to
see established in the community, rather than the ties of friendship. Friendship is selective, and in a group it is taken for granted
that degrees of friendship will vary considerably among the members. In a family, all have equal claims on the affection of the others
— which implies that all have an equal duty to make themselves
lovable. Among the siblings, if the parents are happy together,
affection and loyalty override the essential rivalries that must
occur in development. When the children have become adults and
their dissimilarities have led them into different careers and ways
of life, there remains that mysterious thing called family affection
which links them all together. But when it comes to parents and
children, there is an ambivalence from a very early stage. While
the parents' intent and desire is to love, what the child sometimes
experiences in himself is love and also fear. As Augustine wrote
in the passage which we have quoted from *The Catholic Way of Life*,
fear is the response to coercion, which is itself a response to one's

own fear; and love is a response to instruction/guidance/leading which can only be given when one is open and unafraid. In any human social structure there will inevitably be both a laying down of the law accompanied by penalties for its infringement, and a teaching of the law which is a way of liberation and development. That is why in the *Rule* Augustine concedes that both love and fear are necessary (*necessarium*), necessary because inevitable, human nature and human society being what they are.

So when the prior is admonished to seek rather to be loved than feared he is challenged at a very deep level. The leader's basic attitude to life is called in question by this precept, and he or she will have to look at it closely not once but often. How are leaders to keep coercion to a minimum? And when it has to be used, how can this be done without constricting the self-confidence of another? How can they elicit love when they take a decision or issue a command that can cause fear? How can they dissolve the fear that naturally arises at every threat of diminution? Augustine once said in a sermon: "A master is feared, a father is loved" (Sermon 156, 15). The chief attitude to be avoided by the prior, then, is masterfulness. As we said just now, masterfulness may be prompted by overanxious desire for the good of the brothers and may be prompted by genuine love for them. In that case, he will be overbearing and insensitive. But when masterfulness is a cloak for insecurity and inadequacy — when, that is, it stems from inflated self-love — the result will be imperious domineering and manipulation. In stressing this point explicitly in the sermon and implicitly in the *Rule*, Augustine has behind him the warning to *the elders* by a *fellow elder* in 1 Peter 5:2-3 which has echoes throughout the present paragraph of the precepts: *Tend the flock of God that is your charge, not by constraint but willingly, not for shameful gain but eagerly, not as domineering over those in your charge but being examples to the flock.* Every person in a position of leadership has to examine himself again and again if he desires to be free from self-seeking in the fulfillment of his office.

THE PRIOR IS LEADER, NOT MASTER

That is why Augustine's stress on the role of a father is so important. It is a constant reminder to the leader of the group that he is not its master. His function is to minister to the needs of the brothers and when he does this with great flexibility then he is loved. And more than that, he is strengthened and encouraged in the work that he has to do.

The prior's work is not of his own making; it is laid on him by his community, and through them by God. He is accountable to the group for what he does and for what he makes of the community during his term of office. And, like everyone else, he is accountable to God. When Augustine writes of "the account that [the prior] will have to render to God," he is drawing on Jesus' notion of stewardship which is recorded in the gospels and developed in 1 Peter 5. Both Matthew and Luke have a detailed account of the parable of the talents (Mt 25:14-30, Lk 19:11-26) where the stress is fairly evenly divided between the giver of the talents (who has the first and the last word in the matter) and what is done with them by his servants. And both evangelists emphasize the accountability of stewards to their employers (Mt 24:45-51; Lk 12:42-48 and 16:1). In all these passages the writers stress Jesus' teaching that the gifts are from God and that complete trustworthiness is expected in the receivers. The same point is made by Paul in 1 Corinthians 4:1-2: *This is how you should regard us, as servants of Christ and stewards of the mysteries of God. Moreover it is required of stewards that they be found trustworthy.* 1 Peter 4:10 makes two further points: *As each has received a gift employ it for one another, as good stewards of God's varied grace.* Here, God's gift takes varying forms — it has its own flexibility — and it is to be used for the benefit of others (and not for that of the user). Finally, there is the passage in Hebrews which is echoed in the precept which we are now considering. Here it is the others who are addressed, and the writer tells them how they are to regard those who have particular responsibilities as stewards of the gifts of God: *Obey your leaders and submit to them; for they are keeping watch over your souls, as men who will have to give an account.*

At this point, then, Augustine is reminding the prior that he is not his own master, nor can he be a law unto himself in the way he leads the community. He, like the other monks, is under God in the monastery. He holds the office of prior for the upbuilding of the group and the well-being of each individual. He is to become for them the person who is always available, attentive, and caring. And the monks must themselves constantly bear in mind the tremendous demands that this makes on him. It is small wonder that he will feel himself to be "prostrate at [their] feet."

The prior's charge is a heavy one, yet is it not entirely his. The work of sustaining the monks is above all God's work, and the prior's chief part is to keep the channels open for the incoming of God in their individual and corporate lives. It is for this task that he is accountable to his *praepositus*, God. The monks for their part must aid him in his work; and this is the point which Augustine makes in the following paragraph.

Rule, Chapter VII, 4

This is why
by being the more obedient
you show compassion not only to yourselves but also to him,
for the higher the position held among you
the greater is the peril of him who holds it.

COMPASSION AND OBEDIENCE

Augustine now begins to pull all his threads together, and in this final paragraph of chapter VII he reverts to a theme which he had expressed forcibly in chapter IV, 8 and 9. In these two passages he evoked compassion, contrasting it with cruelty, when he was stating that there are times in the life of a community when action has to be taken against one member, when it would be entirely wrong to concur in what he does. Here in chapter VII, 4 compassion is appealed to as a reason for obedience. In both cases this demand is striking and challenging. What links them together is the underlying theme that unless compassion is brought into play, situations will get out of hand (in cases of sin and sickness in chapter IV, and in regard to the well-being of the whole community in the present passage).

Both the weak and the strong, then, need compassion — and this mercifulness itself penetrates deeply into the area of need of the one to whom it is shown. All have needs, both the weak and the strong; need is part of the human condition and is nothing to be ashamed of in itself. We have already explored the sinner's need which is considered in chapter IV. Here we must look at Augustine's understanding of the prior's need.

Obviously, but not superficially, the first necessity is for the brothers' obedience. The very fact of the prior's position of leadership establishes a relationship between him and the others, and he needs to have their acceptance of him as a person and of his role in the community; he needs their trust and their respect for what he asks of them, their readiness to interpret his orders in accordance with his mind, not with their own. Such obedience is something quite different from subservience, since it requires sensitivity, self-knowledge, integrity, and, above all, patience and confidence. It is impossible for every member of the group to respond to the prior with an equality of personal affection, and their degrees of understanding will vary according to their own nature. But as each one becomes more and more centered upon God his awareness of the needs of others leads to deep compassion — for everyone, including his leader.

It is possible to be aware of the needs of others without compassion, to do so with arrogance and contempt; that can happen when there is no humility. And it is this insight that induces Augustine to couple compassion with obedience. As we said in the previous paragraph, obedience involves so much more than doing as one is ordered to do. It requires also a willingness to give oneself away, a letting go of one's in-built securities, a readiness to take risks with one's self, an abandonment of preconceived ideas and a daring to trust the judgment of others. The monks have to be open to receive their prior as he is, being fully aware of the dimensions of the demands that his office makes of him.

Augustine himself had already been aware of the cost of leadership for many years when he wrote the *Rule*, and it was a concern which he continued to share with others until the end of his life. He saw the problem in his early days as a Christian and became acutely concerned with it when he was ordained. It continued to challenge him while he lived in the monastery in the garden where he could see the difficulties that met him as a priest and that met the prior as the guardian of the community's life; and he recognized that they both faced the same complex situation.[37] In fact he used precisely the same word in relation to himself as priest in 391 and to the prior in 397, and nearly thirty years later he used it again in Sermon 355, 2. In the letter which he addressed to his bishop, Valerius, at the time of his ordination, he said that there was "nothing in this life . . . more difficult, toilsome, and hazardous (*difficilius, laboriosius, periculosius*) than the office of a bishop or priest or deacon" (Letter 21, 1), that such a ministry was "fraught with great hazards" (Letter 21, 2) in that it laid him open to presumptuousness in his dealings with others; and he asked to be allowed time from work because he did "at last recognize [his] weak points and felt it his duty to investigate all the remedies to be found in . . . Scripture: to see that prayer and study procure for [his] soul adequate strength for such dangerous tasks" (*ad tam periculosa negotia tribuatur*). And in 426 his awareness of the dangers of high office were still vivid when he told the Hippo congregation that in his younger days he dreaded episcopal office to such an extent that when there began to be any report of him among the servants of God in any place which was without a bishop, he would not go there. He said that he feared this and acted, insofar as he was able, "so that he might be saved in a lowly place and not imperiled in a high one" (*ut in loco humili salvarer, ne in alto periclitarer*) (Sermon 355, 2).

Yet although from the beginning he was aware of the difficulties inherent in the holding of office he was at the same time confident that protection was available if it was looked for: remedies (*medicamenta*) was the word that he used when he wrote to Valerius (Letter 21, 3). As we have seen, he considered that the cures could be discovered by attentive study of the Bible, and through these writings and their power to change a man's thinking and attitudes it would be possible to build up an immunity to danger.

As early as 386, when he wrote *Order*, he had come to see that a leader needs to exercise his authority "as if one were ashamed to command" and needs to command "as if it were a delight to serve" (II, 8[25]). In 391, it is his very awareness of the hazards that protects him from taking the easy way out and embarking on his clerical ministry "in a mechanical and sycophantic way" (*perfunctorie atque adulatorie*) (Letter 21, 1). By the following year, when he wrote to Aurelius of Carthage, he could say explicitly that he saw the need to avoid praise as much as possible though at the same time he realized that an artificial situation is created when a leader belittles or abases himself unduly; what is required, he wrote, is patience and humility (Letter 22, 7-8). Later, in fact in the year after the writing of the *Rule*, his letter to Eudoxius in Capraria shows deeper insight which applies as much to an abbot and his monks as it does to a priest or a bishop. The one thing necessary, he wrote, is that all is consciously done to the glory of God; and this applies equally to such things as prayer, almsgiving, and service and to forgiving injuries, subduing bad habits, and guarding against temptations (Letter 48, 3). If seeking and expressing the glory of God is one's objective, then it is possible to meet all obstacles and obstructions with endurance and with equanimity (*ibid.*). And the chief means of protection lies in the ability — one can even say, the heroic ability — to bear with each other "in love (*in dilectionem*), for what can he endure who does not endure his brother?" (*ibid.*). The same themes occur also in one of his sermons but with an added dimension. In Sermon 46, 1 Augustine refers to the need to combat self-seeking; and later he speaks of a leader's ability to bear criticism, protests and even hatred, and of the necessity for knowing how to deal with praise, approval, sympathy, and flattery (Sermon 46, 20). However, in Sermon 46, 2 he makes a significant point when he tells his congregation to remember that people in office in the Church are first of all Christians and then leaders: they are Christians for their own benefit, they are leaders for the benefit of others. This stress on what we may call a double stream of consciousness in a leader — and we are concerned principally with a leader in a monastery — is important, for it emphasizes the extreme difficulty of his task. The office itself will require all his strengths, and it will also reveal his weaknesses. The person who cannot face his own weaknesses as they are revealed may rule, but he cannot serve others. Augustine, as we have seen, could face his weaknesses, and it was this that gave him the capacity to be close to other people and to trust himself to them as he sought to serve them. To live for the sake of others, which is the greatest expression of love, is also the paramount demand which God makes of anyone who holds high office, and it is very costing. And so he adds: If I tell you about this grave concern, it is so that you may have compassion on us and pray for us.[38]

THE PRIOR IS AS VULNERABLE AS HIS COMPANIONS

In the monastery, compassion is shown for the leader by the quality of the monks' obedience: "By being the more obedient you show compassion" (*uos magis oboediendo . . . miseremini*). Compassion for the leader is to be built into the life of the community to whom Augustine addresses the *Rule*. In paragraphs 1-3 of this present chapter he has not sketched an ideal prior, nor the ideals that a prior should aim at; what he has shown is the way of life that he envisages for the one who carries the responsibility of leadership in the monastery. If we were to try to make a complete drawing from the lines and curves and shading that Augustine has set down we would not produce a tower of strength but a person whose very vulnerability and dependence enable him to give strength to others: he is a source of strength, or a channel through which strength can pass — but this channel is made of fine bone china and not of reinforced concrete. The prior is as vulnerable as every other member of the group, but it is only those who have recognized their own weakness who will be able to accept with compassion the stresses and strains that beset their leader. The compassion that Augustine evokes is one which says "You and we are one in our frailty; we have one common need, the support of each other." The monks have compassion on themselves as well as on their prior.

Compassion such as this, compassion which is not blind but which sees and accepts to the point of obeying, is a sign of maturity. There are other forms of obedience which are rooted in fear and insecurity; but obedience of the kind that Augustine is seeking to draw out here is only possible when the leader is open to all and when each member is himself open to him — and this is why it is possible for Augustine to say that, in obeying, the monks will show compassion not only to the prior but also to themselves. Compassion can hold all complexities together; it can be patient, tolerant, and understanding because it is rooted in love and in prayer which, for Augustine and for those who follow him, is the whole meaning of their life in the monastery where there is "one soul and one heart entirely centered upon God" (chapter I, 2). The desire for unity, integrity, and service can only be fulfilled when the monks — as individuals, each in his own way, and as a group with a rich pattern of expression — have come to learn the meaning and value of acceptance, consent, and love.

In looking back down the whole length of the *Rule*, or in looking back on the whole of one's life in a monastery, it is possible to see how the exercise of compassion is the solvent of the many and great temptations and stresses that have to be met — the clashes of temperament, disparities of background and education, the claims and counterclaims that are inevitable when a number of people live together, the fact of sin and suffering, the many forms that the search for God and integrity in him can take — in looking back on all of this we are forced to say "If only I had been more compassionate, more considerate, more capable of affirming the value of others." And that itself is one's prayer.

So it is fitting that in coming to the end of his precepts Augustine does pray with his readers, as we shall see in the next and final chapter.

NOTES

1. Peter Salway, *Roman Britain,* Clarendon Press, 1981, page 317; see also A. M. H. Jones, *The Later Roman Empire, 284-602* (3 volumes Blackwell, 1964, reprinted in 2 volumes, 1973), page 835.

2. The earlier passage is in chapter V, 5, where a sick person is warned that he should obey whatever is prescribed for him and not his own inclination.

3. Henry C. Lea, *History of Sacerdotal Celibacy in the Christian Church,* Williams & Norgate (4rd revised edition), 1907, Volume I, page 112.

4. *Institutes* IV, 10, 21; *Conferences* LV, 20.

5. *Conferences* XIX, 1.

6. *Institutes* IV, 23.

7. *Institutes* I, 2.

8. For a valuable discussion of this tradition, see Paul Evdokimov, *L'Amour Fou de Dieu,* Editions du Seuil, 1973, chapter IV.

9. Saint Basil, RB CXV (*Ascetical Works,* page 273).

10. See the *City of God* XIX, 16. Although Basil and Augustine must have had the same household model in mind, the former's servant/slave-master analogy stresses the head's function of command, while Augustine's use of "father" stresses the leader's role as that of one who cares.

11. See Karl Rahner's discussion in *The Religious Life Today,* pages 51-69.

12. Lk 10:16; Jn 13:20.

13. Rom 13:1.7.

14. Augustine's verb in the text is *praetereatur,* and this echoes the Latin version of Lk 10:31.

15. *The Way of the Preacher,* Darton, Longman & Todd, 1979, pages 7-8.

16. See chapter I, 2-7; II, 2.4; III, 2-5; IV, 2.6.11; V, 1-4.6-11; VI, 2-3.

17. See Luc Verheijen, *Nouvelle Approche de la Règle de Saint Augustin,* Abbaye de Bellefontaine, 1980, pages 394-401.

18. *Ibid.,* page 227.

19. *Saint Augustin: l'Aventure de la Raison et de la Grâce,* Études Augustiniennes, 1968, page 236.

20. *Ibid.,* pages 394-339.

21. Concerning the Renunciation of the World 204d and 205a, *Longer Rule* VII and XXVI; *Shorter Rule* CXIII, CCXXVII, CCXXIX.

22. *Institutes* IV, 7-9; *Conferences* II, 11; XX, 8.

23. Chapter V, 9.

24. Chapter I, 5; III, 3-5; VII, 3.

25. See the article by Jacques Leclercq, "The Use of Authority" in John M. Todd's *Problems of Authority,* Darton, Longman & Todd, 1964, pages 246-260.

26. See Mt 20:25-28; Mk 9:35; Lk 22:26; Jn 13:4.13-15.

27. *Science, Religion and Christianity,* Burns & Oates, 1958 page 38.

28. Chapter III, 1.5 (3 times) and V, 8 (twice).

29. Chapter V, 8.

30. The verb used in the Greek text literally means to lay hold of something and help it to stand firm.

31. There is a valuable article on this whole subject by John E. Rotelle, O.S.A. and Edward R. Manning, O.S.A., "The Fraternity, Sacrament of Love" in *Review for Religious* 27 (1968) 393-410.

32. The textual variants are summarized by Luc Verheijen, *La Règle de Saint Augustin*, I, page 436. His reasons for accepting *metum inponat* as the correct reading are given on page 399.

33. See Luc Verheijen, *St. Augustine: Monk, Priest and Bishop*, Augustinian Historical Institute, Villanova University, 1978, page 37.

34. *The Problem of Self-Love in St. Augustine*, Yale University Press, 1980, pages 11-12.

35. *Ibid.*, page 13.

36. Letter 10, 1; *Life of Augustine* 3.

37. In what follows I am indebted to Luc Verheijen, *op. cit., passim.*

38. For the whole passage, see Luc Verheijen, *op. cit.*, page 40.

8

Mature Freedom

Rule, Chapter VIII, 1
May the Lord grant
that you may observe all these things with love,
as lovers of spiritual beauty,
radiating by your good life the sweet odor of Christ,
not like slaves under the law
but as free persons
established in grace.

AUGUSTINE'S PRAYER

We now come to the climax of the *Rule* which takes the form of a prayer for the brothers. It is more than that. It is a prayer which everyone whose monastic life is informed with Augustine's spirituality may make his own: May the Lord grant that we may observe all these things with love, as lovers of spiritual beauty, radiating by our lives the sweet odor of Christ, not like slaves under the law but as free persons established in grace.

It is in this paragraph that the spirituality and the praxis of the *Rule* are summed up. The use of *dilectio* reminds us that love is its meaning. This love is made known in fidelity, in devotion, and in witness, and above all in making Christ known, in extending his life (that is, in becoming his body). Christ is the heart and mind of the community; he is its unity which the daily life of the monks must seek to express. There is no room for a rigid, slavish attitude to the demands of the common life — rather, that life must be characterized by freedom. Yet freedom within the patterns of the common life is an impossibility without the enabling power of the Lord the Spirit — without the free gift of grace, with its power to create unity and to perfect love. It is in the freedom of grace that the seeker can find, the servant can serve, and the monastery can become a living cell of Christ's body, the Church.

These are the matters which Augustine touches on lightly in this last chapter of his precepts.

LOVERS OF SPIRITUAL BEAUTY

The very people whose advantages and disadvantages, quirks, foibles, psychological, and moral inadequacies he has taken into account as he sets down his guidelines for monastic life are the ones whom he knows to be "lovers of spiritual beauty" (*spiritalis pulchritudinis amatores*). The same is true of every generation and holds good today. Our world is different from Augustine's and some of the conditions of living that he takes for granted are no longer acceptable in the twentieth century (the same is true of both Testaments of the Bible, of course); but our humanness has not changed much. All enter a monastery with high ideals "entirely centered upon God" (chapter I, 2), and after that we spend the rest of our life in discovering what sort of a person we are who carry deep longing for God in our heart. We are rarely single-minded, though when we entered we thought that we were. We begin to become single-minded as soon as we make the first discovery of our divided self; and we become more centered upon God in the measure that we increasingly recognize what manner of person we are and then realize that God is with us and in us and is accepting us in love.

Vocation itself is a gift of God, and so is the enabling power to follow it faithfully. "May the Lord grant" (*Donet dominus*) is the beginning of Augustine's prayer. May God grant you the power to live out your vocation in a spirit of love. Here again the key word *dilectio* occurs — the aspect of love that is deeply sensitive and caring and which alone can hold the community together.

Monastic life is a response of love to love, and that is why we can be faithful in it in spite of our own and others' inherent weaknesses. A person who loves is transformed by the one whom he loves and by the creative act of loving; and when we love we find ourselves willing and, often to our surprise, able to absorb the points of view, the needs, and also the dictates of the beloved. These do not necessarily come to us directly from the one who is loved — other people, by their words or their attitudes, may be a source of our understanding of those closest to us. "I did not know until I met X how important Y's work is and how well it is thought of" is a not uncommon remark.

It is in this spirit that Augustine's monastic precepts are meant by him to be accepted. They are not the object of love, but they are a way that he believes to be pleasing to the Lord and in harmony with his love and his will; and they are to be seen by a monk as an expression of his own love for God and for his neighbor.

Here Augustine uses the word observe (*obseruetur*) for the third time. At the beginning he wrote: "These are the things which we give as precepts to be observed" (chapter I, 1); and at the end of his long discussion of what should be done when a monk is behaving very badly and causing scandal, he says that the steps he has suggested are to be observed carefully and faithfully whatever the serious fault that comes to light among the brothers (chapter IV, 10). Now, at the end of the *Rule*, the same word is repeated. Augustine has laid down his precepts and it is they that he desires should be observed; they are an expression of a love that transcends and yet remains immanent in the ordinary every-day affairs of the monastery.

Unity, love, and forgiving acceptance are the qualities that are to characterize the life of the community. Unity centered on God is the destination; love is the road to it; and forgiving acceptances are, as it were, the means of transport, the vehicles by which we travel.

Love is central. Without it, there is no possibility of unity because only love gives the ability to set aside one's own demands and to accept those of others. Love holds together all the desires and longings for good, for happiness, for completion and all the events, people, and things that make up our daily lives. Love acts. Love goes out to meet other people where they are and as they are.

Anyone reading or hearing the precepts attentively must be aware that Augustine had no illusions that the Hippo monks were plaster saints; nevertheless it is possible for him to describe them as "lovers of spiritual beauty." He does not say that they should be, using a verb form; he uses a noun, *amatores* (lovers), thus assuming an existing state of affairs. He knows where their hearts are set and what it is that they desire above all, just as he knows the hindrances in themselves and in others that have to be over-come. The monks' love for the things of God is expressed in their striving.

For a modern reader of the *Rule*, the phrases "spiritual beauty" and "lovers of spiritual beauty" come as something of a surprise because there is, seemingly, nothing that leads up to them. But for Augustine's first readers this was not so, and one may imagine a smile of recognition among the first hearers of the precepts: this was a theme that had been constant in his and their thinking and talking for a long time. And perhaps it ought not to surprise us of a later generation: after all, his best-known words are "Late have I loved Thee, O Beauty, so ancient and so new: late have I loved Thee" (*sero te amaui, pulchritudo tam antiqua et tam noua, sero te amaui*) (*Confessions* X, 27). They were written a few years later than the *Rule*, but they clearly relate to a part of Augustine that had old and deep roots.

Luc Verheijen has shown in detail how it came about that Augustine used the image of beauty and the notion of spiritual beauty to express the goodness, fullness, and transcendence of God, and the manner in which they may be incarnated in the lives of men.[1] The roots lie deep in classical culture, forming the basis of the Pythagorean system of education in which Augustine and his contemporaries were all brought up. At one level it could be said that Augustine was conditioned by his education; at another, it seems true to say that by his nature he was able to respond to his education. Committed to his search for God, beauty for him expressed the utter desirability and the utter loveliness of the One whom he was seeking. By describing God in terms of loveliness Augustine was stating his openness to him, his willingness to be attracted and to respond. And in this he was not unique — his language was that of his contemporaries and he was not breaking new ground in speaking or writing of "spiritual beauty." Nor was he breaking new ground here in calling the monks "lovers of spiritual beauty." The shorter and the longer phrase are to be found in his own writings covering the eleven years that preceded the writing of the *Rule*.

In his book *Order*, which he wrote in 386 as a kind of handbook for his pupils, he said that the observance of precepts is animated by one's love of spiritual beauty, and in the same paragraph he says that it is the contemplation of beauty which makes the soul beautiful (II, 19). In the following year, in his treatise on music, he draws attention to the direct relation between beauty and ordered harmony (*Music* VI, 13). And in number 36 (2) of the *Miscellany of Eighty-three Questions*, which he worked on between 388 and 395, he treats of a relationship between spiritual beauty, liberty, and the imitation of Christ. Thus the terminology of his prayer at the end of the *Rule* would have been one that was familiar to the monks of Hippo. The underlying theme of beauty will continue to attract him, and it finds its fullest expression many years later in the commentary on John's gospel.

> Transcendental beauty [he wrote] is the source of the harmony of the body, the source of universal order, the source of the fine balance of the virtues (especially of wisdom), the source of the unity of the Church which is called to become ever more unified. It is in God that the elect will contemplate the supreme harmony of the Trinity in the peace of unity (*Homilies on the Gospel of John* 14, 9).

For Augustine, all beauty is God's beauty and it is reflected in people as the source of their unity, order, and well-being. And, as we have seen throughout the *Rule*, these are the aims which those who live in the monastery are always to have in mind. The whole of their life is a response to the attraction of beauty.

Monastic life is always a response: it is never, it never can be, self-initiating. Nor is it ever preserved by its own definitions. Whatever structures, rules, regulations — whatever precepts — it may require, these are themselves a response to the attraction of the divine beauty which expresses itself in love.

THE NATURE OF LOVE

Love, Augustine reminds the readers of the *Rule*, expresses itself in a distinctive manner of life. Or, as the New Testament puts it, every Christian's manner of life is to be characterized by love:

> By this will all men know that you are my disciples, if you have love for one another (Jn 13:35).

> This is my commandment, that you love one another as I have loved you (Jn 15:12).

> Owe no one anything, except to love one another; for he who loves his neighbor has fulfilled the law (Rom 13:8).

> Having purified your souls by your obedience to the truth for a sincere love of the brethren, love one another earnestly from the heart (1 Pt 1:22).

> This is the message which you have heard from the beginning, that we should love one another (1 Jn 3:11).

> No man has ever seen God; if we love one another, God abides in us and his love is perfected in us (1 Jn 4:12).

Love such as this is a willed love which stems from God who abides in us and which reaches its full flowering when it is able to control and direct a purified heart that shows utter integrity in its love for truth and for other people.

Love is made known by what it does rather than by what it says. And when Augustine writes to the monks about their "good life" he uses the noun *conuersatio* in the wide sense that is to be found in the New Testament. This word and its related verb form are found in 2 Corinthians 1:12, Galatians 1:13, Ephesians 2:3, 4:22, 1 Timothy 4:12, Hebrews 13:7, James 3:13, 1 Peter 1:15-18, 2:12, 3:1-2-16, 2 Peter 3:11. The Revised Standard Version translates these as "behavior," "life," "manner of life," "conduct," "ways"; and as "life" is the word that implies depth of living as well as variety I have used that to translate Augustine's use of *conuersatio* in this passage of the *Rule*. This is the only place where it occurs in the text, but it is what all the precepts are about: the quality of living of those who are committed to life in the monastery.

RADIANT SELF-GIVING

Augustine's phrasing is poetic at this point. Usually he makes his point by using rhetorical devices, but here he is constrained to use language that transcends reason and emotion, that declares its meaning by overleaping categories. The existing manuscripts of the *Rule* show that scribes and readers have been disconcerted by Augustine's change of style at this point, and it is not clear what word he actually wrote for the one which I have translated as radiating. Verheijen gives *flagrantes* but points out that there are variants in a number of codices.[6] Following his version I have concentrated on *flagrantes* which may be translated as flaming, blazing, glowing, glittering, shining, and, metaphorically, ardent, or eager. But nothing can glitter with a smell, and so one must seek for some word or expression that can contain all the dimensions of Augustine's searching phrase which evokes the many aspects of beauty which he prays may be found in the lives of the monks. The appeal is more than that to the senses, for the consent of the will is involved. So in translation I have used the word radiating with its overtones of radiance as well as of spreading abroad, as coming nearest to the poetry of *flagrantes*. As Augustine once put it in a sermon: "When love is cold the heart is silent but when there is ardent love (*flagrantia charitatis*) the heart makes itself heard" (*Expositions of the Psalms* 38, 14).

Augustine prays that the monks may shine with the *bono odore* of Christ. The phrase is taken from 2 Corinthians 2:15 which itself takes up the Old Testament theme of sacrificial offerings: the smell of a burnt offering (in, for example, Genesis 8:21, Exodus 29:18-25, Leviticus 1:9-13, Numbers 28:2), or of incense (in, for example, Exodus 30:8, Leviticus 16:13, Psalms 141:2, Malachi 1:11), is a token of self-giving to God which is acceptable to him. In the New Testament the word smell (Latin *odor*) has, as Robert J. Daly has pointed out, a technical meaning describing the acceptability of a sacrifice before God.[2]

The theme which Augustine is evoking when he prays that the monks may be radiant with the sweet odor of Christ is thus their boundless self-sacrifice which will spend itself continually for the sake of others. This self-offering, marked with Christlike qualities, will show itself in the quality of their lives, of their good lives. Throughout the *Rule*, Augustine's aim has been to portray the good life — not in an ideal setting but in the midst of all the mixture of circumstances, temperaments, and opportunities that make up the common life. As we have noticed so often, in exploring the precepts, it is the ordinary aspects of humanness which challenge each person to break through into the deeper and wider dimensions of living. The radiant good of their lives lies in its Christ-likeness, in their free self-giving through love.

FREE PERSONS ESTABLISHED IN GRACE

And so now Augustine comes to his deepest insight into the nature of life in the monastery. It is as if he said, I have given you these guidelines. They are not intended to enslave you, to force you to a procrustean bed. They are offered so that you may enter into their meaning and accept their demands with complete freedom of spirit and remain your unique selves while following this route which I have marked out: "Not like slaves under the law but as free persons established in grace" (*non sicut serui sub lege, sed sicut liberi sub gratia constituti*). This phrase expresses what a writer has called the joy, confidence, and high purpose[3] of Augustine's own life which he always longed to share with others after his conversion. Founded on God's gracious mercy, resilience such as this is what gives continuing life to a community, expressing the group's spirit rather than its conduct.

Yet there have been those who have attempted to observe Augustine's precepts *au pied de la lettre*; but to do so is to go contrary to the very important point that he is making in this sentence. To do so is to behave like a slave and it is to cut oneself off from completeness. There have been, and there still are, those who say on entering a monastery, "I only want to do what I am told." But this is not a sign of suppleness but of pathological rigidity which prevents growth to maturity and fullness of life. Eric Fromm calls it the fear of freedom.[4] Such an attitude may be human, for some humans, but it is not the attitude of an integrated human, and it is not Christian since it leaves the grace of God entirely out of account.

It is right that Augustine should set freedom at the climax of his *Rule*, and not at an earlier point in his text; for freedom depends on the integration of personality with the experiences of life in all its dimensions.

First he says that the monks are to "observe" the precepts. He does not use the words obey or conform. The precepts do not form a code of conduct which ensures right behavior, efficiency, and all the rest. They remain pointers leading somewhere; and on the human level it is toward mature freedom that they direct those who follow them. The one thing necessary, if this freedom is to be attained in monastic life, is love (*dilectio*). The whole of the second part of the *Rule* is an exploration of the meaning of love, and when Augustine refers to it again specifically in his final prayer he is simply showing for the last time what it is that will liberate the monks so that they can pursue their monastic vocation. But when you are talking about monastic life the terms of reference always transcend the human level, for the interaction between God and human beings is at the heart of this way of living. So the mature freedom to which the *Rule* points is always many-dimensioned, and that is why Augustine could not evoke freedom without setting it within the sphere of grace.

In *Augustine of Hippo*, Peter Brown discusses Augustine's own development and he concludes:

> For Augustine freedom can only be the culmination of a process of healing. . . . Freedom . . . for Augustine cannot be reduced to a sense of choice: it is a freedom to act fully. Such freedom must involve a transcendence of a sense of choice. For a sense of choice is a symptom of the disintegration of the will: the final union of knowledge and feeling would involve a man in the object of his choice in such a way that any other alternative would be inconceivable.[5]

This expresses clearly what Augustine means when he prays that the precepts may be observed with love in a spirit of freedom rather than in that of slaves. Throughout the *Rule*, as throughout the course of one's life in a monastery, the healing process has been at work in the choices that each member is confronted with. And it is only when choices are motivated by deeply caring love, as one pursues the way of seeking and serving, that one may hope to reach those wholly free moments when there is no choice but an overwhelming compulsion to give oneself away completely. The impulse was there from the beginning — in fact it was a dominant factor at the beginning of one's life in the monastery; but it is only the maturely free person who is able to say from the depths of his being "I could not live in any other way."

Of course, such moments of transcendent freedom are not "saved up for the end" but may occur whenever a person is, as it were, lost in love. We see this happening in disparate events and circumstances as a community lives its continuing life.

In this paragraph of the *Rule* Augustine does not actually write of freedom — he takes the concept for granted and simply refers to the monks as free (*liberi*). It is difficult for twentieth-century people to appreciate the overtones of the words free and freedom as they were used and experienced in the ancient world. The fact of slavery is not part of the social climate in which most people in the world now live;[6] and so we can tend to spiritualize that word as we do also the idea of freedom. But for fourth-century people both slavery and freedom were concrete experiences. Today injustice and oppression have taken the place of legal slavery and challenge the conscience of mankind. In that sense it is possible for us all to experience what it is not to be free. Thus in our attitudes to life, and particularly to the demands of our monastic life, we still have the choice of acceptance in the spirit of a slave (which is characterized by fear and constraint) or in the spirit of one who is free (when the chief characteristic is love, sensitivity, and willingness).

When Augustine wrote the present paragraph of the *Rule* he used one word for free men (*liberi*). This is the word that he had in his Latin Bible at 1 Corinthians 12:13 (*slaves or free*) and 1 Peter 2:16 (*live as free men*), where the stress is on the social status of each one. But in the *Rule*, in which the monks have been challenged deeply and where, finally, Augustine prays implicitly that they may be made whole, the stress of *liberi* is on the spiritual and psychological dimensions into which they have now moved. For that reason I have translated his word as "free persons," not as "free men," in order to underline the depth of experience which monastic life brings to those who follow it. Of course, the modern concept of personality did not exist in Augustine's day and so it would be outside our terms of reference to discuss it in relation to the *Rule*. Nevertheless, from beginning to end his concern is with the monks as they are and with their developing experience of each other, of God and of themselves. When a modern Christian writes, "If the presence of the Holy Spirit in man liberates him, if grace means emancipation from slavery to the deterministic contingencies of the world, membership of the body of Christ also means freedom. Finally, freedom means personal existence,"[7] he is expressing something which Augustine and his monks could readily accept.

Having inner freedom, for Augustine, is never a state that exists *sui generis*. As the New Testament writers had themselves discovered, freedom is always something given. The giver is God who in giving shares himself with us — and this he does while we are still sinners (Rom 5:8). Those who give imply their own acceptance of those who receive — and this is important because God's acceptance of us implies that we may dare to accept ourselves, and it is there that we experience freedom.

FREEDOM: SPONTANEITY IN THE MONASTERY

The experience of freedom manifests itself in a spontaneity which carries us beyond our own barriers and beyond the barriers of others and thus makes possible a common life that is itself a body. As Erich Fromm states in *The Fear of Freedom*:

> Spontaneous activity is the one way in which man can overcome the terror of aloneness without sacrificing the integrity of his self; for in the spontaneous realization of the self man unites himself anew with . . . man, nature, and himself. Love is the foremost component of such spontaneity . . . love as a spontaneous affirmation of others, as the union of the individual with others on the basis of the preservation of the individual self. The dynamic quality of love lies in this very polarity: that it springs from the need for overcoming separateness, that it leads to oneness — and yet that individuality is not eliminated. Work is the other component . . . work as creation in which man becomes one with nature in the act of creation. . . . The basic

dichotomy that is inherent in freedom — the birth of individuality and the pain of aloneness — is dissolved on a higher plane by man's spontaneous action.[8]

This insight, which is in no way influenced by monastic tradition, underlines the soundness of Augustine's instinct in setting freedom at the peak of his precepts.

By now, having reached the end of the *Rule*, many unacceptable ingredients of our lives have been faced. When we have faced them we may find them so intolerable that we turn away, and it is then that we take refuge in slavish rigidity as the only way of being able to survive within the common life. But if we do that we are failing to do the very thing that Augustine has done throughout the *Rule*. What he shows to be the way is the interiorization of every experience that comes to us: from an outer aspect we turn to its inner meaning, from the surface we penetrate to the depth. And it is the deepening of habit that transforms the ordinariness of life into something gloriously different. From the beginning of his Christian awakening Augustine himself had been aware of the downward drag in human nature and its weakening effect on human aspirations. As he once wrote in a letter, "No one is known to another so intimately as he is known to himself, and yet no one is so well known even to himself that he can be sure as to his own conduct on the morrow" (Letter 130, 2, 4). Yet in spite of this, people do go on aspiring, if and when they discover another factor in their lives. Our ability to accept the dark, estranging side of our natures rests on our capacity to be truly and honestly humble, on the ability to admit the sin which law confronts us with in the way that the letter to the Romans describes so poignantly.

HUMILITY IS A GIFT OF GRACE

In chapter VI, 3 of the *Rule* Augustine discusses false humility, and that is the only occasion when he actually mentions the word. Humiliation is referred to in chapter I, 6 and humble birth in chapter III, 5. But humility as a virtue is never named, it is simply taken for granted. It is at home, as it were, in the discussion of the way to unity of heart and mind in chapter I, in the monks' prayer in chapter II, in the simplicity of life in chapter III, in the wrongdoing and compassion of chapter IV, in the service of others in chapter V, and in the forgiving and obedient spirit of chapters VI and VII.

Yet humility itself does not come naturally to us. Trusting humility is itself God's work in us. Thus we come, with Augustine, to the primacy of grace within Christian experience. As Luc Verheijen has pointed out,[9] when the *Rule* came to be written Augustine had already given much thought to this aspect of Christian living. His awareness of the antithesis of law and grace, of fear and love, and of slavery and liberty finds a place in the arguments of *The Catholic Way of Life* 28(56) and 30(60-64), *Order* II, 8, 25, and *The Advantage of Believing* 3(9). In the same period he was expressing the resolution of these antitheses as the operation of grace. The very phrase which we find in the *Rule*, "under grace" (*sub gratia*), occurs altogether thirteen times in his *Commentary on Some Statements in the Letter to the Romans* (written in 394), *Commentary on the Letter to the Galatians* (written at the same time) and in *Miscellany of Eighty-three Questions* (begun in 397).

For Augustine, who was very much aware of his own natural tendencies — and, presumably, the tendencies of those Hippo monks whom he knew so well — what, as Christians, they were able to irradiate to those around them could only be explained in terms of a power bestowed on them by the generosity of God. This is what he means by "grace" which in a sermon he once described as an undeserved gift from him (*Expositions of the Psalms* 31, 2, 6). It would seem that in his early Christian years he recognized grace intuitively and experientially, and it was only with the passing of time that he was able to marry his thought to his experience in this area. His study of the letter to the Romans was begun before he became a bishop, and it was from Paul that he learned the meaning of grace at a deeper level.

For the apostle, grace is something experienced. It is the gift of God which gives the followers of Jesus the power to act as his messengers (Rom 1:4-5). It is grace which has the power to undermine the potency of sin and counteract the downward drag of humanness (3:23-24, 5:15); or, to put it another way, it is grace that liberates us from the power of evil (6:14). It is grace that gives strength to the Christians' resolute joy (5:2). Most important of all, it is grace that enables them simply to be good (5:17), for grace is the way to the goodness and richness of eternal life in Christ (5:20). And finally, Paul declares, grace is the source of the ability that we find in ourselves and in one another, ability which grace itself enables us to use for the upbuilding of the Church (12:6).

It is within this experience of grace as the source of Christian confidence, which Augustine himself entered into through his conversion, that he wrote as he did at the end of his *Rule*. Grace was not something that at that stage of his life was capable of intellectual formulation such as he later expressed.[10] This later stage was conditioned by and the result of years of controversy and hard thinking. Now, when he is himself still on the way to his full development, what he does is to orchestrate the many themes that are the positive elements of his life as part of the — of a — Christian community. When he turned his careful attention to the letter to the Romans he echoed the thought of Paul in writing:

> When man tries to live justly by his own strength without the help of the liberating grace of God, he is then conquered by sins. But in free will he has it in his power to believe in the Liberator and to receive grace, in order that, with Him, who gives him this, freeing and assisting him, he may not sin, and thus may seem to be under the Law, but with the Law or in the Law, fulfill by God's charity that law, which in fear he had not been able to do (*Commentary on Some Statements in the Letter to the Romans* 45).

Here we find all the themes that come together at the end of the *Rule*: law, slavery, and fear over against grace, freedom, and love. The first three characterize man's life lived "by his own strength"; the second group are God's gift and his action.

FREEDOM AND FREE CHOICE

When Augustine writes of free will (*liberum arbitrium*) he is thinking of a human capacity — the power to choose between alternatives; but when he writes of freedom (*libertas*) he sees this as entirely a God-given grace coming from the nature of God himself who, in the passage just quoted, is called "the liberator." The actual conditions of life in which men and women live may in one sense be static and uniform, but how they live that life will depend on choice — whether they decide to rely on following a structured pattern (of their own or of others' making) or whether they decide to be open to the impulse of the Spirit. *Where the Spirit of the Lord is, there is freedom* (2 Cor 3:17). It is as we live within God's gift of freedom that the will is liberated from the downward drag of its humanness or, as Augustine calls it later on, "the fault of the carnal mind" (*The Spirit and the Letter* XIX, 34).

This experience of freedom is not one which once received is never lost. That could only be so if free choice did not exist. Monastic life presents choices all day and every day; and it takes a very long time and wide and deep experience at many levels (as the *Rule* itself has shown) before a monk or nun can discover whether he or she is living that life in freedom. In biblical terms the downward drag is often described as a form of slavery,[11] and the experience of gaining freedom is common to all Christians whatever their social status.[12] (It is impossible for us today to enter into the experience of gaining freedom by manumission, but C. K. Barrett makes an important point when he reminds us that "the freedman . . . was a humble rather than a dignified figure."[13])

In monastic life, the first choosing comes when we prepare to enter, and the moments of choice recur with every event and encounter, trivial or important, of the years that follow. Monastic commitment to poverty, to chastity, and to obedience has to be remade in everything that we do. It has to be worked out with every other member of the group as well as with those outside the community. The commitment that we have undertaken is itself the primary integrating force among all the members. But it cannot be a unifying factor unless both mind and heart make their continual assent to what has been undertaken. It is possible to live in a monastery "with the head" — and members who tend to do this are those who make up its conservative and dogmatic ranks. It is also possible to live entirely "with the heart" — and the ones who tend in this direction weaken stability in the group by a restlessness that can never allow time for things to develop.

At the beginning of the *Rule* Augustine reminded the monks of their unity (chapter I, 2). But what the course of the precepts has shown is how hard it is for heart and mind to become one thing. It is all too easy to think and to be unable to go beyond that point. What goes on in the brain will only be actualized when it is married to what goes on in the heart. And while this is true for each individual, its working out within the group is something that never can be calculated and plotted on a chart, for the great unknown factor is the most important one of all — the operation of God whose temples the monks have become (chapter I, 8). The actualization of oneness among the members remains a miracle rooted in mystery. It is the working of the grace of God, his gift of love to those who dare to give themselves away. Yet in spite of the primary element of mystery in the unifying work of grace, it is possible to see precisely what it is that happens when our thinking and our feeling are joined together; it is then that imagination is released into the sphere of our consciousness. Imagination takes us beyond the boundaries of the self into the inner world of others, enabling us to enter into their thoughts and emotions. It is the use of imagination that gives one the power of discernment and of making judgments, for imagination widens our sympathy.

For this reason, Augustine's precepts do not provide a set of instructions which if followed would produce the model that was in his, the designer's, mind. They were offered to the monks of Hippo as providing general principles which do not have the force of law but describe likely circumstances in which it is possible for God's grace to have full play. The *Rule* is not a code of conduct to be accepted and acted upon but an instrument for measuring human stature.

For this reason it is pusillanimous to look in the *Rule* for a formula that will dictate any precise action. There are in fact very few precise instructions in the text; and it is remarkable that when, in chapter IV, Augustine did attempt to set down exact methods of procedure in one particular set of circumstances the result is very confusing! If heart and mind are "entirely centered upon God" (chapter I, 2) then he "who dwells within" (chapter IV, 6) is free to share his freedom with those who love both him and one another. From the beginning of the *Rule*, Augustine has stressed the within-ness of God, his active presence in each monk. His presence is experienced as the forgiving, comforting, and strengthening activity of love. And men themselves become free, with divine freedom, to the extent that they are compelled by love to forgive, comfort, and strengthen those with whom they have to do. Thus the common life of the monastery is the place of growth.

Augustine's own spirituality was based on a fusion of love and freedom, and his great gift to monasticism lies in the importance which love and freedom have in his *Rule*.

But there is a further activity of God within each person which Augustine seeks to make plain for the monks, and it is this that underlines the final paragraph of the *Rule*.

Rule, Chapter VIII, 2
And so that you may be able to look at yourselves
in this little book

as in a mirror,
it should be read to you once a week
lest you neglect anything through forgetfulness.
When you find that you are doing the things that are written,
give thanks to the Lord,
the giver of all good things.
But when any one of you sees that he has failed in some way,
he should be sorry for the past
and be on his guard for the future,
praying that his sin may be forgiven
and that he may not be led into temptation.

Augustine refers to what he has written as a "little book" (*libellum*), so we know that it was put together in the form of a modern brochure or small book with the text written on each page. It would have been made of parchment or papyrus.[14] It was not a codex and not a volume. Like most guidebooks, it was small and easy to handle. And this guidebook is like all others of its kind: there is much more in it than immediately meets the eye, as we have seen all the way through our exploration, and one needs to go back to it repeatedly.

We can be certain that Augustine did not expect his readers to encounter a precise description of themselves within the pages of the little book. The true outlines of each individual's strengths and weaknesses can rarely be perceived with clarity, and in likening his book to a "mirror" (*speculum*) Augustine is being thoroughly realistic in a way that at first is not easy for us to grasp today. For us, the word mirror implies a clear reflection that omits nothing; but in the fourth century mirrors were more merciful. They were usually made of bronze, but tin and silver were sometimes used, and they had one slightly convex surface which was very highly polished in order to give reflections — but what they revealed was far less than what we see today when we use a looking-glass. Paul's *in a mirror dimly* (1 Cor 13:12) may serve as a reminder of what Augustine's expectations would have been.

If we remember this relative dimness, it is easier to understand Augustine's desire that every monk should hear the *Rule* read aloud once a week. This is the second instance of his regarding verbal repetition as a challenge. The first occurred in chapter VI, 2, when he was discussing the necessity of seeking and receiving forgiveness from a brother whom one has wronged: he says that forgiveness must become part of one's life, for if it does not then frequently-repeated prayers become a mockery. In that passage, and in the *Rule* as a whole, the chief emphasis is laid on each monk's responsibility for the other members of the group. Here, at the end of the *Rule*, Augustine underlines the fact of each one's responsibility for himself — a responsibility which only becomes effective when one is free.

All the precepts reflect the experience of the monks as they are. It is far easier, because more comfortable, to look at the group as a whole than it is to look at oneself. (It is in the first part of the *Rule*, where attention is to a large extent concentrated on the problems of individuals, that the really difficult problems of community life are thrashed out.) Yet throughout the precepts there is a path that leads to the discovery — or, rather, to many discoveries — of one's own self. This path leads right through the heart of each encounter within the monastery. The precepts are, as it were, a cross-check with experience. What Augustine is careful to preserve through the frequent reading of the little book is the opportunity for each monk to grow in self-awareness, for unless he does that both his search and his service are sterile. We dare not ignore what we are.

Discovering what we are is an even more painful experience than discovering what other people are. It is an outrage to one's life as one lives it, like an earthquake or a tornado. But Augustine knows that within the whole of this disintegrating occurrence, whenever it happens, and it will happen many times, it is God himself who is at work, God who is doing the destroying. It is the Spirit of God, he once said in a sermon, "that fights in you against you, against that which is against you in yourself" (Sermon 128, 9). For most of the time we dare not believe that, and we go on fighting and struggling against what is mirrored dimly to us through eyes and ears and all our powers.

And, as Augustine well knew, the acceptance of what we are is the chief factor which actually makes it possible for us to accept other people as they are. This is the stuff of which compassion, so often evoked in the *Rule*, is made. Once he put it very simply: "If we do not forget what we have been, we shall not despair of those that now are what we were" (*Expositions of the Psalms* 50, 24).

The precaution of reading the *Rule* aloud once a week is also advisable, Augustine says, because of men's innate capacity for forgetting (*ne per obliuionem aliquid neglegatis*). Things get neglected because they are forgotten far more often than they are because they are considered worthless. He wants the Hippo monks to have his guidelines in the forefront of their minds. It is difficult for us in the twentieth century, with its glut of reading material and broadcasting, to imagine what the effect of a weekly reading of a little book would have on minds that were for the most part free from the constant pressure of verbal suggestion. Among literate people, weekly repetition may be less than valuable; but Augustine's chief contention remains — we need to seek every means of getting to know ourselves as we are, what we do to other people, and how we react to what they do to us.

Having described the purpose of frequent attention to the *Rule* Augustine ends with a few precepts on the monk's attitude to what he gradually discovers of himself.

Sometimes he will be able to detect a change in his own outlook and behavior which may have moved in either a good or a bad direction. Whether or not he stands condemned of any breach of good behavior is of only minor importance: what matters is the interior motives that prompt action. When tolerance, love, and humility show us what we should do, then we have moved away from our self-regarding and demanding ego and are being drawn by the Lord into an area where all good things can have free play. When we discover that we have indeed been moved by accepting and compassionate concern for our companions, then we may know that God is truly at work in our depths. He, Augustine says, is the "giver (*largitor*) of all good things" (*bonorum omnium*) that we may become aware of in ourselves, and there is only one response to such discoveries — sheer gratitude.

The English language does not help its users to express gratitude. The Latin *agite gratias* stresses the fact that gratitude is an activity, something that requires action if it is to be effective. And it is the acting out of gratitude that in its turn brings about the transformation of our selves. Each movement in the process is a response — spiraling always, not going round in circles. If we begin with an awareness of a great gift given (that is, the ability to transcend the downward drag of humanness in this or that particular), our gratitude to God will express itself in thankful dependence on him and also in the ability to use that gift in an increasing number of situations within the common life of the monastery. And the ability to do that will itself open us to the still fuller enabling which the Spirit can bestow on us because our defenses are falling and we are learning more and more to give ourselves away. And so it could go on, in a perpetual dance of receiving and giving, receiving and giving.

But the perpetual dance is a hope rather than a fact, for we so often break the continuity by our failures. That is why Augustine's instinct is right in suggesting the use of his precepts as a constant challenge; for it is possible to ignore the fact of our failures, to live superficially in the belief that all is well. He has just reminded his readers how easy it is to forget. In some way or other, we all need to have our awareness frequently rekindled — whether by reading the precepts or by any other means. The important thing is to know what we are doing and where we are going. The inexact nature of the *Rule* precludes strict adherence to a detailed set of instructions: every single suggestion or admonition or piece of advice that Augustine has offered to the monks in their garden monastery needed to be, and still needs to be, interpreted in the light of daily experience.

ACCEPTANCE OF FAILURE

And sometimes we shall find that in thought and behavior we have accepted the standards of the world, as Augustine puts it in chapter VI, 3, in the choices we have made. The whole of monastic life is a choosing, and its authenticity as an expression of Christian living is attested in the nature of the choices that all religious make. For that reason Augustine is right to end his precepts with warnings against failure rather than with powerful allusions to what monasticism achieves at its best (grace's gift of mature freedom — chapter VIII, 1). Every choice has failure as one of its alternatives (that statement is not the same thing as saying that white is white and black is black — issues are rarely as clear as that).

The word used for failing is the verb *deesse*, whose general meaning is to fall short. So often, Augustine means, we find that we conform to the situation that he wishes to put right, and not to his advice for the righting of what has gone wrong. And this we know to be very true to experience. Wheat and tares, dark and light, right and wrong, bad and good: we know ourselves to be a compound of all of these things. Paul's personal confusion is the experience of all who are committed to the search and the service of God: *I do not understand my own actions. For I do not do what I want, but I do the very thing I hate* (Rom 7:15).

Yet, as Paul also found, this awareness of weakness and repeated failure throws into relief the merciful bounty of God in bearing with us and bearing us up on our journey toward him. And the final phrases of Augustine's precepts are based on the same overwhelming confidence that enabled Paul to continue on life's journey: *Wretched man that I am! Who will deliver me from this body of death? Thanks be to God through our Lord Jesus Christ* (Rom 7:24-25). Augustine's confidence is the same, though it is expressed less ecstatically: after making the obvious comment that it is right, in the face of failure, to "be sorry for the past" (*doleat de praeterito*) and "be on . . . guard in the future" (*caueat de futuro*), he leads the monks straight into praying that their shortcomings may be forgiven and that they may not be led into temptation.

WE ARE ALL FORGIVEN SINNERS LOVED BY GOD

Augustine ends his little book with the words of the Lord's Prayer. The first noun in both texts is *debitum* whose primary meaning is a debt, something that is owed by someone to someone else. For the monks who have committed themselves to a life entirely centered upon God, each failure in acceptance, in understanding, in compassion, in love, is a failure to give what is due to another. We are all in debt to others; and we are also in debt to God on account of these same failures because we have blocked the channel of his access to others which runs through our selves. Our need for forgiveness is, then, twofold — we need to receive it from our brothers and sisters as well as from God. With God, it is there for the asking; with our brothers and sisters we may sometimes have to wait, as we ourselves may sometimes withhold forgiveness from those who have failed us. But we do not want to be hard, unforgiving, self-centered; and so our first and our last prayer must always be a plea to be enabled not to acquiesce in the temptations that assail us. There is nothing to be ashamed of in being assailed — that is part of the human condition. But we do not want to be overcome. In the one who is striving to be entirely centered upon God, whom he enables by his indwelling to live and move in freedom of spirit, the heart and the mind and the will cry out to him whom the psalmist called *Shepherd of Israel*: come and save us (Ps 80:1-2).

Yet it is for more than salvation that we cry. The first desire for all who enter upon the monastic way is for God himself; and the second desire (which Augustine expressed in his early letter to Nebridius [Letter 10, 2] by the word *deificare* — to be made God) is to be made new. The old materials which make us what we are will always remain, but their renewal and their restored life are what we pray for. A picture painted by an old master remains itself, but in course of time it needs to be restored if it is to continue to mean what it was intended to mean.

Augustine wrote his precepts before he had reached his full maturity yet its themes remained constant within his developing thought and spirituality. I would suggest that the aspirations of every religious — of Augustine himself, of the monks in the garden monastery as well as of those who have come after them — are expressed at the end of the great work, *The Trinity*, which he began in 399, not long after he had written the *Rule*, and which was completed twenty years later:

> I have sought you and desired to see intellectually what I have believed, and I have argued much and toiled much. O Lord my God, my one hope, listen to me lest out of weariness I should stop wanting to seek you, but let me seek your face always, and with ardor. Do you yourself give me the strength to seek, having caused yourself to be found and having given me the hope of finding you more and more. Before you lies my strength and my weakness; preserve the one, heal the other. Before you lies my knowledge and my ignorance; where you have opened to me, receive me as I come in; where you have shut to me, open to me as I knock. Let me remember you, let me understand you, let me love you. Increase these things in me until you refashion me entirely (XV, 51).

NOTES

1. Luc Verheijen, *Nouvelle Approche de la Règle de Saint Augustin*, Abbaye de Bellefontaine, 1980, pages 201-242 (hereafter *Nouvelle Approche*).

2. See *The Origins of the Christian Doctrine of Sacrifice*, Darton, Longman & Todd, 1978, page 63.

3. Quincey Howe, Jr., *Selected Sermons of Saint Augustine*, Gollancz, 1967, page V.

4. *The Fear of Freedom*, Kegan Paul, Trench, Trubner, 1942.

5. Peter Brown, *Religion and Society in the Age of Saint Augustine*, Faber, 1972, pages 373-374.

6. A deeply sensitive description of the experience of slavery is to be found in André Brink's novel *A Chain of Voices*, Faber, 1982, *passim*.

7. John Meyendorff, *Living Tradition*, St. Vladimir's Seminary Press, 1970, page 179.

8. Erich Fromm, *The Fear of Freedom*, page 225.

9. See *Nouvelle Approche*, page 59.

10. (a) In Augustine's study, *The Spirit and the Letter*, of the year 412, he defines grace as "the action of the life-giving Spirit" (XIX, 34). Earlier in the text he wrote: "It is given not because we have done good works, but in order that we may have the power to do them, not because we have fulfilled the law, but in order that we may fulfill it" (16). And further on he works out the sequence by which grace operates: "By grace comes healing of the soul from sin's sickness; by the healing of the soul comes freedom of choice; by freedom of choice comes the love of righteousness; by the love of righteousness comes the working of the law" (52). See Burnaby, *Augustine, Later Works*, pages 220, 206 and 236.

(b) Near the end of his life, in 426, he wrote: "The grace of God through Jesus Christ our Lord must be understood as that by which alone men are delivered from evil, and without which they do absolutely no good thing . . . not only in order that they may know the manifestation of . . . what should be done, but . . . in order that by its enabling they may do with love what they know" (*Correction and Grace* 2, 3).

11. See Jn 8:34; Rom 6:17.20; 7:14.

12. See Rom 6:18; 1 Cor 7:22; Gal 5:1; 1 Pt 2:16.

13. *The First Epistle to the Corinthians*, A. & C. Black, 2nd edition, 1971, page 171.

14. See Rich's *Dictionary of Roman and Greet Antiquities*, page 379.